CHARTER OF THE

Basic Documents in World Politics

Basic Documents in World Politics reproduces foundational documents that have had a major impact on the character and course of world politics, together with interpretive essays by major scholars. The essays, all previously unpublished, range over the historical context within which the documents were written and their evolving influence in shaping the contemporary world. The goal is to make the documents and controversies they have spawned accessible to newcomers, while contributing to scholarly debates about their meaning and significance.

Previous volume in the series:
Charter of the United Nations, edited by Ian Shapiro and Joseph Lampert (2014)

Forthcoming:
The Bretton Woods Agreement, edited by Naomi Lamoreaux and Ian Shapiro

CHARTER OF THE NORTH ATLANTIC TREATY ORGANIZATION

Together with Scholarly Commentaries and Essential Historical Documents

Edited and with an Introduction by
IAN SHAPIRO AND ADAM TOOZE

Yale UNIVERSITY PRESS/NEW HAVEN & LONDON

The contributors to this volume gratefully acknowledge assistance from The Edward J. and Dorothy Clarke Kempf Fund at Yale University.

Copyright © 2018 by Ian Shapiro and Adam Tooze.
All rights reserved.
This book may not be reproduced, in whole or in part, including illustrations, in any form (beyond that copying permitted by Sections 107 and 108 of the U.S. Copyright Law and except by reviewers for the public press), without written permission from the publishers.

Yale University Press books may be purchased in quantity for educational, business, or promotional use. For information, please e-mail sales.press@yale.edu (U.S. office) or sales@yaleup.co.uk (U.K. office).

Designed by Mary Valencia.
Set in Joanna and Eureka Sans types by Westchester Publishing Services.
Printed in the United States of America.

Library of Congress Control Number: 2017955556
ISBN 978-0-300-22852-6 (paperback : alk. paper)

A catalogue record for this book is available from the British Library.

This paper meets the requirements of ANSI/NISO Z39.48-1992 (Permanence of Paper).

10 9 8 7 6 5 4 3 2 1

Contents

Introduction
Ian Shapiro and Adam Tooze, **vii**

Documents

The North Atlantic Treaty, Washington, DC, April 4, 1949 **3**
Speech Delivered by Former British Prime Minister Winston Churchill,
 Fulton, Missouri, March 5, 1946 **7**
The Pentagon Paper, Washington, DC, April 1, 1948 **18**
Speech Delivered by Prime Minister and Foreign Minister of Belgium
 Paul-Henri Spaak, Paris, September 28, 1948 **22**
Nationwide Radio Address Delivered by Secretary of State Acheson,
 March 18, 1949 **31**
Speeches Delivered at the Treaty Signing Ceremony, Washington, DC, April 4,
 1949 **40**
Statement by President Truman on the Coming into Effect of the North
 Atlantic Treaty, Washington, DC, August 24, 1949 **57**
North Atlantic Military Committee Decision on M.C. 48 (Final),
 November 22, 1954 **58**
C.M. (55) 15 (Final), "Security Within the North Atlantic Treaty
 Organization," March 8, 1955 **74**
Report of the Committee of Three on Non-Military Cooperation in NATO,
 New York, December 1956 **81**
Meeting of the North Atlantic Council at the Level of Foreign Ministers
 Final Communiqué, Turnberry, Scotland, June 7, 1990 **108**
Declaration on a Transformed North Atlantic Alliance Issued by the Heads
 of State and Government Participating in the Meeting of the North
 Atlantic Council, London, July 6, 1990 **116**
The Alliance's New Strategic Concept, London, November 8, 1991 **122**
The Alliance's Strategic Concept, Washington, DC, April 24, 1999 **140**
Strategic Concept for the Defence and Security of the Members of the North
 Atlantic Treaty Organization, Lisbon, November 19, 2010 **162**

Part I The Evolution of the Alliance

1. NATO's Radical Response to the Nuclear Revolution
   Francis J. Gavin, 177
2. NATO and Nuclear Proliferation, 1949–1968
   Alexandre Debs and Nuno P. Monteiro, 193
3. The Contest over NATO's Future: The US, France, and the Concept of Pan-Europeanism after the Fall of the Berlin Wall, 1989–1990
   Mary Elise Sarotte, 212

Part II Current Challenges

4. Toward an Open and Accountable NATO
   Ian Davis, 231
5. The North Atlantic Treaty Organization: Is NATO a Force Fit for a New Century?
   General Sir Graeme Lamb, 253
6. Organizational Survival: NATO's Pragmatic Functionalism
   Joanna Spear, 265
7. NATO's Charter: Adaptable but Limited
   James Goldgeier, 288
8. NATO, Regionalism, and the Responsibility to Protect
   Anne Orford, 302
9. Conclusion: Another Cold War? NATO and the New Russia
   Adam Tooze and Ian Shapiro, 328

List of Contributors 343

Index 347

Introduction

Ian Shapiro and Adam Tooze

NATO is the most powerful military alliance in history. Signed by the Western powers in April 1949, the North Atlantic Treaty famously declares that an attack on one will be deemed an attack on all, triggering obligations to assist the endangered nation "by taking forthwith, individually and in concert with the other Parties, such action as it deems necessary, including the use of armed force."[1] NATO's twelve original members have since been joined by several waves of additional signatories, so that today twenty-nine countries fall under its mutual-protection umbrella. NATO headquarters are in Brussels, Belgium, though its Supreme Allied Commander Europe is always an American, the first SACEUR being no less a figure than Dwight Eisenhower.[2]

NATO was an artifact and accelerant of the solidifying postwar standoff between the United States and the Soviet Union that soon became the Cold War.[3] Greece and Turkey joined the alliance three years after its founding, but it was West Germany's inclusion in May 1955 that was, as Norwegian Foreign Minister Halvard Lange said at the time, a "decisive turning point in the history of our continent." As the contributions to this volume attest, NATO would outlive the geopolitics that spawned it to become a major architect of the post–Cold War world.

The Soviets saw NATO as a threat from the beginning. Having tried, and failed, to prevent its formation, they then sought with no more success to limit NATO's reach. They made numerous proposals for combined European security arrangements centered on a unified Germany, including, as a last-ditch effort, an application to join the alliance themselves, which the British, French, and Americans dismissed out of hand. General Hastings Ismay captured prevailing sentiment with the remark that "the Soviet request to join NATO is like an unrepentant burglar requesting to join the police force."[4] The USSR established the Warsaw Pact the week after the West Germans joined the alliance.[5]

NATO was exceptional from the start. Perhaps more than any other country, the United States had exemplified Lord Palmerston's dictum that nations have no permanent friends or allies, only permanent interests.[6] For a century and a half, Americans had heeded George Washington's advice, in his farewell address, to "steer clear of permanent alliances with any portion of the foreign world."[7] Political leaders had learned that foreign entanglements are a tough sell to American electorates, for the most part avoiding them like the plague. US participation in World War I had been as reluctant as it was controversial. Victory did little to erode American antipathy for international commitments. The US Senate dashed Woodrow Wilson's dream of a new era of engagement by rejecting the League of Nations envisaged in the Treaty of Versailles. Nor was there any American appetite for ongoing alliances with the powers that had defeated Germany and its allies.

The US entered World War II just as grudgingly. President Franklin D. Roosevelt's desire to assist in the fight against Hitler had been an uphill battle in Congress into the first years of the war. Many senators and representatives reflected widespread public sentiment, endorsed by US Ambassador to Britain Joseph Kennedy, that this was not America's fight.[8] It was Hitler who declared war on the United States four days after the Japanese attack on Pearl Harbor in December 1941, finally rendering debates about American participation in another European war moot. None of this history suggested that, soon after the war, the United States would become the midwife and leader of a permanent alliance of a dozen countries that could be dragged into hostilities if any suffered an attack.

A safer bet, at the time, would have been on international institutions. Roosevelt had worked hard, in the last years of his life, to ensure that Woodrow Wilson's stillborn dream would not be replicated after World War II. FDR died six months before the United Nations Charter came into force in October 1945, but President Harry S. Truman quickly threw his weight behind the institution it envisaged as "the essential organization to keep the peace." Tens of millions had been killed and untold devastation wrought by two world wars, making it imperative that the leading powers create "sensible machinery for the settlement of disputes among nations." Truman insisted that "we can no longer permit any nation, or groups of nations, to attempt to settle their arguments with bombs and bayonets."[9]

Within four years Truman was preparing for exactly that eventuality by creating NATO. The US did not abandon the fledgling UN institutions, to be sure, but Truman made it clear that the US would not count on them. The day after the signing of the North Atlantic Treaty was made public, Secretary of State Dean Acheson declared in a radio speech that "obstructive" Soviet tactics in the Security Council were hobbling the organization and posing a clear threat to European security. Recent experience made it clear that "the control of Europe by a single aggressive, unfriendly power would constitute an intolerable threat to the national security of the United States."[10]

Another lesson justifying the need for the alliance was that "if the free nations do not stand together, they will fall one by one." Acheson invoked a Senate resolution the previous year that had declared "the best deterrent to aggression is the certainty that immediate and effective counter-measures will be taken against those who violate the peace," and expressly encouraged the administration to press for "the development of collective self-defense and regional arrangements within the United Nations framework." Acheson dismissed inevitable criticism that the pact was a smokescreen for aggressive American designs as "a malicious misrepresentation or a fantastic misunderstanding of the nature and aims of American society." On the contrary, by backing the UN, reconstituting the European and world economies, and facing down the Soviets, the United States was "waging peace with a vigor and on a scale without precedent." The North Atlantic Treaty was integral to that endeavor.[11]

The challenge that NATO faced was, however, enormous. The Red Army was the most formidable conventional force the world had ever seen. It maintained 175 divisions in some state of readiness at a time when the Western armies were almost completely demobilized. In 1949 British Field Marshal Bernard Montgomery could scrape together a force of no more than ten divisions to face a spearhead invasion force of at least twenty-five Soviet divisions, with many more echeloned to the rear.[12] To make matters worse, the Soviets tested their first nuclear weapon in August 1949, four months after the North Atlantic Treaty was signed, and their first hydrogen bomb four years later. They soon went on to develop ten closed cities, known as "Atomgrads," in which they pursued the research and built up the stockpiles that supported their side in the deterrence logic of mutual assured destruction (MAD).

The famous 1950 National Security Council memorandum NSC 68, on which US Cold War security strategy was based, presumed Soviet superiority well into the coming decade. Faced with this preponderance, NATO at first opted for an ambitious conventional military buildup. But when the costs and political difficulty of rearming West Germany (formally known as the Federal Republic of Germany) became apparent, this was rapidly overtaken from the winter of 1953–1954 by the "New Look" strategy that relied above all on asymmetric massive nuclear retaliation.[13] From its inception, therefore, the danger of nuclear war hung over NATO and the Cold War confrontation. Despite the efforts toward disarmament and détente, and the brief flirtation with denuclearizing the standoff entertained by Ronald Reagan and Mikhail Gorbachev in Geneva and Reykjavik in the mid-1980s, the threat was never removed. The nuclear shadow that had been there from the start never lifted, fueling macabre debates in the West over whether or not we would be "better Red than dead," as Bertrand Russell famously contended.[14]

As Francis Gavin points out in chapter 1 of this volume, the Cold War nuclear standoff led NATO to adopt two radical strategies: first, a preannounced commitment to massive, preemptive use of nuclear weapons against Soviet military assets in the first hours of a war; and second, NATO's role as a vehicle to suppress nuclear proliferation within and, ultimately, beyond the alliance. The first strategy lived in some disharmony with the second, because the heavy reliance on threatening early and massive use of nuclear weapons intensified the desire of NATO members for their own nuclear options. The resulting tensions persisted throughout the Cold War, generating numerous predicaments and crises, but Gavin argues that they nonetheless helped stabilize geopolitics in what had been the world's cauldron of war, Central Europe.

In chapter 2, Alexandre Debs and Nuno Monteiro explore the relations between the US reliance on overwhelming nuclear force and its efforts to limit proliferation within and beyond NATO. Their particular focus is on the period until 1968, when negotiations for the Treaty on the Non-Proliferation of Nuclear Weapons (NPT) were concluded. During this period, Washington followed a two-pronged nonproliferation approach within NATO. On the one hand, the US reinforced its commitment to the security of any ally considering nuclear weapons. On the other hand, especially from the mid-1960s onward, American policymakers tried to condition this commitment on the ally's abandoning nuclear ambitions. This strategy did not always work, as Debs and Monteiro note. The French insisted on developing their own nuclear deterrent, which the US accepted because Moscow was not unduly concerned by it. But West Germany was another matter. Nuclearization in the Federal Republic might well have produced conflict with the Soviets, and the Americans, accordingly, forbade it. They also tried to extend their umbrella logic beyond NATO, again with mixed success. The Swedes were convinced to abandon their clandestine nuclear weapons program in 1966 (it was wound down by 1972). But the Americans failed with Israel, which refused to sign the NPT and defied the Nixon administration's efforts to halt its nuclear program.

The Soviet Union's dissolution in December 1991 took NATO's raison d'être with it. Debate over its mission, composition, and perhaps even existence became inevitable. The French had always had an ambivalent relationship with the alliance. Aside from the nuclear issue, President Charles de Gaulle had at different times withdrawn the French fleets, and eventually all French armed forces, from NATO command, and demanded that non-French NATO forces leave the country. France remained within the alliance and maintained secret agreements about cooperation in the event of war, but it came as no surprise after 1989 that French President François Mitterrand, a Socialist, favored radical rethinking of the need for NATO. As Mary Sarotte notes in chapter 3, Mitterrand thought that the time was ripe to overcome longstanding European divisions. He argued for a new pan-Europeanism, including the creation or expansion of pan-European security institutions, which could eventually include Russia.

Skepticism of the need for NATO would continue as a perpetual post–Cold War theme, particularly on the European left. In August 2015 Jeremy Corbyn made it part of his successful bid for the Labour Party leadership in the UK that NATO "should have shut up shop in 1990 along with the Warsaw Pact."[15] But Sarotte notes that the Americans never seriously contemplated that course. Indeed, no serious contender for high office in the US would question NATO's centrality to American national security until Donald Trump's arrival on the scene in 2016. President George Herbert Walker Bush and West German chancellor Helmut Kohl insisted that NATO continue to dominate European security, and that the continued presence of NATO's troops in Europe necessarily meant that of their nuclear weapons as well. The result was the perpetuation of a vision of European security based on a classic Cold War institution, NATO. Mitterrand's project of a pan-European security institution died.

Nor did the accession to NATO of every former member of the Warsaw Pact, bar Russia, put an end to the matter. In 2008 the alliance announced that it looked forward to the addition of both Georgia and Ukraine.[16] This fueled Russian paranoia and antagonism toward the West, strengthening President Vladimir Putin's hand when Ukraine collapsed into civil war in 2014, and he moved to annex Crimea rather than risk losing access to Russia's only warm-water naval base on the Black Sea at Sevastopol.[17] Whether Sarotte's path not taken could have forestalled these developments will never be known. In any case, by the end of 2014 US relations with Russia had deteriorated into the familiar Cold War pattern of confrontation and containment, despite

President Barack Obama's announced determination to "reset" them as a central part of his foreign policy on assuming office five years earlier.[18] Donald Trump flirted with the proposition that NATO should be disbanded during the 2016 primaries.[19] But by the time he won the Republican nomination it seemed clear that his own version of the reset would be limited to insisting that member states meet their financial commitments to defense spending, not abandoning the alliance.[20]

If NATO is here to stay, questions inevitably arise about its governance. Ian Davis notes in chapter 4 that while transparency has been a burning public policy issue in the advanced democracies over the last decade or so, this has not extended to defense institutions or intergovernmental organizations, including NATO. Indeed, NATO is one of the few major intergovernmental bodies that entirely lack a basic information disclosure policy. Davis notes that NATO's transparency deficit exists at four levels: within the closed inner workings of the alliance; as a result of Cold War legacy secrecy and classification rules; through poor budgetary controls and nonexistent performance metrics; and weak parliamentary and public oversight, including sluggish mechanisms of engagement and outreach by NATO itself. This lack of transparency leads to failures of monitoring and other inefficiencies, including lack of accountability and vulnerability to capture by special interests. It may also increase the vulnerability and malleability of public opinion in foreign affairs at a time when current security threats, from Afghanistan to countering Islamic militants in the Middle East, are matters of perception and judgment rather than fact. Davis concludes by proposing reforms that would increase NATO's transparency, mitigating some of these difficulties.

However we assess Davis's proposals, he is surely right that NATO's post–Cold War expansion has not been accompanied by systematic reflection on its purpose. Graeme Lamb takes up this deficit in chapter 5, asking whether the alliance, as structured and authorized in the late 1940s, still makes sense in today's world and, if so, what its purpose in fact is. He starts with a discussion of the history of "global policing efforts" before NATO and during the Cold War. During the Cold War, NATO's MAD strategy led to relative peace, sustaining a fragile set of rules that were accepted, for the most part, by all sides. This stands in stark contrast to today's world, in which threats emanate less from states and more from stateless terrorism and cyber-warfare. This is a world in which it is unlikely that NATO's large complement of members will continue to be able to act as one. Moreover, Lamb argues that as a conventional military force, NATO is ill equipped to meet today's threats, which often emanate from, and perpetuate, failed and failing states. NATO stands in need of restructuring. Lamb concludes that if the will and resources to undertake this are not forthcoming, which until now has been the case, NATO is a waste of money and might as well be disbanded.

Joanna Spear offers a more sanguine assessment of NATO's post–Cold War evolution in chapter 6. Rather than remaining an institution with clear goals and objectives as it was during the Cold War, she notes that NATO has become a "pragmatic functionalist" organization, taking on issues that help to perpetuate its role in the Western security architecture. Since the 1990s, NATO members have been more consistently and actively involved in military activities than during the first forty years of the alliance's existence, when no military operations were undertaken. Spear notes that NATO has always been crisis-ridden, despite the geostrategic commonalities that held it together in the face of the Soviet threat. Since that dissipated, the alliance has survived the loss of its core mission by manufacturing a laundry list of new things to do: crisis prevention and management, humanitarian operations, peacekeeping, Combined Joint Task Forces, security sector reform, counterterrorism, counterpiracy, counterproliferation, transformation, Smart Defense, cyber-security, energy security, and combating organized crime.

James Goldgeier also offers an encouraging assessment of NATO's post–Cold War evolution in chapter 7. He notes that because would-be members must demonstrate commitments to democracy and the rule of law, the prospect of NATO membership has created incentives for beneficial reform in Central and Eastern Europe. As for the mission, the treaty's Article 5 mutual-aid provision had outlived its usefulness in his view and has appropriately been replaced by a more expansive commitment to humanitarian intervention even when no NATO member is threatened. The precedent was Kosovo in 1999. When Albanian Muslims there faced ethnic cleansing and the prospect of mass killings at the hands of Serb armies and militias, NATO bombed Serbia, ending the threat. This action was declared "illegal but legitimate" after the fact by the Independent International Commission on Kosovo appointed by the Swedish government on the initiative of Prime Minister Göran Persson.[21] Since then, NATO has engaged in missions that have neither involved the threat of armed attack nor taken place near the territory of member states; it remains a work in progress. Goldgeier welcomes this evolution, arguing that NATO should foster a robust network of partnerships worldwide to deal with global threats to the prosperity and security of its member states.

In chapter 8, Anne Orford digs more deeply into NATO's evolution from a Cold War defensive alliance into an enforcer of the Responsibility to Protect (R2P). This is the doctrine, affirmed by the UN in the wake of such events as the 1994 Rwandan genocide and the Yugoslav civil war of 1991–2001, that governments have an affirmative obligation to protect their populations from genocide, war crimes, crimes against humanity, and ethnic cleansing, and that the international community is authorized to intervene when they do not. In 2006 the UN Security Council asserted the right to authorize such intervention, and in March 2011 it exercised this authority by sanctioning NATO intervention in Libya in response to allegations of the imminent slaughter of civilians by Muammar Gaddafi's forces in Benghazi.

Orford begins by exploring NATO's evolution from a regional alliance geared exclusively to its members' interests to its embrace of the more universalist vision that informs the UN Charter. Then she analyzes the Kosovo intervention as a turning point in the history both of NATO and of international law relating to intervention. Next she turns to the Libyan intervention. She notes that, once empowered by the Security Council, NATO went beyond its mandate to prevent civilian slaughter in Benghazi by assisting the forces that sought, and eventually achieved, Gaddafi's overthrow. The resulting controversy throws the unresolved debate over NATO's future role into sharp relief. At a minimum, the alliance is increasingly seen as the armed wing of the European Union, committed to the welfare not only of North Atlantic populations but also of the populations of neighboring territories. But the Libyan intervention has opened up the possibility of a more extensive global agenda. Orford cautions that these debates should not lead us to lose sight of the reality that NATO unapologetically uses force in the service of protecting the economic and national security of the alliance.

We take Orford's caution seriously, exploring it further in the final chapter. There we argue that Kosovo lulled NATO into a false sense of security and that the Libyan intervention and subsequent fallout shed a more accurate and more sobering light on NATO as the police force for humanitarian intervention in the name of R2P. Whether or not it should be disbanded entirely, as the Corbyns of this world contend, Lamb and Davis are right that its mission and governance stand in need of fundamental reassessment. Even if NATO were to return to some variant of its more traditional role, at a minimum Article 5 and the alliance's stance toward Russia are in need of rethinking. Donald Trump's election to the US presidency in 2016 suggested that the time for that reassessment had arrived.

Notes

1. Article 5, North Atlantic Treaty, Washington, DC, April 4, 1949; see below.
2. Alexander M. Bielakowski, "Eisenhower: The First NATO SACEUR," *War and Society*, Vol. 22, No. 2 (2004), pp. 95–108.
3. The term *Cold War* originated with a prescient article by George Orwell, "You and the Atomic Bomb," that appeared in the *Tribune* (UK) on October 19, 1945, http://orwell.ru/library/articles/ABomb/english/e_abomb.
4. Memo by Lord Ismay on Russian admission to NATO, http://www.nato.int/60years/doc/5-Soviet-Union-s-request-to-join%20NATO/Transcript%20of%20Lord%20Ismay's%20Memo.pdf.
5. BBC, "On This Day," May 5, 1955, http://news.bbc.co.uk/onthisday/hi/dates/stories/may/9/newsid_2519000/2519979.stm.
6. "We have no eternal allies, and we have no perpetual enemies. Our interests are eternal and perpetual, and those interests it is our duty to follow." Viscount Palmerston, speech to the House of Commons on the Treaty of Adrianople, March 1, 1848, http://hansard.millbanksystems.com/commons/1848/mar/01/treaty-of-adrianople-charges-against.
7. George Washington's Farewell Address, *American Daily Advertiser*, September 19, 1796, the Avalon Project, Yale Law Library, http://avalon.law.yale.edu/18th_century/washing.asp.
8. See Susan Dunn, *1940: FDR, Willkie, Lindbergh, Hitler: The Election amid the Storm* (New Haven: Yale University Press, 2013), pp. 21–70, 259–75.
9. Harry S. Truman, Address to the United Nations Conference on International Organization at San Francisco, April 25, 1945; in Ian Shapiro and Joseph Lampert, eds., *Charter of the United Nations: Together with Scholarly Commentaries and Essential Historical Documents* (New Haven: Yale University Press, 2014), pp. 10–13.
10. "Nationwide Radio Address Delivered by Secretary of State Acheson, March 18, 1949," Truman Library NATO Documents; see Documents section in this volume, pp. 31–39.
11. Ibid.
12. Phillip A. Karber and Jerald A. Combs, "The United States, NATO, and the Soviet Threat to Western Europe: Military Estimates and Policy Options, 1945–1963," *Diplomatic History*, Vol. 22, No. 3 (1998), pp. 399–429.
13. Beatrice Heuser, "The Development of NATO's Nuclear Strategy," *Contemporary European History*, Vol. 4, No. 1 (March 1995), pp. 37–66.
14. Bertrand Russell, *Has Man a Future?* (Nottingham: Spokesman, 2001), pp. 42–51.
15. Jim Pickard, "Jeremy Corbyn: There Is a Thirst for Debate in the Party," *Financial Times*, August 23, 2015, http://www.ft.com/intl/cms/s/0/5e7c3ca6-4999-11e5-9b5d-89a026fda5c9.html?siteedition=uk#axzz3jxc5mbxe.
16. See "Final Communiqué," press release from the meeting of the North Atlantic Council at the level of foreign ministers held at NATO headquarters in Brussels on December 3, 2008, http://www.nato.int/cps/en/natolive/official_texts_46247.htm; and Stephen Brown and Missy Ryan, "Ukraine Crisis: West and Russia Accuse Each Other of 'Coercing' Unstable Ukraine," NBC News, February 1, 2014, http://worldnews.nbcnews.com/_news/2014/02/01/22533424-ukraine-crisis-west-and-russia-accuse-each-other-of-coercing-unstable-nation?lite.
17. "When the infrastructure of a military bloc is moving toward our borders, it causes us some concerns and questions. We need to take some steps in response. NATO ships would have ended up in the city of Russian navy glory, Sevastopol." Vladimir Putin quoted in "Putin Says Annexation of Crimea Partly in Response to NATO Enlargement," Reuters, April 17, 2014, http://www.reuters.com/article/2014/04/17/us-russia-putin-nato-idUSBREA3G22A20140417.
18. James Marson and Andrey Ostroukh, "Putin Blasts West's 'Containment' Policy," *Wall Street Journal*, December 5, 2014, p. A7, http://online.wsj.com/public/resources/documents/print/WSJ_-A007-20141205.pdf.

19. See Philip Rucker and Robert Costa, "Trump Questions Need for NATO, Outlines Noninterventionist Foreign Policy," *Washington Post*, March 21, 2016, https://www.washingtonpost.com/news/post-politics/wp/2016/03/21/donald-trump-reveals-foreign-policy-team-in-meeting-with-the-washington-post/?utm_term=.8e72ffcb2380.

20. David Sanger and Maggie Haberman, "Trump Sets Conditions for Defending NATO Allies against Attack," *New York Times*, July 20, 2016, http://www.nytimes.com/2016/07/21/us/politics/donald-trump-issues.html?_r=0.

21. For the commission's findings, see their *Kosovo Report* (New York: Oxford University Press, 2001), pp. 3–4.

DOCUMENTS

THE NORTH ATLANTIC TREATY

WASHINGTON, DC, APRIL 4, 1949

(Source: NATO)

The Parties to this Treaty reaffirm their faith in the purposes and principles of the Charter of the United Nations and their desire to live in peace with all peoples and all governments.

They are determined to safeguard the freedom, common heritage and civilisation of their peoples, founded on the principles of democracy, individual liberty and the rule of law. They seek to promote stability and well-being in the North Atlantic area.

They are resolved to unite their efforts for collective defence and for the preservation of peace and security. They therefore agree to this North Atlantic Treaty:

Article 1

The Parties undertake, as set forth in the Charter of the United Nations, to settle any international dispute in which they may be involved by peaceful means in such a manner that international peace and security and justice are not endangered, and to refrain in their international relations from the threat or use of force in any manner inconsistent with the purposes of the United Nations.

Article 2

The Parties will contribute toward the further development of peaceful and friendly international relations by strengthening their free institutions, by bringing about a better understanding of the principles upon which these institutions are founded, and by promoting conditions of stability and well-being. They will seek to eliminate conflict in their international economic policies and will encourage economic collaboration between any or all of them.

Article 3

In order more effectively to achieve the objectives of this Treaty, the Parties, separately and jointly, by means of continuous and effective self-help and mutual aid, will maintain and develop their individual and collective capacity to resist armed attack.

Article 4

The Parties will consult together whenever, in the opinion of any of them, the territorial integrity, political independence or security of any of the Parties is threatened.

Article 5

The Parties agree that an armed attack against one or more of them in Europe or North America shall be considered an attack against them all and consequently they agree that, if such an armed attack occurs, each of them, in exercise of the right of individual or collective self-defence recognised by Article 51 of the Charter of the United Nations, will assist the Party or Parties so attacked by taking forthwith, individually and in concert with the other Parties, such action as it deems necessary, including the use of armed force, to restore and maintain the security of the North Atlantic area.

Any such armed attack and all measures taken as a result thereof shall immediately be reported to the Security Council. Such measures shall be terminated when the Security Council has taken the measures necessary to restore and maintain international peace and security.

Article 6[1]

For the purpose of Article 5, an armed attack on one or more of the Parties is deemed to include an armed attack:

- on the territory of any of the Parties in Europe or North America, on the Algerian Departments of France[2] (2), on the territory of or on the Islands under the jurisdiction of any of the Parties in the North Atlantic area north of the Tropic of Cancer;

- on the forces, vessels, or aircraft of any of the Parties, when in or over these territories or any other area in Europe in which occupation forces of any of the Parties were stationed on the date when the Treaty entered into force or the Mediterranean Sea or the North Atlantic area north of the Tropic of Cancer.

Article 7

This Treaty does not affect, and shall not be interpreted as affecting in any way the rights and obligations under the Charter of the Parties which are members of the United Nations, or the primary responsibility of the Security Council for the maintenance of international peace and security.

Article 8

Each Party declares that none of the international engagements now in force between it and any other of the Parties or any third State is in conflict with the provisions of this Treaty, and undertakes not to enter into any international engagement in conflict with this Treaty.

Article 9

The Parties hereby establish a Council, on which each of them shall be represented, to consider matters concerning the implementation of this Treaty. The Council shall be so organised as to be able to meet promptly at any time. The Council shall set up such subsidiary bodies as may be necessary; in particular it shall establish immediately a defence committee which shall recommend measures for the implementation of Articles 3 and 5.

Article 10

The Parties may, by unanimous agreement, invite any other European State in a position to further the principles of this Treaty and to contribute to the security of the North Atlantic area to accede to this Treaty. Any State so invited may become a Party to the Treaty by depositing its instrument of accession with the Government of the United States of America. The Government of the United States of America will inform each of the Parties of the deposit of each such instrument of accession.

Article 11

This Treaty shall be ratified and its provisions carried out by the Parties in accordance with their respective constitutional processes. The instruments of ratification shall be deposited as soon as possible with the Government of the United States of America, which will notify all the other signatories of each deposit. The Treaty shall enter into force between the States which have ratified it as soon as the ratifications of the majority of the signatories, including the ratifications of Belgium, Canada, France, Luxembourg, the Netherlands, the United Kingdom and the United States, have been deposited and shall come into effect with respect to other States on the date of the deposit of their ratifications.[3]

Article 12

After the Treaty has been in force for ten years, or at any time thereafter, the Parties shall, if any of them so requests, consult together for the purpose of reviewing the Treaty, having regard for the factors then affecting peace and security in the North Atlantic area, including the development of universal as well as regional arrangements under the Charter of the United Nations for the maintenance of international peace and security.

Article 13

After the Treaty has been in force for twenty years, any Party may cease to be a Party one year after its notice of denunciation has been given to the Government of the United States of America, which will inform the Governments of the other Parties of the deposit of each notice of denunciation.

Article 14

This Treaty, of which the English and French texts are equally authentic, shall be deposited in the archives of the Government of the United States of America. Duly certified copies will be transmitted by that Government to the Governments of other signatories.

Notes

1. The definition of the territories to which Article 5 applies was revised by Article 2 of the Protocol to the North Atlantic Treaty on the accession of Greece and Turkey signed on October 22, 1951.
2. On January 16, 1963, the North Atlantic Council noted that insofar as the former Algerian Departments of France were concerned, the relevant clauses of this Treaty had become inapplicable as from July 3, 1962.
3. The Treaty came into force on August 24, 1949, after the deposition of the ratifications of all signatory states.

SPEECH DELIVERED BY FORMER BRITISH PRIME MINISTER WINSTON CHURCHILL

"THE SINEWS OF PEACE"

FULTON, MISSOURI, MARCH 5, 1946

(Reproduced with permission of Curtis Brown, London, on behalf of the Estate of Winston S. Churchill. © The Estate of Sir Winston Churchill)

I am glad to come to Westminster College this afternoon, and am complimented that you should give me a degree. The name "Westminster" is somehow familiar to me. I seem to have heard of it before. Indeed, it was at Westminster that I received a very large part of my education in politics, dialectic, rhetoric, and one or two other things. In fact we have both been educated at the same, or similar, or, at any rate, kindred establishments.

It is also an honour, perhaps almost unique, for a private visitor to be introduced to an academic audience by the President of the United States. Amid his heavy burdens, duties, and responsibilities—unsought but not recoiled from—the President has travelled a thousand miles to dignify and magnify our meeting here to-day and to give me an opportunity of addressing this kindred nation, as well as my own countrymen across the ocean, and perhaps some other countries too. The President has told you that it is his wish, as I am sure it is yours, that I should have full liberty to give my true and faithful counsel in these anxious and baffling times. I shall certainly avail myself of this freedom, and feel the more right to do so because any private ambitions I may have cherished in my younger days have been satisfied beyond my wildest dreams. Let me, however, make it clear that I have no official mission or status of any kind, and that I speak only for myself. There is nothing here but what you see.

I can therefore allow my mind, with the experience of a lifetime, to play over the problems which beset us on the morrow of our absolute victory in arms, and to try to make sure with what strength I have that what has been gained with so much sacrifice and suffering shall be preserved for the future glory and safety of mankind.

The United States stands at this time at the pinnacle of world power. It is a solemn moment for the American Democracy. For with primacy in power is also joined an awe inspiring accountability to the future. If you look around you, you must feel not only the sense of duty done but also you must feel anxiety lest you fall below the level of achievement. Opportunity is here now, clear and shining for both our countries. To reject it or ignore it or fritter it away will bring upon us all the long reproaches of the after-time. It is necessary that constancy of mind, persistency of purpose, and the grand simplicity of decision shall guide and rule the conduct of the English-speaking peoples in peace as they did in war. We must, and I believe we shall, prove ourselves equal to this severe requirement.

When American military men approach some serious situation they are wont to write at the head of their directive the words "over-all strategic concept." There is wisdom in this, as it leads to clarity of thought. What then is the over-all strategic concept which we should inscribe today? It is nothing less than the safety and welfare, the freedom and progress, of all the homes and families of all the men and women in all the lands. And here I speak particularly of the myriad cottage or apartment homes where the wage-earner strives amid the accidents and difficulties of life to guard his wife and children from privation and bring the family up in the fear of the Lord, or upon ethical conceptions which often play their potent part.

To give security to these countless homes, they must be shielded from the two giant marauders, war and tyranny. We all know the frightful disturbances in which the ordinary family is plunged when the curse of war swoops down upon the bread-winner and those for whom he works and contrives. The awful ruin of Europe, with all its vanished glories, and of large parts of Asia glares us in the eyes. When the designs of wicked men or the aggressive urge of mighty States dissolve over large areas the frame of civilised society, humble folk are confronted with difficulties with which they cannot cope. For them all is distorted, all is broken, even ground to pulp.

When I stand here this quiet afternoon I shudder to visualise what is actually happening to millions now and what is going to happen in this period when famine stalks the earth. None can compute what has been called "the unestimated sum of human pain." Our supreme task and duty is to guard the homes of the common people from the horrors and miseries of another war. We are all agreed on that.

Our American military colleagues, after having proclaimed their "over-all strategic concept" and computed available resources, always proceed to the next step—namely, the method. Here again there is widespread agreement. A world organisation has already been erected for the prime purpose of preventing war, UNO, the successor of the League of Nations, with the decisive addition of the United States and all that that means, is already at work. We must make sure that its work is fruitful, that it is a reality and not a sham, that it is a force for action, and not merely a frothing of words, that it is a true temple of peace in which the shields of many nations can some day be hung up, and not merely a cockpit in a Tower of Babel. Before we cast away the solid assurances of national armaments for self-preservation we must be certain that our temple is built, not upon shifting sands or quagmires, but upon the rock. Anyone can see with his eyes open that our path will be difficult and also long, but if we persevere together as we did in the two world wars—though not, alas, in the interval between them—I cannot doubt that we shall achieve our common purpose in the end.

I have, however, a definite and practical proposal to make for action. Courts and magistrates may be set up but they cannot function without sheriffs and constables. The United Nations Organisation must immediately begin to be equipped with an international armed force. In such a matter we can only go step by step, but we must begin now. I propose that each of the Powers and States should be invited to delegate a certain number of air squadrons to the service of the world organisation. These squadrons would be trained and prepared in their own countries, but would move around in rotation from one country to another. They would wear the uniform of their own countries but with different badges. They would not be required to act against their own nation, but in other respects they would be directed by the world organisation. This might be started on a modest scale and would grow as confidence grew. I wished to see this done after the First World War, and I devoutly trust it may be done forthwith.

It would nevertheless be wrong and imprudent to entrust the secret knowledge or experience of the atomic bomb, which the United States, Great Britain, and Canada now share, to the world organisation, while it is still in its infancy. It would be criminal madness to cast it adrift in this still agitated and un-united world. No one in any country has slept less well in their beds because this knowledge and the method and the raw materials to apply it, are at present largely retained in American hands. I do not believe we should all have slept so soundly had the positions been reversed and if some Communist or neo-Fascist State monopolised for the time being these dread agencies. The fear of them alone might easily have been used to enforce totalitarian systems upon the free democratic world, with consequences appalling to human imagination. God has willed that this shall not be and we have at least a breathing space to set our house in order before this peril has to be encountered: and even then, if no effort is spared, we should still possess so formidable a superiority as to impose effective deterrents upon its employment, or threat of employment, by others. Ultimately, when the essential brotherhood of man is truly embodied and expressed in a world organisation with all the necessary practical safeguards to make it effective, these powers would naturally be confided to that world organisation.

Now I come to the second danger of these two marauders which threatens the cottage, the home, and the ordinary people—namely, tyranny. We cannot be blind to the fact that the liberties enjoyed by individual citizens throughout the British Empire are not valid in a considerable number of countries, some of which are very powerful. In these States control is enforced upon the common people by various kinds of all-embracing police governments. The power of the State is exercised without restraint, either by dictators or by compact oligarchies operating through a privileged party and a political police. It is not our duty at this time when difficulties are so numerous to interfere forcibly in the internal affairs of countries which we have not conquered in war. But we must never cease to proclaim in fearless tones the great principles of freedom and the rights of man which are the joint inheritance of the English-speaking world and which through Magna Carta, the Bill of Rights, the Habeas Corpus, trial by jury, and the English common law find their most famous expression in the American Declaration of Independence.

All this means that the people of any country have the right, and should have the power by constitutional action, by free unfettered elections, with secret ballot, to choose or change the character or form of government under which they dwell; that freedom of speech and thought should reign; that courts of justice, independent of the executive, unbiased by any party, should administer laws which have received the broad assent of large majorities or are consecrated by time and custom. Here are the title deeds of freedom which should lie in every cottage home. Here is the message of the British and American peoples to mankind. Let us preach what we practise—let us practise what we preach.

I have now stated the two great dangers which menace the homes of the people: War and Tyranny. I have not yet spoken of poverty and privation which are in many cases the prevailing anxiety. But if the dangers of war and tyranny are removed, there is no doubt that science and co-operation can bring in the next few years to the world, certainly in the next few decades newly taught in the sharpening school of war, an expansion of material well-being beyond anything that has yet occurred in human experience. Now, at this sad and breathless moment, we are plunged in the hunger and distress which are the aftermath of our stupendous struggle; but this will pass and may pass quickly, and there is no reason except human folly or sub-human crime which should deny to all the nations the inauguration and enjoyment of an age of plenty. I have often used words which I learned fifty years ago from a great Irish-American orator, a friend of mine, Mr. Bourke Cockran. "There is enough for all. The earth is a generous mother; she will provide in plentiful abundance food for all her children if they will but cultivate her soil in justice and in peace." So far I feel that we are in full agreement.

Now, while still pursuing the method of realising our overall strategic concept, I come to the crux of what I have travelled here to Say. Neither the sure prevention of war, nor the continuous rise of world organisation will be gained without what I have called the fraternal association of the English-speaking peoples. This means a special relationship between the British Commonwealth and Empire and the United States. This is no time for generalities, and I will venture to be precise. Fraternal association requires not only the growing friendship and mutual understanding between our two vast but kindred Systems of society, but the continuance of the intimate relationship between our military advisers, leading to common study of potential dangers, the similarity of weapons and manuals of instructions, and to the interchange of officers and cadets at technical colleges. It should carry with it the continuance of the present facilities for mutual security by the joint use of all Naval and Air Force bases in the possession of either country all over the world. This would perhaps double the mobility of the American Navy and Air Force. It would greatly expand that of the British Empire Forces and it might well lead, if and as the world calms down, to important financial savings. Already we use together a large number of islands; more may well be entrusted to our joint care in the near future.

The United States has already a Permanent Defence Agreement with the Do-minion of Canada, which is so devotedly attached to the British Commonwealth and Empire. This Agreement is more effective than many of those which have often been made under formal alliances. This principle should be extended to all British Commonwealths with full reciprocity. Thus, whatever happens, and thus only, shall we be secure ourselves and able to work together for the high and simple causes that are dear to us and bode no ill to any. Eventually there may come—I feel eventually there will come—the principle of common citizenship, but that we may be content to leave to destiny, whose outstretched arm many of us can already clearly see.

There is however an important question we must ask ourselves. Would a special relationship between the United States and the British Commonwealth be inconsistent with our over-riding loyalties to the World Organisation? I reply that, on the contrary, it is probably the only means by which that organisation will achieve its full stature and strength. There are already the special United States relations with Canada which I have just mentioned, and there are the special relations between the United States and the South American Republics. We British have our twenty years Treaty of Collaboration and Mutual Assistance with Soviet Russia. I agree with Mr. Bevin, the Foreign Secretary of Great Britain, that it might well be a fifty years Treaty so far as we are concerned. We aim at nothing but mutual assistance and collaboration. The British have an alliance with Portugal unbroken since 1384, and which produced fruitful results at critical moments in the late war. None of these clash with the general interest of a world agreement, or a world organisation; on the contrary they help it. "In my father's house are many mansions." Special associations between members of the United Nations which have no aggressive point against any other country, which harbour no design incompatible with the Charter of the United Nations, far from being harmful, are beneficial and, as I believe, indispensable.

I spoke earlier of the Temple of Peace. Workmen from all countries must build that temple. If two of the workmen know each other particularly well and are old friends, if their families are inter-mingled, and if they have "faith in each other's purpose, hope in each other's future and charity towards each other's shortcomings"—to quote some good words I read here the other day-why cannot they work together at the common task as friends and partners? Why cannot they share their tools and thus increase each other's working powers? Indeed they must do so or else the temple may not be built, or, being built, it may collapse, and we shall all be proved again unteachable and have to go and try to learn again for a third time in a school of war, incomparably more rigorous than that from which we have just been released. The dark ages may return, the Stone Age may return on the gleaming wings of science, and what might now shower immeasurable material blessings upon mankind, may even bring about its total destruction. Beware, I say; time may be short. Do not let us take the course of allowing events to drift along until it is too late. If there is to be a fraternal association of the kind I have described, with all the extra strength and security which both our countries can derive from it, let us make sure that that great fact is known to the world, and that it plays its part in steadying and stabilising the foundations of peace. There is the path of wisdom. Prevention is better than cure.

A shadow has fallen upon the scenes so lately lighted by the Allied victory. Nobody knows what Soviet Russia and its Communist international organisation intends to do in the immediate future, or what are the limits, if any, to their expansive and proselytising tendencies. I have a strong admiration and regard for the valiant Russian people and for my wartime comrade, Marshal Stalin. There is deep sympathy and goodwill in Britain—and I doubt not here also—towards the peoples of all the Russias and a resolve to persevere through many differences and rebuffs in establishing lasting friendships. We understand the Russian need to be secure on her western frontiers by the removal of all possibility of German aggression. We welcome Russia to her rightful place among the leading nations of the world. We welcome her flag upon the seas. Above all, we welcome constant, frequent and growing contacts between the Russian people and our own people on both sides of the Atlantic. It is my duty however, for I am sure you would wish me to state the facts as I see them to you, to place before you certain facts about the present position in Europe.

From Stettin in the Baltic to Trieste in the Adriatic, an iron curtain has descended across the Continent. Behind that line lie all the capitals of the ancient states of Central and Eastern Europe. Warsaw, Berlin, Prague, Vienna, Budapest, Belgrade, Bucharest and Sofia, all these famous cities and the populations around them lie in what I must call the Soviet sphere, and all are subject in one form or another, not only to Soviet influence but to a very high and, in many cases, increasing measure of control from Moscow. Athens alone-Greece with its immortal glories-is free to decide its future at an election under British, American and French observation. The Russian-dominated Polish Government has been encouraged to make enormous and wrongful inroads upon Germany, and mass expulsions of millions of Germans on a scale grievous and undreamed-of are now taking place. The Communist parties, which were very small in all these Eastern States of Europe, have been raised to pre-eminence and power far beyond their numbers and are seeking everywhere to obtain totalitarian control. Police governments are prevailing in nearly every case, and so far, except in Czechoslovakia, there is no true democracy.

Turkey and Persia are both profoundly alarmed and disturbed at the claims which are being made upon them and at the pressure being exerted by the Moscow Government. An attempt is being made by the Russians in Berlin to build up a quasi-Communist party in their zone of Occupied Germany by showing special favours to groups of left-wing German leaders. At the end of the fighting last June, the American and British Armies withdrew westwards, in accordance with an earlier agreement, to a depth at some points of 150 miles upon a front of nearly four hundred miles, in order to allow our Russian allies to occupy this vast expanse of territory which the Western Democracies had conquered.

If now the Soviet Government tries, by separate action, to build up a pro-Communist Germany in their areas, this will cause new serious difficulties in the British and American zones, and will give the defeated Germans the power of putting themselves up to auction between the Soviets and the Western Democracies. Whatever conclusions may be drawn from these facts—and facts they are—this is certainly not the Liberated Europe we fought to build up. Nor is it one which contains the essentials of permanent peace.

The safety of the world requires a new unity in Europe, from which no nation should be permanently outcast. It is from the quarrels of the strong parent races in Europe that the world wars we have witnessed, or which occurred in former times, have sprung. Twice in our own lifetime we have seen the United States, against their wishes and their traditions, against arguments, the force of which it is impossible not to comprehend, drawn by irresistible forces, into these wars in time to secure the victory of the good cause, but only after frightful slaughter and devastation had occurred. Twice the United States has had to send several millions of its young men across the Atlantic to find the war; but now war can find any nation, wherever it may dwell between dusk and dawn. Surely we should work with conscious purpose for a grand pacification of Europe, within the structure of the United Nations and in accordance with its Charter. That I feel is an open cause of policy of very great importance.

In front of the iron curtain which lies across Europe are other causes for anxiety. In Italy the Communist Party is seriously hampered by having to Support the Communist-trained Marshal Tito's claims to former Italian territory at the head of the Adriatic. Nevertheless the future of Italy hangs in the balance. Again one cannot imagine a regenerated Europe without a strong France. All my public life I have worked for a Strong France and I never lost faith in her destiny, even in the darkest hours. I will not lose faith now. However, in a great number of countries, far from the Russian frontiers and throughout the world, Communist fifth columns are established and work in complete unity and absolute obedience to the directions they receive from the Communist centre. Except in the British Commonwealth and in the United States where Communism is in its infancy, the Communist parties or fifth columns constitute a growing challenge and peril to Christian civilisation. These are sombre facts for anyone to have to recite on the morrow of a victory gained by so much splendid comradeship in arms and in the cause of freedom and democracy; but we should be most unwise not to face them squarely while time remains.

The outlook is also anxious in the Far East and especially in Manchuria. The Agreement which was made at Yalta, to which I was a party, was extremely favourable to Soviet Russia, but it was made at a time when no one could say that the German war might not extend all through the summer and autumn of 1945 and when the Japanese war was expected to last for a further 18 months from the end of the German war. In this country you are all so well-informed about the Far East, and such devoted friends of China, that I do not need to expatiate on the situation there.

I have felt bound to portray the shadow which, alike in the west and in the east, falls upon the world. I was a high minister at the time of the Versailles Treaty and a close friend of Mr. Lloyd-George, who was the head of the British delegation at Versailles. I did not myself agree with many things that were done, but I have a very Strong impression in my mind of that situation, and I find it painful to contrast it with that which prevails now. In those days there were high hopes and unbounded confidence that the wars were over, and that the League of Nations would become all-powerful. I do not see or feel that same confidence or even the same hopes in the haggard world at the present time.

On the other hand I repulse the idea that a new war is inevitable; still more that it is imminent. It is because I am sure that our fortunes are still in our own hands and that we hold the power to save the future, that I feel the duty to speak out now that I have the occasion and the opportunity to do so. I do not believe that Soviet Russia desires war. What they desire is the fruits of war and the indefinite expansion of their power and doctrines. But what we have to consider here to-day while time remains, is the permanent prevention of war and the establishment of conditions of freedom and democracy as rapidly as possible in all countries. Our difficulties and dangers will not be removed by closing our eyes to them. They will not be removed by mere waiting to see what happens; nor will they be removed by a policy of appeasement. What is needed is a settlement, and the longer this is delayed, the more difficult it will be and the greater our dangers will become.

From what I have seen of our Russian friends and Allies during the war, I am convinced that there is nothing they admire so much as strength, and there is nothing for which they have less respect than for weakness, especially military weakness. For that reason the old doctrine of a balance of power is unsound. We cannot afford, if we can help it, to work on narrow margins, offering temptations to a trial of strength. If the Western Democracies stand together in strict adherence to the principles of the United Nations Charter, their influence for furthering those principles will be immense and no one is likely to molest them. If however they become divided or falter in their duty and if these all-important years are allowed to slip away then indeed catastrophe may overwhelm us all.

Last time I saw it all coming and cried aloud to my own fellow-countrymen and to the world, but no one paid any attention. Up till the year 1933 or even 1935, Germany might have been saved from the awful fate which has overtaken her and we might all have been spared the miseries Hitler let loose upon mankind. There never was a war in all history easier to prevent by timely action than the one which has just desolated such great areas of the globe. It could have been prevented in my belief without the firing of a single shot, and Germany might be powerful, prosperous and honoured to-day; but no one would listen and one by one we were all sucked into the awful whirlpool. We surely must not let that happen again. This can only be achieved by reaching now, in 1946, a good understanding on all points with Russia under the general authority of the United Nations Organisation and by the maintenance of that good understanding through many peaceful years, by the world instrument, supported by the whole strength of the English-speaking world and all its connections. There is the solution which I respectfully offer to you in this Address to which I have given the title "The Sinews of Peace."

Let no man underrate the abiding power of the British Empire and Commonwealth. Because you see the 46 millions in our island harassed about their food supply, of which they only grow one half, even in war-time, or because we have difficulty in restarting our industries and export trade after six years of passionate war effort, do not suppose that we shall not come through these dark years of privation as we have come through the glorious years of agony, or that half a century from now, you will not see 70 or 80 millions of Britons spread about the world and united in defence of our traditions, our way of life, and of the world causes which you and we espouse. If the population of the English-speaking Commonwealths be added to that of the United States with all that such co-operation implies in the air, on the sea, all over the globe and in science and in industry, and in moral force, there will be no quivering, precarious balance of power to offer its temptation to ambition or adventure. On the contrary, there will be an overwhelming assurance of security. If we adhere faithfully to the Charter of the United Nations and walk forward in sedate and sober strength seeking no one's land or treasure, seeking to lay no arbitrary control upon the thoughts of men; if all British moral and material forces and convictions are joined with your own in fraternal association, the high-roads of the future will be clear, not only for us but for all, not only for our time, but for a century to come.

THE PENTAGON PAPER[1]
WASHINGTON, DC, APRIL 1, 1948

(Source: *Foreign Relations of the United States*, 1948, Western Europe, Volume III, David H. Stauffer, Ralph R. Goodwin, Marvin W. Kranz, Howard McGaw Smyth, Frederick Aandahl, and Charles S. Sampson, eds., Washington: United States Government Printing Office, 1974, Document 63)

The purpose of this paper is to recommend a course of action adequate to give effect to the declaration of March 17 by the President of support for the free nations of Europe. The recommendations made will require close consultation with political leaders of both parties in order that whatever policy is formulated may be a truly bipartisan American policy.

RECOMMENDATIONS

1. Diplomatic approaches to be made by the Government of the United States to the signatories of the Five-Power Treaty signed at Brussels on March 17, 1948 in order to secure their approval to its extension in the manner outlined below and to inform them of plans for the conclusion of a collective defense agreement for the North Atlantic Area, details of which are given below.

2. An immediate approach then to be made to Norway, Sweden, Denmark and Iceland, and (if the Italian elections are over) also to Italy, through diplomatic channels, by the United States, United Kingdom and France, with the consent of Benelux, with the object of explaining to them the scheme for a declaration by the President on the lines of that recommended in paragraph 3 below, and of ascertaining whether they

would be prepared in such circumstances to accede to the Five-Power Treaty in the near future and to enter into negotiations for the North Atlantic Collective Defense Agreement.

3. The President to announce that invitations had been issued to the United Kingdom, France, Canada, Norway, Sweden, Denmark, Iceland, The Netherlands, Belgium, Luxembourg, Eire, Italy, and Portugal (provided that secret inquiries had established the fact that these countries would be prepared to accept the invitations) to take part in a conference with a view to the conclusion of a collective Defense Agreement for the North Atlantic Area designed to give maximum effect, as between the parties, to the provisions of the United Nations Charter.

In his statement the President would include a declaration of American intention, in the light of the obligations assumed by the signatories of the Five-Power Treaty and pending the conclusion of the Defense Agreement, to regard any action in the North Atlantic Area which it considers an armed attack against a signatory of the Five-Power Treaty as an armed attack against the United States to be dealt with by the United States under Article 51 of the United Nations Charter. Pending agreement upon collective defense measures, the United States would determine the immediate measures which it would take individually. The declaration would state that the United States would be disposed to extend similar support to any other free democracy in Western Europe which acceded to the Five-Power Treaty.

If, as a result of the inquiries referred to in Paragraph 2 above, it appears that Norway, Sweden, Denmark, Iceland, and Italy, or any of them, do not wish to accede to the Five-Power Treaty at this stage, consideration would need to be given, in the light of the views of each of the above states, to the extension to them of some assurance of immediate support in case of an armed attack against them which they resisted resolutely. In any event, the declaration would be so phrased as to avoid inviting aggression against any other free country in Europe.

4. Simultaneously with this declaration an Anglo-American declaration to be made to the effect that the two countries are not prepared to countenance any attack on the political independence or territorial integrity of Greece, Turkey, or Iran, and that in the event of such an attack and pending the possible negotiation of some general Middle Eastern security system, they would feel bound fully to support these states under Article 51 of the Charter of the United Nations.

5. It is contemplated that the Defense Agreement referred to in paragraph 3 above would contain the following main provisions:

a. Preamble combining some of the features of the preamble to the Five-Power Treaty and making it clear that the main object of the instrument would be to preserve western civilization in the geographical area covered by the agreement. The Preamble should also refer to the desirability of the conclusion of further defense agreements under Article 51 of the Charter of the United Nations to the end that all free nations should eventually be covered by such agreements.

b. Provision that each Party shall regard any action in the area covered by the agreement, which it considers an armed attack against any other Party, as an armed attack against itself and that each Party accordingly undertakes to assist in meeting the attack in the exercise of the inherent right of individual or collective self defense recognized by Article 51 of the Charter.

c. Provision following the lines of Article III, paragraph 2 of the Rio Treaty to the effect that, at the request of the State or States directly attacked, and until coordinated measures have been agreed upon, each one of the Parties shall determine the immediate measures which it will individually take in fulfillment of the obligation contained in the preceding paragraph and in accordance with the principle of mutual solidarity.

d. Provision to the effect that action taken under the agreement shall, as provided in Article 51 of the Charter, be promptly reported to the Security Council and cease when the Security Council shall have taken the necessary steps to maintain or restore peace and security.

e. Delineation of the area covered by the agreement to include: (1) the continental territory in Europe or North America of any Party, (2) any territory in Europe occupied by the forces of any party, (3) the islands in the North Atlantic whether sovereign or belonging to any Party, and (4) the waters of the North Atlantic and the air space over them. (This would include Spitzbergen and other Norwegian Islands, Iceland, Greenland, Newfoundland and Alaska.)

f. Provision for consultation between all the parties in the event of any party considering that its territorial integrity or political independence is threatened by armed attack or indirect aggression in any part of the world.

    g. Provision for the establishment of such agencies as may be necessary for effective implementation of the agreement including the working out of plans for prompt and effective action under b and c above.

    h. Duration of ten years, with automatic renewal for five-year periods unless denounced.

6. When circumstances permit, Germany (or the three Western Zones), Austria (or the three Western Zones) and Spain should be invited to adhere to the Five-Power Treaty and to the Defense Agreement for the North Atlantic Area. This objective, which should not be publicly disclosed, could be provided for by a suitable accession clause in the Defense Agreement.

7. Military conversations to be initiated in the immediate future with parties to the Five-Power Treaty with a view initially to strengthening their collective security through coordinating military production and supply.

Note

1. Secret talks between Canada, the United Kingdom and the United States, held between March 25 and April 1, 1948, led to the recommendations in the document.

SPEECH DELIVERED BY PRIME MINISTER AND FOREIGN MINISTER OF BELGIUM PAUL-HENRI SPAAK
"WHY WE FEAR RUSSIA" OR "THE FEAR SPEECH" DELIVERED AT THE THIRD SESSION OF THE GENERAL ASSEMBLY OF THE UNITED NATIONS, PARIS, SEPTEMBER 28, 1948

(Source: *Vital Speeches of the Day*, Vol. XV, No. 1, October 1948, pp. 8–11)

The representatives who spoke at the beginning of this general debate on many occasions stressed the atmosphere of great anxiety in which our work has begun. How could it be otherwise with so many deceived hopes and so many problems that have remained without solution?

After a week of general debate, perhaps it is permissible to question where we are and whether we have effected any progress. Some speakers have come to this rostrum in order to stress their persistent faith in the principles of the Charter. Others have drawn their conclusions with serenity and with courage. Others have delivered their usual recriminations.

If, at this stage of the general debate, I were to ask myself what is the prevailing feeling, I would say that it seems to me, alas, that the atmosphere of lack of comprehension which more and more is dividing the United Nations has only increased still further, has only still further deepened. And I would not hesitate to say that there is perhaps no greater feeling of disillusionment, no more painful feeling, than to see that a society such as ours cannot succeed unless, at its base, there is not only tolerance but also the possibility of understanding one another's point of view.

In this atmosphere of lack of comprehension, who is the more guilty party? Who is not making any effort to understand the point of view of the opposing party? Mr. Bevin said yesterday from this very rostrum—and I can but repeat his words—that the countries which stress that they belong to the Western, the democratic civilization, in the classic sense of the word, have nothing for which to reproach themselves. It is we who wish the free circulation of human beings; it is we who wish the free circulation of ideas; it is we who are ready to submit ourselves to the examination, to the investigation, to the judgment of everyone—to the examination of our policies, of our ideals. It is not we who close ourselves to this examination; it is not we who shut ourselves up behind an iron curtain; it is not we who elude such an attempt to understand; it is not we who do not wish, on the basis of this understanding, to co-operate.

It is quite certain that there is a complete lack of comprehension of the western world on the part of the Union of Soviet Socialist Republics, and the speech of Mr. Vishinsky was an eloquent testimony to this. Perhaps it may seem impertinent for the representative of a modest country to wish to reply to the representative of the Union of Soviet Socialist Republics. But perhaps, after all, it is better that the representative of a small country should reply to the USSR representative, since, I believe, no one will be able to find in my attitude any intention of provocation on the part of Belgium of the Union of Soviet Socialist Republics. That would be, indeed, ridiculous.

But the speech of Mr. Vishinsky can be understood in only two ways. Either it is a speech of propaganda, or else it is a sincere speech. And in both cases this speech deserves an answer, because, if it is a propaganda speech, then we also have the right to make use of this rostrum to indulge in counter-propaganda; and, if it is a sincere speech, then it reveals such a lack of comprehension of our spirit, it shows such an ignorance of our wishes, of our thoughts, of the thoughts of the Western European countries, that it is imperative to redress these mistakes and to allow the Union of Soviet Socialist Republics to base its policies on an accurate understanding of what is happening and of what is being thought in a part of the world.

After Mr. Bevin, I would reply: We do not wish to discuss the communist regime. We consider that, for many countries, communism is a test which is perhaps necessary, but we believe that it is a test which the Western world can avoid, through which it need not go. Without discussing the merits of the regime, I should like to assert that, after having struggled in this last war against fascism and against Hitlerism, we do not propose to submit ourselves to any other totalitarian or authoritarian doctrine. We are in favor of liberal democracy; that is to say, we believe—and we believe with all our force and with all our conscience—in the necessity of building a political society based on liberty of thought, on liberty of writing, on liberty of reunion and on liberty of association. We want free elections; we want a government responsible to the people; we want respect for human dignity; we want a state that serves the human being and not a human being that serves the state—and still less do we want a man who serves a single party.

This regime has vast advantages. It allows all manner of progress, both economic and social. It repudiates intolerance. It repudiates the use of force and the use of violence. It shows confidence in good sense and in human wisdom. I recognize that this regime is perhaps the most difficult political regime to achieve, and I also recognize that it offers certain inconveniences, certain disadvantages, and perhaps even certain dangers. In my country, liberty of thought and liberty of writing includes even liberty to write and think differently from what is generally admitted. But in order to struggle against a mistake, we do not believe that we should base ourselves on the might of the police, of censorship, or of the tribunals. Still less do we believe that we should base ourselves on propaganda which spreads lies and errors. We believe that we must base ourselves on propaganda that spreads truth. It is because we have this great confidence in the wisdom of human beings that we believe that truthful propaganda will triumph over everything.

All this—this spirit in which we live, the principles which are ours, the truths which we respect and protect and defend—must be understood if one wishes to judge our political action.

Mr. Vishinsky has spoken a lot of the war-mongering campaigns which allegedly exist in the United States, in the United Kingdom—and he did not fail to mention even France, Belgium, Luxembourg and other countries such as the Netherlands.

Very frankly, as far as my country is concerned, I do not know a single political party, I do not know a single responsible political personality, I do not know a single man who exercises influence in the leadership of public opinion—I do not know a single one who is a war-monger. I have never heard, I have never seen, I have never read in the press of my country or in speeches delivered in my country any sentence that could make one believe that Belgium would participate in a campaign of war-mongering against any other country. But I believe that in this field we must not lose a sense of nuance. We must not confound the feeling that a war might start with the will that a war should start. We must not mistake the possibility of envisaging a war and the fact of desiring it. We must not even confuse the will to prepare for war and the will to provoke war.

Of course, in the Union of Soviet Socialist Republics what is read in the papers and what is heard in speeches is greatly exaggerated. I have applied myself to listening with the closest attention, with the greatest respect, to the words of the USSR representative, but I have also re-read his speech and I have noticed that, nevertheless, he attributes extraordinary importance to certain facts which, in a country of liberty, go more or less unnoticed.

Mr. Vishinsky denounces passionately certain articles which have appeared in the American press, and he says that in these articles we have with singular frankness enumerated the bases from which the Soviet Union would be bombed. We have also shown the distances over which these planes would fly. We have also indicated that Moscow is so many miles' distance from Tripoli and so on and so forth. Mr. Vishinsky enumerates the range of action of the United States planes, and he says that this is a war-mongering campaign to point out in precise figures the distances which exist between London and Moscow and Moscow and Tripoli. I should like to put to the representative of the USSR a single question. Does he wish to give me an assurance that the General Staff of the Soviet Union has not evaluated the distance from Moscow to London, and that there are not calculations made by the General Staffs which reveal so eloquently in the American press the distances which exist between the various cities? But there is not only the war-mongering propaganda, there is also the five power pact—the Brussels pact—and Mr. Vishinsky said that those who conceived such treaties, those who built up such blocs and conducted such policies were encouraging the instigators of war and the organizers of a new war. This lamentation of the Soviet Union is not very subtle, because it is tantamount to saying that as long as the Soviet Union signs alliances with its neighboring countries, so long as the Soviet Union signs defensive treaties with Poland, Czechoslovakia and Yugoslavia and other countries of eastern Europe, all these are peaceful policies. When, on the contrary, Belgium, Luxembourg or the Netherlands sign alliances with France and the United Kingdom, that, of course, is a war-mongering policy.

I have two arguments to make against this statement, and they are both decisive. One, in refutation of such propaganda, is that when we signed the five power pact, the Brussels pact, we did nothing but comply strictly with the letter of Article 51 of the Charter. Article 51 of the Charter states:

> "Nothing in the present Charter shall impair the inherent right of individual or collective self-defense . . ."

This is the Charter which the Soviet Union and the other countries of eastern Europe signed together with us. This is where we are authorized to organize our mutual self-defense, whether it be individual or collective. It is on the basis of Article 51 of the Charter that we have confined and that we have conceived our Brussels pact.

I believe that this juridical provision is sufficient to authorize the spirit of our agreement, but is there anyone in this Assembly, anyone in the world, who might believe that Luxembourg, or that the Netherlands, or that Belgium wish to participate in an aggressive war. Does one forget where we come from, does one forget the two contests we have suffered within twenty-five years? Does one forget that though we have been victorious we have, nevertheless, been occupied for four long years and that our countries have come out of every war ravaged and decimated? Does anyone really believe that we could survive a third world war? Of course not. Nobody can believe such a thing, and Mr. Bevin said so very eloquently. Nobody can believe that the Brussels pact conceived in March of last year is of an aggressive nature. Everybody knows that we wish to join our forces in order to defend ourselves.

The delegation of the USSR must not seek complicated explanations of our policy. I will explain to this delegation what is the basis of our policy. I will say, in terms which perhaps are cool ones, in terms which I believe that the small nations alone can employ, what is the basis of our policy. It is fear; the fear of you, the fear of your Government, the fear of your policy. If I may use this word, it is because the fear to which I refer is not the fear of a coward. It is not the fear of a country that trembles, a country that is ready to ask for mercy or pity. It is the fear of someone who can and must have that fear, of one who looks ahead, the fear of one who considers the horror and tragedy that will face them in the future.

Do you know why we fear? It is because you speak of imperialism often, and what is the definition of imperialism? What is the current notion, the generally accepted notion of imperialism? It is usually that of a great country that effects conquests, that expands its influence throughout the world. What is the reality of this conception? There is only one great power that has emerged from the war having conquered other territories and that power is the USSR. It is during this war, and because of this war, that you have annexed the Balkan countries, that you seized a portion of Finland, and that you seized a portion of Poland. It is because of your policy that you reached Warsaw, that you reached Sofia, and that you reached Bucharest. It is because of this policy that you occupy Berlin and you are not ready to quit Berlin and Vienna, and it is because of this policy that you assert your right to participate in the Ruhr. It is because of all this that we feel you are on the very banks of the Rhine and, therefore, we cannot understand why you ask us why we are fearful.

The truth is that your foreign policy is now more audacious and more ambitious than the foreign policy of the Tsars themselves. We also fear because of the policy you pursue in this Assembly. We also fear because of the use and the abuse that you make of the right that has been given to you in San Francisco, the use and the abuse of the veto. We fear because in this Assembly you have arisen as the champions of the doctrine of absolute national sovereignty, and we ask you, how can an international organization function and fulfill the purposes that belong to it if this antiquated doctrine, this absolute doctrine, this reactionary doctrine prevails? Such an international organization can only function when all nations, small, medium and large, have recognized that above their own personal will there is the international law. So long as any nation wishes to impose its will or to place its will above the majority of nations, that organization will not give the results we hoped it would give.

It has not sufficed to make use or abuse of the veto. It has not sufficed that you proclaim this principle of absolute sovereignty against international law. You have also systematically refused to co-operate with the United Nations every time that this Assembly, against your feelings or against your views, has made a recommendation. You have contended that the Korean Commission or the Balkan Commission has not offered any tangible result. How could it offer any tangible result, because from the outset you have refused to co-operate with them?

We fear because of all this. We fear because by your conduct you have rendered this Organization ineffective. We fear because the problems before this Assembly have remained unsolved, because even when a solution is proposed by the majority of the United Nations, you have refused to adhere to this solution. We have feared because we have placed all our hopes and our confidence in the defensive organization of the

United Nations and through the policy you have pursued you are forbidding us to seek our security and our salvation within the framework of this Organization, but making us seek it within the framework of a regional arrangement. We fear you because in every country represented here you are maintaining a fifth column besides which the Hitlerite fifth column is nothing but a Boy Scout organization, if I might say so. There is not a single spot in the world, whether in Asia, whether in Europe, or whether in Africa, where a Government represented here fails to find difficulties, and where these difficulties are [not] being still further aggravated by you. Whereas these Governments represented here seek to co-operate, in every one of our countries there is a group of individuals who are not only representatives and defenders of your foreign policy, which is not perhaps a very grave fault, but they do not miss an opportunity to weaken the countries to which they belong, morally, politically and socially, and you, the USSR and the eastern European countries and the communist parties of the world have shown exactly what you can do in your opposition and in your attacks against the Marshall plan.

I do not have many illusions. I know that in certain sections of the press throughout the world I shall most likely be called an instrument of American policy or a pawn of Wall Street. But I assert that the position taken by the Union of Soviet Socialist Republics against the Marshall Plan is the basest, the saddest, the most disquieting policy that could be imagined. The hopes of the world are portrayed by sixteen countries pursuing one aim, that of national rehabilitation. In spite of all statements to the contrary, we can see clearly that without the Marshall Plan these countries would be lost. Instead of going into complicated debates on the Marshall Plan, instead of delving into the American Press, it would perhaps be more logical to seek an explanation of the Marshall Plan in the words of General Marshall himself. When he spoke for the first time of this Plan which was to become the Marshall Plan, he said that it is logical that the United States should do all it can to reestablish the economic health of the world, without which political stability and peace cannot be ensured. Our policy is against no country; it is against no doctrine; it is against famine, poverty, despair and chaos. Its purpose is the resurrection of an active economy throughout the world.

Whatever the future of the Marshall Plan, the words said on that day are words which will shed honor on the head of the American State Department and the policy for which we have the greatest respect and gratitude. We know that this policy speaks for the country which has twice in twenty-five years sent soldiers to fight for liberty and independence. This is the policy inspired by Wilson and by Roosevelt. It was this same policy that made UNRRA and Lend-Lease. Now it is offering Europe its greatest and only hope of salvation.

And that is why we fear. I repeat, rather grossly speaking, that is why we are afraid.

In a speech made during the war, President Roosevelt enumerated the Four Freedoms which should, according to him, bring confidence and prosperity to the world. One of these freedoms was the "Freedom from Fear." I must admit that when that speech was made I did not understand its entire purport; I did not understand its depth. But today, a few years later at the time when the Third General Assembly of the United Nations is meeting, I know what tremendous service would be rendered to the world if one succeeded, once and for all in freeing us from fear.

If this freedom from fear is to become a reality, may I tell the representatives of the Union of Soviet Socialist Republics that the Union of Soviet Socialist Republics must play a vital part. We do not only expect one to proclaim that one is for the United Nations Charter, that one is for freedom. We want these words translated into action. In this Assembly we should like to begin a real, genuine co-operation based on mutual understanding and mutual respect for one another.

Is this a pessimistic speech? Does this mean that I believe that all is lost? Of course not. Whatever has been said in this general debate, whatever meaning one might attribute to the words spoken, whatever one's feelings, we all have the same respect for peace and the same desire to co-operate. Whatever the frankness of my words, I believe that these peaceful speeches were genuinely sincere. I believe we are too close to the war, too close to the suffering which we have gone through, too close to our dead, our orphans and widows, too close to all this to be insincere when we speak of peace and co-operation.

What frightens me is that I understand that at this time humanity knows what should be done in order that it be saved. Humanity would like to do it. But its tragic destiny seems to render it incapable of doing it.

Nevertheless, at the time when this Third Session of the General Assembly is meeting, we should strive to undertake something, even at the time when we feel that our illusions are being slowly lost. Of course, we must not be too ambitious; we must not, at this stage, attempt to change a situation that we have all allowed to deteriorate year by year. But, within the framework of our everyday task, within the framework of the Third Session of the General Assembly we should try to resolve certain problems and we should begin by a spectacular coup. We should start with a compromise.

I know that in certain quarters compromises are not looked on with favor, but how can we come to agreement with one another, when we are so different from one another, if we fail to seek a compromise?

I have noted that our agenda is heavily overloaded. In parentheses, may I say that our Organization is dealing with too many secondary problems. Would it not do better to tackle the more essential and immediate problems? Perhaps I am naive in saying so. Nevertheless, you may see a reasonable element in the proposal that I am about to make. The Assembly seems to abhor everything that smells of a revision of the Charter or an abrogation of the veto. One believes that certain countries might always be in the minority. But I do not believe that this is the case. I do not think this fear is justified. I believe it is exaggerated, and I say so quite frankly. I know that there are a number of delegations in this Assembly which would like to come nearer to the theses propounded by certain countries, if only they could see that these are reasonable and dependable. But even though this fear is exaggerated, I understand that it can exist. And, even though we believe that this Organization can only function if the Charter is revised, even though we believe that this Organization can only exist on condition that the veto is abrogated, we are willing to renounce this proposal. We will make an effort to apply the Charter as it emerged from San Francisco. We are willing to renounce something which we consider essential. But on the other hand, we hope that you will promise to collaborate on the basis of the Charter as it now stands. Not only as it stands in the letter, but also in the spirit. This means that you will not object ceaselessly to the admission of new members, that you will not prevent certain countries from participating in our work; this means that, during this Session, you will collaborate in drawing up a resolution that will allow these countries to participate in our work. We need you to make a success of our task. We enjoin you not to sabotage the work. Promise us your co-operation. Promise us that you will help us to start off on a new tack. In striving to understand one another and to come closer to one another, perhaps our fear will disappear and we will again have the faith we had at San Francisco.

Let us make this new start together before it is too late. I believe it is time for us to do so.

Official interpretation from French

NATIONWIDE RADIO ADDRESS DELIVERED BY SECRETARY OF STATE ACHESON

MARCH 18, 1949

(Source: Address by the Honorable Dean G. Acheson, Secretary of State, March 18, 1949; SSF:SRC; Harry S. Truman Papers, Truman Library)

The text of the proposed North Atlantic Pact was made public today. I welcome this opportunity to talk with my fellow citizens about it. It has taken many months to work out this text with the representatives of the other nations involved. First Mr. Lovett and then I met with the ambassadors of England, Canada, France, Belgium, the Netherlands and Luxembourg. Recently the Ambassador of Norway joined in these discussions. These talks had to be conducted in private and in confidence, so that each of us could speak freely and frankly on matters of vital importance to our countries. It is for this compelling reason that public discussion of the text of the pact by your representatives has not been possible up to this time.

That restraint no longer applies. The treaty and its implications can now be fully discussed. Public opinion can now be formed on the basis of complete information. Only in this way can your government have what former secretary of State Stimson has termed "the understanding support of the American people," which is essential to the success of any policy.

I think the American people will want to know the answers to three principal questions about this pact: How did it come about and why is it necessary? What are its terms? Will it accomplish its purpose?

The paramount purposes of the pact are peace and security. If peace and security can be achieved in the North Atlantic area, we shall have gone a long way to secure peace and security in other areas as well.

The achievement of peace and security means more than that in the final outcome we shall have prevented war and brought about the settlement of international disputes by peaceful means. There must be conviction of people everywhere that war will be prevented and that disputes will be settled peacefully. In the most practical terms, true international peace and security require a firm belief by the peoples of the world that they will not be subjected to unprovoked attack, to coercion and intimidation, to interference in their own affairs. Peace and security require confidence in the future, based on the assurance that the peoples of the world will be permitted to improve their conditions of life, free from fear that the fruits of their labor may be taken from them by alien hands.

These are goals of our own foreign policy which President Truman has emphasized many times, most recently in his inaugural address when he spoke of the hope that we could help create "the conditions that will lead eventually to personal freedom and happiness for all mankind." These are also the purposes of the United Nations, whose members are pledged "to maintain international peace and security" and to promote the economic and social advancement of all peoples."

These purposes are intimately related to the origins of the United Nations. As the Second World War neared its end, the peoples who bore the brunt of the fighting were sick of the horror, the brutality, the tragedy of war. Out of that revulsion came the determination to create a system that would go as far as humanly possible in insuring international peace and security.

The United Nations seeks to maintain peace and security by enjoining its members from using force to settle international disputes. Moreover, it insists that they acknowledge tolerance and cooperation as the guiding principles in the conduct of nations.

The members are expected to settle differences by the exercise of reason and adjustment, according to the principles of justice and law. This requires a spirit of tolerance and restraint on the part of all its members.

But, as in any other institution which presupposes restraint, violence or obstruction can be used to defeat the basic undertaking. This happens in personal relations, in families, communities, churches, politics, and everywhere in human life. If the system is used in ways it was not intended to be used, there is grave danger that the system will be disrupted.

That applies to the United Nations. The system is not working as effectively as we hoped because one of its members has attempted to prevent it from working. By obstructive tactics and the misuse of the veto, the Soviet Union has seriously interfered with the work of the Security Council in maintaining international peace and security.

But the United Nations is a flexible instrument. Although the actions of the Soviet Union have disturbed the work of the United Nations, it is strong enough to be an effective instrument for peace. It is the instrument by which we hope world peace will be achieved. The Charter recognizes the importance of regional arrangements consistent with the purposes and principles of the Charter. Such arrangements can greatly strengthen it.

The Atlantic pact is a collective self-defense arrangement among the countries of the North Atlantic area. It is aimed at coordinating the exercise of the right of self-defense specifically recognized in Article 51 of the United Nations Charter. It is designed to fit precisely into the framework of the United Nations and to assure practical measures for maintaining peace and security in harmony with the Charter.

It is the firm intention of the parties to carry out the pact in accordance with the provisions of the United Nations Charter and in a manner which will advance its purposes and principles.

Already one such arrangement under the Charter has been established with United States participation. The twenty-one American republics in reorganizing their regional system have specifically brought it within the framework of the United Nations Charter. We are now joining in the formation of a second arrangement, pertaining to the North Atlantic area, likewise within the framework of the United Nations.

It is important to keep in mind that the really successful national and international institutions are those that recognize and express underlying realities. The North Atlantic community of nations is such a reality. It is based on the affinity and natural identity of interests of the North Atlantic powers.

The North Atlantic treaty which will formally unite them is the product of at least 350 years of history and perhaps more. There developed on our Atlantic Coast a community, which has spread across the continent, connected with Western Europe by common institutions and moral and ethical beliefs. Similarities of this kind are not superficial, but fundamental. They are the strongest kind of ties, because they are based on moral conviction, on acceptance of the same values in life.

The very basis of Western civilization, which we share with the other nations bordering on the North Atlantic, and which all of us share with many other nations, is the ingrained spirit of restraint and tolerance. This is the opposite of the Communist belief that coercion by force is a proper method of hastening the inevitable. Western civilization has lived by mutual restraint and tolerance. This civilization permits and stimulates free inquiry and bold experimentation. It creates the environment of freedom, from which flows the greatest amount of ingenuity, enterprise and accomplishment.

These principles of democracy, individual liberty and rule of law have flourished in the Atlantic community. They have universal validity. They are shared by other free nations and find expression on a universal basis in the Charter of the United Nations; they are the standards by which its members have solemnly agreed to be judged. They are the elements out of which are forged the peace and the welfare of mankind.

Added to this profoundly important basis of understanding is another unifying influence—the effect of living on the sea. The sea does not separate people as much as it joins them, through trade, through travel, through mutual understanding and common interests.

For this second reason, as well as the first, North America and Western Europe have formed the two halves of what is in reality one community, and have maintained an abiding interest with each other.

It is clear that the North Atlantic pact is not an improvisation. It is the statement of the facts and lessons of history. We have learned our history lesson from two world wars in less than half a century. That experience has taught us that the control of Europe by a single aggressive, unfriendly power would constitute an intolerable threat to the national security of the United States. We participated in those two great wars to preserve the integrity and independence of the European half of the Atlantic community in order to preserve the integrity and independence of the American half. It is a simple fact, proved by experience, that an outside attack on one member of this community is an attack upon all members.

We have also learned that if the free nations do not stand together, they will fall one by one. The stratagem of the aggressor is to keep his intended victims divided, or better still, to set them quarreling with each other. Then they can be picked off one by one without arousing unified resistance. We and the free nations of Europe are determined that history shall not repeat itself in that melancholy particular.

As President Truman has said: "If we can make it sufficiently clear, in advance, that any armed attack affecting our national security would be met by overwhelming force, the armed attack might never occur." The same thought was expressed by the Foreign Relations Committee of the Senate last year in its report recommending approval of Senate Resolution 239. "The committee is convinced," the report said, "that the horrors of another world war can be avoided with certainty only by preventing war from starting. The experience of World War I and World War II suggests that the best deterrent to aggression is the certainty that immediate and effective countermeasures will be taken against those who violate the peace." That resolution, adopted by an overwhelming vote of the Senate, expressly encourages the development of collective self-defense and regional arrangements within the United Nations framework and the participation of the United States in those arrangements. Now what are the principal provisions of the North Atlantic Pact? I should like to summarize them.

First, the pact is carefully and conscientiously designed to conform in every particular with the Charter of the United Nations. This is made clear in the first article of the pact, which reiterates and reaffirms the basic principles of the Charter. The participating countries at the very outset of their association state again that they will settle all their international disputes, not only among themselves but with any nation, by peaceful means, in accordance with the provisions of the Charter. This declaration sets the whole tone and purpose of the treaty.

The second article is equally fundamental. The associated countries assert that they will preserve and strengthen their free institutions, and will see to it that the fundamental principles upon which free institutions are founded are better understood everywhere. They also agree to eliminate conflicts in their economic life and to promote economic cooperation among themselves. Here is the ethical essence of the treaty—the common resolve to preserve, strengthen and make understood the very basis of tolerance, restraint and freedom—the really vital things with which we are concerned.

This purpose is further extended in Article 3, in which the participating countries pledge themselves to self-help and mutual aid. In addition to strengthening their free institutions, they will take practical steps to maintain and develop their own capacity and that of their partners to resist aggression. They also agree to consult together when the integrity or security of any of them is threatened. The treaty sets up a council, consisting of all the members, and other machinery for consultation and for carrying out the provisions of the pact.

Now successful resistance to aggression in the modern world requires modern arms and trained military forces. As a result of the recent war, the European countries joining in the pact are generally deficient in both requirements. The treaty does not bind the United States to any arms program. But we all know that the United States is now the only democratic nation with the resources and productive capacity to help the free nations of Europe to recover their military strength.

Therefore, we expect to ask the Congress to supply our European partners some of the weapons and equipment they need to resist aggression. We also expect to recommend military supplies for other free nations which will cooperate with us in safeguarding peace and security.

In the compact world of today the security of the United States cannot be defined in terms of boundaries and frontiers. A serious threat to international peace and security anywhere in the world is of direct concern to this country. Therefore it is our policy to help free peoples to maintain their integrity and independence, not only in Western Europe, not only in the Americas, but wherever the aid we are able to provide can be effective. Our actions in supporting the integrity and independence of Greece, of Turkey, of Iran, are expressions of that determination. Our interest in the security of these countries has been made clear, and we shall continue to pursue that policy.

In providing military assistance to other countries, both inside and outside the North Atlantic pact, we will give clear priority to the requirements of economic recovery. We will carefully balance the military assistance program with the capacity and requirements of the total economy, both at home and abroad.

But to return to the treaty, Article 5 deals with the possibility, which unhappily cannot be excluded, that the nations joining together in the pact may have to face the eventuality of an armed attack. In this article, they agree that an armed attack on any of them, in Europe or North America, will be considered an attack on all of them. In the event of such an attack, each of them will take, individually and in concert with the other parties, whatever action it deems necessary to restore and maintain the security of the North Atlantic area, including the use of armed force.

Now this does not mean that the United States would be automatically at war if one of the nations covered by the pact is subject to armed attack.

Under our Constitution, the Congress alone has the power to declare war. We would be bound to take promptly the action which we deemed necessary to restore and maintain security in the North Atlantic area. That decision would be taken in accordance with our constitutional procedures. The factors which would have to be considered would be, on the one side, the gravity of the armed attack; on the other, the action which we believed necessary to restore and maintain the security of the North Atlantic area. That is the end to be achieved. We are bound to do what in our honest judgment is necessary to reach that result. If we should be confronted again with a calculated armed attack such as we have seen twice in the Twentieth Century, I should not suppose that we would decide that any action other than the use of armed force would be effective either as an exercise of the right of self-defense or as necessary to restore the peace and security of the North Atlantic area. That decision will rest where the Constitution has placed it.

Now this is not a legalistic question. It is a question we have frequently faced, the question of faith and principle in carrying out treaties. Those who decide it will have the responsibility for taking all appropriate action under the treaty. Such a responsibility requires the exercise of will—a will disciplined by the undertaking solemnly contracted to do what they decide is necessary to restore and maintain the peace and security of the North Atlantic area. That is our obligation under Article 5. That is equally our duty and our obligation to our own country.

All of these provisions of the pact are subject to the overriding provisions of the United Nations Charter. Any measures for self-defense taken under the treaty will be reported to the Security Council of the United Nations. These measures will continue only until the Security Council, with its primary responsibility, takes the necessary action to restore peace and maintain security.

The treaty has no time limit, but after it has been in effect twenty years any member can withdraw on one year's notice. It also provides that after it has been in existence for ten years, it will be reviewed in the circumstances prevailing at that time. Additional countries may be admitted to the pact by agreement of all the parties already signatories.

These are the principal provisions of the treaty.

Now will the treaty accomplish its purpose?

No one can say with certainty. We can only act on our convictions. The United States Government and the Governments with which we are associated in this treaty are convinced that it is an essential measure for strengthening the United Nations, deterring aggression, and establishing the sense of security necessary for the restoration of the economic and political health of the world.

It seems absurd that it should be necessary in this era of popular education and highly developed communications to deal with allegations which have no relation to the truth and could not stand even the crudest test of measurement against realities.

I refer here to the allegations that this treaty conceals aggressive designs on the part of its authors with respect to other countries. Anyone with the most elementary knowledge of the processes of democratic government knows that democracies do not and cannot plan aggressive wars. But for those from whom such knowledge may have been withheld I must make the following categoric and unequivocal statement, for which I stand with the full measure of my responsibility in the office which I hold:

This country is not planning to make war against anyone. It is not seeking war. It abhors war. It does not hold war to be inevitable. Its policies are devised with the specific aim of bridging by peaceful means the tremendous differences which beset international society at this time.

Allegations that aggressive designs lie behind this country's signature of the Atlantic pact can rest only on a malicious misrepresentation or a fantastic misunderstanding of the nature and aims of American society.

This treaty is designed to help toward the goal envisioned by President Truman when he said: "As our stability becomes manifest, as more and more nations come to know the benefits of democracy and to participate in growing abundance, I believe that those countries which now oppose us will abandon their delusions and join with the free nations of the world in a just settlement of international differences."

To bring that time to pass, we are determined, that on the one hand, we will make it unmistakably clear that immediate and effective countermeasures will be taken against those who violate the peace, and on the other, that we will wage peace vigorously and relentlessly.

Too often peace has been thought of as a negative condition—the mere absence of war. We know now that we cannot achieve peace by taking negative attitudes. Peace is positive, and it has to be waged with all our thought, energy and courage, and with the conviction that war is not inevitable.

Under the leadership of President Truman the United States is waging peace with a vigor and on a scale without precedent. While the war was being fought this country took the initiative in the organization of the United Nations and related agencies for the collective and cooperative conduct of international affairs. We withdrew our military forces, except those required for occupational duties, and quickly reduced our military establishment to about one-tenth its wartime size. We contributed generously to post-war relief and rehabilitation.

But when events called for firmness as well as generosity the United States waged peace by pledging its aid to free nations threatened by aggression, and took prompt and vigorous action to fulfill that pledge. We have actively sought and are actively seeking to make the United Nations an effective instrument of international cooperation. We proposed, and, with the eager cooperation of sixteen other nations, put into effect a great concerted program for economic recovery and the spiritual reinvigoration of Europe. We joined the other American republics, and we now join with Western Europe, in treaties to strengthen the United Nations and to insure international peace and security.

The United States is waging peace by promoting measures for the revival and expansion of world trade on a sound and beneficial basis. We are preparing to carry out an energetic program to apply modern skills and techniques to what President Truman has called the "primitive and stagnant" economies of vast areas, so that they will yield a better and richer life for their peoples.

The United States is waging peace by throwing its full strength and energy into the struggle, and we shall continue to do so.

We sincerely hope that we can avoid strife, but we cannot avoid striving for what is right. We devoutly hope that we can have genuine peace, but we cannot be complacent about the present uneasy and troubled peace.

A secure and stable peace is not a goal we can reach all at once and for all time. It is a dynamic state, produced by effort and faith, with courage and justice. The struggle is continuous and hard. The prize is never irrevocably ours.

To have this genuine peace we must constantly work for it. But we must do even more. We must make it clear that armed attack will be met by collective defense, prompt and effective.

That is the meaning of the North Atlantic pact.

SPEECHES DELIVERED AT THE TREATY SIGNING CEREMONY
WASHINGTON, DC, APRIL 4, 1949

(Source: NATO)

BY DEAN ACHESON, SECRETARY OF STATE OF THE UNITED STATES

On behalf of the Government and the people of the United States, I warmly welcome to our country and our capital the Foreign Ministers who have assembled here to sign the North Atlantic Treaty.

We are honored by their presence, both as individuals who have done much for peace and as representatives of nations and peoples who have contributed notably to the welfare and progress of mankind.

We are met together to consummate a solemn act. Those who participated in the drafting of this treaty must leave to others judgment of the significance and value of this act. They cannot appraise the achievement but they can and should declare the purposes of their minds and hearts.

It was, I think, their purpose—like the purpose of those who chart the stars—not to create what they record, but to set down realities for the guidance of men, whether well- or ill-disposed.

For those who seek peace it is a guide to refuge and strength, a very present help in trouble. For those who set their feet upon the path of aggression, it is a warning that if it must needs be that offenses come, then woe unto them by whom the offense cometh.

For the reality which is set down here is not created here. The reality is the unity of belief, of spirit, of interest of the community of nations represented here. It is the product of many centuries of common thought and of the blood of many simple and brave men and women.

The reality lies not in the common pursuit of a material goal or of a power to dominate others. It lies in the affirmation of moral and spiritual values which govern the kind of life they propose to lead and which they propose to defend, by all possible means, should that necessity be thrust upon them. Even this purpose is a fact which has been demonstrated twice in this present century.

It is well that these truths be known. The purpose of this treaty is to publish them and give them form.

From this act, taken here today, will flow increasing good for all peoples. From this joining of many wills in one purpose will come new inspiration for the future. New strength and courage will accrue not only to the peoples of the Atlantic community but to all peoples of the world community who seek for themselves, and for others equally, freedom and peace.

BY PAUL-HENRI SPAAK, PRIME MINISTER AND MINISTER OF FOREIGN AFFAIRS OF BELGIUM

In signing the North Atlantic pact, we are going to participate in the most important political event that has occurred since the creation of the United Nations.

The great defensive alliance about to be created is an essential milestone on the road leading to the consolidation of peace.

The peoples of the world have therefore the right to rejoice over it.

The North Atlantic pact conforms with the letter and the spirit of the San Francisco Charter since, inspired solely by a sense of defense, it is, through the magnitude of the forces which it brings together, of a nature to discourage any future aggressor and since it gives to Article 51, which proclaims the right to legitimate individual and collective defense, a practical and effective form without which it would be but a mockery.

The new pact is purely defensive. It is directed against no one. It threatens no one: it should therefore disturb no one, save, of course, any person or persons who might foster the criminal idea of having recourse to war. To be convinced of this, one has only to read it, but one must do so without a preconceived idea.

The peoples here represented detest war, and their Governments share their sentiments.

War is a hateful and absurd thing. It settles nothing, and its consequences constitute almost as heavy a burden for the conquerors as for the conquered. Democracies are essentially pacific. Where peoples have something to say, where thought is not in chains and opposition muzzled, the idea that an aggressive policy could be pursued is inconceivable. If the whole world accepted and practiced the democratic principles which are ours, there would be no more war. But until that is the case, we have the right and the duty to be prudent and prepared.

Twice within less than 25 years the democracies of Western Europe, the United States of America, and Canada have faced terrible dangers. Twice the civilization that they represent, their way of life and of thought have been jeopardized. Twice it has required military miracles to save them. Twice an overblind trust has all but ruined them. It would be unpardonable to ignore the repeated lessons of history.

Those who today are angered or saddened because the principles of universal collective security contemplated in the United Nations Charter are to be supplemented by a system more restricted, but having the same goal and observing the same principles, will find some subjects for reflection in the signing of the pact. They will regret, perhaps, having seen the rostrum of the United Nations transformed into an instrument of propaganda in which vehemence and insult have frequently replaced the essential desire for cooperation; perhaps also they will regret that the abuse of the veto and refusal to collaborate have so often rendered ineffective the decisions of the Security Council or the recommendations of the Assembly.

The United Nations remain our great hope.

We continue to desire and to believe that one day all nations may find their security in this world organization and that all Governments, having at last recognized the precedence of international law over their own will, may make of the United Nations the mighty instrument that we have always wished for.

But until that day, no one can contest our right to gather together and organize in one corner of the world all the forces of those who, having finally and wholly renounced all idea of aggressive warfare, do not wish to find themselves one day without defense before an attack upon them.

The North Atlantic pact is an act of faith in the destiny of Western civilization. Based on the exercise of civil and political liberties, on respect for the human person, it cannot perish.

The North Atlantic pact places in the service of this civilization and of peace the most powerful means of defense that has ever been created. That is why, in the name of an overwhelming majority of the Belgian people, I shall sign it in a few moments with confidence and pride.

BY LESTER B. PEARSON, CANADIAN SECRETARY OF STATE FOR EXTERNAL AFFAIRS

Last week the Parliament of Canada, with only two dissenting voices, endorsed the treaty which we sign here today. This virtual unanimity reflected the views of the Canadian people who feel deeply and instinctively that this treaty is not a pact for war, but a pledge for peace and progress.

The North Atlantic Treaty was born out of fear and frustration; fear of the aggressive and subversive policies of Communism and the effect of those policies on our own peace and security and well-being; frustration over the obstinate obstruction by Communist states of our efforts to make the United Nations function effectively as a universal security system. This treaty, though born of fear and frustration, must, however, lead to positive social, economic, and political achievements if it is to live; achievements which will extend beyond the time of emergency which gave it birth or the geographical area which it now includes.

This treaty does not of itself ensure peace. It does, however, give us the promise of far greater security and stability than we possess today. By our combined efforts, we must convert this promise into performance or the treaty will remain no more than yet another expression of high but unattained ideals. That will not happen to our North Atlantic pact if each of us accepts the challenge it proclaims; if each of us, with trust in the good will and peaceful policies of the others, will strive to make it something more than words. We know that we can do this. If it were not so, we would not today be giving this pledge to stand together in danger and to work together in peace.

We, in this North Atlantic community, the structure of which we now consolidate, must jealously guard the defensive and progressive nature of our league. There can be no place in this group for power politics or imperialist ambitions on the part of any of its members. This is more than a treaty for defense. We must, of course, defend ourselves, and that is the first purpose of our pact; but, in doing so, we must never forget that we are now organizing force for peace, so that peace can one day be preserved without force.

We are a North Atlantic community of twelve nations, and three hundred and fifty million people. We are strong in our lands and resources, in our industry and manpower. We are strong above all in our common tradition of liberty, in our common belief in the dignity of the individual, in our common heritage of social and political thought, and in our resolve to defend our freedoms together. Security and progress, however, like peace and war, are indivisible. So there must be nothing narrow or exclusive about our league, no slackening of our interest in the welfare and security of all friendly people.

The North Atlantic community is part of the world community and as we grow stronger to preserve the peace, all free men grow stronger with us. The world today is too small, too interdependent, for even regional isolation.

This treaty is a forward move in man's progress from the wasteland of his postwar world, to better, safer ground. But as we reach the distant pastures, we see greener ones far on. As we reach the summit of this lofty peak, higher ones loom up beyond. We are forever climbing the ever mounting slope and must not rest until we reach the last objective of a sane and moral world.

Our treaty is no mere Maginot Line against annihilation, no mere fox hole from fear, but the point from which we start for yet one more attack on all those evil forces that would block our way to justice and to peace.

In that spirit, and with great pride, I sign this treaty as the delegate and the servant of my country.

BY GUSTAV RASMUSSEN, MINISTER OF FOREIGN AFFAIRS OF DENMARK

When today, on behalf of Denmark, I sign the North Atlantic Treaty, I do so because it is an instrument of peace, and because it has no other purpose than defense in case an armed attack should occur against any one of the signatory powers.

Under Article 1 of the Treaty, the parties undertake to settle any international dispute by peaceful means. As has been recently said by a high American official, behind this pledge stand the character and policies of the countries which are parties to the treaty. The very nature of their institutions makes a calculated plan of aggression a virtual impossibility.

The North Atlantic Treaty contains a solemn reaffirmation of the pledges given by those countries under the United Nations Charter. The treaty is therefore designed to strengthen the system of the United Nations. It constitutes a cornerstone in the fundamental structure of general security.

Twice in this century, the United States of America has gone to war in order to come to the aid of the democratic nations of Europe in their fight against aggression.

By this treaty the United States has in advance expressed her readiness also in the future to stand by democratic and peace-loving peoples, and has thereby contributed in a magnanimous way to the maintenance of peace.

This goal, the preservation of peace, is also Denmark's, in deep accord with the ardent desire and old tradition of the Danish nation.

BY ROBERT SCHUMAN, MINISTER OF FOREIGN AFFAIRS OF FRANCE

The history of contemporary France is a succession of aggressions she endured and of attempts she has made to avoid them.

Three times in seventy years she has been invaded. The first time, she was the sole victim of the aggressor. From 1914 to 1918 half of our continent was submerged under the wave of aggression. And the last war overflowed Europe; the invasion became transcontinental, not only because of alliances, but also because of the immensity of the means of action. Invasion crosses neutral frontiers; neither distance nor natural obstacles can stop it any longer.

In the past, the peoples menaced by it too often allowed themselves to be surprised by it. The teaching of experience has led them to draw together. They have placed their confidence in international organization for peace and security. France has constantly supported these efforts and nurtured this great hope. She remains fervently attached to it because she is convinced that in the end humanity will submit to the exigencies of solidarity.

But she is obliged also to recognize that collective organizations, as they function today, have not yet acquired the necessary efficacy. The Charter envisages the possibility of regional pacts. It authorizes its members to organize individually or collectively for self-defense in conformity with the principles of the Charter.

France ardently desires that the United Nations may become one day strong enough to assure by itself peace and security in the world, thus rendering any individual initiative unnecessary.

But, meanwhile, the Governments which bear the fearsome responsibility of guarding the independence of their countries have no right to put their trust in partial guarantees. It would be criminal for them to neglect a single opportunity, or a possible aid, for the preservation of peace.

The exclusive concern of France is to make impossible any invasion of her own territory or of the territory of peace-loving nations. Our aim cannot be restricted to the winning of a war which might be forced upon us, a war which, even if we win it, would leave Europe ravaged and depopulated. We want to avoid such a war by becoming, together, strong enough to safeguard peace.

Who, in justice, could reproach us for such an attempt? What sincere friend could take offense at it? In the past, France has been sufficiently respectful of her obligations and true to her friendships, sufficiently alerted also by dreadful experience, to be beyond all suspicion.

There is no contradiction between two treaties when both have as their object to guarantee the security of the same country but are concluded with different guarantors. The multiplicity of possible risks necessitates a multiplicity of precautions. This answer we gave to Germany when, in 1935, she took objection to the Franco-Russian treaty, incompatible, according to her, with the Locarno pact. Today, we give it to the U.S.S.R. with whom we remain bound by a defense pact against a possible German menace and by the obligation we accepted never to associate ourselves with any threat directed against her. We shall scrupulously honor this obligation. When we expand the network of our friendships, old and new, do we in fact repudiate a friendship which does not satisfy all our need for security? Is it a threat to anyone when we take out insurance against all risks, when we organize a system of common defense against any attack, whatever its nature?

We are uniting with the intention of providing a common and reciprocal protection. We want to discourage in advance any aggression, by making it more and more dangerous for the aggressor. Only a potential aggressor could legitimately consider it aimed at him. Our conscience is clear. In signing this pact, France solemnly proclaims her absolute determination to maintain peace. It is not for herself alone that France wants peace, for she knows that peace has become the indivisible property of all, and that, by allowing it to be compromised by one of us, we would all lose it together.

Nations are more and more convinced that their fates are closely bound together, that their salvation and their welfare can no longer be based upon an egotistical and aggressive nationalism, but must rest upon the progressive application of human solidarity.

BY BJARNI BENEDIKTSSON, MINISTER OF FOREIGN AFFAIRS OF ICELAND

The nations who are now forming this new brotherhood are unlike each other in many respects: some of them are the greatest and most powerful in the world—others are small and weak.

None is smaller or weaker than my one—the Icelandic nation. My people are unarmed and have been unarmed since the days of our Viking forefathers. We neither have nor can have an army. My country has never waged war on any country and as an unarmed country we neither can nor will declare war against any nation as we stated when entering the United Nations. In truth we are quite unable to defend ourselves from any foreign armed attack.

There was, therefore, hesitation in our minds as to whether there was a place for us as participants in this defensive pact. But our country is under certain circumstances of vital importance for the safety of the North Atlantic area. In the last war Great Britain took over the defense of Iceland, and later we concluded an agreement with the United States Government for military protection of Iceland during the war. Our participation in this pact shows that for our own sake, as well as for the sake of others, we want similar arrangements in case of a new war, which we all indeed hope and pray never will occur.

But it is not only this realistic reason which has decided our attitude. We also want to make it crystal clear that we belong, and want to belong, to this free community of free nations which now is being formally founded.

It is a fact, as I said before, that we are unlike each other in many respects but there are many things which bind us solidly together.

We all face the same danger. In this world of ours, where distances have vanished, peace indeed is indivisible. The same disruptive elements are everywhere at this sinister work. Everywhere they are accusing us, who are working for peace, of being warmongers.

When we were discussing this pact in the Parliament of Iceland, those elements tried with force to hinder that venerable institution in its work. Such violence has never before been tried against the thousand-year-old Parliament of Iceland.

The misguided crowd which tried this pretended they were shouting for peace. This contradictory behavior of throwing stones with your hands while you are clamoring for peace with your lips is not in accordance with Icelandic tradition, nor is it in conformity with Western culture. We all know where those habits originate, and this mentality certainly is the greatest menace to the world today.

But it is not only this threat to world peace and human well-being which unites us. Neither is it only the fact that we all live in the same part of the world. There are stronger bonds which bind us together.

We all belong to the same culture. We would all prefer to lose our lives rather than lose our freedom, either as individuals or nations. We all believe in friendly cooperation among nations. We all want peace for all the world and well-being for mankind.

Therefore, we gather here today hopefully to sign this solemn treaty.

BY CARLO SFORZA, MINISTER OF FOREIGN AFFAIRS OF ITALY

The Italian nation, after two World Wars, in the space of one generation, looks with confidence and hope to this treaty; it sees in it a decisive step towards the advent of peace in a free and united world.

This Pact is a complex and articulate instrument in which the will prevails to discourage, through our unity, any aggressive move, preposterous and unlikely as this may appear. To the very few who in good faith still hesitate, be it enough to remind that, had this treaty existed in 1914 and in 1939, there wouldn't have been the battles which spread ruins from Italy to England, from France to Russia.

It is not without significance that the European peoples should have apprehended with joy that this treaty would be signed on the free American soil. It helps everybody realize that oceans are becoming small lakes and that even the most different historical formations represent no more than a variety of folklore in front of the necessity of uniting, all of us, in order to save our most cherished common patrimony: peace and democracy.

Signing a pact, however, is not enough. Life shall have to circulate through it, as a result of a constant free collaboration in the service of peace between all its members, present and future.

It is within the spirit of this Pact, that two of its signatories, the French and the Italians, signed a week ago in Paris a treaty of economic cooperation between Italy and France. Not only would we fail the spirit of the Pact, we would also belittle its force if we considered it only as a protective umbrella. We must pray to God that this pact will prove to be like the English Magna Carta: on one side intangible, on the other side a continuous creation.

The North Atlantic pact will constitute one among the noblest and most generous events in human history if all its members will show—within and outside the Pact—that the melancholy history of Europe has taught them this supreme lesson: that no nation in the world can feel secure in its prosperity and peace if all its neighbors are not as safely marching towards the same goals of prosperity and security.

BY JOSEPH BECH, MINISTER OF FOREIGN AFFAIRS OF LUXEMBOURG

Grouped around the most powerful democracy in the world, the states signatory to the Atlantic pact constitute at once the most formidable and the most sincerely peaceful coalition of material and moral forces that has ever been set up by nations to insure their security and to spare the world the horrors of war.

In the absence of any coercive force belonging to the United Nations, the treaty of assistance and mutual aid among the twelve Western countries constitutes the most effective guarantee possible for them, a guarantee that is essential in a world where distrust prevails, a world divided by political and ideological conceptions that are radically opposed, with all the risks and dangers that this state of things and of mind involves.

The nations of the West never wanted this division. It is not their concern that other nations have a regime different from theirs, and they ask only normal relations with the East. If, a year ago, five of them placed themselves on the defensive in concluding the Brussels pact, and if, today, the United States and Canada are in their turn joining the ten European countries to organize collective defense and the maintenance of peace, security, and liberty in the North Atlantic community, it is because their unceasing efforts to find common solutions with the countries of the East in important matters have encountered constant intransigence and because, in a word, the policy of conciliation followed by the Western countries has found no echo in the East.

These causes which have given birth to our pact determine and limit its purpose and scope.

The North Atlantic pact is the logical supplement to the Brussels pact.

Like the latter, its purpose is both to prevent war from breaking out, by establishing a balance between the forces confronting each other, and to win any war of aggression that may be directed against one or all of the signatory states.

The defensive alliance that we are concluding today cannot of course establish true peace, which is more than the absence of war, but, like other similar alliances in the past, it may give the world a salutary period of lasting truce. I am sure that that is the fervent desire of the signatories to this pact, all of whom believe that peaceful coexistence of the two regimes is possible and all of whom wish it.

With the aid given to Europe by the Marshall Plan, the Atlantic pact opens a new era of the closest solidarity between the democratic countries of Europe and the New World.

Nothing proves better this ineluctable solidarity of the destinies of our countries than the fact that the United States, breaking with a tradition two centuries old, is concluding a military alliance in peacetime. That is an event of extraordinary historical significance for the United States and of the utmost importance for Europe.

The peoples of Europe note with profound gratitude what the presence at their sides of this mighty and generous country signifies.

They approve and acclaim the pact, and accept the real risks and the heavy obligations that it imposes upon them. They accept it with active faith in the necessity for and the efficacy of the union that has been achieved.

It is in this same spirit that, with the prior assent of nine-tenths of the members of the Luxembourg Parliament, I set the signature of my small country beside those of so many friendly nations at the bottom of this instrument of peace, the Atlantic pact.

BY DIRK U. STIKKER, MINISTER OF FOREIGN AFFAIRS OF THE NETHERLANDS

The treaty we are about to sign marks the end of an illusion: the hope that the United Nations would, by itself, ensure international peace.

Regretfully, we were driven to the conclusion that the Charter, though essential, is not enough, in the world as it is, to protect those vital principles for which we of the Western world who have gathered here, stand.

Therefore, we felt it our duty to make this treaty. So far from merely marking the end of an illusion, it most especially marks the birth of a new hope of enduring peace.

Its opponents are clamoring that this treaty aims at war. That is a lie. Its aim is peace—peace, not after a new war, but peace now, and from now on.

We who are vitally interested in the security of the North Atlantic area, henceforth stand united in our resolve to repel aggression, just as we stand united in our resolve not to attack others.

Such, then, is the treaty's unshakable moral basis. We shall sign with a clear conscience in the face of God.

Various aspects of the new treaty are being explained by my fellow speakers. Let me add and stress this:

Together we are determined in our mutual interest to gird the North Atlantic with a chain of strength. That chain is, necessarily, as strong as its weakest link. Let us then strive together, on a basis of equal treatment for all, to uphold the strength of the strongest links, and to increase that of the weakest, for weak links are a common peril. This is a dictate of plain common sense.

Here, as in so many other fields of international cooperation and integration, the Netherlands will not be found wanting. As we have participated in making and implementing the Brussels pact, and Benelux, the Organization for European Economic Cooperation, and a Western European Federation (to name only these), so shall we participate in making the treaty now before us a living and inspiring reality. We know that you all in turn will not fail us.

We rejoice at the thought that at last the truth prevails that the North Atlantic is a highway that unites, not a barrier that divides. We rejoice at the thought that North Americans and Western Europeans have found each other in a common edifice dedicated to peace. Freedom from fear is being brought nearer to all of us today.

Let me close with a word of Netherlands gratitude to all those who have labored towards bringing us here together. In saying this, I am thinking not only of the negotiators, whom I thank most warmly, but also, and no less of those enlightened men who built that massive pedestal of popular support on which this treaty now securely stands: members of Congress, parliamentarians, moulders and interpreters of public opinion in all our countries.

And so, with a humble prayer for God's merciful blessing, I declare the Netherlands Government's readiness to sign this treaty for peace.

BY HALVARD M. LANGE, MINISTER OF FOREIGN AFFAIRS OF NORWAY

As I am about to sign, on behalf of the Norwegian Government, the North Atlantic pact, I strongly feel that it is a logical sequence to a line which we have followed since the liberation of our country in May, 1945. The five long years of Nazi occupation had given our people a new and deeper conception of freedom, law, and democracy.

And so we were determined that never again must Norway risk the loss of her freedom and all that goes with it.

With great faith and hope the Norwegian Government had taken an active part in the United Nations Conference in San Francisco. When after many divergencies the nations represented there reached agreement and the Charter was solemnly signed, we sincerely believed that a foundation had been laid upon which we—allies and friends of the great war—could build together a future of peace and freedom.

We believe today as firmly as ever in the rightness of the words and spirit of that great Charter and in the fundamental soundness and necessity of the universal idea of the United Nations.

We cannot close our eyes, however, to the fact, that—for reasons which we all know—the United Nations cannot today give us or any other nation the security to which we had confidently looked forward.

Under these circumstances my country temporarily had to look for a greater measure of security, beyond that provided by membership in the United Nations.

Our first thought, naturally, was to turn to our neighbors and friends in the north of Europe to see what the three of us together could do. As we Norwegians saw it, the best solution would be a Scandinavian regional pact under the Charter of the United Nations, in some way affiliated with the great Western democracies, to which we are so closely related economically, culturally, and ideologically.

As we could not fully agree, however, on the basis for such a Scandinavian defense union and on the necessity of establishing solidarity with a broader and stronger regional defense grouping, the logical solution for Norway was to join the North Atlantic pact.

We have a longer coastline on the North Atlantic than any other country. Our experience through the centuries has been that the ocean did not separate. On the contrary, for us it has been the highway of commercial and cultural intercourse.

Before doing so, we asked ourselves some searching questions:

Can the proposed pact offer the protection we need if the worst should happen? Will our obligations under the pact be within our means, without jeopardizing our economic reconstruction program?

We further asked: Is the pact in full accordance with the Charter of the United Nations?

And, last but not least, is the proposed pact of a clearly defensive nature? Will it promote our foremost aim: Peace with freedom?

Studying the text of the pact, we found satisfactory answers to all these questions.

We felt convinced that the prospective signers of the pact considered the preservation of peace and freedom their foremost aim. They would regard any idea of aggression contrary to their most basic instincts and fundamental policies.

Our pact is a pact of peace. It is directed against no nation. It is directed solely against aggression itself.

The moment the United Nations through the common efforts of all its member nations is capable of functioning in accordance with the intention of its founders and with the letter and spirit of the Charter, at that moment the need for such regional arrangements will become much less urgent, and will ultimately be eliminated altogether.

The overwhelming majority of the Norwegian people deeply believes that the signing of the Atlantic pact is an event which may decisively influence the course of history and hasten the day when all nations can work together for peace and freedom.

On this solemn occasion I wish to take the opportunity to express our deep-felt appreciation of the tremendous contribution of the United States of America during and after the war.

The scope and vision of the undertakings which the United States have originated for the reconstruction and stabilization of a war-torn world, have seldom been equaled in human history.

BY JOSÉ CAEIRO DA MATTA, MINISTER OF FOREIGN AFFAIRS OF PORTUGAL

The Government of Portugal, which I have the honor to represent here on this occasion, received with pleasure the invitation extended by the Government of the United States in its name and in the name of Belgium, Canada, France, Luxembourg, the Netherlands, Norway, and the United Kingdom, to take part in the North Atlantic pact.

The time has now come where we see the concept of this pact become a reality; and, before our signatures are affixed to it, allow me to say a few words in the name of Portugal.

To President Truman, who, with his strong personality, so well symbolizes in this hour the clear political vision and the decisive entry of the

United States into this undertaking, go the cordial greetings of the Government and people of Portugal.

My country, in accepting the invitation extended to her to take her place among the original participating nations in the Atlantic pact, was not—I can affirm—concerned exclusively with considerations of her own security: she did so much more because of her recognition of the need of giving her cooperation to this great effort. More than ever it is necessary to defend the principles and the positions which those peoples that are the depository of the ideals of Western civilization occupy in the world. It can be said that there is now being repeated around the shores of the Atlantic—and on a much vaster scale—the picture which the ancient peoples knew at the time when the finest conquests of the human mind and the highest exponents of civilization were centered in the small but fertile area of the classical world.

Portugal is an Atlantic country whose activities throughout the long centuries of history took place to a great extent on the broad sea which forms her boundary. To those countries to which we are bound by the seaways of the Atlantic, we are brought near by friendly relations. The memory of our first contacts with some of them is lost in the night of time. With one of them we can point to centuries of the closest collaboration.

Europe, which has such a great moral heritage to defend, Europe, reduced in political values, struggling against the greatest and most dangerous mental epidemic of all times, which threatens to destroy the flower of our culture, Europe is anxiously seeking a formula for peace. Her moral forces are now exerted in the will to correct her ills. And the evidence of what might be a disquieting shadow on her horizon finds her facing with courage and decision the reality of her present position, appreciative and grateful for the moral and material solidarity nobly offered to her from this side of the Atlantic.

Portugal wishes to assert that she sees in the North Atlantic pact, not only an instrument of defense and international cooperation, but also, for the reasons and for the aims which govern it, a precious instrument for peace. And she considers herself fortunate to be able to find that, once again, none of the instruments on which her foreign relations are based is in conflict with its letter or its spirit.

May the thought which has made of these nations living examples of true social progress, in work, in freedom, and in peace, keep intact the ties which are being formed today and ensure that this pact may bear the fruit which we expect of it.

BY ERNEST BEVIN, SECRETARY OF STATE FOR FOREIGN AFFAIRS OF THE UNITED KINGDOM

In appending my signature to this pact today, I am doing so on behalf of a free parliamentary nation, and I am satisfied that the step we are taking has the almost unanimous approval of the British people.

Like other signatories, my country has had forced upon it the great task of fighting two world wars against aggression within a period of a quarter of a century.

The cost in human life and treasure was appalling. Succeeding generations in the period following each struggle over a wide area of the world were thrown into a state of uncertainty and harassed by wars of nerves and civil wars.

The common people (who only want to live in peace) have been unable to follow their peaceful pursuits or to sleep safely in their beds.

They have seen their constitutions crushed—constitutions in which they thought they had made their liberty secure.

We have witnessed a period in which, while the countries represented here have been striving to rehabilitate the world and to restore it to prosperity and sanity, they have been constantly frustrated in their efforts.

We have all tried with a genuine desire and firm purpose to build an effective United Nations.

We have endeavored to make its machinery work and to create such confidence in this great world organisation as will enable it to establish security for all the peoples of the world.

But so far our hopes have not been fully realised.

What course then was open to us?

We had to get together and build with such material as was available to us, and this material was happily at hand in this great Atlantic community, with a common outlook and desire for peace.

Countries whose representatives are signing this great pact today are composed of peace-loving peoples with spiritual affinities, but who also have great pride in their skill and their production and in their achievements in mastering the forces of nature and harnessing the great resources of the world for the benefit of mankind.

Our peoples do not glorify war, but they will not shrink from it if aggression is threatened.

This pact is a concrete proof of the determination of a group of like-minded nations never to fight one another.

These nations are, in addition, linked with many other peoples, who equally will never indulge in aggression.

All these peoples are united in a common line of thought and desire.

Today is not only the day of the signature of this pact, it is also a day of solemn thought—and, may I say, of consecration for peace and resistance to aggression.

Speaking for the British people, I can assure you that they have agreed to make their contribution to the pool for peace.

Although this pact is called the Atlantic pact and is defined as covering the Atlantic area, I must repeat what I stated recently in the British House of Commons, that it does not minimise either our interest in or determination to support others not included in this pact, with whom we have had long years of friendship and alliances.

We are in the process of enthroning and making paramount the use of reason as against force.

The day may come when all the world will accept that view.

Today will bring a great feeling of relief to millions of people.

At last democracy is no longer a series of isolated units.

It has become a cohesive organism, determined to fulfil its great purpose.

But it is not the final end.

We shall pursue with every endeavour the building up of a truly universal United Nations, to which this group of countries will be no mean contributor.

In the solemnity of this moment, I put my signature to this pact in the name of a people who join with other signatories for the preservation of the great freedoms, and in giving an assurance to mankind of our determination to assist all the peoples of the world to live in understanding and good-neighborliness.

STATEMENT BY PRESIDENT TRUMAN ON THE COMING INTO EFFECT OF THE NORTH ATLANTIC TREATY
WASHINGTON, DC, AUGUST 24, 1949

(Source: Statement by President Truman on the Coming into Effect of the North Atlantic Treaty, August 24, 1949; Public Papers, Harry S. Truman Papers, Truman Library)

With the deposit of instruments of ratification by Denmark, France, Italy, and Portugal, the North Atlantic Treaty today enters into effect. This is a momentous occasion not only for all the signatories of the treaty, but for all peoples who share our profound desire for stability and peaceful development.

By this treaty we are not only seeking to establish freedom from aggression and from the use of force in the North Atlantic community, but we are also actively striving to promote and preserve peace throughout the world. In these endeavors, we are acting within the framework of the United Nations Charter, which imposes on us all the most solemn obligations.

These obligations, which bind us to settle international disputes by peaceful means, to refrain from the threat or use of force against the territory or independence of any country, and to support the United Nations in any action it may take to preserve peace, are all clearly stated in the North Atlantic Treaty.

Today, as this treaty comes into effect, it seems particularly appropriate to rededicate ourselves to the carrying out of the great task we have set for ourselves—the preservation of stability and peace. No nation need fear the results of our cooperation toward this end. On the contrary, the more closely the nations of the Atlantic community can work together for peace, the better for all people everywhere.

NORTH ATLANTIC MILITARY COMMITTEE
DECISION ON M.C. 48 (FINAL)
A REPORT BY THE MILITARY COMMITTEE ON THE MOST EFFECTIVE PATTERN OF NATO MILITARY STRENGTH FOR THE NEXT FEW YEARS
NOVEMBER 22, 1954

(Source: NATO)

INTRODUCTION

1. In December 1953, the North Atlantic Council invited the Military Committee to press on with their reassessment of the most effective pattern of military strength for the next few years within the resources which it is anticipated will be made available and to keep the Council informed of their progress. The NATO military authorities therefore initiated a series of studies which they intend making over the next few years, on which to base this reassessment. This report covers the first of this series of studies. The Military Committee, after having reviewed these first studies, has arrived at certain broad conclusions which relate primarily to forces which will be employed in Europe and has encountered certain problems, including among others those relating to sea communications and Air Defense, which should be investigated further. Although in initiating these studies the NATO Commanders were directed to gear the studies to a possible war in 1957, the year 1957 has no particular significance, and in this report, therefore, the Military Committee has dealt with the broad issues involved in NATO defense over the next few years.

THE DEFENSIVE AIMS OF NATO

2. Defense preparations in the North Atlantic Treaty area aim at providing:

   a. A major deterrent to aggression.

   b. A successful forward defense in Europe against Soviet military aggression, and an assurance that if war is thrust upon NATO by the U.S.S.R. NATO will be able to exploit fully its land, sea and air power and thus assure defeat of the Soviets.

   c. A high measure of confidence and security during the cold war.

3. To achieve these aims we must convince the Soviets that:

   a. They cannot quickly overrun Europe.

   b. In the event of aggression they will be subjected immediately to devastating counter-attack employing atomic weapons.

PROBABLE NATURE AND DURATION OF FUTURE WAR INVOLVING NATO

4. The primary consideration affecting the Military Committee studies is that during the period under consideration an appreciable number of atomic weapons,* along with the capability to deliver them, will become available both to NATO and to the Soviets. From its studies the Military Committee has concluded that the advent of atomic weapons systems will drastically change the conditions of modern war.

The destructive power of these weapons, particularly the thermonuclear ones, and the difficulties of defense against them pose entirely new problems, not only of a military nature but political, economic and psychological as well.

* The term "atomic weapons" whenever appearing is understood to mean atomic and thermonuclear weapons and, as appropriate, includes those delivered by aircraft, guided missiles, rockets and artillery.

5. The problem of the air defense of Europe will form the subject of a separate report. There does not exist in Europe today an air defense system which would be sufficiently effective against a determined air attack, and it is considered that existing types of active air defense systems will not alone be able to provide such a defense. It will, of course, be essential to employ all available air defense weapons, supplemented by adequate passive defense preparations, and to coordinate their use with counter-air operations. At

this time the counter-air offensive is the most important factor in the overall air defense. The only presently feasible way of stopping an enemy from delivering atomic weapons against selected targets in Europe is to destroy his means of delivery at source. This will require early atomic counter-attack against the enemy's delivery system.

6. As the initiation of a war by NATO would be contrary to the fundamental principles of the Alliance, it has been ruled out as a possibility. War, therefore, can come only as a result of Communist aggression either intentional or as a result of miscalculation. In the face of NATO's great and growing power in the field of atomic weapons, the Soviets' only hope of winning such a war would rest upon their sudden destruction of NATO's ability to counter-attack immediately and decisively with atomic weapons. There is a remote possibility that the Soviets might attempt to take advantage of their preponderance in land and tactical air forces to overrun Europe without employing atomic weapons in the hope that by so doing the Allies would also refrain from using these weapons. In this contingency our studies indicate that NATO would be unable to prevent the rapid overrunning of Europe unless NATO immediately employed these weapons both strategically and tactically.

7. The Soviets must realize this. There is little doubt, therefore, that should they provoke a war involving NATO, it would be initiated by an atomic onslaught against which NATO would have to react in kind. This would result in an intensive initial phase of operations—approximately thirty days or less—in which each side would strive to deliver a large portion of its accumulated stockpiles of atomic weapons as rapidly and effectively as possible in an effort to neutralize the opponent's atomic delivery capability. Instead, therefore, of the gradually increasing rate of destruction prevalent in recent wars of prolonged mobilization and attrition, maximum destruction would occur within the first few days or weeks as both sides strove to exploit their accumulated atomic stockpiles to gain atomic superiority. In addition to this atomic exchange both sides would initiate operations of their land, sea and air forces to achieve strategic advantage and to be prepared to conduct continued operations.

8. It is considered that the scale of devastation resulting from this initial atomic exchange, when supplemented by continued attacks, may well be so great that the side gaining superiority in this field would probably be able to prevent the enemy regaining the initiative. Thus, the loser in the initial exchange might possibly capitulate. However, despite the destruction

wrought during the initial phase, it is probable that hostilities would not cease. In this case there would be a subsequent period of readjustment and follow-up, the exact nature of which would largely depend on the outcome of the initial phase. Hence, we visualize that a future war involving NATO will probably consist of two phases. The initial phase would include an intensive exchange of atomic weapons between the two groups of adversaries as each strove to gain atomic superiority. By the end of this phase, the atomic stockpiles of the weaker side will have been virtually expended. In a war between NATO and the Soviets within the next few years, our superiority in atomic weapons and in our ability to deliver them should provide a major advantage in this phase, and should be adequate to provide us with a residual for use in the subsequent phase of operations. This subsequent phase would consist of a period of readjustment and follow-up leading to a conclusion of the war. The duration and the outcome of this phase will depend on the relative advantage achieved in the initial phase and our ability to continue to supply our forces in the U.K. and Europe.

9. As it cannot safely be assumed that hostilities will terminate at the end of the initial phase, our forces must be prepared to conduct subsequent operations of a much longer duration. Our ability, however, to defeat the enemy will depend on our ability to survive and gain superiority in the initial phase. Thus our peacetime force pattern must be designed primarily to achieve success during this initial phase and emphasis must be placed upon development of the forces which can participate most effectively in these operations.

FACTORS AFFECTING THE OUTCOME OF THE INITIAL PHASE

10. Should the Soviets decide to start a war involving NATO they will possess certain important advantages. These advantages may be summed up as follows:

    a. The Initiative. The ability to choose the time, place, and type of attack has always been important. In a future war employing atomic weapons the possession of the initiative will be even more important than it has been in the past.

    b. Surprise. Surprise is directly related to the possession of the initiative. In the atomic age, when the warning of a surprise air attack would be measured in minutes and when our ability to withstand the first blow would depend on our being in an effective alert status, the degree of surprise attained by the enemy could greatly influence the outcome of the war. The Military Committee considers that a surprise onslaught with atomic weapons constitutes the most dangerous threat the West has to face, and that the Soviets would not jeopardize the attainment of surprise by any major pre-deployment of their forces.

    c. Monolithic Political System. The Soviet political system, with its power of immediate decision and its advantage of strict security, as compared with the free and democratic system of the NATO type which must obtain decisions through group action, provides an initial advantage of great importance in achieving surprise.

    d. Superiority in Land and Tactical Air Forces. The preponderance of the Soviets in land and tactical air forces is a major advantage to them, particularly in relation to their aim of rapidly overrunning the European Continent.

11. In any examination of how these advantages can best be offset and overcome, it is essential to keep in mind that in the event of war the primary tasks of the NATO forces would be not only to survive the enemy's initial attacks, but also to retaliate immediately with atomic weapons. To be able to carry out these tasks successfully, it is necessary for NATO to take measures to:

    a. Develop an effective intelligence system to provide NATO with the best possible analysis of Soviet capabilities, intentions and operations.

    b. Ensure to the maximum extent possible the security of their vitally important strategic air forces and atomic striking forces in Europe. The most important measures to be taken are the establishment of a satisfactory alert system, the improvement of intelligence and communications, the initiation of adequate active and passive air defense measures, and the dispersion of vital atomic delivery forces.

    c. Ensure that, in the event of aggression, NATO forces would be able to initiate immediate defensive and retaliatory operations including the use of atomic weapons.

    d. Develop 'forces in being' in Europe which would be capable of effectively contributing to success in the initial phase and of preventing the rapid overrunning of Europe. To do this, these forces must be highly trained, mobile, have an integrated atomic capability* and be properly positioned in depth. In this respect the importance of obtaining a German contribution to these forces cannot be too strongly emphasized.

* The ability to integrate the delivery of atomic weapons with the delivery of present type weapons. This involves the integration of intelligence and communications systems, and a common tactical doctrine.

FACTORS AFFECTING THE OUTCOME OF SUBSEQUENT OPERATIONS

12. The Military Committee has not yet been able to give detailed study to the nature of operations subsequent to the initial phase of a war. However, it appears that at this point the advantage would be on our side. The Soviets would probably still be considerably superior numerically in field armies. On the other hand, the NATO countries should still be superior to the Soviets in the fields of atomic delivery capability and production capacity and should be in possession of superiority in strategic air and at sea. Should NATO attain these advantages the Soviets would be seriously handicapped in their ability to maintain the offensive because of the vulnerability of their tactical formations, transportation systems and lines of communication to continued atomic attacks.

13. The objective of our air operations subsequent to the initial phase should, therefore, be to continue attacks on the Soviets' industry, communications, and centers of control, in order that they could not remobilize sufficiently to overcome our atomic superiority. If these attacks are successful the Soviet totalitarian political system, dependent on highly centralized control and communications, might be incapable of continuing to give cohesive direction to the Soviet armed forces, or of performing the essential functions of civil government. Finally, it is possible that at this time serious defections of dissident groups within the Soviet Union and among the enslaved satellite peoples might occur. The latter will be more likely to develop if our atomic success is promptly exploited by land operations designed to link up with such groups. The greater Allied residual capacity in atomic stockpiles, and production and manpower would enable NATO to keep exerting ever increasing pressure with these ends in view.

14. Should NATO attain the above advantages the Soviets would generally be on the defensive both strategically and tactically—a condition that must lead to their final defeat.

EXAMINATION OF SOVIET CAPABILITIES AND PROBABLE STRATEGY

15. It is now necessary to examine the capabilities of the Soviet forces in the atomic concept of warfare outlined above, and to consider the probable

strategy that would be employed. Then, in the light of the conclusions reached, it should be possible to: formulate a NATO strategy to counter the Soviet threat; devise a pattern of NATO forces to implement this strategy and still be within the NATO resources likely to be available; and finally make recommendations on the measures which must be taken to attain this force pattern.

16. On the assumption that for the next three to five years the Soviet military build-up conforms to present trends, the Soviet armed forces should be capable towards the end of that period of effectively carrying out the following offensive operations during the opening stages of war:

    a. Intensive atomic strategic air attacks against the vital centers and atomic bases of NATO. It is expected that surprise would be utilized to the full.

    b. Widespread attacks by the Soviet army and tactical air forces against NATO countries in Europe. In carrying out these attacks the enemy will have a superiority of at least 2 to 1 on the ground, and an appreciable numerical superiority in aircraft, and will have the great advantage of possessing the initiative. Moreover, the Soviet tactical air forces will be capable of delivering atomic weapons.

    c. Attacks against Allied naval forces, naval bases, ports and merchant shipping.

17. Since it is considered that a surprise attack would give the Soviets the best chance of gaining dominance in the vital atomic field and would be the worst condition that NATO might have to face, it has been assumed that Soviet strategy would be based on surprise. It would probably be on the following lines:

    a. A strategic air offensive with the aim of:

        (1) Destruction of vital allied centers and the war-making capacity of the United States, the United Kingdom and Canada and their overseas bases, giving highest priority to the destruction of the Allied atomic capability.

        (2) Isolation of the European battlefield by attacks against NATO lines of communication in the Atlantic and Mediterranean, and against Allied ports and harbors in Europe, North Africa and North America.

b. Defense of the U.S.S.R.
   c. Destruction of the forces of Allied Command Europe, and acquisition of vital strategic areas in Europe and the Middle East.
   d. Offensive naval operations, particularly with submarines, against Allied naval forces, ports and merchant shipping.
   e. Strategic defensive in other areas.

THE TASK OF NATO FORCES IN EUROPE

18. In planning the future development and organization of NATO forces it is essential not to lose sight of the primary aim of the Alliance which is to prevent war. Within this aim the primary role of the NATO forces in Europe must be that of an effective deterrent. These forces must, therefore, be so organized, disposed, trained and equipped that the Soviets, in taking account of them in their plans, must come to the conclusion that, even with superior numbers and the advantage of surprise, their chances of obtaining a quick decision in the European theater are small and that such an attempt would involve grave risks to the Soviet Union.

19. We must not assume, however, that even in these circumstances the Soviets might not precipitate a war, in which case the forces which had been built up and deployed to act as a deterrent must be capable of immediately and successfully carrying out their wartime role of preventing the rapid overrunning of Europe.

20. This clearly establishes that essential NATO forces must first of all be forces-in-being. Moreover, it is clear from an analysis of the Capabilities Study of the Supreme Allied Commander Europe that, to offset the great numerical superiority of the Soviets in land and tactical air forces, NATO forces-in-being must be equipped with an integrated atomic capability.

21. To be effective tactically in their wartime role, these forces-in-being must be capable of:

   a. Surviving the initial attack. This will entail implementing in peacetime passive defense measures such as dispersion and protection, obtaining maximum warning of attack, and establishing an effective alerts system.
   b. Participating effectively in the battle for air superiority. They must be able, in conjunction with the operations of strategic air forces, to

establish air superiority, primarily by attacking the enemy's air complex at source with atomic weapons.

  c. Preventing the rapid overrunning of Europe. An analysis of the Study of the Supreme Allied Commander Europe has led the Military Committee to conclude that this could be accomplished, within the NATO resources that could be made available, by the use of highly trained and mobile forces with an integrated atomic capability, properly deployed in depth and immediately ready to fight with maximum intensity on D-Day and in the early phases. There is reason to believe that, when employed by such forces, particularly when NATO land forces are operating on ground of their own choosing and on pre-selected and prepared defensive zones, atomic weapons will favor NATO's planned system of defense on the battlefield since, as a general principle, if an enemy wishes to advance against a strongly defended position he must concentrate. In an atomic war, concentration would expose his forces to heavy losses from atomic attack. On the other hand, the dispersion required to provide adequate protection against atomic attack would force the enemy to adopt tactics for advancing which would be less effective than concentrated penetrations.

22. An examination, in the light of the above, of the forces likely to be at the disposal of Allied Command Europe leads to the conclusion that with the quantities of atomic weapons estimated to be available to these forces in the next few years, it lies within NATO's power to provide an effective deterrent in Europe and, should war come despite the deterrent, to prevent a rapid overrunning of Europe provided that:

  a. The ability to make immediate use of atomic weapons is ensured. Our studies have indicated that without their immediate use we could not successfully defend Europe within the resources available. Any delay in their use even measured in hours could be fatal. Therefore, in the event of a war involving NATO it is militarily essential that NATO forces should be able to use atomic and thermonuclear weapons in their defense from the outset.

  b. A German contribution will be provided. It has been evident from all past NATO military studies that, insofar as the Central European theater is concerned, a German contribution would be necessary, even for the strategy of holding the Rhine-Ijssel line. Up till now NATO has been obliged to accept this strategy, even though it neither includes the vital industrial areas of the Ruhr, nor provides adequate defense in depth for Western Europe. The advent of tactical atomic weapons alone would not enable NATO to hold even the Rhine-Ijssel line without a German contribution. The advent of new weapons, plus a German contribution, however, will for the first time enable NATO to adopt a real forward strategy with a main line of defense well to the East of the Rhine-Ijssel. This is vital to a successful defense in Central and Northern Europe and to the basic NATO strategy.

c. Certain essential measures necessary to enable our present forces to fight effectively in an atomic war are taken. The most important of these measures (except certain additional measures relating to air defense which will be covered in a later report) are set out in the Enclosure to this Report. The Supreme Allied Commander Europe has prepared a more detailed list of these measures, which the Military Committee has noted as the basis which he will use for further action.

23. If and only if these actions are taken will NATO forces in Europe provide an effective deterrent and have a reasonable expectation of preventing the rapid overrunning of Europe should war come despite the deterrent.

24. It has not yet been possible for an assessment to be made of the costs involved in carrying out the measures necessary to enable our forces in Europe to fight effectively in an atomic war. Many of the most important of these measures are not ones involving heavy expenditures in either money or resources; others will be costly.

CONTROL OF SEA COMMUNICATIONS

25. In considering the pattern of the NATO naval forces required over the next few years for the accomplishment of essential naval tasks, the Military Committee encountered certain very important problems. These require further study to insure that naval force patterns and capabilities are kept abreast of latest advances and the naval requirements of atomic warfare.

26. The basic tasks of the NATO Naval Commanders are to control and exploit the seas for NATO purposes and to deny their use to the enemy. To achieve this, they must protect and maintain the flow of Allied shipping in the Atlantic, Channel, and Mediterranean, ensure the support and reinforcement of NATO forces in Europe, control and exploit vital sea areas, and deny to the enemy the use of sea areas essential to his operations. In

order to participate most effectively in a future war involving NATO, naval forces-in-being must be capable during the initial phase of carrying out powerful offensive operations against such targets as enemy naval bases and confined areas and of establishing Allied supremacy at sea.

27. In the Capabilities Studies prepared by Supreme Allied Commander Atlantic and Commanders-in-Chief Channel, they imply that, with the forces anticipated to be available to them within the next few years, they will not be able to provide adequate protection for the amount of shipping which present plans require them to safeguard in the initial phase of a war. On the other hand, the Supreme Allied Commander Atlantic will possess a considerable offensive capability which he plans to use to the maximum extent to reduce the threat to shipping and thus to compensate in part for his deficiency in defensive forces and to lighten the escort burden. These offensive forces are also of importance as a component of the forces-in-being required to act as a deterrent.

28. In a war developing into a period of sustained operations, the timely arrival in Europe of reinforcements and supplies from overseas would be essential. This would require coordinated operations to protect essential Allied shipping and naval forces against losses critical to the maintenance of the civilian population and to the successful continuation of the war. In the initial phase, however, the essential military and civilian requirements must be met to the greatest extent possible from stockpiles and local sources in order to reduce the necessity of bringing a great volume of shipping into the United Kingdom and the ports of Allied Command Europe. A reliable estimate of the minimum resulting shipping requirements both for the initial phase and subsequent operations is urgently needed before a useful assessment can be made of the forces required to protect shipping during a future war.

29. Another factor of determining influence on the composition and operations of naval forces will be the effect of atomic attacks on ports and unloading facilities. While all lines of communications will be exposed to similar hazards, ports, in particular, are likely to be high priority targets for the enemy. As it appears improbable that they can be adequately defended during the period under consideration, the damage inflicted may well be so great that in the early stages of a war seaborne supplies will have to be largely handled through secondary harbors and over beaches. This would greatly reduce the total tonnage that could be properly handled and will

also have an effect on the types of vessels required. Moreover, it would be dangerous to send in large convoys in excess of the rates which could be handled expeditiously under these conditions, since such convoys or groupings of ships awaiting unloading would themselves be excellent targets for enemy air and submarine attacks. The probable extent of damage to ports from atomic attack is now being studied. An evaluation of the resultant capacity of ports, anchorages, and beaches will then determine the amount of shipping which it will be possible to handle. A related problem is that the atomic threat is likely to lead, on the outbreak of war, to an immediate exodus of merchant shipping from major European ports. These problems need further investigation as they may well have an influence on the composition of NATO naval forces.

30. Further studies are necessary to determine how naval forces expected to be available in the next few years can be used to the greatest advantage in performing essential naval tasks. These studies must take into account new developments in naval techniques and weapons in order that NATO naval forces will be kept abreast of the latest technical advances in naval warfare under atomic conditions.

31. At this stage, therefore, it is necessary to defer final conclusions with respect to the present Capabilities Studies of the NATO Naval Commanders. The Military Committee is initiating further studies and will report on them to the Council in their next assessment of the NATO force pattern.

CONCLUSIONS

32. As a result of its recent study of the impact of new weapons on a war involving NATO, the Military Committee has reached the following conclusions:

    a. Superiority in atomic weapons and the capability to deliver them will be the most important factor in a major war in the foreseeable future.

    b. Surprise will be a major factor in any future war involving NATO, and the degree of surprise attained by the enemy could greatly influence the outcome of the war. The ability of NATO to withstand and react to the first blow will depend on the extent of the resistance of our populations to such action and the state of preparedness of our forces at the time of the enemy's surprise attack.

c. Should war occur, it will most likely consist of two phases:

   - a relatively short initial phase of intensive atomic exchange;
   - a subsequent phase involving operations of indeterminable length and of lesser intensity. The ultimate victory however, would probably have been determined by the outcome of the initial phase.

   d. Should war occur, the best defense against atomic attack lies in the ability of the Allied nations to reduce the threat at source by immediate and intensive atomic counter-attack.

33. In face of the threat of such a war, the primary aim of NATO, must more than ever before, be to prevent war. This aim can only be achieved if the Allied nations are so powerful in the vital elements of modern warfare that the enemy will conclude that he has little hope of winning a war involving NATO. This means that NATO must be able to withstand the initial Soviet onslaught, to deliver decisive atomic counter-attacks against the war-making capacity of the enemy, and to prevent the rapid overrunning of Europe.

34. In developing the pattern of NATO military strength in Europe which would be most effective in the type of war envisaged for the next few years and which would be within the available resources, priority must be given to the provision of forces in being capable of effectively contributing to success in the initial phase. Other forces are required to contribute to subsequent operations, but, in view of the importance of the initial phase and taking into account the limited resources which it is anticipated will be available, the build-up of these forces must be given a lower priority.

35. The forces in being must be characterized by:

   a. Atomic delivery forces adequately protected from initial attack and constantly ready to launch an immediate counterattack.

   b. Systems in operation designed to ensure early warning of attack.

   c. Forces which will have an integrated atomic capability, will have been properly equipped, trained, and deployed in depth, and will be maintained in a high state of readiness.

36. If measures are taken to provide NATO forces in Europe of the above pattern and if a German contribution is available, it is considered that, by

the use of atomic weapons from the outset of hostilities, the forces of Allied Command Europe could provide a successful forward defense in Europe. Insofar as the Central and Northern European commands are concerned, this would enable NATO, for the first time, to establish a major defensive line well to the east of the Rhine-Ijssel, which is vital to defense of these commands and to the control of the Baltic exits.

37. It is militarily essential that NATO forces should be able to use atomic and thermo-nuclear weapons in their defense and that NATO military authorities should be authorized to plan and make preparations on the assumption that atomic and thermo-nuclear weapons will be used in defense from the outset.

38. The Military Committee is initiating further studies dealing with NATO naval problems. Until these studies are completed and assessed it is necessary to defer conclusions with respect to the recent Capabilities Studies of the NATO Naval Commanders.

39. The most effective pattern of all NATO forces must, of course, be examined continuously in the light of the new problems posed by the advent of atomic weapons.

RECOMMENDATIONS

40. The Military Committee recommends that the North Atlantic Council:

    a. Approve the above conclusions, noting the significance of the assumption in paragraph 37.

    b. Approve in principle the measures in the Enclosure to the report as being those most necessary to adapt our military forces for a future major war; and note that the Supreme Allied Commander Europe has prepared a detailed list of Program Recommendations which he will use as a basis for further study and action.

    c. Note the Military Committee's action in initiating further studies of NATO naval problems.

    d. Note that the Military Committee is initiating such action as lies within its authority to adapt NATO forces for an atomic war.

    e. Note that the Military Committee will submit a later Report on Air Defense.

    f. Note that this report is only the first of a series that the Military Committee intends to make in the future.

ENCLOSURE

MINIMUM MEASURES NECESSARY TO INCREASE THE DETERRENT AND DEFENSIVE VALUE OF NATO FORCES

1. Atomic Capability. The forces of NATO should be provided with an integrated atomic capability for use as rapidly as possible in order to give them maximum deterrent power and the ability to participate effectively in an immediate atomic counter-offensive in the event of war.

2. The Alert System. A fully effective alert system must be provided, as surprise will be extremely important in an atomic war. NATO must be able to react immediately to a warning by initiating all possible passive defense measures and by preparing to launch counteroffensive operations against the enemy's air complex the moment after positive evaluation of attack has been made. The effectiveness of this alert system will be a major factor in the initial phase of a war.

3. Warning of Attack. In the event of war it will be essential for Allied forces to obtain the maximum possible warning of enemy attack. All measures contributing to the achievement of early warning must, therefore, be given high priority. In particular, the following measures are recommended:

    a. Increased emphasis be placed on the improvement of Allied intelligence systems, and on improvement in methods of rapid communication of such intelligence within NATO.

    b. Steps be taken to ensure that the main NATO radar net will be completed and adequately manned.

    c. The currently planned radar cover be extended and completed as necessary.

4. Forces-in-Being. Priority must be given to forces-in-being. These forces must have an integrated atomic capability and must be so organized, equipped, trained, and deployed in depth that they fulfill to the maximum extent practicable their dual role of a deterrent force and a force capable of surviving and countering the enemy's initial onslaught. An effective German contribution to these forces-in-being is essential, and must be provided as soon as possible. The provision of all forces other than forces-in-being should be accorded a lower priority.

5. Measures to Enable NATO Forces to Survive Soviet Atomic Attack. In view of the increasing Soviet atomic capability and the probability of a

future war opening with surprise atomic attacks, it is essential that the necessary dispersal and redeployment measures are taken to ensure the survival of NATO forces during the initial phase of hostilities. We must readjust our tactical disposition, improve and augment both passive and active defense measures, and increase unit dispersion and mobility. These measures apply to all forces, air, land and sea alike. We must particularly guard our air forces against such attack by basing them on as many different air fields as possible, by dispersing them to the maximum extent possible on these airfields, and by improving their ability to redeploy to and operate from alternate bases at immediate notice.

C.M. (55) 15 (FINAL)
"SECURITY WITHIN THE NORTH ATLANTIC TREATY ORGANIZATION"
MARCH 8, 1955

(Source: NATO)

ENCLOSURE A: SECURITY AGREEMENT BY THE PARTIES TO THE NORTH ATLANTIC TREATY

1. The parties to the North Atlantic Treaty, having formed an organization for the purpose of uniting their military efforts for their collective defence, and realising that the effective planning for this defence entails the exchange of classified information among the parties, agree that they will protect and safeguard the classified information of the others; will make every effort to ensure that they will maintain the security classifications established by any party with respect to information of that party's origin; will safeguard accordingly such information; will not exploit such information for production for other than military purposes; and will not disclose such information to another nation without the consent of the originator. This Agreement applies to information disclosed by any party to another party on and after the date of acceptance of this Agreement by the parties.

2. It is agreed, in respect of classified information communicated by one party to another, that the recipient nation shall use its best endeavours within the framework of its laws and rules to prevent any loss of patent rights in the information. Specifically, it is declared and agreed that:

(a) any rights of the originator to obtain patent protection in the recipient nation in respect of the information communicated are not, and will not be, prejudiced by virtue of the introduction of the information into such nation;

(b) each party, when so requested by another and to the extent consistent with its laws and rules, will use its best endeavours:

(i) to have maintained in secrecy any patent application in the recipient nation in respect of information for so long as may be desired by the party of origin; and

(ii) to supply, upon request of the originator, reports of the manner in which the information embodied in a patent application has been used or disclosed.

ENCLOSURE B: THE BASIC PRINCIPLES AND MINIMUM STANDARDS OF SECURITY

Introduction

1. This document lays down the basic principles and minimum standards of security to be applied in an appropriate manner by all members of the North Atlantic Treaty Organization so that each may be assured that a common standard of protection is established in each nation.

2. The principal objectives of protective security are to safeguard:

(a) classified information from espionage, compromise, or unauthorized disclosure; and

(b) important installations from sabotage and malicious willful damage.

3. The foundations of sound national security are:

(a) a national security organization responsible for:

(i) the collection and recording of intelligence regarding espionage, sabotage, terrorist and other subversive activities; and

(ii) information and advice to governments on the nature of the threats to security and the means of protection against them;

(b) regular collaboration among government departments and agencies to agree:

(i) what information, assets and resources need to be protected; and

(ii) common standards of protection.

4. Care and experience are needed in the selection of information to be protected and the assessment of the degree of protection it requires. It is fundamental that the degree of protection should correspond with the security importance of the information to be protected. The classification system is the instrument for giving effect to this principle; a similar system of classification ought to be followed in the planning of counter-sabotage so that the greatest measure of protection is given to the most important installations and to the most sensitive points within them.

Major Principles

5. The security measures adopted in each nation must:

(a) extend to all persons having access to classified information, information-carrying media, to all premises containing such information and important installations;

(b) be designed to detect persons whose employment might endanger the security of classified information and important installations and provide for their exclusion or removal;

(c) prevent any unauthorized person from having access to classified information;

(d) ensure that classified information is disseminated solely on the basis of the need-to-know principle, which is fundamental to all aspects of security.

Organization of Security
Common Minimum Standards

6. Each nation should ensure that common minimum standards of security are observed in all its government departments and agencies so that classified information can be passed in the confidence that it will be handled with equal care. Such minimum standards should include criteria for the clearance of personnel and procedures for the protection of classified information.

Co-ordination of Information on Espionage, Sabotage, Terrorist and Other Subversive Activities

7. All information and records on espionage, sabotage, terrorist and other subversive activities in each nation should be so centralised that they can readily be applied to any question relating to the appointment and continued employment of persons in government service or to the protection of classified information and of installations.

Personnel Security
Clearance of Personnel

8. All persons, civilian and military, who require access to information classified CONFIDENTIAL or above must be appropriately cleared before such access is authorized. This clearance should be designed to determine whether such individuals are of:

(a) unquestioned loyalty; and
(b) such character, habits, associations and discretion as to cast no doubt upon their trust-worthiness in the handling of classified information.

Particularly close scrutiny in the clearance procedures should be given to persons:

(c) to be granted access to TOP SECRET information;
(d) occupying positions involving constant access to a considerable volume of information classified SECRET;
(e) who may be vulnerable to pressure from foreign or other sources, e.g. due to former residence or past associations.

In the circumstances outlined in sub-paragraphs (c), (d) and (e) above, the fullest practicable practicable use should be made of the technique of background investigation.

9. When persons are employed in circumstances in which they may have access to classified information (e.g. security guards, messengers, maintenance personnel, etc.) consideration must be given to their first being appropriately security cleared.

Records of Personnel Clearances

10. All establishments handling classified information should maintain a register of the clearances granted to the personnel assigned thereto. Each

clearance should be reviewed as the occasion demands to ensure that it conforms with the current standards applicable to the person's employment, and should be re-examined as a matter of priority whenever new information is received which indicates that continued employment on classified work is no longer consistent with the interests of security.

Security Instruction of Personnel

11. All personnel employed in positions where they have access to classified information should be thoroughly instructed, upon employment and at regular intervals, in the need for security and the procedures for accomplishing it. It is a useful procedure to require that all such personnel should certify in writing that they fully understand the security regulations relevant to their employment.

Security Status of Personnel

12. Procedures should be established to ensure that when adverse information becomes known concerning an individual, it is determined whether the individual is employed on classified work, and the authority concerned informed.

Supervision of Staff

13. Supervising officials should have the duty of knowing those of their staff who are engaged on classified work and of recording and reporting any incidents, associations or habits likely to have a bearing on security.

Removal of Personnel

14. Persons who are considered to be security risks or those about whose loyalty or trustworthiness there is reasonable doubt, should be excluded or removed from positions where they might endanger security.

Physical Security
Need for Protection

15. The degree of physical security measures applied depends in particular on the classification and volume of the information held. Therefore care must be taken to avoid over-classification and classification must be subject to regular review. All government departments should follow uniform practices regarding the classification, including down-

grading and declassification, custody, transmission and disposal of information requiring protection.

Inspection

16. Before leaving areas containing classified information unattended, persons having custody of such information must ensure that it is securely stored and that all locking devices are secure. Further independent inspections should be carried out after working hours.

Building Security

17. Buildings which house classified information must be protected against unauthorized access. The nature of the protection, e.g. barring of windows, locks for doors, guards at entrances, automated access control systems, security inspections and patrols, alarm systems, intrusion detection systems, watch-dogs, will depend on:

   (a) the classification, volume and location of the information in a particular building;
   (b) the quality of the containers for this information; and
   (c) the character of the building.

Emergency Plans

18. Complete plans should be prepared in advance for the protection of classified information during a local or national emergency.

Classified information Entrusted to Persons and Organizations Outside the Government

19. The standards for the protection of classified information entrusted to persons and organizations outside the government, e.g. consultants, industry, universities, should be comparable to those laid down for government departments.

Counter-Sabotage and Safeguards Against Malicious Wilful Damage

20. Physical precautions for the protection of important installations are the best protective security safeguards against sabotage and malicious wilful damage and clearance of personnel alone is not an effective substitute. The national security organisation should collect intelligence regarding sabotage, terrorist and other subversive activities.

Protection of Information on Key Points

21. The distribution of industrial information of military significance, which might be translated into bombing, sabotage or terrorist targets, should be controlled by means of a policy designed to hamper the compilation by potential enemies of a Key Points List.

REPORT OF THE COMMITTEE OF THREE ON NON-MILITARY COOPERATION IN NATO
NEW YORK, DECEMBER 1956
(Source: NATO)

CHAPTER I: GENERAL INTRODUCTION

1. The Committee on Non-Military Cooperation, set up by the North Atlantic Council at its session of May 1956, was requested: "to advise the Council on ways and means to improve and extend NATO cooperation in non-military fields and to develop greater unity within the Atlantic Community."

2. The Committee has interpreted these terms of reference as requiring it: to examine and re-define the objectives and needs of the Alliance, especially in the light of current international developments; and to make recommendations for strengthening its internal solidarity, cohesion and unity.

3. The Committee hopes that the report and recommendations which it now submits will make NATO's purely defensive and constructive purposes better understood in non-NATO countries, thereby facilitating and encouraging steps to lessen international tension. The events of the last few months have increased this tension and reduced hopes, which had been raised since Stalin's death, of finding a secure and honorable basis for competitive and ultimately for cooperative co-existence with the Communist world. The effort to this end, however, must go on.

4. Inter-Allied relations have also undergone severe strains. The substance of this report was prepared by the Committee of Three in the course of its meetings and inter-governmental consultations last September. Subsequent events have reinforced the Committee's conviction that the Atlantic Community can develop greater unity only by working constantly to achieve common policies by full and timely consultation on issues of common concern. Unless this is done, the very framework of cooperation in NATO, which has contributed so greatly to the cause of freedom, and which is so vital to its advancement in the future,[1] will be endangered.

5. The foundation of NATO, on which alone a strong superstructure can be built, is the political obligation that its members have taken for collective defence: to consider that an attack on one is an attack on all which will be met by the collective action of all. There is a tendency at times to overlook the far-reaching importance of this commitment, especially during those periods when the danger of having to invoke it may seem to recede.

6. With this political commitment for collective defence as the cornerstone of the foreign and defence policies of its members, NATO has a solid basis for existence. It is true, of course, that the ways and means by which the obligation is to be discharged may alter as political or strategic conditions alter, as the threat to peace changes its character or its direction. However, any variations in plans and strategic policies which may be required need not weaken NATO or the confidence of its members in NATO and in each other; providing, and the proviso is decisive, that each member retains its will and its capacity to play its full part in discharging the political commitment for collective action against aggression which it undertook when it signed the Pact; providing also—and recent events have shown that this is equally important—that any changes in national strategy or policy which affect the coalition are made only after collective consideration.

7. The first essential, then, of a healthy and developing NATO lies in the whole-hearted acceptance by all its members of the political commitment for collective defence, and in the confidence which each has in the will and ability of the others to honour that commitment if aggression should take place.

8. This is our best present deterrent against military aggression, and consequently the best assurance that the commitment undertaken will not be engaged.

9. However, this deterrent role of NATO, based on solidarity and strength, can be discharged only if the political and economic relations between its members are cooperative and close. An Alliance in which the members ignore each other's interests or engage in political or economic conflict, or harbour suspicions of each other, cannot be effective either for deterrence or defence. Recent experience makes this clearer than ever before.

10. It is useful, in searching for ways and means of strengthening NATO unity and understanding, to recall the origin and the aims of the Organisation.

11. The Treaty which was signed in Washington in 1949 was a collective response—we had learned that a purely national response was insufficient for security—to the fear of military aggression by the forces of the USSR and its allies. These forces were of overwhelming strength. The threat to Greece, the capture of Czechoslovakia, the blockade of Berlin, and the pressure against Yugoslavia showed that they were also aggressive.

12. While fear may have been the main urge for the creation of NATO, there was also the realisation conscious or instinctive that in a shrinking nuclear world it was wise and timely to bring about a closer association of kindred Atlantic and Western European nations for other than defence purposes alone; that a partial pooling of sovereignty for mutual protection should also promote progress and cooperation generally. There was a feeling among the government and peoples concerned that this close unity was both natural and desirable; that the common cultural traditions, free institutions and democratic concepts which were being challenged, and were marked for destruction by those who challenged them, were things which should also bring the NATO nations closer together, not only for their defence but for their development. There was, in short, a sense of Atlantic Community, alongside the realisation of an immediate common danger.

13. Any such feeling was certainly not the decisive, or even the main impulse in the creation of NATO. Nevertheless, it gave birth to the hope that NATO would grow beyond and above the emergency which brought it into being.

14. The expression of this hope is found in the Preamble and in Articles 2 and 4 of the Treaty. These two Articles, limited in their terms but with at least the promise of the grand design of an Atlantic Community, were included because of this insistent feeling that NATO must become more than a military alliance.

They reflected the very real anxiety that if NATO failed to meet this test, it would disappear with the immediate crisis which produced it, even though the need for it might be as great as ever.

15. From the very beginning of NATO, then, it was recognised that while defence cooperation was the first and most urgent requirement, this was not enough. It has also become increasingly realised since the Treaty was signed that security is today far more than a military matter. The strengthening of political consultation and economic cooperation, the development of resources, progress in education and public understanding, all these can be as important, or even more important, for the protection of the security of a nation, or an alliance, as the building of a battleship or the equipping of an army.

16. These two aspects of security—civil and military—can no longer safely be considered in watertight compartments, either within or between nations. Perhaps NATO has not yet fully recognised their essential interrelationship, or done enough to bring about that close and continuous contact between its civil and military sides which is essential if it is to be strong and enduring.

17. North Atlantic political and economic cooperation, however, let alone unity, will not be brought about in a day or by a declaration, but by creating over the years and through a whole series of national acts and policies, the habits and traditions and precedents for such cooperation and unity. The process will be a slow and gradual one at best; slower than we might wish. We can be satisfied if it is steady and sure. This will not be the case, however, unless the member governments—especially the more powerful ones—are willing to work, to a much greater extent than hitherto, with and through NATO for more than purposes of collective military defence.

18. While the members of NATO have already developed various forms of non-military cooperation between themselves and have been among the most active and constructive participants in various international organisations, NATO as such has been hesitant in entering this field, particularly in regard to economic matters. Its members have been rightly concerned to avoid duplication and to do, through other existing international organisations, the things which can best be done in that way.

19. Recently, however, the members of NATO have been examining and re-examining the purposes and the needs of the Organisation in the light of certain changes in Soviet tactics and policies which have taken place

since the death of Stalin, and of the effect of the present turmoil in Eastern Europe on this development.

20. These changes have not diminished the need for collective military defence but they have faced NATO with an additional challenge in which the emphasis is largely non-military in character. NATO must recognise the real nature of the developments which have taken place. An important aspect of the new Soviet policies of competitive co-existence is an attempt to respond to positive initiatives of the Western nations aimed at improving, in an atmosphere of freedom, the lot of the economically less-developed countries, and at establishing a just and mutually beneficial trading system in which all countries can prosper. The Soviet Union is now apparently veering towards policies designed to ensnare these countries by economic means and by political subversion, and to fasten on them the same shackles of Communism from which certain members of the Soviet bloc are now striving to release themselves. The members of NATO must maintain their vigilance in dealing with this form of penetration.

21. Meanwhile some of the immediate fears of large-scale all-out military aggression against Western Europe have lessened. This process has been facilitated by evidence that the Soviet Government has realised that any such all-out aggression would be met by a sure, swift and devastating retaliation, and that there could be no victory in a war of this kind with nuclear weapons on both sides. With an increased Soviet emphasis on non-military or paramilitary methods, a review is needed of NATO's ability to meet effectively the challenge of penetration under the guise of coexistence, with its emphasis on conflict without catastrophe.

22. Certain questions now take on a new urgency. Have NATO's needs and objectives changed, or should they be changed? Is the Organisation operating satisfactorily in the altered circumstances of 1956? If not what can be done about it? There is the even more far-reaching question: "Can a loose association of sovereign states hold together at all without the common binding force of fear?"

23. The Committee has been examining these questions in the light of its firm conviction that the objectives which governments had in mind when the Pact was signed remain valid; that NATO is as important now to its member states as it was at that time.

24. The first of these objectives—as has already been pointed out—is security, based on collective action with adequate armed forces both for deterrence and defence.

25. Certainly NATO unity and strength in the pursuit of this objective remain as essential as they were in 1949. Soviet tactics may have changed; but Soviet armed might and ultimate objectives remain unchanged. Moreover, recent events in Eastern Europe show that the Soviet Union will not hesitate in certain circumstances to use force and the threat of force.

Therefore the military strength of NATO must not be reduced, though its character and capabilities should be constantly adapted to changing circumstances. Strengthening the political and economic side of NATO is an essential complement to—not a substitute for—continuous cooperation in defence.

26. In spite of these recent events Soviet leaders may place greater emphasis on political, economic and propaganda action.

There is no evidence, however, that this will be permitted to prejudice in any way the maintenance of a high level of military power in its most modern form as a base for Soviet activity in these other fields.

27. We should welcome changes in Soviet policies if they were genuinely designed to ease international tensions. But we must remember that the weakening and eventual dissolution of NATO remains a major Communist goal. We must therefore remain on guard so long as Soviet leaders persist in their determination to maintain a preponderance of military power for the achievement of their own political objectives and those of their allies.

28. This brings us again to the second and long-term aim of NATO: the development of an Atlantic Community whose roots are deeper even than the necessity for common defence. This implies nothing less than the permanent association of the free Atlantic peoples for the promotion of their greater unity and the protection and the advancement of the interests which, as free democracies, they have in common.

29. If we are to secure this long-term aim, we must prevent the centrifugal forces of opposition or indifference from weakening the Alliance. NATO has not been destroyed, or even weakened, by the threats or attacks of its enemies. It has faltered at times through the lethargy or complacency of its members: through dissension or division between them; by putting narrow national considerations above the collective interest. It could be destroyed by these forces, if they were allowed to subsist. To combat these tendencies, NATO must be used by its members, far more

than it has been used, for sincere and genuine consultation and cooperation on questions of common concern. For this purpose, resolution is more important than resolutions; will than words.

30. The problem, however, goes deeper than this. NATO countries are faced by a political as well as a military threat. It comes from the revolutionary doctrines of Communism which have by careful design of the Communist leaders over many years been sowing seeds of falsehood concerning our free and democratic way of life. The best answer to such falsehoods is a continuing demonstration of the superiority of our own institutions over Communist ones. We can show by word and deed that we welcome political progress, economic advancement and orderly social change and that the real reactionaries of this day are these Communist regimes which, adhering to an inflexible pattern of economic and political doctrine, have been more successful in destroying freedom than in promoting it.

31. We must, however, realise that falsehoods concerning our institutions have sometimes been accepted at face value and that there are those, even in the non-Communist world, who under the systematic influence of Communist propaganda do not accept our own analysis of NATO's aims and values. They believe that while NATO may have served a useful defensive deterrent role in the Stalinist era, it is no longer necessary even for the security of its members; that it is tending now to become an agency for the pooling of the strength and resources of the "colonial" powers in defence of imperial privileges, racial superiority, and Atlantic hegemony under the leadership of the United States. The fact that we know these views to be false and unjustified does not mean that NATO and its governments should not do everything they can to correct and counteract them.

32. NATO should not forget that the influence and interests of its members are not confined to the area covered by the Treaty, and that common interests of the Atlantic Community can be seriously affected by developments outside the Treaty area.

> Therefore, while striving to improve their relations with each other, and to strengthen and deepen their own unity, they should also be concerned with harmonising their policies in relation to other areas, taking into account the broader interests of the whole international community; particularly in working through the United Nations and elsewhere for the maintenance of international peace and security and for the solution of the problems that now divide the world.

33. In following this course, NATO can show that it is more than a defence organisation acting and reacting to the ebb and flow of the fears and dangers arising out of Soviet policy. It can prove its desire to cooperate fully with other members of the international community in bringing to reality the principles of the Charter of the United Nations. It can show that it is not merely concerned with preventing the cold war from deteriorating into a shooting one; or with defending itself if tragedy should take place, but that it is even more concerned with seizing the political and moral initiative to enable all countries to develop in freedom, and to bring about a secure peace for all nations.

34. Our caution in accepting without question the pacific character of any Soviet moves, our refusal to dismantle our defences before we are convinced that conditions of international confidence have been restored, will, particularly after the events in Hungary, be understood by all people of sincerity and goodwill. What would not be understood is any unwillingness on our part to seek ways and means of breaking down the barriers with a view to establishing such confidence.

35. The coming together of the Atlantic nations for good and constructive purposes—which is the basic principle and ideal underlying the NATO concept—must rest on and grow from deeper and more permanent factors than the divisions and dangers of the last ten years. It is a historical, rather than a contemporary, development, and if it is to achieve its real purpose, it must be considered in that light and the necessary conclusions drawn. A short-range view will not suffice.

36. The fundamental historical tact underlying development is that the nation state, by itself and relying exclusively on national policy and national power, is inadequate for progress or even for survival in the nuclear age. As the founders of the North Atlantic Treaty foresaw, the growing interdependence of states, politically and economically as well as militarily, calls for an ever increasing measure of international cohesion and cooperation. Some states may be able to enjoy a degree of political and economic independence when things are going well. No state, however powerful, can guarantee its security and its welfare by national action alone.

37. This basic fact underlies our report and the recommendations contained therein which appear in the subsequent chapters.

38. It has not been difficult to make these recommendations. It will be far more difficult for the member governments to carry them into effect.

This will require, on their part, the firm conviction that the transformation of the Atlantic Community into a vital and vigorous political reality is as important as any purely national purpose. It will require, above all, the will to carry this conviction into the realm of practical governmental policy.

CHAPTER II: POLITICAL COOPERATION
I. Introduction

39. If there is to be vitality and growth in the concept of the Atlantic Community, the relations between the members of NATO must rest on a solid basis of confidence and understanding. Without this there cannot be constructive or solid political cooperation.

40. The deepening and strengthening of this political cooperation does not imply the weakening of the ties of NATO members with other friendly countries or with other international associations, particularly the United Nations. Adherence to NATO is not exclusive or restrictive. Nor should the evolution of the Atlantic Community through NATO prevent the formation of even closer relationships among some of its members, for instance within groups of European countries. The moves toward Atlantic cooperation and European unity should be parallel and complementary, not competitive or conflicting.

41. Effective and constructive international cooperation requires a resolve to work together for the solution of common problems. There are special ties between NATO members, special incentives and security interests, which should make this task easier than it otherwise would be. But its successful accomplishment will depend largely on the extent to which member governments, in their own policies and actions, take into consideration the interests of the Alliance. This requires not only the acceptance of the obligation of consultation and cooperation whenever necessary, but also the development of practices by which the discharge of this obligation becomes a normal part of governmental activity.

42. It is easy to profess devotion to the principle of political—or economic—consultation in NATO. It is difficult and has in fact been shown to be impossible, if the proper conviction is lacking, to convert the profession into practice. Consultation within an alliance means more than exchange of information, though that is necessary. It means more than letting the NATO Council know about national decisions that have already been taken; or trying to enlist support for those decisions. It means the

discussion of problems collectively, in the early stages of policy formation, and before national positions become fixed. At best, this will result in collective decisions on matters of common interest affecting the Alliance. At the least, it will ensure that no action is taken by one member without a knowledge of the views of the others.

II. Consultation on Foreign Policies
A. *Scope and Character of Political Consultation*

43. The essential role of consultation in fostering political cooperation was clearly defined by an earlier NATO Committee on the North Atlantic Community in 1951: ". . . The achievement of a closer degree of coordination of the foreign policies of the members of the North Atlantic Treaty, through the development of the 'habit of consultation' on matters of common concern, would greatly strengthen the solidarity of the North Atlantic Community and increase the individual and collective capacity of its members to serve the peaceful purposes for which NATO was established. In the political field, this means that while each North Atlantic government retains full freedom of action and decision with respect to its own policy, the aim should be to achieve, through exchanging information and views, as wide an area of agreement as possible in the formulation of policies as a whole."

> "Special attention must be paid, as explicitly recognised in Article 4 of the Treaty, to matters of urgent and immediate importance to the members of NATO, and to 'emergency' situations where it may be necessary to consult closely on national lines of conduct affecting the interests of members of NATO as a whole. There is a continuing need, however, for effective consultation at an early stage on current problems, in order that national policies may be developed and action taken on the basis of a full awareness of the attitudes and interests of all the members of NATO. While all members of NATO have a responsibility to consult with their partners on appropriate matters, a large share of responsibility for such consultation necessarily rests on the more powerful members of the Community."

44. These words were written five years ago. They hold true now more than ever before. If we can say that they have not been ignored by NATO we must also recognise that the practice of consulting has not so developed in the NATO Council as to meet the demands of political changes and world

trends. The present need, therefore, is more than simply broadening the scope and deepening the character of consultation. There is a pressing requirement for all members to make consultation in NATO an integral part of the making of national policy. Without this the very existence of the North Atlantic Community may be in jeopardy.

45. It should, however, be remembered that collective discussion is not an end in itself, but a means to the end of harmonising policies. Where common interests of the Atlantic Community are at stake consultation should always seek to arrive at timely agreement on common lines of policy and action.

46. Such agreement, even with the closest possible cooperation and consultation, is not easy to secure. But it is essential to the Atlantic Alliance that a steady and continuous effort be made to bring it about. There cannot be unity in defence and disunity in foreign policy.

47. There are, of course, certain practical limitations to consultation in this field. They are sufficiently obvious in fact to make it unnecessary to emphasise them in words. Indeed the danger is less that they will be minimised or evaded than that they will be exaggerated and used to justify practices which unnecessarily ignore the common interest.

48. One of these limitations is the hard fact that ultimate responsibility for decision and action still rests on national governments. It is conceivable that a situation of extreme emergency may arise where action must be taken by one government before consultation is possible with the others.

49. Another limitation is the difficulty, and indeed the unwisdom, of trying to specify in advance all the subjects and all the situations where consultation is necessary; to separate by area or by subject the matters of NATO concern from those of purely national concern; to define in detail the obligations and duties of consultation. These things have to work themselves out in practice. In this process, experience is a better guide than dogma.

50. The essential thing is that on all occasions and in all circumstances member governments, before acting or even before pronouncing, should keep the interest and the requirements of the Alliance in mind. If they have not the desire and the will to do this, no resolutions or recommendations or declarations by the Council or any Committee of the Council will be of any great value.

51. On the assumption, however, that this will and this desire do exist, the following principles and practices in the field of political consultation are recommended:

a. members should inform the Council of any development which significantly affects the Alliance. They should do this, not merely as formality but as a preliminary to effective political consultation;

b. both individual member governments and the Secretary General should have the right to raise for discussion in the Council any subject which is of common NATO interest and not of a purely domestic character;

c. a member government should not, without adequate advance consultation, adopt firm policies or make major political pronouncements on matters which significantly affect the Alliance or any of its members, unless circumstances make such prior consultation obviously and demonstrably impossible;

d. in developing their national policies, members should take into consideration the interest and views of other governments, particularly those most directly concerned, as expressed in NATO consultation, even where no community of views or consensus has been reached in the Council;

e. where a consensus has been reached, it should be reflected in the formation of national policies. When for national reasons the consensus is not followed, the government concerned should offer an explanation to the Council. It is even more important that where an agreed and formal recommendation has emerged from the Council's discussions, governments should give it full weight in any national actions or policies related to the subject of that recommendation.

B. Annual Political Appraisal

52. To strengthen the process of consultation, it is recommended that Foreign Ministers, at each Spring meeting, should make an appraisal of the political progress of the Alliance and consider the lines along which it should advance.

53. To prepare for this discussion, the Secretary General should submit an annual report

a. analysing the major political problems of the Alliance;

b. reviewing the extent to which member governments have consulted and cooperated on such problems;

c. indicating the problems and possible developments which may require future consultation, so that difficulties might be resolved and positive and constructive initiative taken.

54. Member governments, through their Permanent Representatives, should give the Secretary General such information and assistance, including that of technical experts, as he may require in preparing his report.

C. Preparation for Political Consultation

55. Effective consultation also requires careful planning and preparation of the agenda for meetings of the Council both in Ministerial and permanent session. Political questions coming up for discussion in the Council should so far as practicable be previously reviewed and discussed; so that representatives may have background information on the thinking both of their own and of other governments. When appropriate, drafts of resolutions should be prepared in advance as a basis for discussion. Additional preparatory work will also be required for the annual political appraisal referred to in the preceding section.

56. To assist the Permanent Representatives and the Secretary General in discharging their responsibilities for political consultation, there should be constituted under the Council a Committee of Political Advisers from each delegation, aided when necessary by specialists from the capitals. It would meet under the chairmanship of a member of the International Staff appointed by the Secretary General, and would include among its responsibilities current studies such as those on trends of Soviet policy.

III. Peaceful Settlement of Inter-member Disputes

57. In the development of effective political cooperation in NATO, it is of crucial importance to avoid serious inter-member disputes and to settle them quickly and satisfactorily when they occur. The settlement of such disputes is in the first place the direct responsibility of the member governments concerned, under both the Charter of the United Nations (Article XXXIII) and the North Atlantic Treaty (Article 1). To clarify NATO's responsibilities in dealing with disputes which have not proved capable of settlement directly and to enable NATO, if necessary, to help in the settlement of such disputes, the Committee recommends that the Council adopt a resolution under Article I of the Treaty on the following lines:

    a. re-affirming the obligation of members to settle by peaceful means any disputes between themselves;

    b. declaring their intention to submit any such disputes, which have not proved capable of settlement directly, to good offices procedures within the NATO framework before resorting to any other international agency; except for disputes of a legal character for submission to a judicial tribunal, and those disputes of an economic character for which attempts at settlement might best be made initially in the appropriate specialised economic organisation;

c. recognising the right and duty of member government and of the Secretary General to bring to the attention of the Council matters which in their opinion may threaten the solidarity or effectiveness of the Alliance;

d. empowering the Secretary General to offer his good offices informally at any time to the parties in dispute, and with their consent to initiate or facilitate procedures of inquiry, mediation, conciliation, or arbitration, and e. empowering the Secretary General, where he deems it appropriate for the purpose outlined in d. above, to use the assistance of not more than three Permanent Representatives chosen by him in each instance.

IV. Parliamentary Associations and the Parliamentary Conference

58. Among the best supporters of NATO and its purposes are those Members of Parliament who have had a chance at first hand to see some of its activities and to learn of its problems, and to exchange views with their colleagues from other parliaments.

In particular, the formation of national Parliamentary Associations and the activities of the Conference of Members of Parliament from NATO countries have contributed to the development of public support for NATO and solidarity among its members.

59. In order to maintain a close relationship of Parliamentarians with NATO, the following arrangements are recommended:

a. that the Secretary General continue to place the facilities of NATO Headquarters at the disposal of Parliamentary Conferences and give all possible help with arrangements for their meetings;

b. that invited representatives of member governments and the Secretary General and other senior NATO civil and military officers attend certain of these meetings. In this way the Parliamentarians would be informed on the state of the Alliance and the problems before it, and the value of their discussions would be increased.

CHAPTER III: ECONOMIC COOPERATION
I. Introduction

60. Political cooperation and economic conflict are not reconcilable. Therefore, in the economic as well as in the political field there must be a genuine desire among the members to work together and a readiness to consult on questions of common concern based on the recognition of common interests.

61. These common economic interests shared by the members of NATO call for:

> a. cooperative and national action to achieve healthy and expanding economies, both to promote the well-being and self-confidence of the Atlantic peoples and to serve as the essential support for an adequate defence effort;
> b. the greatest possible freedom in trade and payments and in the movement of manpower and long-term capital;
> c. assistance to economically underdeveloped areas for reasons of enlightened self-interest and to promote better relations among peoples; and
> d. policies which will demonstrate, under conditions of competitive co-existence, the superiority of free institutions in promoting human welfare and economic progress.

62. A recognition of these common NATO interests, and collective and individual efforts to promote them, need not in any way prejudice close economic relations with non-NATO countries. Economic, like political, cooperation is and must remain wider than NATO. At the same time, the NATO countries have an interest in any arrangements for especially close economic cooperation among groups of European member nations. It should be possible as it is desirable for such special arrangements to promote rather than conflict with the wider objectives of Article 2 of our Treaty, which are of basic importance to the stability and well-being, not only of the North Atlantic area, but of the whole non-Communist world.

II. NATO and Other Organisations

63. While the purposes and principles of Article 2 are of vital importance, it is not necessary that member countries pursue them only through action in NATO itself. It would not serve the interests of the Atlantic Community

for NATO to duplicate the operating functions of other international organisations designed for various forms of economic cooperation. NATO members play a major part in all these agencies, whose membership is generally well adapted to the purposes they serve.

64. Nor do there now appear to be significant new areas for collective economic action requiring execution by NATO itself. In fact, the common economic concern of the member nations will often best be fostered by continued and increased collaboration both bilateral and through organisations other than NATO. This collaboration should be reinforced, however, by NATO consultation whenever economic issues of special interest to the Alliance are involved, particularly those which have political or defence implications or affect the economic health of the Atlantic Community as a whole. This, in turn, requires a substantial expansion of exchange of information and views in NATO in the economic as well as in the political field. Such economic consultation should seek to secure a common approach on the part of member governments where the questions are clearly related to the political and security interests of the Alliance. Action resulting from such a common approach, however, should normally be taken by governments either directly or through other international organisations.

65. NATO, as such, should not seek to establish formal relations with these other organisations, and the harmonising of attitudes and actions should be left to the representatives of the NATO governments therein. Nor is it necessary or desirable for NATO members to form a "bloc" in such organisations. This would only alienate other friendly governments. There should, however, be consultation in NATO when economic issues of special political or strategic importance to NATO arise in other organisations and in particular before meetings at which there may be attempts to divide or weaken the Atlantic Alliance, or prejudice its interests.

III. Conflicts in Economic Policies of NATO Countries

66. NATO has a positive interest in the resolution of economic disputes which may have political or strategic repercussions damaging to the Alliance. These are to be distinguished from disagreements on economic policy which are normally dealt with through direct negotiations or by multilateral discussions in other organisations. Nothing would be gained by merely having repeated in NATO the same arguments made in other and more technically qualified organisations. It should however, be open to any member or to the Secretary General to raise in NATO issues on which

they feel that consideration elsewhere is not making adequate progress and that NATO consultation might facilitate solutions contributing to the objectives of the Atlantic Community. The procedures for peaceful settlement of political disputes discussed in the previous chapter should also be available for major disputes of an economic character which are appropriate for NATO consideration.

IV. Scientific and Technical Cooperation

67. One area of special importance to the Atlantic Community is that of science and technology. During the last decade, it has become ever clearer that progress in this field can be decisive in determining the security of nations and their position in world affairs. Such progress is also vital if the Western world is to play its proper role in relation to economically underdeveloped areas.

68. Within the general field of science and technology, there is an especially urgent need to improve the quality and to increase the supply of scientists, engineers and technicians. Responsibility for recruitment, training and utilisation of scientific and technical personnel is primarily a national rather than an international matter. Nor is it a responsibility solely of national governments. In the member countries with federal systems, state and provincial governments play the major part, and many of the universities and institutes of higher learning in the Atlantic area are independent institutions free from detailed control by governments. At the same time, properly designed measures of international cooperation could stimulate individual member countries to adopt more positive policies and, in some cases, help guide them in the most constructive directions.

69. Certain activities in this connection are already being carried out by other organisations. Progress in this field, however, is so crucial to the future of the Atlantic Community that NATO members should ensure that every possibility of fruitful cooperation is examined. As a first concrete step, therefore, it is recommended that a conference be convened composed of one or at the most two outstanding authorities, private or governmental, from each country in order:

> a. to exchange information and views concerning the most urgent problems in the recruitment, training and utilisation of scientists, engineers and technicians, and the best means, both long-term and short-term, of solving those problems;

b. to foster closer relations among the participants with a view to continued interchange of experience and stimulation of constructive work in member countries; and

c. to propose specific measures for future international cooperation in this field, through NATO or other international organizations.

V. Consultation on Economic Problems

70. It is agreed that the Atlantic Community has a positive concern with healthy and accelerated development in economically underdeveloped areas, both inside and outside the NATO area. The Committee feels, however, that NATO is not an appropriate agency for administering programs of assistance for economic development, or even for systematically concerning the relevant policies of member nations. What member countries can and should do is to keep each other and the Organisation informed of their programs and policies in this field. When required, NATO should review the adequacy of existing action in relation to the interests of the Alliance.

71. The economic interests of the Atlantic Community cannot be considered in isolation from the activities and policies of the Soviet bloc. The Soviets are resorting all too often to the use of economic measures designed to weaken the Western Alliance, or to create in other areas a high degree of dependence on the Soviet world. In this situation it is more than ever important that NATO countries actively develop their own constructive commercial and financial policies. In particular, they should avoid creating situations of which the Soviet bloc countries might take advantage to the detriment of the Atlantic Community and of other non-Communist countries. In this whole field of competitive economic co-existence member countries should consult together more fully in order to determine their course deliberately and with the fullest possible knowledge.

72. There has been a considerable evolution in NATO's arrangements for regular economic consultation. In addition, a number of economic matters have been brought before the Council for consideration on an ad hoc basis. No substantial new machinery in this field is called for. However, in view of the extended range of topics for regular exchange of information and consultation described above, there should be established under the Council a Committee of Economic Advisers. This group should be entrusted with preliminary discussion, on a systematic basis, of the matters outlined above, together with such tasks as many be assigned by the

Council or approved by the Council at the Committee's request. It would absorb any continuing function of the Committee of Technical Advisers.

Since its duties would not be full-time, member governments could be represented normally by officials mainly concerned with the work of other international economic organisations.

Membership, however, should be flexible, the Committee being composed, when appropriate, of specialists from the capitals on particular topics under consideration.

CHAPTER IV: CULTURAL COOPERATION

73. A sense of community must bind the people as well as the institutions of the Atlantic nations. This will exist only to the extent that there is a realisation of their common cultural heritage and of the values of their free way of life and thought. It is important, therefore, for the NATO countries to promote cultural cooperation among their peoples by all practical means in order to strengthen their unity and develop maximum support for the Alliance. It is particularly important that this cultural cooperation should be wider than continental. This, however, does not preclude particular governments from acting on a more limited multilateral or even bilateral basis to strengthen their own cultural relations within the broader Atlantic framework. The Committee welcomes the measures for cultural cooperation within the Atlantic Community which have been initiated by private individuals and non-governmental groups. These should be encouraged and increased.

74. To further cultural collaboration, the Committee suggests that member governments be guided by the following general principles:

    a. government activities in this field should not duplicate but should support and supplement private efforts;

    b. member governments should give priority to those projects which require joint NATO action, and thus contribute to a developing sense of community;

    c. in developing new activities in the cultural field, NATO can most fruitfully place the main emphasis on inspiring and promoting transatlantic contacts;

    d. there should be a realistic appreciation of the financial implications of cultural projects.

75. In order to develop public awareness and understanding of NATO and the Atlantic Community, the Council should work out arrangements for NATO courses and seminars for teachers.

76. NATO and its member governments should broaden their support of other educational and related activities such as the NATO Fellowship and Scholarship Program; creation of university chairs of Atlantic studies; visiting professorships; government-sponsored programs for the exchange of persons, especially on a transatlantic basis; use of NATO information materials in schools; and establishment of special NATO awards for students.

77. Governments should actively promote closer relations between NATO and youth organisations and a specialist should be added to the International Staff in this connection.

Conferences under NATO auspices of representatives of youth organisations such as that of July, 1956, should be held from time to time.

78. In the interests of promoting easier and more frequent contacts among the NATO peoples, governments should review and, if possible, revise their foreign exchange and other policies which restrict travel.

79. In view of the importance of promoting better understanding and goodwill between NATO service personnel, it would be desirable, in cooperation with the military authorities, to extend exchanges of such personnel beyond the limits of normal training programs. Such exchanges might, at first step, be developed by governments on a bilateral basis. In addition, member governments should seek the assistance of the Atlantic Treaty Association and other voluntary organisations in the further development of such exchanges.

80. Cultural projects which have a common benefit should be commonly financed. Agreed cultural projects initiated by a single member government or a private organisation, such as the recent seminar held at Oxford or the Study conference sponsored by the Atlantic Treaty Association on "The Role of the School in the Atlantic Community," should receive financial support from NATO where that is necessary to supplement national resources.

CHAPTER V: COOPERATION IN THE INFORMATION FIELD

81. The people of the member countries must know about NATO if they are to support it. Therefore they must be informed not only of NATO's

aspirations, but of its achievements. There must be substance for an effective NATO information programme and resources to carry it out. The public should be informed to the greatest possible extent of significant results achieved through NATO consultation.

82. NATO information activities should be directed primarily to public opinion in the NATO area. At the same time an understanding outside the NATO area of the objectives and accomplishments of the Organisation is necessary if it is to be viewed sympathetically, and if its activities are not to be misinterpreted.

83. The important task of explaining and reporting NATO activities rests primarily on national information services. They cannot discharge this task if member governments do not make adequate provisions in their national programmes for that purpose. It is essential, therefore, that such provision be made. NATO can and should assist national governments in this work. The promotion of information about, and public understanding of NATO and the Atlantic Community should, in fact, be a joint endeavor by the Organisation and its members.

84. One of NATO's functions should be to coordinate the work of national information services in fields of common interest. Governments should pool their experiences and views in NATO to avoid differences in evaluation and emphasis. This is particularly important in the dissemination of information about NATO to other countries. Coordinated policy should underline the defensive character of our Alliance and the importance of its non-military aspects. It should cover also replies to anti-NATO propaganda and the analysis of Communist moves and statements which affect NATO.

85. In its turn, the NATO Information Division must be given the resources by governments as well as their support, without which it could not discharge these new tasks and should not be asked to do so.

86. In order to facilitate cooperation between the NATO Information Division and national information services, the following specific measures are recommended:

    a. an Officer should be designated by each national information service to maintain liaison with NATO and to be responsible for the dissemination of NATO information material;

    b. governments should submit to NATO the relevant information programmes which they plan to implement, for discussion in the

Committee on Information and Cultural Relations. Representatives of national information services should take part in these discussions;

   c. within the NATO Information Division budget, provision should be made for a translation fund so that NATO information material can be translated into the non-official languages of the Alliance, according to reasonable requirements of the member governments;

   d. NATO should, on request, provide national services with special studies on matters of common interest.

87. The journalists' tours sponsored by NATO should be broadened to include others in a position to influence public opinion, such as trade and youth leaders, teachers and lecturers. Closer relations between private organisations supporting NATO and the NATO Information Division should also be encouraged.

CHAPTER VI: ORGANISATION AND FUNCTIONS

88. The Committee considers that NATO in its present form is capable of discharging the non-military functions required of it. Structural changes are not needed. The machine is basically satisfactory. It is for governments to make use of it.

89. At the same time, certain improvements in the procedures and functioning of the Organisation will be required if the recommendations of this report are to be fully implemented. The proposals in this Chapter are submitted for this purpose.

A. Meetings of the Council

90. More time should be allowed for Ministerial Meetings. Experience has shown that, without more time, important issues on the agenda cannot be adequately considered. Decisions concerning some of them will not be reached at all, or will be reached only in an unclear form.

91. Efforts should be made to encourage discussion rather than simply declarations of policy prepared in advance. Arrangements for meetings should be made with this aim in view. For most sessions, the numbers present should be sharply restricted.

> In order to facilitate free discussion, when Ministers wish to speak in a language other than French or English, consecutive translation into one of these official languages should be provided by interpreters from their own delegations.

92. Meetings of Foreign Ministers should be held whenever required, and occasionally in locations other than NATO Headquarters. Ministers might also participate more frequently in regular Council meetings, even though not all of them may find it possible to attend such meetings at the same time. The Council of Permanent Representatives has powers of effective decision: in other words, the authority of the Council as such is the same whether governments are represented by Ministers or by their Permanent Representatives. Thus there should be no firm or formal line between Ministerial and other meetings of the Council.

B. Strengthening the Links between the Council and Member Governments

93. It is indispensable to the kind of consultations envisaged in this report that Permanent Representatives should be in a position to speak authoritatively and to reflect the current thinking of their governments. Differences in location and in constitutional organisation make impossible any uniform arrangements in all member governments. In some cases it might be desirable to designate a high official in the national capital to be concerned primarily with NATO affairs. The purpose would be to help both in fostering NATO consultations whenever national policies impinge on the common interest of the Atlantic Community, and in translating the results of such consultation into effective action within the national governments.

94. To ensure the closest possible connection between current thinking in the governments and consultations in the Council, there might be occasional Council Meetings with the participation of specially designated officials or the permanent heads of foreign ministries.

C. Preparation for Council Meetings

95. Items on the agenda of Ministerial Meetings should be thoroughly examined by Permanent Representatives and relevant proposals prepared before Ministers meet. For this purpose it may be found desirable for governments to send senior experts to consult on agenda items before the meetings take place.

96. The preparation of questions for discussion in the Council should be assisted by appropriate use of the Council's Committees of Political and Economic Advisers. (Recommendations on the establishment of these Committees are set forth in Chapter II, paragraph 56, and Chapter III, paragraph 72.)

97. In the case of consultations on special subjects, more use should be made of senior experts from national capitals to assist permanent delegations by calling them, on an ad hoc basis, to do preparatory work. Informal discussions among specialists with corresponding responsibilities are a particularly valuable means of concerning governmental attitudes in the early stages of policy formation.

98. Member governments should make available to one another through NATO "basic position material" for background information. This would help the Alliance as a whole in the consideration of problems of common concern and would assist individual governments to understand more fully the reasons for the position adopted by any member country on a particular issue which might be its special concern, but which might also affect in varying degrees other members of NATO.

D. The Secretary General and the International Staff

99. To enable the Organisation to make its full contribution, the role of the Secretary General and the International Staff needs to be enhanced.

100. It is recommended that the Secretary General preside over meetings of the Council in Ministerial session, as he does now in other sessions. Such a change with respect to the conduct of the Council's business would follow naturally from the new responsibilities of the Secretary General, arising out of the recommendations of this report. It is also warranted by the Secretary General's unique opportunities for becoming familiar with the problems and the activities of the Alliance as a whole.

101. It would, however, still be desirable to have one Minister chosen each year as President of the Council in accordance with the present practice of alphabetical rotation. This Minister, as President, would continue to have especially close contact with the Secretary General during and between Ministerial Meetings, and would, as at present, act as the spokesman of the Council on all formal occasions. He would also preside at the formal opening and closing of Ministerial sessions of the Council.

102. In addition:

   a. the Secretary General should be encouraged to propose items for NATO consultation in the fields covered by this report and should be responsible for promoting and directing the process of consultation;

   b. in view of these responsibilities member governments should undertake to keep the Secretary General fully and currently informed through their permanent delegations of their governments' thinking on questions of common concern to the Alliance;

c. attention is also called to the additional responsibilities of the Secretary General, recommended in connection with the annual political appraisal (Chapter II, paragraph 52), and the peaceful settlement of disputes (Chapter II, paragraph 57).

103. The effective functioning of NATO depends in large measure on the efficiency, devotion and morale of its Secretariat. Acceptance of the recommendations in this report would impose on the Secretariat new duties and responsibilities. Governments must, therefore, be prepared to give the International Staff all necessary support, both in finance and personnel. If this is not done, the recommendations of the report, even if accepted by governments, will not be satisfactorily carried out.

ANNEX: COUNCIL RESOLUTIONS

1. Resolution on the Peaceful Settlement of Disputes and Differences between Members of the North Atlantic Treaty Organisation Whereas the parties to the North Atlantic Treaty, under Article I of that treaty, have undertaken "to settle any international disputes in which they may be involved by peaceful means in such a manner that international peace and security and justice are not endangered";

Whereas the parties have further undertaken to seek to eliminate conflicts in their international economic policies and will encourage economic collaboration between any or all of them;

Whereas NATO unity and strength in the pursuit of these objectives remain essential for continuous cooperation in military and non-military fields;

The North Atlantic Council:

Reaffirms the obligations of all its members, under Article I of the Treaty, to settle by peaceful means any dispute between themselves;

Decides that such disputes which have not proved capable of settlement directly be submitted to good offices procedures within the NATO framework before member governments resort to any other international agency except for disputes of a legal character appropriate for submission to a judicial tribunal and those disputes of an economic character for which attempts at settlement might best be made initially in the appropriate specialised economic organisations;

Recognises the right and duty of member governments and of the Secretary General to bring to its attention matters which in their opinion may threaten the solidarity or effectiveness of the Alliance;

Empowers the Secretary General to offer his good offices informally at any time to member governments involved in a dispute and with their consent to initiate or facilitate procedures of inquiry, mediation, conciliation, or arbitration;

Authorises the Secretary General where he deems it appropriate for the purpose outlined in the preceding paragraph to use the assistance of not more than three permanent representatives chosen by him in each instance.

RESOLUTION ON THE REPORT OF THE COMMITTEE OF THREE ON NON-MILITARY COOPERATION IN NATO

Whereas the North Atlantic Council at its meeting in Paris on May 5 established a Committee composed of the Foreign Ministers of Italy, Canada and Norway to advise the Council on ways and means to improve and extend NATO cooperation in non-military fields and to develop greater unity within the Atlantic Community;

Whereas the Committee of Three has now reported on the task assigned to it and has submitted to the Council a number of recommendations on such ways and means to improve and extend NATO cooperation in non-military fields;

The North Atlantic Council:

Takes note of the Report of the Committee of Three; and

Approves its recommendations; and

Invites the Council in Permanent Session to implement in the light of the comments made by governments the principles and recommendations contained in the Report; and

Invites the Secretary General to draw up for consideration by the Council such further specific proposals as may be required for the implementation of these recommendations and to report periodically on the compliance with these recommendations by governments. Authorises the Committee of Three to publish their report.

Note

1. The outstanding instances are the Organisation for European Cooperation and Development (OECD) (which includes all NATO countries and four others); the General Agreement on Tariffs and Trade (GATT); the International Monetary Fund (IMF); the International Bank for Reconstruction and Development (IBRD); the International Finance Corporation (IFC); and the various other United Nations agencies including the Economic Commission for Europe. Several NATO members participate actively in the Colombo Plan for promoting economic development in Asia. Most members are taking an active part in technical assistance programmes and are also participating in discussions of proposals for the creation of a Special United Nations Fund for Economic Development (SUNFED).

MEETING OF THE NORTH ATLANTIC COUNCIL AT THE LEVEL OF FOREIGN MINISTERS FINAL COMMUNIQUÉ

TURNBERRY, SCOTLAND, JUNE 7, 1990

(Source: NATO)

1. The historic events that have occurred since we met last December in Brussels confirm that Europe is entering a new era. The countries of Central and Eastern Europe are taking decisive steps to establish democratic institutions, hold free elections and promote political pluralism and market-oriented economic policies. Germany is peacefully and democratically moving towards unity. We welcome the expansion and deepening of political exchanges at all levels. The visits to NATO by the Soviet, Czechoslovak and Polish Foreign Ministers exemplify this broadened dialogue. We look to further such opportunities in the future. A continent divided for four decades is searching for new patterns and structures of cooperation. These positive trends are having repercussions beyond Europe: democracy, the search for peaceful solutions and respect for human values are gaining ground in other parts of the world as well. Our Alliance remains vitally important as an instrument both for ensuring the security of its members and the stability of Europe and as a keystone of our efforts to build a new European order of peace. At this meeting, we have looked ahead to both continuing and new Alliance tasks in support of the positive changes in Europe, in preparation for the decisions to be taken by our Heads of State and Government next month in London. To that end, we have confirmed our agreement on the following points.

2. We strongly emphasise that we attach the highest priority to the conclusion this year of a CFE treaty. This must encompass all subjects under negotiation, and result in substantial, binding, verifiable reductions of conventional forces in Europe, thus eliminating destabilising disparities and the capability to launch a surprise attack or initiate large-scale offensive action. Such a treaty would be a dramatic advance towards greater stability and security in Europe. That goal is within sight, and it is now imperative that the remaining obstacles to its achievement be removed. We remain ready to take account of the stated interests of the other participants and to explore all open issues on the basis of a willingness on all sides to make reasonable compromises. We have therefore instructed our negotiators in Vienna to pursue new approaches to mutually acceptable solutions, in particular on aircraft, armour and verification. We call on the Soviet Union to cooperate in reaching agreement on all substantive issues this Summer, in order that progress can be made on the broader agenda for the construction of a new Europe, including a CSCE Summit later this year.

3. Allied governments will continue to work for substantive results in the CSBM negotiations, in the form of an agreement later this year. To that end, Allies have recently proposed a series of innovative cooperative measures, such as a mechanism for discussion of unusual activities of a military nature and annual implementation assessment meetings. We will continue to build on the contributions to confidence-building flowing from the Military Doctrine Seminar held in January in the framework of the CSBM negotiations in order to further expand military contacts and exchanges on military matters.

4. As soon as a CFE agreement is reached, Allies will be prepared to undertake follow-on negotiations to further enhance security and stability in Europe. The objectives of these follow-on negotiations, and of our further quest for European security, including through conventional arms control, will be considered at our meeting of Heads of State and Government.

5. We welcome the progress attained at the US–Soviet Summit held last week and, in particular, the agreement on major outstanding issues governing a START treaty that will result in deep reductions in both sides' strategic nuclear weapons and greatly expand bilateral military transparency in that area, as well as agreement to begin further talks on strategic nuclear forces specifically devoted to achieving a more stable strategic balance after the current treaty is completed. We took special note of the

progress represented by the signature at that Summit meeting of verification protocols for treaties limiting nuclear testing and expressed our satisfaction with the bilateral agreement that will drastically reduce both sides' stocks of chemical weapons.

6. We believe the US–Soviet agreement on reducing chemical weapons stockpiles will provide great impetus towards the earliest possible conclusion of the convention for an effectively verifiable, global and comprehensive ban on chemical weapons now being negotiated, which remains our goal. All Allies hereby state their intention to be among the original signatories to the convention and to promote its early entry into force. We call on all other states to undertake a similar commitment. We reaffirm our determination to work to prevent the proliferation of nuclear and chemical weapons and of missiles capable of carrying such weapons.

7. We will pursue the "Open Skies" initiative, convinced that such a regime would make a significant contribution to the openness and transparency we wish to encourage. We therefore regret that our efforts to reach such an agreement have thus far not been successful and look to the Soviet Union to join with us to take the steps necessary to create an "Open Skies" regime that will increase calculability, mutual confidence and the security of all participants.

8. Recognising that the verification of arms control treaties is destined to become a long-term task for the Alliance, we have decided to establish a coordination mechanism for this purpose.

9. We agree on the crucial importance of the political and economic reforms underway in the states of Central and Eastern Europe and the Soviet Union. The continued progress of these states towards becoming democratic and economically prosperous partners cooperating with us will be an important element in the future security and stability of Europe. We are prepared to support their efforts to integrate their economies more closely into the world economy and to widen and deepen the scope of our cooperation with them as they progress, thus contributing to the success of their reform programmes.

10. We strongly hope that the processes of economic reorientation and development and of democratic institution-building in these countries, necessarily complicated and uneven, will successfully overcome periods of uncertainty and potential instability. The historic changes already underway and the prospects for further positive developments have not removed all grounds for concern about the stability and security of Europe. More-

over, we cannot be oblivious to the fact that the Soviet Union will retain substantial military capabilities, which it is continuing to modernise and which have implications for our defence.

11. The need to maintain our common defence remains vital. The Alliance's role in preventing conflict, precluding the use or threat of force against any of its members and guaranteeing stability will continue to be essential. That role is built upon the principle of the indivisibility of security for all member countries and embodies an indispensable link between North America and European democracies. For the foreseeable future, the prevention of war will continue to require an appropriate mix of survivable and effective conventional and nuclear forces, at the lowest levels consistent with our security needs. Our resolve, our commitment to the equitable and widespread sharing of responsibilities, and our solidarity with which we have maintained adequate collective defence arrangements for so long, including the presence of significant North American conventional and nuclear forces in Europe, will continue to be crucial factors in the maintenance of peace in Europe.

12. The military risks facing the Alliance have already decreased substantially, and implementation of a successful CFE agreement would result in a further dramatic improvement. The principles of Alliance security set out in May 1989 in the Comprehensive Concept of Arms Control and Disarmament are the basis for our further work in assessing the implications of the changing situation in Europe for our strategy. Thus, those governments among us participating in the Defence Planning Committee welcome its recent decision to undertake a review of NATO's military strategy, and the means of implementing it, in the emerging circumstances. They also welcome the invitation to the NATO Military Authorities to undertake a study of the possibilities for greater use of multi-national forces. They endorse the US President's recent proposal that negotiations on US and Soviet short-range nuclear weapon systems in Europe begin shortly after a CFE agreement is concluded.

13. We see the CSCE process as an important framework for far-reaching reforms and stability and as a central element in the construction of a new Europe, along with other European institutions including the Alliance itself. The function of the CSCE will be complementary to that of the Alliance. The CSCE, having from the outset served to ease the burden of the division of Europe, will now become even more vital as an instrument for developing structures for a Europe whole and free and for cooperation

within a united continent. The Allies look forward to an early outcome to the CFE negotiations which are taking place in the CSCE framework and to continued progress in the talks on confidence and security-building measures, which, along with results of CSCE inter-sessional activities, will lay the necessary basis for the CSCE Summit this year. The Summit should reflect the new role of the CSCE and take appropriate decisions. Furthermore, it is the hope of the Allies that the "2 + 4" process will be completed prior to the CSCE Summit. That Summit will help consolidate the changes that have taken place in Central and Eastern Europe, and provide substantial new impetus to the CSCE process in all main areas of the Helsinki Final Act. To this end, implementation in letter and spirit of all CSCE obligations by all CSCE participating states remains essential. Meanwhile, we believe that the time has now come to determine the modalities of institutionalisation without depriving the process of its flexibility and balance. A number of valuable proposals have been raised within the framework of Alliance consultations for the further development of the CSCE process and for enhancing regional cooperation efforts. They include a consultation mechanism on a high level as well as other arrangements in specific fields of cooperation. Our governments continue to develop these ideas as our preparations continue for the CSCE Summit. We are pleased that other CSCE participants are equally developing their ideas. We welcome the decision of the Foreign Ministers of the 35 CSCE states at their meeting in Copenhagen on 5th June 1990 to establish a preparatory Committee for the Summit, and for Ministers of the "35" to meet in the United States this Autumn.

14. Welcoming agreement at the recent Bonn Conference on Economic Cooperation in Europe on fundamental principles to guide the conversion from planned to market-oriented economies, we fully support the efforts of the Copenhagen meeting of the Conference on the Human Dimension now underway to reinforce and extend the protection and guarantee of human rights and individual freedoms. Allies place particular importance on resolutions concerning the right to free and fair elections held at regular intervals, a commitment to the rule of law, and rights of persons belonging to national minorities among many proposals put forward for consideration at the Copenhagen meeting. We hope that the Palma de Mallorca meeting on the Mediterranean will contribute to enhancing cooperation also in that region. We also welcome the interest recently expressed by the Albanian Government in associating itself with the CSCE process and the

commitments therein. We look to the Albanian Government to demonstrate its willingness to comply with all existing CSCE commitments, including those on human rights.

15. We note with pride that after 40 years as a divided city, Berlin is finally growing together again. The Berlin Wall has come down. This heralds the long-awaited ending of the post-war era and of the division of Germany and of Europe. The realisation of the unity of Germany has always been a primary goal of our Alliance. Therefore, on the basis of our close and continuing consultations within the Alliance, we are united in actively supporting the progress that has already been achieved in the process of German unification; we also support the efforts underway in the "2 + 4" talks to seek a final settlement under international law terminating the Four Power rights and responsibilities relating to Berlin and Germany as a whole, and without the establishment of constraints on the sovereignty of Germany. A united Germany must have the right, recognised in the Helsinki Final Act, to choose to be a party to a treaty of alliance. We believe that European stability, as well as the wishes of the German people, requires that a unified Germany be a full member of this Alliance, including its integrated military structure, without prejudice to stated positions about nondeployment of NATO forces on the present GDR territory. The security guarantee provided by Articles 5 and 6 of the North Atlantic Treaty will extend to all the territory of a united Germany. We seek no unilateral advantage from German unity and are prepared to demonstrate this, taking into account legitimate Soviet security interests. A free and democratic Germany will be an essential element of a peaceful order in Europe in which no state need harbour fears for its security against its neighbours. We underline the importance of the points on German unification discussed with the Soviet leadership in Washington, which fully reflect our consultations.

16. We express the wish that the problems accompanying the difficult internal transition of the Soviet Union be solved in a constructive manner and to the satisfaction of all concerned. In this context, we firmly support the expectations and aspirations of the Baltic peoples. It is our understanding that the leaders of Lithuania and the Soviet Union have indicated their willingness to begin a dialogue upon the suspension and not retraction by the Lithuanian leadership of the implementation of their declaration of independence. We appeal to all parties to show flexibility and enter into true dialogue to reach an early solution.

17. Our activities in the scientific and environmental fields, known as NATO's "Third Dimension," remain of major benefit to our member nations and are an expression of their solidarity. In the spirit of the 40th Anniversary Summit Declaration we shall pursue measures to invite scientific experts from Central and Eastern Europe to participate in work on the environment connected with pilot studies within the framework of the Committee on the Challenges of Modern Society.

18. The NATO Summit in May 1989 launched a Democratic Institutions Fellowship programme intended to help qualified applicants from Central and Eastern Europe, as well as those from Alliance countries, to study our democratic values and way of life. We intend to pursue this initiative and are pleased with the strong response it has received in its first year.

19. Mindful of the continuing need to inform our publics better about the work and objectives of the Alliance, we expressed our strong support for the network of Atlantic Committees and Associations brought together under the Atlantic Treaty Association. We are convinced that they have a vital role to play in deepening public understanding of the role of the Alliance. We underline the great value of the exchange of views in the North Atlantic Assembly on issues facing the Alliance.

20. The developments which we are now witnessing and of which we have been and will continue to be among the principal architects, are producing far-reaching changes in the political and military fundamentals of European security, and consequently in the conditions under which our Alliance is required to work.

These changes call into question neither the necessity for maintaining the Alliance nor the permanence of its fundamental features. We will keep our Alliance dynamic and cohesive and will continue to foster a solid and fruitful transatlantic relationship between North America and an increasingly united Europe. We will remain cognisant of the need for intra-Alliance cooperation and assistance. We must continue, in the face of historic change, to deepen and strengthen our political consultation and, where appropriate, coordination.

Thus, while ensuring that the permanent principles which form the basis of our Alliance and guarantee its effectiveness are preserved, we must today adapt it to the enormous changes now taking place. We have already begun this process in the political and defence spheres, as demonstrated by our Ministerial consultations this Spring. We have shown ourselves ready, through the arms control negotiations in which we are participating or which we are preparing to initiate, to adjust the size of the Allies' conventional and nuclear forces. We have noted that the Defence Ministers who participate in the Nuclear Planning Group and the Defence Planning Committee have decided to reconsider their strategy. Although the prevention of war will always remain our fundamental task, the changing European environment now requires of us a broader approach to security based as much on constructive peace-building as on peace-keeping.

21. We recognise, against the background of the changes now taking place in Europe, that the modifications in certain aspects of the Alliance's policies and functioning will form part of a broader pattern of adaptation within the Organization. This process should encompass all activities of our Alliance and must be consistent with the principles which we have declared to be permanent and with the requirements of the new era upon which we are embarking. We have, therefore, instructed our Council in Permanent Session to oversee the work in hand, with a view to ensuring that it is effectively coordinated, and to report regularly to us on the progress made.

22. We express our deep appreciation for the warm hospitality provided by the Government of the United Kingdom.

DECLARATION ON A TRANSFORMED NORTH ATLANTIC ALLIANCE ISSUED BY THE HEADS OF STATE AND GOVERNMENT PARTICIPATING IN THE MEETING OF THE NORTH ATLANTIC COUNCIL
"THE LONDON DECLARATION"
LONDON, JULY 6, 1990

(Source: NATO)

1. Europe has entered a new, promising era. Central and Eastern Europe is liberating itself. The Soviet Union has embarked on the long journey toward a free society. The walls that once confined people and ideas are collapsing. Europeans are determining their own destiny. They are choosing freedom. They are choosing economic liberty. They are choosing peace. They are choosing a Europe whole and free. As a consequence, this Alliance must and will adapt.

2. The North Atlantic Alliance has been the most successful defensive alliance in history. As our Alliance enters its fifth decade and looks ahead to a new century, it must continue to provide for the common defence. This Alliance has done much to bring about the new Europe. No-one, however, can be certain of the future. We need to keep standing together, to extend the long peace we have enjoyed these past four decades. Yet our Alliance must be even more an agent of change. It can help build the structures of a more united continent, supporting security and stability with the strength of our shared faith in democracy, the rights of the individual, and the peaceful resolution of disputes. We reaffirm that security and stability do not lie solely in the military dimension, and we intend to enhance the political component of our Alliance as provided for by Article 2 of our Treaty.

3. The unification of Germany means that the division of Europe is also being overcome. A united Germany in the Atlantic Alliance of free democracies and part of the growing political and economic integration of the European Community will be an indispensable factor of stability, which is needed in the heart of Europe. The move within the European Community towards political union, including the development of a European identity in the domain of security, will also contribute to Atlantic solidarity and to the establishment of a just and lasting order of peace throughout the whole of Europe.

4. We recognise that, in the new Europe, the security of every state is inseparably linked to the security of its neighbours. NATO must become an institution where Europeans, Canadians and Americans work together not only for the common defence, but to build new partnerships with all the nations of Europe. The Atlantic Community must reach out to the countries of the East which were our adversaries in the Cold War, and extend to them the hand of friendship.

5. We will remain a defensive alliance and will continue to defend all the territory of all of our members. We have no aggressive intentions and we commit ourselves to the peaceful resolution of all disputes. We will never in any circumstance be the first to use force.

6. The member states of the North Atlantic Alliance propose to the member states of the Warsaw Treaty Organization a joint declaration in which we solemnly state that we are no longer adversaries and reaffirm our intention to refrain from the threat or use of force against the territorial integrity or political independence of any state, or from acting in any other manner inconsistent with the purposes and principles of the United Nations Charter and with the CSCE Final Act. We invite all other CSCE member states to join us in this commitment to non-aggression.

7. In that spirit, and to reflect the changing political role of the Alliance, we today invite President Gorbachev on behalf of the Soviet Union, and representatives of the other Central and Eastern European countries to come to Brussels and address the North Atlantic Council. We today also invite the governments of the Union of Soviet Socialist Republics, the Czech and Slovak Federal Republic, the Hungarian Republic, the Republic of Poland, the People's Republic of Bulgaria and Romania to come to NATO, not just to visit, but to establish regular diplomatic liaison with NATO. This will make it possible for us to share with them our thinking and deliberations in this historic period of change.

8. Our Alliance will do its share to overcome the legacy of decades of suspicion. We are ready to intensify military contacts, including those of NATO Military Commanders, with Moscow and other Central and Eastern European capitals.

9. We welcome the invitation to NATO Secretary General Manfred Wörner to visit Moscow and meet with Soviet leaders.

10. Military leaders from throughout Europe gathered earlier this year in Vienna to talk about their forces and doctrine. NATO proposes another such meeting this Autumn to promote common understanding. We intend to establish an entirely different quality of openness in Europe, including an agreement on 'Open Skies.'

11. The significant presence of North American conventional and US nuclear forces in Europe demonstrates the underlying political compact that binds North America's fate to Europe's democracies. But, as Europe changes, we must profoundly alter the way we think about defence.

12. To reduce our military requirements, sound arms control agreements are essential. That is why we put the highest priority on completing this year the first treaty to reduce and limit conventional armed forces in Europe (CFE) along with the completion of a meaningful CSBM package. These talks should remain in continuous session until the work is done. Yet we hope to go further. We propose that, once a CFE Treaty is signed, follow-on talks should begin with the same membership and mandate, with the goal of building on the current agreement with additional measures, including measures to limit manpower in Europe. With this goal in mind, a commitment will be given at the time of signature of the CFE Treaty concerning the manpower levels of a unified Germany.

13. Our objective will be to conclude the negotiations on the follow-on to CFE and CSBMs as soon as possible and looking to the follow-up meeting of the CSCE to be held in Helsinki in 1992. We will seek through new conventional arms control negotiations, within the CSCE framework, further far-reaching measures in the 1990s to limit the offensive capability of conventional armed forces in Europe, so as to prevent any nation from maintaining disproportionate military power on the continent. NATO's High Level Task Force will formulate a detailed position for these follow-on conventional arms control talks. We will make provisions as needed for different regions to redress disparities and to ensure that no one's security is harmed at any stage. Furthermore, we will continue to explore broader

arms control and confidence-building opportunities. This is an ambitious agenda, but it matches our goal: enduring peace in Europe.

14. As Soviet troops leave Eastern Europe and a treaty limiting conventional armed forces is implemented, the Alliance's integrated force structure and its strategy will change fundamentally to include the following elements:

- NATO will field smaller and restructured active forces. These forces will be highly mobile and versatile so that Allied leaders will have maximum flexibility in deciding how to respond to a crisis. It will rely increasingly on multinational corps made up of national units.
- NATO will scale back the readiness of its active units, reducing training requirements and the number of exercises.
- NATO will rely more heavily on the ability to build up larger forces if and when they might be needed.

15. To keep the peace, the Alliance must maintain for the foreseeable future an appropriate mix of nuclear and conventional forces, based in Europe, and kept up to date where necessary. But, as a defensive Alliance, NATO has always stressed that none of its weapons will ever be used except in self-defence and that we seek the lowest and most stable level of nuclear forces needed to secure the prevention of war.

16. The political and military changes in Europe, and the prospects of further changes, now allow the Allies concerned to go further. They will thus modify the size and adapt the tasks of their nuclear deterrent forces. They have concluded that, as a result of the new political and military conditions in Europe, there will be a significantly reduced role for substrategic nuclear systems of the shortest range. They have decided specifically that, once negotiations begin on short range nuclear forces, the Alliance will propose, in return for reciprocal action by the Soviet Union, the elimination of all its nuclear artillery shells from Europe.

17. New negotiations between the United States and the Soviet Union on the reduction of short-range nuclear forces should begin shortly after a CFE agreement is signed. The Allies concerned will develop an arms control framework for these negotiations which takes into account our requirements for far fewer nuclear weapons, and the diminished need for substrategic nuclear systems of the shortest range.

18. Finally, with the total withdrawal of Soviet stationed forces and the implementation of a CFE agreement, the Allies concerned can reduce their

reliance on nuclear weapons. These will continue to fulfill an essential role in the overall strategy of the Alliance to prevent war by ensuring that there are no circumstances in which nuclear retaliation in response to military action might be discounted. However, in the transformed Europe, they will be able to adopt a new NATO strategy making nuclear forces truly weapons of last resort.

19. We approve the mandate given in Turnberry to the North Atlantic Council in Permanent Session to oversee the ongoing work on the adaptation of the Alliance to the new circumstances. It should report its conclusions as soon as possible.

20. In the context of these revised plans for defence and arms control, and with the advice of NATO Military Authorities and all member states concerned, NATO will prepare a new Allied military strategy moving away from 'forward defence,' where appropriate, towards a reduced forward presence and modifying 'flexible response' to reflect a reduced reliance on nuclear weapons. In that connection, NATO will elaborate new force plans consistent with the revolutionary changes in Europe. NATO will also provide a forum for Allied consultation on the upcoming negotiations on short-range nuclear forces.

21. The Conference on Security and Cooperation in Europe (CSCE) should become more prominent in Europe's future, bringing together the countries of Europe and North America. We support a CSCE Summit later this year in Paris which would include the signature of a CFE agreement and would set new standards for the establishment, and preservation, of free societies. It should endorse, inter alia:

- CSCE principles on the right to free and fair elections;
- CSCE commitments to respect and uphold the rule of law;
- CSCE guidelines for enhancing economic cooperation, based on the development of free and competitive market economies; and
- CSCE cooperation on environmental protection.

22. We further propose that the CSCE Summit in Paris decide how the CSCE can be institutionalised to provide a forum for wider political dialogue in a more united Europe. We recommend that CSCE governments establish:

- a programme for regular consultations among member governments at the Heads of State and Government or Ministerial level, at least

once each year, with other periodic meetings of officials to prepare for and follow up on these consultations;
- a schedule of CSCE review conferences once every two years to assess progress toward a Europe whole and free;
- a small CSCE secretariat to coordinate these meetings and conferences;
- a CSCE mechanism to monitor elections in all the CSCE countries, on the basis of the Copenhagen Document;
- a CSCE Centre for the Prevention of Conflict that might serve as a forum for exchanges of military information, discussion of unusual military activities, and the conciliation of disputes involving CSCE member states; and
- a CSCE parliamentary body, the Assembly of Europe, to be based on the existing parliamentary assembly of the Council of Europe, in Strasbourg, and to include representatives of all CSCE member states.

The sites of these new institutions should reflect the fact that the newly democratic countries of Central and Eastern Europe form part of the political structures of the new Europe.

23. Today, our Alliance begins a major transformation. Working with all the countries of Europe, we are determined to create enduring peace on this continent.

THE ALLIANCE'S NEW STRATEGIC CONCEPT
AGREED BY THE HEADS OF STATE AND GOVERNMENT PARTICIPATING IN THE MEETING OF THE NORTH ATLANTIC COUNCIL
LONDON, NOVEMBER 8, 1991

(Source: NATO)

At their meeting in London in July 1990, NATO's Heads of State and Government agreed on the need to transform the Atlantic Alliance to reflect the new, more promising, era in Europe. While reaffirming the basic principles on which the Alliance has rested since its inception, they recognised that the developments taking place in Europe would have a far-reaching impact on the way in which its aims would be met in future. In particular, they set in hand a fundamental strategic review. The resulting new Strategic Concept is set out below.

PART I: THE STRATEGIC CONTEXT
The New Strategic Environment

1. Since 1989, profound political changes have taken place in Central and Eastern Europe which have radically improved the security environment in which the North Atlantic Alliance seeks to achieve its objectives. The USSR's former satellites have fully recovered their sovereignty. The Soviet Union and its Republics are undergoing radical change. The three Baltic Republics have regained their independence. Soviet forces have left Hungary and Czechoslovakia and are due to complete their withdrawal from Poland and Germany by 1994. All the countries that were formerly adversaries of NATO have dismantled the Warsaw Pact and rejected

ideological hostility to the West. They have, in varying degrees, embraced and begun to implement policies aimed at achieving pluralistic democracy, the rule of law, respect for human rights and a market economy. The political division of Europe that was the source of the military confrontation of the Cold War period has thus been overcome.

2. In the West, there have also been significant changes. Germany has been united and remains a full member of the Alliance and of European institutions. The fact that the countries of the European Community are working towards the goal of political union, including the development of a European security identity, and the enhancement of the role of the WEU are important factors for European security. The strengthening of the security dimension in the process of European integration, and the enhancement of the role and responsibilities of European members of the Alliance are positive and mutually reinforcing. The development of a European security identity and defence role, reflected in the strengthening of the European pillar within the Alliance, will not only serve the interests of the European states but also reinforce the integrity and effectiveness of the Alliance as a whole.

3. Substantial progress in arms control has already enhanced stability and security by lowering arms levels and increasing military transparency and mutual confidence (including through the Stockholm CDE agreement of 1986, the INF Treaty of 1987 and the CSCE agreements and confidence and security-building measures of 1990). Implementation of the 1991 START Treaty will lead to increased stability through substantial and balanced reductions in the field of strategic nuclear arms. Further far-reaching changes and reductions in the nuclear forces of the United States and the Soviet Union will be pursued following President Bush's September 1991 initiative. Also of great importance is the Treaty on Conventional Armed Forces in Europe (CFE), signed at the 1990 Paris Summit; its implementation will remove the Alliance's numerical inferiority in key conventional weapon systems and provide for effective verification procedures. All these developments will also result in an unprecedented degree of military transparency in Europe, thus increasing predictability and mutual confidence. Such transparency would be further enhanced by the achievement of an Open Skies regime. There are welcome prospects for further advances in arms control in conventional and nuclear forces, and for the achievement of a global ban on chemical weapons, as well as restricting de-stabilising arms exports and the proliferation of certain weapons technologies.

4. The CSCE process, which began in Helsinki in 1975, has already contributed significantly to overcoming the division of Europe. As a result of the Paris Summit, it now includes new institutional arrangements and provides a contractual frame-work for consultation and cooperation that can play a constructive role, complementary to that of NATO and the process of European integration, in preserving peace.

5. The historic changes that have occurred in Europe, which have led to the fulfilment of a number of objectives set out in the Harmel Report, have significantly improved the overall security of the Allies. The monolithic, massive and potentially immediate threat which was the principal concern of the Alliance in its first forty years has disappeared. On the other hand, a great deal of uncertainty about the future and risks to the security of the Alliance remain.

6. The new Strategic Concept looks forward to a security environment in which the positive changes referred to above have come to fruition. In particular, it assumes both the completion of the planned withdrawal of Soviet military forces from Central and Eastern Europe and the full implementation by all parties of the 1990 CFE Treaty. The implementation of the Strategic Concept will thus be kept under review in the light of the evolving security environment and in particular progress in fulfilling these assumptions. Further adaptation will be made to the extent necessary.

Security Challenges and Risks

7. The security challenges and risks which NATO faces are different in nature from what they were in the past. The threat of a simultaneous, full-scale attack on all of NATO's European fronts has effectively been removed and thus no longer provides the focus for Allied strategy. Particularly in Central Europe, the risk of a surprise attack has been substantially reduced, and minimum Allied warning time has increased accordingly.

8. In contrast with the predominant threat of the past, the risks to Allied security that remain are multi-faceted in nature and multi-directional, which makes them hard to predict and assess. NATO must be capable of responding to such risks if stability in Europe and the security of Alliance members are to be preserved. These risks can arise in various ways.

9. Risks to Allied security are less likely to result from calculated aggression against the territory of the Allies, but rather from the adverse consequences of instabilities that may arise from the serious economic,

social and political difficulties, including ethnic rivalries and territorial disputes, which are faced by many countries in central and eastern Europe. The tensions which may result, as long as they remain limited, should not directly threaten the security and territorial integrity of members of the Alliance. They could, however, lead to crises inimical to European stability and even to armed conflicts, which could involve outside powers or spill over into NATO countries, having a direct effect on the security of the Alliance.

10. In the particular case of the Soviet Union, the risks and uncertainties that accompany the process of change cannot be seen in isolation from the fact that its conventional forces are significantly larger than those of any other European State and its large nuclear arsenal comparable only with that of the United States. These capabilities have to be taken into account if stability and security in Europe are to be preserved.

11. The Allies also wish to maintain peaceful and non-adversarial relations with the countries in the Southern Mediterranean and Middle East. The stability and peace of the countries on the southern periphery of Europe are important for the security of the Alliance, as the 1991 Gulf war has shown. This is all the more so because of the build-up of military power and the proliferation of weapons technologies in the area, including weapons of mass destruction and ballistic missiles capable of reaching the territory of some member states of the Alliance.

12. Any armed attack on the territory of the Allies, from whatever direction, would be covered by Articles 5 and 6 of the Washington [North Atlantic] Treaty. However, Alliance security must also take account of the global context. Alliance security interests can be affected by other risks of a wider nature, including proliferation of weapons of mass destruction, disruption of the flow of vital resources and actions of terrorism and sabotage. Arrangements exist within the Alliance for consultation among the Allies under Article 4 of the Washington Treaty and, where appropriate, coordination of their efforts including their responses to such risks.

13. From the point of view of Alliance strategy, these different risks have to be seen in different ways. Even in a non-adversarial and cooperative relationship, Soviet military capability and build-up potential, including its nuclear dimension, still constitute the most significant factor of which the Alliance has to take account in maintaining the strategic balance in Europe. The end of East–West confrontation has, however, greatly reduced the risk

of major conflict in Europe. On the other hand, there is a greater risk of different crises arising, which could develop quickly and would require a rapid response, but they are likely to be of a lesser magnitude.

14. Two conclusions can be drawn from this analysis of the strategic context. The first is that the new environment does not change the purpose or the security functions of the Alliance, but rather underlines their enduring validity. The second, on the other hand, is that the changed environment offers new opportunities for the Alliance to frame its strategy within a broad approach to security.

PART II: ALLIANCE OBJECTIVES AND SECURITY FUNCTIONS
The Purpose of the Alliance

15. NATO's essential purpose, set out in the Washington Treaty and reiterated in the London Declaration, is to safeguard the freedom and security of all its members by political and military means in accordance with the principles of the United Nations Charter. Based on common values of democracy, human rights and the rule of law, the Alliance has worked since its inception for the establishment of a just and lasting peaceful order in Europe. This Alliance objective remains unchanged.

The Nature of the Alliance

16. NATO embodies the transatlantic link by which the security of North America is permanently tied to the security of Europe. It is the practical expression of effective collective effort among its members in support of their common interests.

17. The fundamental operating principle of the Alliance is that of common commitment and mutual co-operation among sovereign states in support of the indivisibility of security for all of its members. Solidarity within the Alliance, given substance and effect by NATO's daily work in both the political and military spheres, ensures that no single Ally is forced to rely upon its own national efforts alone in dealing with basic security challenges. Without depriving member states of their right and duty to assume their sovereign responsibilities in the field of defence, the Alliance enables them through collective effort to enhance their ability to realise their essential national security objectives.

18. The resulting sense of equal security amongst the members of the Alliance, regardless of differences in their circumstances or in their national military capabilities relative to each other, contributes to overall

stability within Europe and thus to the creation of conditions conducive to increased co-operation both among Alliance members and with others. It is on this basis that members of the Alliance, together with other nations, are able to pursue the development of co-operative structures of security for a Europe whole and free.

The Fundamental Tasks of the Alliance

19. The means by which the Alliance pursues its security policy to preserve the peace will continue to include the maintenance of a military capability sufficient to prevent war and to provide for effective defence; an overall capability to manage successfully crises affecting the security of its members; and the pursuit of political efforts favouring dialogue with other nations and the active search for a co-operative approach to European security, including in the field of arms control and disarmament.

20. To achieve its essential purpose, the Alliance performs the following fundamental security tasks:

> I. To provide one of the indispensable foundations for a stable security environment in Europe, based on the growth of democratic institutions and commitment to the peaceful resolution of disputes, in which no country would be able to intimidate or coerce any European nation or to impose hegemony through the threat or use of force.
>
> II. To serve, as provided for in Article 4 of the North Atlantic Treaty, as a transatlantic forum for Allied consultations on any issues that affect their vital interests, including possible developments posing risks for members' security, and for appropriate co-ordination of their efforts in fields of common concern.
>
> III. To deter and defend against any threat of aggression against the territory of any NATO member state.
>
> IV. To preserve the strategic balance within Europe.

21. Other European institutions such as the EC, WEU and CSCE also have roles to play, in accordance with their respective responsibilities and purposes, in these fields. The creation of a European identity in security and defence will underline the preparedness of the Europeans to take a greater share of responsibility for their security and will help to reinforce transatlantic solidarity. However the extent of its membership and of its capabilities gives NATO a particular position in that it can perform all four core security functions. NATO is the essential forum for consultation

among the Allies and the forum for agreement on policies bearing on the security and defence commitments of its members under the Washington Treaty.

22. In defining the core functions of the Alliance in the terms set out above, member states confirm that the scope of the Alliance as well as their rights and obligations as provided for in the Washington Treaty remain unchanged.

PART III: A BROAD APPROACH TO SECURITY
Protecting Peace in a New Europe

23. The Alliance has always sought to achieve its objectives of safeguarding the security and territorial integrity of its members, and establishing a just and lasting peaceful order in Europe, through both political and military means. This comprehensive approach remains the basis of the Alliance's security policy.

24. But what is new is that, with the radical changes in the security situation, the opportunities for achieving Alliance objectives through political means are greater than ever before. It is now possible to draw all the consequences from the fact that security and stability have political, economic, social, and environmental elements as well as the indispensable defence dimension. Managing the diversity of challenges facing the Alliance requires a broad approach to security. This is reflected in three mutually reinforcing elements of Allied security policy; dialogue, co-operation, and the maintenance of a collective defence capability.

25. The Alliance's active pursuit of dialogue and co-operation, underpinned by its commitment to an effective collective defence capability, seeks to reduce the risks of conflict arising out of misunderstanding or design; to build increased mutual understanding and confidence among all European states; to help manage crises affecting the security of the Allies; and to expand the opportunities for a genuine partnership among all European countries in dealing with common security problems.

26. In this regard, the Alliance's arms control and disarmament policy contributes both to dialogue and to co-operation with other nations, and thus will continue to play a major role in the achievement of the Alliance's security objectives. The Allies seek, through arms control and disarmament, to enhance security and stability at the lowest possible level of forces consistent with the requirements of defence. Thus, the Alliance will

continue to ensure that defence and arms control and disarmament objectives remain in harmony.

27. In fulfilling its fundamental objectives and core security functions, the Alliance will continue to respect the legitimate security interests of others, and seek the peaceful resolution of disputes as set forth in the Charter of the United Nations. The Alliance will promote peaceful and friendly international relations and support democratic institutions. In this respect, it recognizes the valuable contribution being made by other organizations such as the European Community and the CSCE, and that the roles of these institutions and of the Alliance are complementary.

Dialogue

28. The new situation in Europe has multiplied the opportunities for dialogue on the part of the Alliance with the Soviet Union and the other countries of Central and Eastern Europe. The Alliance has established regular diplomatic liaison and military contacts with the countries of Central and Eastern Europe as provided for in the London Declaration. The Alliance will further promote dialogue through regular diplomatic liaison, including an intensified exchange of views and information on security policy issues. Through such means the Allies, individually and collectively, will seek to make full use of the unprecedented opportunities afforded by the growth of freedom and democracy throughout Europe and encourage greater mutual understanding of respective security concerns, to increase transparency and predictability in security affairs, and thus to reinforce stability. The military can help to overcome the divisions of the past, not least through intensified military contacts and greater military transparency. The Alliance's pursuit of dialogue will provide a foundation for greater co-operation throughout Europe and the ability to resolve differences and conflicts by peaceful means.

Co-operation

29. The Allies are also committed to pursue co-operation with all states in Europe on the basis of the principles set out in the Charter of Paris for a New Europe. They will seek to develop broader and productive patterns of bilateral and multilateral co-operation in all relevant fields of European security, with the aim, inter alia, of preventing crises or, should they arise, ensuring their effective management. Such partnership between the

members of the Alliance and other nations in dealing with specific problems will be an essential factor in moving beyond past divisions towards one Europe whole and free. This policy of co-operation is the expression of the inseparability of security among European states. It is built upon a common recognition among Alliance members that the persistence of new political, economic or social divisions across the continent could lead to future instability, and such divisions must thus be diminished.

Collective Defence

30. The political approach to security will thus become increasingly important. Nonetheless, the military dimension remains essential. The maintenance of an adequate military capability and clear preparedness to act collectively in the common defence remain central to the Alliance's security objectives. Such a capability, together with political solidarity, is required in order to prevent any attempt at coercion or intimidation, and to guarantee that military aggression directed against the Alliance can never be perceived as an option with any prospect of success. It is equally indispensable so that dialogue and co-operation can be undertaken with confidence and achieve their desired results.

Management of Crisis and Conflict Prevention

31. In the new political and strategic environment in Europe, the success of the Alliance's policy of preserving peace and preventing war depends even more than in the past on the effectiveness of preventive diplomacy and successful management of crises affecting the security of its members. Any major aggression in Europe is much more unlikely and would be preceded by significant warning time. Though on a much smaller scale, the range and variety of other potential risks facing the Alliance are less predictable than before.

32. In these new circumstances there are increased opportunities for the successful resolution of crises at an early stage. The success of Alliance policy will require a coherent approach determined by the Alliance's political authorities choosing and co-ordinating appropriate crisis management measures as required from a range of political and other measures, including those in the military field. Close control by the political authorities of the Alliance will be applied from the outset and at all stages.

Appropriate consultation and decision making procedures are essential to this end.

33. The potential of dialogue and co-operation within all of Europe must be fully developed in order to help to defuse crises and to prevent conflicts since the Allies' security is inseparably linked to that of all other states in Europe. To this end, the Allies will support the role of the CSCE process and its institutions. Other bodies including the European Community, Western European Union and United Nations may also have an important role to play.

PART IV: GUIDELINES FOR DEFENCE
Principles of Alliance Strategy

34. The diversity of challenges now facing the Alliance thus requires a broad approach to security. The transformed political and strategic environment enables the Alliance to change a number of important features of its military strategy and to set out new guidelines, while reaffirming proven fundamental principles. At the London Summit, it was therefore agreed to prepare a new military strategy and a revised force posture responding to the changed circumstances.

35. Alliance strategy will continue to reflect a number of fundamental principles. The Alliance is purely defensive in purpose: none of its weapons will ever be used except in self-defence, and it does not consider itself to be anyone's adversary. The Allies will maintain military strength adequate to convince any potential aggressor that the use of force against the territory of one of the Allies would meet collective and effective action by all of them and that the risks involved in initiating conflict would outweigh any foreseeable gains. The forces of the Allies must therefore be able to defend Alliance frontiers, to stop an aggressor's advance as far forward as possible, to maintain or restore the territorial integrity of Allied nations and to terminate war rapidly by making an aggressor reconsider his decision, cease his attack and withdraw. The role of the Alliance's military forces is to assure the territorial integrity and political independence of its member states, and thus contribute to peace and stability in Europe.

36. The security of all Allies is indivisible: an attack on one is an attack on all. Alliance solidarity and strategic unity are accordingly crucial prerequisites for collective security. The achievement of the Alliance's objectives depends critically on the equitable sharing of roles, risks and

responsibilities, as well as the benefits, of common defence. The presence of North American conventional and US nuclear forces in Europe remains vital to the security of Europe, which is inseparably linked to that of North America. As the process of developing a European security identity and defence role progresses, and is reflected in the strengthening of the European pillar within the Alliance, the European members of the Alliance will assume a greater degree of the responsibility for the defence of Europe.

37. The collective nature of Alliance defence is embodied in practical arrangements that enable the Allies to enjoy the crucial political, military and resource advantages of collective defence, and prevent the renationalisation of defence policies, without depriving the Allies of their sovereignty. These arrangements are based on an integrated military structure as well as on co-operation and co-ordination agreements. Key features include collective force planning; common operational planning; multinational formations; the stationing of forces outside home territory, where appropriate on a mutual basis; crisis management and reinforcement arrangements; procedures for consultation; common standards and procedures for equipment, training and logistics; joint and combined exercises; and infrastructure, armaments and logistics co-operation.

38. To protect peace and to prevent war or any kind of coercion, the Alliance will maintain for the foreseeable future an appropriate mix of nuclear and conventional forces based in Europe and kept up to date where necessary, although at a significantly reduced level. Both elements are essential to Alliance security and cannot substitute one for the other. Conventional forces contribute to war prevention by ensuring that no potential aggressor could contemplate a quick or easy victory, or territorial gains, by conventional means. Taking into account the diversity of risks with which the Alliance could be faced, it must maintain the forces necessary to provide a wide range of conventional response options. But the Alliance's conventional forces alone cannot ensure the prevention of war. Nuclear weapons make a unique contribution in rendering the risks of any aggression incalculable and unacceptable. Thus, they remain essential to preserve peace.

The Alliance's New Force Posture

39. At the London Summit, the Allies concerned agreed to move away, where appropriate, from the concept of forward defence towards a reduced

forward presence, and to modify the principle of flexible response to reflect a reduced reliance on nuclear weapons. The changes stemming from the new strategic environment and the altered risks now facing the Alliance enable significant modifications to be made in the missions of the Allies' military forces and in their posture.

The Missions of Alliance Military Forces

40. The primary role of Alliance military forces, to guarantee the security and territorial integrity of member states, remains unchanged. But this role must take account of the new strategic environment, in which a single massive and global threat has given way to diverse and multi-directional risks. Alliance forces have different functions to perform in peace, crisis and war.

41. In peace, the role of Allied military forces is to guard against risks to the security of Alliance members; to contribute towards the maintenance of stability and balance in Europe; and to ensure that peace is preserved. They can contribute to dialogue and co-operation throughout Europe by their participation in confidence-building activities, including those which enhance transparency and improve communication; as well as in verification of arms control agreements. Allies could, further, be called upon to contribute to global stability and peace by providing forces for United Nations missions.

42. In the event of crises which might lead to a military threat to the security of Alliance members, the Alliance's military forces can complement and reinforce political actions within a broad approach to security, and thereby contribute to the management of such crises and their peaceful resolution. This requires that these forces have a capability for measured and timely responses in such circumstances; the capability to deter action against any Ally and, in the event that aggression takes place, to respond to and repel it as well as to reestablish the territorial integrity of member states.

43. While in the new security environment a general war in Europe has become highly unlikely, it cannot finally be ruled out. The Alliance's military forces, which have as their fundamental mission to protect peace, have to provide the essential insurance against potential risks at the minimum level necessary to prevent war of any kind, and, should aggression occur, to restore peace. Hence the need for the capabilities and the appropriate mix of forces already described.

Guidelines for the Alliance's Force Posture

44. To implement its security objectives and strategic principles in the new environment, the organization of the Allies' forces must be adapted to provide capabilities that can contribute to protecting peace, managing crises that affect the security of Alliance members, and preventing war, while retaining at all times the means to defend, if necessary, all Allied territory and to restore peace. The posture of Allies' forces will conform to the guidelines developed in the following paragraphs.

45. The size, readiness, availability and deployment of the Alliance's military forces will continue to reflect its strictly defensive nature and will be adapted accordingly to the new strategic environment including arms control agreements. This means in particular:

> a. that the overall size of the Allies' forces, and in many cases their readiness, will be reduced;
>
> b. that the maintenance of a comprehensive in-place linear defensive posture in the central region will no longer be required. The peacetime geographical distribution of forces will ensure a sufficient military presence throughout the territory of the Alliance, including where necessary forward deployment of appropriate forces. Regional considerations and, in particular, geostrategic differences within the Alliance will have to be taken into account, including the shorter warning times to which the northern and southern regions will be subject compared with the central region and, in the southern region, the potential for instability and the military capabilities in the adjacent areas.

46. To ensure that at this reduced level the Allies' forces can play an effective role both in managing crises and in countering aggression against any Ally, they will require enhanced flexibility and mobility and an assured capability for augmentation when necessary. For these reasons:

> a. Available forces will include, in a limited but militarily significant proportion, ground, air and sea immediate and rapid reaction elements able to respond to a wide range of eventualities, many of which are unforeseeable. They will be of sufficient quality, quantity and readiness to deter a limited attack and, if required, to defend the territory of the Allies against attacks, particularly those launched without long warning time.

b. The forces of the Allies will be structured so as to permit their military capability to be built up when necessary. This ability to build up by reinforcement, by mobilising reserves, or by reconstituting forces, must be in proportion to potential threats to Alliance security, including the possibility albeit unlikely, but one that prudence dictates should not be ruled out of a major conflict. Consequently, capabilities for timely reinforcement and resupply both within Europe and from North America will be of critical importance.

c. Appropriate force structures and procedures, including those that would provide an ability to build up, deploy and draw down forces quickly and discriminately, will be developed to permit measured, flexible and timely responses in order to reduce and defuse tensions. These arrangements must be exercised regularly in peacetime.

d. In the event of use of forces, including the deployment of reaction and other available reinforcing forces as an instrument of crisis management, the Alliance's political authorities will, as before, exercise close control over their employment at all stages. Existing procedures will be reviewed in the light of the new missions and posture of Alliance forces.

Characteristics of Conventional Forces

47. It is essential that the Allies' military forces have a credible ability to fulfil their functions in peace, crisis and war in a way appropriate to the new security environment. This will be reflected in force and equipment levels; readiness and availability; training and exercises; deployment and employment options; and force build-up capabilities, all of which will be adjusted accordingly. The conventional forces of the Allies will include, in addition to immediate and rapid reaction forces, main defence forces, which will provide the bulk of forces needed to ensure the Alliance's territorial integrity and the unimpeded use of their lines of communication; and augmentation forces, which will provide a means of reinforcing existing forces in a particular region. Main defence and augmentation forces will comprise both active and mobilisable elements.

48. Ground, maritime and air forces will have to co-operate closely and combine and assist each other in operations aimed at achieving agreed objectives. These forces will consist of the following:

a. **Ground forces**, which are essential to hold or regain territory. The majority will normally be at lower states of readiness and, overall, there will be a greater reliance on mobilization and reserves. All categories of ground forces will require demonstrable combat effectiveness together with an appropriately enhanced capability for flexible deployment.

b. **Maritime forces**, which because of their inherent mobility, flexibility and endurance, make an important contribution to the Alliance's crisis response options. Their essential missions are to ensure sea control in order to safeguard the Allies' sea lines of communication, to support land and amphibious operations, and to protect the deployment of the Alliance's sea-based nuclear deterrent.

c. **Air forces**, whose ability to fulfil their fundamental roles in both independent air and combined operations counter-air, air interdiction and offensive air support as well as to contribute to surveillance, reconnaissance and electronic warfare operations, is essential to the overall effectiveness of the Allies' military forces. Their role in supporting operations, on land and at sea, will require appropriate long-distance airlift and air refuelling capabilities. Air defence forces, including modern air command and control systems, are required to ensure a secure air defence environment.

49. In light of the potential risks it poses, the proliferation of ballistic missiles and weapons of mass destruction should be given special consideration. Solution of this problem will require complementary approaches including, for example, export control and missile defences.

50. Alliance strategy is not dependent on a chemical warfare capability. The Allies remain committed to the earliest possible achievement of a global, comprehensive, and effectively verifiable ban on all chemical weapons. But, even after implementation of a global ban, precautions of a purely defensive nature will need to be maintained.

51. In the new security environment and given the reduced overall force levels in future, the ability to work closely together, which will facilitate the cost effective use of Alliance resources, will be particularly important for the achievement of the missions of the Allies' forces. The Alliance's collective defence arrangements in which, for those concerned, the integrated military structure, including multinational forces, plays the key role, will be essential in this regard. Integrated and multinational European structures, as they are further developed in the context of an emerging

European Defence Identity, will also increasingly have a similarly important role to play in enhancing the Allies' ability to work together in the common defence. Allies' efforts to achieve maximum co-operation will be based on the common guidelines for defence defined above. Practical arrangements will be developed to ensure the necessary mutual transparency and complementarity between the European security and defence identity and the Alliance.

52. In order to be able to respond flexibly to a wide range of possible contingencies, the Allies concerned will require effective surveillance and intelligence, flexible command and control, mobility within and between regions, and appropriate logistics capabilities, including transport capacities. Logistic stocks must be sufficient to sustain all types of forces in order to permit effective defence until resupply is available. The capability of the Allies concerned to build-up larger, adequately equipped and trained forces, in a timely manner and to a level appropriate to any risk to Alliance security, will also make an essential contribution to crisis management and defence. This capability will include the ability to reinforce any area at risk within the territory of the Allies and to establish a multinational presence when and where this is needed. Elements of all three force categories will be capable of being employed flexibly as part of both intra-European and transatlantic reinforcement. Proper use of these capabilities will require control of the necessary lines of communication as well as appropriate support and exercise arrangements. Civil resources will be of increasing relevance in this context.

53. For the Allies concerned, collective defence arrangements will rely increasingly on multinational forces, complementing national commitments to NATO. Multinational forces demonstrate the Alliance's resolve to maintain a credible collective defence; enhance Alliance cohesion; reinforce the transatlantic partnership and strengthen the European pillar. Multinational forces, and in particular reaction forces, reinforce solidarity. They can also provide a way of deploying more capable formations than might be available purely nationally, thus helping to make more efficient use of scarce defence resources. This may include a highly integrated, multinational approach to specific tasks and functions.

Characteristics of Nuclear Forces

54. The fundamental purpose of the nuclear forces of the Allies is political: to preserve peace and prevent coercion and any kind of war. They

will continue to fulfil an essential role by ensuring uncertainty in the mind of any aggressor about the nature of the Allies' response to military aggression. They demonstrate that aggression of any kind is not a rational option. The supreme guarantee of the security of the Allies is provided by the strategic nuclear forces of the Alliance, particularly those of the United States; the independent nuclear forces of the United Kingdom and France, which have a deterrent role of their own, contribute to the overall deterrence and security of the Allies.

55. A credible Alliance nuclear posture and the demonstration of Alliance solidarity and common commitment to war prevention continue to require widespread participation by European Allies involved in collective defence planning in nuclear roles, in peacetime basing of nuclear forces on their territory and in command, control and consultation arrangements. Nuclear forces based in Europe and committed to NATO provide an essential political and military link between the European and the North American members of the Alliance. The Alliance will therefore maintain adequate nuclear forces in Europe. These forces need to have the necessary characteristics and appropriate flexibility and survivability, to be perceived as a credible and effective element of the Allies' strategy in preventing war. They will be maintained at the minimum level sufficient to preserve peace and stability.

56. The Allies concerned consider that, with the radical changes in the security situation, including conventional force levels in Europe maintained in relative balance and increased reaction times, NATO's ability to defuse a crisis through diplomatic and other means or, should it be necessary, to mount a successful conventional defence will significantly improve. The circumstances in which any use of nuclear weapons might have to be contemplated by them are therefore even more remote. They can therefore significantly reduce their sub-strategic nuclear forces. They will maintain adequate sub-strategic forces based in Europe which will provide an essential link with strategic nuclear forces, reinforcing the trans-Atlantic link. These will consist solely of dual capable aircraft which could, if necessary, be supplemented by offshore systems. Sub-strategic nuclear weapons will, however, not be deployed in normal circumstances on surface vessels and attack submarines. There is no requirement for nuclear artillery or ground-launched short-range nuclear missiles and they will be eliminated.

PART V: CONCLUSION

57. This Strategic Concept reaffirms the defensive nature of the Alliance and the resolve of its members to safeguard their security, sovereignty and territorial integrity. The Alliance's security policy is based on dialogue; co-operation; and effective collective defence as mutually reinforcing instruments for preserving the peace. Making full use of the new opportunities available, the Alliance will maintain security at the lowest possible level of forces consistent with the requirements of defence. In this way, the Alliance is making an essential contribution to promoting a lasting peaceful order.

58. The Allies will continue to pursue vigorously further progress in arms control and confidence-building measures with the objective of enhancing security and stability. They will also play an active part in promoting dialogue and co-operation between states on the basis of the principles enunciated in the Paris Charter.

59. NATO's strategy will retain the flexibility to reflect further developments in the politico-military environment, including progress in the moves towards a European security identity, and in any changes in the risks to Alliance security. For the Allies concerned, the Strategic Concept will form the basis for the further development of the Alliance's defence policy, its operational concepts, its conventional and nuclear force posture and its collective defence planning arrangements.

THE ALLIANCE'S STRATEGIC CONCEPT
APPROVED BY THE HEADS OF STATE AND GOVERNMENT PARTICIPATING IN THE MEETING OF THE NORTH ATLANTIC COUNCIL IN WASHINGTON D.C.
WASHINGTON, DC, APRIL 24, 1999

(Source: NATO)

INTRODUCTION

1. At their Summit meeting in Washington in April 1999, NATO Heads of State and Government approved the Alliance's new Strategic Concept.

2. NATO has successfully ensured the freedom of its members and prevented war in Europe during the 40 years of the Cold War. By combining defence with dialogue, it played an indispensable role in bringing East–West confrontation to a peaceful end. The dramatic changes in the Euro-Atlantic strategic landscape brought by the end of the Cold War were reflected in the Alliance's 1991 Strategic Concept. There have, however, been further profound political and security developments since then.

3. The dangers of the Cold War have given way to more promising, but also challenging prospects, to new opportunities and risks. A new Europe of greater integration is emerging, and a Euro-Atlantic security structure is evolving in which NATO plays a central part. The Alliance has been at the heart of efforts to establish new patterns of cooperation and mutual understanding across the Euro-Atlantic region and has committed itself to essential new activities in the interest of a wider stability. It has shown the depth of that commitment in its efforts to put an end to the immense human suffering created by conflict in the Balkans. The years since the end of the Cold War have also witnessed important developments in arms

control, a process to which the Alliance is fully committed. The Alliance's role in these positive developments has been underpinned by the comprehensive adaptation of its approach to security and of its procedures and structures. The last ten years have also seen, however, the appearance of complex new risks to Euro-Atlantic peace and stability, including oppression, ethnic conflict, economic distress, the collapse of political order, and the proliferation of weapons of mass destruction.

4. The Alliance has an indispensable role to play in consolidating and preserving the positive changes of the recent past, and in meeting current and future security challenges. It has, therefore, a demanding agenda. It must safeguard common security interests in an environment of further, often unpredictable change. It must maintain collective defence and reinforce the transatlantic link and ensure a balance that allows the European Allies to assume greater responsibility. It must deepen its relations with its partners and prepare for the accession of new members. It must, above all, maintain the political will and the military means required by the entire range of its missions.

5. This new Strategic Concept will guide the Alliance as it pursues this agenda. It expresses NATO's enduring purpose and nature and its fundamental security tasks, identifies the central features of the new security environment, specifies the elements of the Alliance's broad approach to security, and provides guidelines for the further adaptation of its military forces.

PART I: THE PURPOSE AND TASKS OF THE ALLIANCE

6. NATO's essential and enduring purpose, set out in the Washington Treaty, is to safeguard the freedom and security of all its members by political and military means. Based on common values of democracy, human rights and the rule of law, the Alliance has striven since its inception to secure a just and lasting peaceful order in Europe. It will continue to do so. The achievement of this aim can be put at risk by crisis and conflict affecting the security of the Euro-Atlantic area. The Alliance therefore not only ensures the defence of its members but contributes to peace and stability in this region.

7. The Alliance embodies the transatlantic link by which the security of North America is permanently tied to the security of Europe. It is the practical expression of effective collective effort among its members in support of their common interests.

8. The fundamental guiding principle by which the Alliance works is that of common commitment and mutual co-operation among sovereign states in support of the indivisibility of security for all of its members. Solidarity and cohesion within the Alliance, through daily cooperation in both the political and military spheres, ensure that no single Ally is forced to rely upon its own national efforts alone in dealing with basic security challenges. Without depriving member states of their right and duty to assume their sovereign responsibilities in the field of defence, the Alliance enables them through collective effort to realise their essential national security objectives.

9. The resulting sense of equal security among the members of the Alliance, regardless of differences in their circumstances or in their national military capabilities, contributes to stability in the Euro-Atlantic area. The Alliance does not seek these benefits for its members alone, but is committed to the creation of conditions conducive to increased partnership, cooperation, and dialogue with others who share its broad political objectives.

10. To achieve its essential purpose, as an Alliance of nations committed to the Washington Treaty and the United Nations Charter, the Alliance performs the following fundamental security tasks:

> **Security**: To provide one of the indispensable foundations for a stable Euro-Atlantic security environment, based on the growth of democratic institutions and commitment to the peaceful resolution of disputes, in which no country would be able to intimidate or coerce any other through the threat or use of force.
>
> **Consultation**: To serve, as provided for in Article 4 of the Washington Treaty, as an essential transatlantic forum for Allied consultations on any issues that affect their vital interests, including possible developments posing risks for members' security, and for appropriate co-ordination of their efforts in fields of common concern.
>
> **Deterrence and Defence**: To deter and defend against any threat of aggression against any NATO member state as provided for in Articles 5 and 6 of the Washington Treaty.

And in order to enhance the security and stability of the Euro-Atlantic area:

> • **Crisis Management**: To stand ready, case-by-case and by consensus, in conformity with Article 7 of the Washington Treaty, to contrib-

ute to effective conflict prevention and to engage actively in crisis management, including crisis response operations.
- **Partnership**: To promote wide-ranging partnership, cooperation, and dialogue with other countries in the Euro-Atlantic area, with the aim of increasing transparency, mutual confidence and the capacity for joint action with the Alliance.

11. In fulfilling its purpose and fundamental security tasks, the Alliance will continue to respect the legitimate security interests of others, and seek the peaceful resolution of disputes as set out in the Charter of the United Nations. The Alliance will promote peaceful and friendly international relations and support democratic institutions. The Alliance does not consider itself to be any country's adversary.

PART II: STRATEGIC PERSPECTIVES
The Evolving Strategic Environment

12. The Alliance operates in an environment of continuing change. Developments in recent years have been generally positive, but uncertainties and risks remain which can develop into acute crises. Within this evolving context, NATO has played an essential part in strengthening Euro-Atlantic security since the end of the Cold War. Its growing political role; its increased political and military partnership, cooperation and dialogue with other states, including with Russia, Ukraine and Mediterranean Dialogue countries; its continuing openness to the accession of new members; its collaboration with other international organisations; its commitment, exemplified in the Balkans, to conflict prevention and crisis management, including through peace support operations: all reflect its determination to shape its security environment and enhance the peace and stability of the Euro-Atlantic area.

13. In parallel, NATO has successfully adapted to enhance its ability to contribute to Euro-Atlantic peace and stability. Internal reform has included a new command structure, including the Combined Joint Task Force (CJTF) concept, the creation of arrangements to permit the rapid deployment of forces for the full range of the Alliance's missions, and the building of the European Security and Defence Identity (ESDI) within the Alliance.

14. The United Nations (UN), the Organisation for Security and Cooperation in Europe (OSCE), the European Union (EU), and the Western

European Union (WEU) have made distinctive contributions to Euro-Atlantic security and stability. Mutually reinforcing organisations have become a central feature of the security environment.

15. The United Nations Security Council has the primary responsibility for the maintenance of international peace and security and, as such, plays a crucial role in contributing to security and stability in the Euro-Atlantic area.

16. The OSCE, as a regional arrangement, is the most inclusive security organisation in Europe, which also includes Canada and the United States, and plays an essential role in promoting peace and stability, enhancing cooperative security, and advancing democracy and human rights in Europe. The OSCE is particularly active in the fields of preventive diplomacy, conflict prevention, crisis management, and post-conflict rehabilitation. NATO and the OSCE have developed close practical cooperation, especially with regard to the international effort to bring peace to the former Yugoslavia.

17. The European Union has taken important decisions and given a further impetus to its efforts to strengthen its security and defence dimension. This process will have implications for the entire Alliance, and all European Allies should be involved in it, building on arrangements developed by NATO and the WEU. The development of a common foreign and security policy (CFSP) includes the progressive framing of a common defence policy. Such a policy, as called for in the Amsterdam Treaty, would be compatible with the common security and defence policy established within the framework of the Washington Treaty. Important steps taken in this context include the incorporation of the WEU's Petersberg tasks into the Treaty on European Union and the development of closer institutional relations with the WEU.

18. As stated in the 1994 Summit declaration and reaffirmed in Berlin in 1996, the Alliance fully supports the development of the European Security and Defence Identity within the Alliance by making available its assets and capabilities for WEU-led operations. To this end, the Alliance and the WEU have developed a close relationship and put into place key elements of the ESDI as agreed in Berlin. In order to enhance peace and stability in Europe and more widely, the European Allies are strengthening their capacity for action, including by increasing their military capabilities. The increase of the responsibilities and capacities of the European Allies with respect to security and defence enhances the security environment of the Alliance.

19. The stability, transparency, predictability, lower levels of armaments, and verification which can be provided by arms control and non-proliferation agreements support NATO's political and military efforts to achieve its strategic objectives. The Allies have played a major part in the significant achievements in this field. These include the enhanced stability produced by the CFE Treaty, the deep reductions in nuclear weapons provided for in the START treaties; the signature of the Comprehensive Test Ban Treaty, the indefinite and unconditional extension of the Nuclear Non-Proliferation Treaty, the accession to it of Belarus, Kazakhstan, and Ukraine as non-nuclear weapons states, and the entry into force of the Chemical Weapons Convention. The Ottawa Convention to ban anti-personnel landmines and similar agreements make an important contribution to alleviating human suffering. There are welcome prospects for further advances in arms control in conventional weapons and with respect to nuclear, chemical, and biological (NBC) weapons.

Security Challenges and Risks

20. Notwithstanding positive developments in the strategic environment and the fact that large-scale conventional aggression against the Alliance is highly unlikely, the possibility of such a threat emerging over the longer term exists. The security of the Alliance remains subject to a wide variety of military and non-military risks which are multi-directional and often difficult to predict. These risks include uncertainty and instability in and around the Euro-Atlantic area and the possibility of regional crises at the periphery of the Alliance, which could evolve rapidly. Some countries in and around the Euro-Atlantic area face serious economic, social and political difficulties. Ethnic and religious rivalries, territorial disputes, inadequate or failed efforts at reform, the abuse of human rights, and the dissolution of states can lead to local and even regional instability. The resulting tensions could lead to crises affecting Euro-Atlantic stability, to human suffering, and to armed conflicts. Such conflicts could affect the security of the Alliance by spilling over into neighbouring countries, including NATO countries, or in other ways, and could also affect the security of other states.

21. The existence of powerful nuclear forces outside the Alliance also constitutes a significant factor which the Alliance has to take into account if security and stability in the Euro-Atlantic area are to be maintained.

22. The proliferation of NBC weapons and their means of delivery remains a matter of serious concern. In spite of welcome progress in

strengthening international non-proliferation regimes, major challenges with respect to proliferation remain. The Alliance recognises that proliferation can occur despite efforts to prevent it and can pose a direct military threat to the Allies' populations, territory, and forces. Some states, including on NATO's periphery and in other regions, sell or acquire or try to acquire NBC weapons and delivery means. Commodities and technology that could be used to build these weapons of mass destruction and their delivery means are becoming more common, while detection and prevention of illicit trade in these materials and know-how continues to be difficult. Non-state actors have shown the potential to create and use some of these weapons.

23. The global spread of technology that can be of use in the production of weapons may result in the greater availability of sophisticated military capabilities, permitting adversaries to acquire highly capable offensive and defensive air, land, and sea-borne systems, cruise missiles, and other advanced weaponry. In addition, state and non-state adversaries may try to exploit the Alliance's growing reliance on information systems through information operations designed to disrupt such systems. They may attempt to use strategies of this kind to counter NATO's superiority in traditional weaponry.

24. Any armed attack on the territory of the Allies, from whatever direction, would be covered by Articles 5 and 6 of the Washington Treaty. However, Alliance security must also take account of the global context. Alliance security interests can be affected by other risks of a wider nature, including acts of terrorism, sabotage and organised crime, and by the disruption of the flow of vital resources. The uncontrolled movement of large numbers of people, particularly as a consequence of armed conflicts, can also pose problems for security and stability affecting the Alliance. Arrangements exist within the Alliance for consultation among the Allies under Article 4 of the Washington Treaty and, where appropriate, co-ordination of their efforts including their responses to risks of this kind.

PART III: THE APPROACH TO SECURITY IN THE 21ST CENTURY

25. The Alliance is committed to a broad approach to security, which recognises the importance of political, economic, social and environmental factors in addition to the indispensable defence dimension. This broad approach forms the basis for the Alliance to accomplish its fundamental security tasks effectively, and its increasing effort to develop effective

cooperation with other European and Euro-Atlantic organisations as well as the United Nations. Our collective aim is to build a European security architecture in which the Alliance's contribution to the security and stability of the Euro-Atlantic area and the contribution of these other international organisations are complementary and mutually reinforcing, both in deepening relations among Euro-Atlantic countries and in managing crises. NATO remains the essential forum for consultation among the Allies and the forum for agreement on policies bearing on the security and defence commitments of its members under the Washington Treaty.

26. The Alliance seeks to preserve peace and to reinforce Euro-Atlantic security and stability by: the preservation of the transatlantic link; the maintenance of effective military capabilities sufficient for deterrence and defence and to fulfil the full range of its missions; the development of the European Security and Defence Identity within the Alliance; an overall capability to manage crises successfully; its continued openness to new members; and the continued pursuit of partnership, cooperation, and dialogue with other nations as part of its co-operative approach to Euro-Atlantic security, including in the field of arms control and disarmament.

The Transatlantic Link

27. NATO is committed to a strong and dynamic partnership between Europe and North America in support of the values and interests they share. The security of Europe and that of North America are indivisible. Thus the Alliance's commitment to the indispensable transatlantic link and the collective defence of its members is fundamental to its credibility and to the security and stability of the Euro-Atlantic area.

The Maintenance of Alliance Military Capabilities

28. The maintenance of an adequate military capability and clear preparedness to act collectively in the common defence remain central to the Alliance's security objectives. Such a capability, together with political solidarity, remains at the core of the Alliance's ability to prevent any attempt at coercion or intimidation, and to guarantee that military aggression directed against the Alliance can never be perceived as an option with any prospect of success.

29. Military capabilities effective under the full range of foreseeable circumstances are also the basis of the Alliance's ability to contribute to conflict prevention and crisis management through non–Article 5 crisis

response operations. These missions can be highly demanding and can place a premium on the same political and military qualities, such as cohesion, multinational training, and extensive prior planning, that would be essential in an Article 5 situation. Accordingly, while they may pose special requirements, they will be handled through a common set of Alliance structures and procedures.

The European Security and Defence Identity

30. The Alliance, which is the foundation of the collective defence of its members and through which common security objectives will be pursued wherever possible, remains committed to a balanced and dynamic transatlantic partnership. The European Allies have taken decisions to enable them to assume greater responsibilities in the security and defence field in order to enhance the peace and stability of the Euro-Atlantic area and thus the security of all Allies. On the basis of decisions taken by the Alliance, in Berlin in 1996 and subsequently, the European Security and Defence Identity will continue to be developed within NATO. This process will require close cooperation between NATO, the WEU and, if and when appropriate, the European Union. It will enable all European Allies to make a more coherent and effective contribution to the missions and activities of the Alliance as an expression of our shared responsibilities; it will reinforce the transatlantic partnership; and it will assist the European Allies to act by themselves as required through the readiness of the Alliance, on a case-by-case basis and by consensus, to make its assets and capabilities available for operations in which the Alliance is not engaged militarily under the political control and strategic direction either of the WEU or as otherwise agreed, taking into account the full participation of all European Allies if they were so to choose.

Conflict Prevention and Crisis Management

31. In pursuit of its policy of preserving peace, preventing war, and enhancing security and stability and as set out in the fundamental security tasks, NATO will seek, in cooperation with other organisations, to prevent conflict, or, should a crisis arise, to contribute to its effective management, consistent with international law, including through the possibility of conducting non–Article 5 crisis response operations. The Alliance's preparedness to carry out such operations supports the broader objective of reinforcing and extending stability and often involves the participation of

NATO's Partners. NATO recalls its offer, made in Brussels in 1994, to support on a case-by-case basis in accordance with its own procedures, peacekeeping and other operations under the authority of the UN Security Council or the responsibility of the OSCE, including by making available Alliance resources and expertise. In this context NATO recalls its subsequent decisions with respect to crisis response operations in the Balkans. Taking into account the necessity for Alliance solidarity and cohesion, participation in any such operation or mission will remain subject to decisions of member states in accordance with national constitutions.

32. NATO will make full use of partnership, cooperation and dialogue and its links to other organisations to contribute to preventing crises and, should they arise, defusing them at an early stage. A coherent approach to crisis management, as in any use of force by the Alliance, will require the Alliance's political authorities to choose and co-ordinate appropriate responses from a range of both political and military measures and to exercise close political control at all stages.

Partnership, Cooperation, and Dialogue

33. Through its active pursuit of partnership, cooperation, and dialogue, the Alliance is a positive force in promoting security and stability throughout the Euro-Atlantic area. Through outreach and openness, the Alliance seeks to preserve peace, support and promote democracy, contribute to prosperity and progress, and foster genuine partnership with and among all democratic Euro-Atlantic countries. This aims at enhancing the security of all, excludes nobody, and helps to overcome divisions and disagreements that could lead to instability and conflict.

34. The Euro-Atlantic Partnership Council (EAPC) will remain the overarching framework for all aspects of NATO's cooperation with its Partners. It offers an expanded political dimension for both consultation and cooperation. EAPC consultations build increased transparency and confidence among its members on security issues, contribute to conflict prevention and crisis management, and develop practical cooperation activities, including in civil emergency planning, and scientific and environmental affairs.

35. The Partnership for Peace is the principal mechanism for forging practical security links between the Alliance and its Partners and for enhancing interoperability between Partners and NATO. Through detailed

programmes that reflect individual Partners' capacities and interests, Allies and Partners work towards transparency in national defence planning and budgeting; democratic control of defence forces; preparedness for civil disasters and other emergencies; and the development of the ability to work together, including in NATO-led PfP operations. The Alliance is committed to increasing the role the Partners play in PfP decision-making and planning, and making PfP more operational. NATO has undertaken to consult with any active participant in the Partnership if that Partner perceives a direct threat to its territorial integrity, political independence, or security.

36. Russia plays a unique role in Euro-Atlantic security. Within the framework of the NATO–Russia Founding Act on Mutual Relations, Cooperation and Security, NATO and Russia have committed themselves to developing their relations on the basis of common interest, reciprocity and transparency to achieve a lasting and inclusive peace in the Euro-Atlantic area based on the principles of democracy and co-operative security. NATO and Russia have agreed to give concrete substance to their shared commitment to build a stable, peaceful and undivided Europe. A strong, stable and enduring partnership between NATO and Russia is essential to achieve lasting stability in the Euro-Atlantic area.

37. Ukraine occupies a special place in the Euro-Atlantic security environment and is an important and valuable partner in promoting stability and common democratic values. NATO is committed to further strengthening its distinctive partnership with Ukraine on the basis of the NATO–Ukraine Charter, including political consultations on issues of common concern and a broad range of practical cooperation activities. The Alliance continues to support Ukrainian sovereignty and independence, territorial integrity, democratic development, economic prosperity and its status as a non-nuclear weapons state as key factors of stability and security in central and eastern Europe and in Europe as a whole.

38. The Mediterranean is an area of special interest to the Alliance. Security in Europe is closely linked to security and stability in the Mediterranean. NATO's Mediterranean Dialogue process is an integral part of NATO's co-operative approach to security. It provides a framework for confidence building, promotes transparency and cooperation in the region, and reinforces and is reinforced by other international efforts. The Alliance is committed to developing progressively the political, civil, and military

aspects of the Dialogue with the aim of achieving closer cooperation with, and more active involvement by, countries that are partners in this Dialogue.

Enlargement

39. The Alliance remains open to new members under Article 10 of the Washington Treaty. It expects to extend further invitations in coming years to nations willing and able to assume the responsibilities and obligations of membership, and as NATO determines that the inclusion of these nations would serve the overall political and strategic interests of the Alliance, strengthen its effectiveness and cohesion, and enhance overall European security and stability. To this end, NATO has established a programme of activities to assist aspiring countries in their preparations for possible future membership in the context of its wider relationship with them. No European democratic country whose admission would fulfil the objectives of the Treaty will be excluded from consideration.

Arms Control, Disarmament, and Non-Proliferation

40. The Alliance's policy of support for arms control, disarmament, and non-proliferation will continue to play a major role in the achievement of the Alliance's security objectives. The Allies seek to enhance security and stability at the lowest possible level of forces consistent with the Alliance's ability to provide for collective defence and to fulfil the full range of its missions. The Alliance will continue to ensure that as an important part of its broad approach to security defence and arms control, disarmament, and non-proliferation objectives remain in harmony. The Alliance will continue to actively contribute to the development of arms control, disarmament, and non-proliferation agreements as well as to confidence and security building measures. The Allies take seriously their distinctive role in promoting a broader, more comprehensive and more verifiable international arms control and disarmament process. The Alliance will enhance its political efforts to reduce dangers arising from the proliferation of weapons of mass destruction and their means of delivery. The principal non-proliferation goal of the Alliance and its members is to prevent proliferation from occurring or, should it occur, to reverse it through diplomatic means. The Alliance attaches great importance to the continuing validity and the full implementation by all parties of the CFE Treaty as an essential element in ensuring the stability of the Euro-Atlantic area.

PART IV: GUIDELINES FOR THE ALLIANCE'S FORCES PRINCIPLES OF ALLIANCE STRATEGY

41. The Alliance will maintain the necessary military capabilities to accomplish the full range of NATO's missions. The principles of Allied solidarity and strategic unity remain paramount for all Alliance missions. Alliance forces must safeguard NATO's military effectiveness and freedom of action. The security of all Allies is indivisible: an attack on one is an attack on all. With respect to collective defence under Article 5 of the Washington Treaty, the combined military forces of the Alliance must be capable of deterring any potential aggression against it, of stopping an aggressor's advance as far forward as possible should an attack nevertheless occur, and of ensuring the political independence and territorial integrity of its member states. They must also be prepared to contribute to conflict prevention and to conduct non–Article 5 crisis response operations. The Alliance's forces have essential roles in fostering cooperation and understanding with NATO's Partners and other states, particularly in helping Partners to prepare for potential participation in NATO-led PfP operations. Thus they contribute to the preservation of peace, to the safeguarding of common security interests of Alliance members, and to the maintenance of the security and stability of the Euro-Atlantic area. By deterring the use of NBC weapons, they contribute to Alliance efforts aimed at preventing the proliferation of these weapons and their delivery means.

42. The achievement of the Alliance's aims depends critically on the equitable sharing of the roles, risks and responsibilities, as well as the benefits, of common defence. The presence of United States conventional and nuclear forces in Europe remains vital to the security of Europe, which is inseparably linked to that of North America. The North American Allies contribute to the Alliance through military forces available for Alliance missions, through their broader contribution to international peace and security, and through the provision of unique training facilities on the North American continent. The European Allies also make wide-ranging and substantial contributions. As the process of developing the ESDI within the Alliance progresses, the European Allies will further enhance their contribution to the common defence and to international peace and stability including through multinational formations.

43. The principle of collective effort in Alliance defence is embodied in practical arrangements that enable the Allies to enjoy the crucial political,

military and resource advantages of collective defence, and prevent the renationalisation of defence policies, without depriving the Allies of their sovereignty. These arrangements also enable NATO's forces to carry out non–Article 5 crisis response operations and constitute a prerequisite for a coherent Alliance response to all possible contingencies. They are based on procedures for consultation, an integrated military structure, and on co-operation agreements. Key features include collective force planning; common funding; common operational planning; multinational formations, headquarters and command arrangements; an integrated air defence system; a balance of roles and responsibilities among the Allies; the stationing and deployment of forces outside home territory when required; arrangements, including planning, for crisis management and reinforcement; common standards and procedures for equipment, training and logistics; joint and combined doctrines and exercises when appropriate; and infrastructure, armaments and logistics cooperation. The inclusion of NATO's Partners in such arrangements or the development of similar arrangements for them, in appropriate areas, is also instrumental in enhancing cooperation and common efforts in Euro-Atlantic security matters.

44. Multinational funding, including through the Military Budget and the NATO Security Investment Programme, will continue to play an important role in acquiring and maintaining necessary assets and capabilities. The management of resources should be guided by the military requirements of the Alliance as they evolve.

45. The Alliance supports the further development of the ESDI within the Alliance, including by being prepared to make available assets and capabilities for operations under the political control and strategic direction either of the WEU or as otherwise agreed.

46. To protect peace and to prevent war or any kind of coercion, the Alliance will maintain for the foreseeable future an appropriate mix of nuclear and conventional forces based in Europe and kept up to date where necessary, although at a minimum sufficient level. Taking into account the diversity of risks with which the Alliance could be faced, it must maintain the forces necessary to ensure credible deterrence and to provide a wide range of conventional response options. But the Alliance's conventional forces alone cannot ensure credible deterrence. Nuclear weapons make a unique contribution in rendering the risks of aggression against the

Alliance incalculable and unacceptable. Thus, they remain essential to preserve peace.

The Alliance's Force Posture
The Missions of Alliance Military Forces

47. The primary role of Alliance military forces is to protect peace and to guarantee the territorial integrity, political independence and security of member states. The Alliance's forces must therefore be able to deter and defend effectively, to maintain or restore the territorial integrity of Allied nations and in case of conflict to terminate war rapidly by making an aggressor reconsider his decision, cease his attack and withdraw. NATO forces must maintain the ability to provide for collective defence while conducting effective non–Article 5 crisis response operations.

48. The maintenance of the security and stability of the Euro-Atlantic area is of key importance. An important aim of the Alliance and its forces is to keep risks at a distance by dealing with potential crises at an early stage. In the event of crises which jeopardise Euro-Atlantic stability and could affect the security of Alliance members, the Alliance's military forces may be called upon to conduct crisis response operations. They may also be called upon to contribute to the preservation of international peace and security by conducting operations in support of other international organisations, complementing and reinforcing political actions within a broad approach to security.

49. In contributing to the management of crises through military operations, the Alliance's forces will have to deal with a complex and diverse range of actors, risks, situations and demands, including humanitarian emergencies. Some non–Article 5 crisis response operations may be as demanding as some collective defence missions. Well-trained and well-equipped forces at adequate levels of readiness and in sufficient strength to meet the full range of contingencies as well as the appropriate support structures, planning tools and command and control capabilities are essential in providing efficient military contributions. The Alliance should also be prepared to support, on the basis of separable but not separate capabilities, operations under the political control and strategic direction either of the WEU or as otherwise agreed. The potential participation of Partners and other non-NATO nations in NATO-led operations as well as possible operations with Russia would be further valuable elements of NATO's contribution to managing crises that affect Euro-Atlantic security.

50. Alliance military forces also contribute to promoting stability throughout the Euro-Atlantic area by their participation in military-to-military contacts and in other cooperation activities and exercises under the Partnership for Peace as well as those organised to deepen NATO's relationships with Russia, Ukraine and the Mediterranean Dialogue countries. They contribute to stability and understanding by participating in confidence-building activities, including those which enhance transparency and improve communication; as well as in verification of arms control agreements and in humanitarian de-mining. Key areas of consultation and cooperation could include inter alia: training and exercises, interoperability, civil-military relations, concept and doctrine development, defence planning, crisis management, proliferation issues, armaments cooperation as well as participation in operational planning and operations.

Guidelines for the Alliance's Force Posture

51. To implement the Alliance's fundamental security tasks and the principles of its strategy, the forces of the Alliance must continue to be adapted to meet the requirements of the full range of Alliance missions effectively and to respond to future challenges. The posture of Allies' forces, building on the strengths of different national defence structures, will conform to the guidelines developed in the following paragraphs.

52. The size, readiness, availability and deployment of the Alliance's military forces will reflect its commitment to collective defence and to conduct crisis response operations, sometimes at short notice, distant from their home stations, including beyond the Allies' territory. The characteristics of the Alliance's forces will also reflect the provisions of relevant arms control agreements. Alliance forces must be adequate in strength and capabilities to deter and counter aggression against any Ally. They must be interoperable and have appropriate doctrines and technologies. They must be held at the required readiness and deployability, and be capable of military success in a wide range of complex joint and combined operations, which may also include Partners and other non-NATO nations.

53. This means in particular:

> a. that the overall size of the Allies' forces will be kept at the lowest levels consistent with the requirements of collective defence and other Alliance missions; they will be held at appropriate and graduated readiness;

b. that the peacetime geographical distribution of forces will ensure a sufficient military presence throughout the territory of the Alliance, including the stationing and deployment of forces outside home territory and waters and forward deployment of forces when and where necessary. Regional and, in particular, geostrategic considerations within the Alliance will have to be taken into account, as instabilities on NATO's periphery could lead to crises or conflicts requiring an Alliance military response, potentially with short warning times;

c. that NATO's command structure will be able to undertake command and control of the full range of the Alliance's military missions including through the use of deployable combined and joint HQs, in particular CJTF headquarters, to command and control multinational and multiservice forces. It will also be able to support operations under the political control and strategic direction either of the WEU or as otherwise agreed, thereby contributing to the development of the ESDI within the Alliance, and to conduct NATO-led non–Article 5 crisis response operations in which Partners and other countries may participate;

d. that overall, the Alliance will, in both the near and long term and for the full range of its missions, require essential operational capabilities such as an effective engagement capability; deployability and mobility; survivability of forces and infrastructure; and sustainability, incorporating logistics and force rotation. To develop these capabilities to their full potential for multinational operations, interoperability, including human factors, the use of appropriate advanced technology, the maintenance of information superiority in military operations, and highly qualified personnel with a broad spectrum of skills will be important. Sufficient capabilities in the areas of command, control and communications as well as intelligence and surveillance will serve as necessary force multipliers;

e. that at any time a limited but militarily significant proportion of ground, air and sea forces will be able to react as rapidly as necessary to a wide range of eventualities, including a short-notice attack on any Ally. Greater numbers of force elements will be available at appropriate levels of readiness to sustain prolonged operations, whether within or beyond Alliance territory, including through rotation of deployed forces. Taken together, these forces must also be of sufficient quality, quantity and readiness to contribute to deterrence and to defend against limited attacks on the Alliance;

f. that the Alliance must be able to build up larger forces, both in response to any fundamental changes in the security environment and for limited requirements, by reinforcement, by mobilising reserves, or by reconstituting forces when necessary. This ability must be in proportion to potential threats to Alliance security, including potential long-term developments. It must take into account the possibility of substantial improvements in the readiness and capabilities of military forces on the periphery of the Alliance. Capabilities for timely reinforcement and resupply both within and from Europe and North America will remain of critical importance, with a resulting need for a high degree of deployability, mobility and flexibility;

g. that appropriate force structures and procedures, including those that would provide an ability to build up, deploy and draw down forces quickly and selectively, are necessary to permit measured, flexible and timely responses in order to reduce and defuse tensions. These arrangements must be exercised regularly in peacetime;

h. that the Alliance's defence posture must have the capability to address appropriately and effectively the risks associated with the proliferation of NBC weapons and their means of delivery, which also pose a potential threat to the Allies' populations, territory, and forces. A balanced mix of forces, response capabilities and strengthened defences is needed;

i. that the Alliance's forces and infrastructure must be protected against terrorist attacks.

Characteristics of Conventional Forces

54. It is essential that the Allies' military forces have a credible ability to fulfil the full range of Alliance missions. This requirement has implications for force structures, force and equipment levels; readiness, availability, and sustainability; training and exercises; deployment and employment options; and force build-up and mobilisation capabilities. The aim should be to achieve an optimum balance between high readiness forces capable of beginning rapidly, and immediately as necessary, collective defence or non–Article 5 crisis response operations; forces at different levels of lower readiness to provide the bulk of those required for collective defence, for

rotation of forces to sustain crisis response operations, or for further reinforcement of a particular region; and a longer-term build-up and augmentation capability for the worst case but very remote scenario of large scale operations for collective defence. A substantial proportion of Alliance forces will be capable of performing more than one of these roles.

55. Alliance forces will be structured to reflect the multinational and joint nature of Alliance missions. Essential tasks will include controlling, protecting, and defending territory; ensuring the unimpeded use of sea, air, and land lines of communication; sea control and protecting the deployment of the Alliance's sea-based deterrent; conducting independent and combined air operations; ensuring a secure air environment and effective extended air defence; surveillance, intelligence, reconnaissance and electronic warfare; strategic lift; and providing effective and flexible command and control facilities, including deployable combined and joint headquarters.

56. The Alliance's defence posture against the risks and potential threats of the proliferation of NBC weapons and their means of delivery must continue to be improved, including through work on missile defences. As NATO forces may be called upon to operate beyond NATO's borders, capabilities for dealing with proliferation risks must be flexible, mobile, rapidly deployable and sustainable. Doctrines, planning, and training and exercise policies must also prepare the Alliance to deter and defend against the use of NBC weapons. The aim in doing so will be to further reduce operational vulnerabilities of NATO military forces while maintaining their flexibility and effectiveness despite the presence, threat or use of NBC weapons.

57. Alliance strategy does not include a chemical or biological warfare capability. The Allies support universal adherence to the relevant disarmament regimes. But, even if further progress with respect to banning chemical and biological weapons can be achieved, defensive precautions will remain essential.

58. Given reduced overall force levels and constrained resources, the ability to work closely together will remain vital for achieving the Alliance's missions. The Alliance's collective defence arrangements in which, for those concerned, the integrated military structure plays the key role, are essential in this regard. The various strands of NATO's defence planning need to be effectively coordinated at all levels in order to ensure the preparedness of the forces and supporting structures to carry out the full

spectrum of their roles. Exchanges of information among the Allies about their force plans contribute to securing the availability of the capabilities needed for the execution of these roles. Consultations in case of important changes in national defence plans also remain of key importance. Cooperation in the development of new operational concepts will be essential for responding to evolving security challenges. The detailed practical arrangements that have been developed as part of the ESDI within the Alliance contribute to close allied co-operation without unnecessary duplication of assets and capabilities.

59. To be able to respond flexibly to possible contingencies and to permit the effective conduct of Alliance missions, the Alliance requires sufficient logistics capabilities, including transport capacities, medical support and stocks to deploy and sustain all types of forces effectively. Standardisation will foster cooperation and cost-effectiveness in providing logistic support to allied forces. Mounting and sustaining operations outside the Allies' territory, where there may be little or no host-nation support, will pose special logistical challenges. The ability to build-up larger, adequately equipped and trained forces, in a timely manner and to a level able to fulfil the full range of Alliance missions, will also make an essential contribution to crisis management and defence. This will include the ability to reinforce any area at risk and to establish a multinational presence when and where this is needed. Forces of various kinds and at various levels of readiness will be capable of flexible employment in both intra-European and transatlantic reinforcement. This will require control of lines of communication, and appropriate support and exercise arrangements.

60. The interaction between Alliance forces and the civil environment (both governmental and non-governmental) in which they operate is crucial to the success of operations. Civil–military cooperation is interdependent: military means are increasingly requested to assist civil authorities; at the same time civil support to military operations is important for logistics, communications, medical support, and public affairs. Cooperation between the Alliance's military and civil bodies will accordingly remain essential.

61. The Alliance's ability to accomplish the full range of its missions will rely increasingly on multinational forces, complementing national commitments to NATO for the Allies concerned. Such forces, which are applicable to the full range of Alliance missions, demonstrate the Alliance's resolve to maintain a credible collective defence; enhance Alliance cohesion; and

reinforce the transatlantic partnership and strengthen the ESDI within the Alliance. Multinational forces, particularly those capable of deploying rapidly for collective defence or for non–Article 5 crisis response operations, reinforce solidarity. They can also provide a way of deploying more capable formations than might be available purely nationally, thus helping to make more efficient use of scarce defence resources. This may include a highly integrated, multinational approach to specific tasks and functions, an approach which underlies the implementation of the CJTF concept. For peace support operations, effective multinational formations and other arrangements involving Partners will be valuable. In order to exploit fully the potential offered by multinational formations, improving interoperability, inter alia through sufficient training and exercises, is of the highest importance.

Characteristics of Nuclear Forces

62. The fundamental purpose of the nuclear forces of the Allies is political: to preserve peace and prevent coercion and any kind of war. They will continue to fulfil an essential role by ensuring uncertainty in the mind of any aggressor about the nature of the Allies' response to military aggression. They demonstrate that aggression of any kind is not a rational option. The supreme guarantee of the security of the Allies is provided by the strategic nuclear forces of the Alliance, particularly those of the United States; the independent nuclear forces of the United Kingdom and France, which have a deterrent role of their own, contribute to the overall deterrence and security of the Allies.

63. A credible Alliance nuclear posture and the demonstration of Alliance solidarity and common commitment to war prevention continue to require widespread participation by European Allies involved in collective defence planning in nuclear roles, in peacetime basing of nuclear forces on their territory and in command, control and consultation arrangements. Nuclear forces based in Europe and committed to NATO provide an essential political and military link between the European and the North American members of the Alliance. The Alliance will therefore maintain adequate nuclear forces in Europe. These forces need to have the necessary characteristics and appropriate flexibility and survivability, to be perceived as a credible and effective element of the Allies' strategy in preventing war. They will be maintained at the minimum level sufficient to preserve peace and stability.

64. The Allies concerned consider that, with the radical changes in the security situation, including reduced conventional force levels in Europe and increased reaction times, NATO's ability to defuse a crisis through diplomatic and other means or, should it be necessary, to mount a successful conventional defence has significantly improved. The circumstances in which any use of nuclear weapons might have to be contemplated by them are therefore extremely remote. Since 1991, therefore, the Allies have taken a series of steps which reflect the post–Cold War security environment. These include a dramatic reduction of the types and numbers of NATO's sub-strategic forces including the elimination of all nuclear artillery and ground-launched short-range nuclear missiles; a significant relaxation of the readiness criteria for nuclear-roled forces; and the termination of standing peacetime nuclear contingency plans. NATO's nuclear forces no longer target any country. Nonetheless, NATO will maintain, at the minimum level consistent with the prevailing security environment, adequate sub-strategic forces based in Europe which will provide an essential link with strategic nuclear forces, reinforcing the transatlantic link. These will consist of dual capable aircraft and a small number of United Kingdom Trident warheads. Sub-strategic nuclear weapons will, however, not be deployed in normal circumstances on surface vessels and attack submarines.

PART V: CONCLUSION

65. As the North Atlantic Alliance enters its sixth decade, it must be ready to meet the challenges and opportunities of a new century. The Strategic Concept reaffirms the enduring purpose of the Alliance and sets out its fundamental security tasks. It enables a transformed NATO to contribute to the evolving security environment, supporting security and stability with the strength of its shared commitment to democracy and the peaceful resolution of disputes. The Strategic Concept will govern the Alliance's security and defence policy, its operational concepts, its conventional and nuclear force posture and its collective defence arrangements, and will be kept under review in the light of the evolving security environment. In an uncertain world the need for effective defence remains, but in reaffirming this commitment the Alliance will also continue making full use of every opportunity to help build an undivided continent by promoting and fostering the vision of a Europe whole and free.

STRATEGIC CONCEPT FOR THE DEFENCE AND SECURITY OF THE MEMBERS OF THE NORTH ATLANTIC TREATY ORGANIZATION
LISBON, NOVEMBER 19, 2010
(Source: NATO)

ACTIVE ENGAGEMENT, MODERN DEFENCE
Preface

We, the Heads of State and Government of the NATO nations, are determined that NATO will continue to play its unique and essential role in ensuring our common defence and security. This Strategic Concept will guide the next phase in NATO's evolution, so that it continues to be effective in a changing world, against new threats, with new capabilities and new partners:

- It reconfirms the bond between our nations to defend one another against attack, including against new threats to the safety of our citizens.
- It commits the Alliance to prevent crises, manage conflicts and stabilize post-conflict situations, including by working more closely with our international partners, most importantly the United Nations and the European Union.
- It offers our partners around the globe more political engagement with the Alliance, and a substantial role in shaping the NATO-led operations to which they contribute.
- It commits NATO to the goal of creating the conditions for a world without nuclear weapons but reconfirms that, as long as there are nuclear weapons in the world, NATO will remain a nuclear Alliance.

- It restates our firm commitment to keep the door to NATO open to all European democracies that meet the standards of membership, because enlargement contributes to our goal of a Europe whole, free and at peace.
- It commits NATO to continuous reform towards a more effective, efficient and flexible Alliance, so that our taxpayers get the most security for the money they invest in defence.

The citizens of our countries rely on NATO to defend Allied nations, to deploy robust military forces where and when required for our security, and to help promote common security with our partners around the globe. While the world is changing, NATO's essential mission will remain the same: to ensure that the Alliance remains an unparalleled community of freedom, peace, security and shared values.

Core Tasks and Principles

1. NATO's fundamental and enduring purpose is to safeguard the freedom and security of all its members by political and military means. Today, the Alliance remains an essential source of stability in an unpredictable world.

2. NATO member states form a unique community of values, committed to the principles of individual liberty, democracy, human rights and the rule of law. The Alliance is firmly committed to the purposes and principles of the Charter of the United Nations, and to the Washington Treaty, which affirms the primary responsibility of the Security Council for the maintenance of international peace and security.

3. The political and military bonds between Europe and North America have been forged in NATO since the Alliance was founded in 1949; the transatlantic link remains as strong, and as important to the preservation of Euro-Atlantic peace and security, as ever. The security of NATO members on both sides of the Atlantic is indivisible. We will continue to defend it together, on the basis of solidarity, shared purpose and fair burden-sharing.

4. The modern security environment contains a broad and evolving set of challenges to the security of NATO's territory and populations. In order to assure their security, the Alliance must and will continue fulfilling effectively three essential core tasks, all of which contribute to safeguarding Alliance members, and always in accordance with international law:

1. **Collective defence.** NATO members will always assist each other against attack, in accordance with Article 5 of the Washington Treaty. That commitment remains firm and binding. NATO will deter and defend against any threat of aggression, and against emerging security challenges where they threaten the fundamental security of individual Allies or the Alliance as a whole.

2. **Crisis management.** NATO has a unique and robust set of political and military capabilities to address the full spectrum of crises before, during and after conflicts. NATO will actively employ an appropriate mix of those political and military tools to help manage developing crises that have the potential to affect Alliance security, before they escalate into conflicts; to stop ongoing conflicts where they affect Alliance security; and to help consolidate stability in post-conflict situations where that contributes to Euro-Atlantic security.

3. **Cooperative security.** The Alliance is affected by, and can affect, political and security developments beyond its borders. The Alliance will engage actively to enhance international security, through partnership with relevant countries and other international organisations; by contributing actively to arms control, non-proliferation and disarmament; and by keeping the door to membership in the Alliance open to all European democracies that meet NATO's standards.

5. NATO remains the unique and essential transatlantic forum for consultations on all matters that affect the territorial integrity, political independence and security of its members, as set out in Article 4 of the Washington Treaty. Any security issue of interest to any Ally can be brought to the NATO table, to share information, exchange views and, where appropriate, forge common approaches.

6. In order to carry out the full range of NATO missions as effectively and efficiently as possible, Allies will engage in a continuous process of reform, modernisation and transformation.

The Security Environment

7. Today, the Euro-Atlantic area is at peace and the threat of a conventional attack against NATO territory is low. That is an historic success for the policies of robust defence, Euro-Atlantic integration and active partnership that have guided NATO for more than half a century.

8. However, the conventional threat cannot be ignored. Many regions and countries around the world are witnessing the acquisition of substantial, modern military capabilities with consequences for international stability and Euro-Atlantic security that are difficult to predict. This includes the proliferation of ballistic missiles, which poses a real and growing threat to the Euro-Atlantic area.

9. The proliferation of nuclear weapons and other weapons of mass destruction, and their means of delivery, threatens incalculable consequences for global stability and prosperity. During the next decade, proliferation will be most acute in some of the world's most volatile regions.

10. Terrorism poses a direct threat to the security of the citizens of NATO countries, and to international stability and prosperity more broadly. Extremist groups continue to spread to, and in, areas of strategic importance to the Alliance, and modern technology increases the threat and potential impact of terrorist attacks, in particular if terrorists were to acquire nuclear, chemical, biological or radiological capabilities.

11. Instability or conflict beyond NATO borders can directly threaten Alliance security, including by fostering extremism, terrorism, and trans-national illegal activities such as trafficking in arms, narcotics and people.

12. Cyber attacks are becoming more frequent, more organised and more costly in the damage that they inflict on government administrations, businesses, economies and potentially also transportation and supply networks and other critical infrastructure; they can reach a threshold that threatens national and Euro-Atlantic prosperity, security and stability. Foreign militaries and intelligence services, organised criminals, terrorist and/or extremist groups can each be the source of such attacks.

13. All countries are increasingly reliant on the vital communication, transport and transit routes on which international trade, energy security and prosperity depend. They require greater international efforts to ensure their resilience against attack or disruption. Some NATO countries will become more dependent on foreign energy suppliers and in some cases, on foreign energy supply and distribution networks for their energy needs. As a larger share of world consumption is transported across the globe, energy supplies are increasingly exposed to disruption.

14. A number of significant technology-related trends including the development of laser weapons, electronic warfare and technologies that

impede access to space appear poised to have major global effects that will impact on NATO military planning and operations.

15. Key environmental and resource constraints, including health risks, climate change, water scarcity and increasing energy needs, will further shape the future security environment in areas of concern to NATO and have the potential to significantly affect NATO planning and operations.

Defence and Deterrence

16. The greatest responsibility of the Alliance is to protect and defend our territory and our populations against attack, as set out in Article 5 of the Washington Treaty. The Alliance does not consider any country to be its adversary. However, no one should doubt NATO's resolve if the security of any of its members were to be threatened.

17. Deterrence, based on an appropriate mix of nuclear and conventional capabilities, remains a core element of our overall strategy. The circumstances in which any use of nuclear weapons might have to be contemplated are extremely remote. As long as nuclear weapons exist, NATO will remain a nuclear alliance.

18. The supreme guarantee of the security of the Allies is provided by the strategic nuclear forces of the Alliance, particularly those of the United States; the independent strategic nuclear forces of the United Kingdom and France, which have a deterrent role of their own, contribute to the overall deterrence and security of the Allies.

19. We will ensure that NATO has the full range of capabilities necessary to deter and defend against any threat to the safety and security of our populations. Therefore, we will:

- maintain an appropriate mix of nuclear and conventional forces;
- maintain the ability to sustain concurrent major joint operations and several smaller operations for collective defence and crisis response, including at strategic distance;
- develop and maintain robust, mobile and deployable conventional forces to carry out both our Article 5 responsibilities and the Alliance's expeditionary operations, including with the NATO Response Force;
- carry out the necessary training, exercises, contingency planning and information exchange for assuring our defence against the full range of conventional and emerging security challenges, and provide appropriate visible assurance and reinforcement for all Allies;

- ensure the broadest possible participation of Allies in collective defence planning on nuclear roles, in peacetime basing of nuclear forces, and in command, control and consultation arrangements;
- develop the capability to defend our populations and territories against ballistic missile attack as a core element of our collective defence, which contributes to the indivisible security of the Alliance. We will actively seek cooperation on missile defence with Russia and other Euro-Atlantic partners;
- further develop NATO's capacity to defend against the threat of chemical, biological, radiological and nuclear weapons of mass destruction;
- develop further our ability to prevent, detect, defend against and recover from cyber-attacks, including by using the NATO planning process to enhance and coordinate national cyber-defence capabilities, bringing all NATO bodies under centralized cyber protection, and better integrating NATO cyber awareness, warning and response with member nations;
- enhance the capacity to detect and defend against international terrorism, including through enhanced analysis of the threat, more consultations with our partners, and the development of appropriate military capabilities, including to help train local forces to fight terrorism themselves;
- develop the capacity to contribute to energy security, including protection of critical energy infrastructure and transit areas and lines, cooperation with partners, and consultations among Allies on the basis of strategic assessments and contingency planning;
- ensure that the Alliance is at the front edge in assessing the security impact of emerging technologies, and that military planning takes the potential threats into account;
- sustain the necessary levels of defence spending, so that our armed forces are sufficiently resourced;
- continue to review NATO's overall posture in deterring and defending against the full range of threats to the Alliance, taking into account changes to the evolving international security environment.

Security through Crisis Management

20. Crises and conflicts beyond NATO's borders can pose a direct threat to the security of Alliance territory and populations. NATO will therefore

engage, where possible and when necessary, to prevent crises, manage crises, stabilize post-conflict situations and support reconstruction.

21. The lessons learned from NATO operations, in particular in Afghanistan and the Western Balkans, make it clear that a comprehensive political, civilian and military approach is necessary for effective crisis management. The Alliance will engage actively with other international actors before, during and after crises to encourage collaborative analysis, planning and conduct of activities on the ground, in order to maximise coherence and effectiveness of the overall international effort.

22. The best way to manage conflicts is to prevent them from happening. NATO will continually monitor and analyse the international environment to anticipate crises and, where appropriate, take active steps to prevent them from becoming larger conflicts.

23. Where conflict prevention proves unsuccessful, NATO will be prepared and capable to manage ongoing hostilities. NATO has unique conflict management capacities, including the unparalleled capability to deploy and sustain robust military forces in the field. NATO-led operations have demonstrated the indispensable contribution the Alliance can make to international conflict management efforts.

24. Even when conflict comes to an end, the international community must often provide continued support, to create the conditions for lasting stability. NATO will be prepared and capable to contribute to stabilisation and reconstruction, in close cooperation and consultation wherever possible with other relevant international actors.

25. To be effective across the crisis management spectrum, we will:

- enhance intelligence sharing within NATO, to better predict when crises might occur, and how they can best be prevented;
- further develop doctrine and military capabilities for expeditionary operations, including counterinsurgency, stabilization and reconstruction operations;
- form an appropriate but modest civilian crisis management capability to interface more effectively with civilian partners, building on the lessons learned from NATO-led operations. This capability may also be used to plan, employ and coordinate civilian activities until conditions allow for the transfer of those responsibilities and tasks to other actors;
- enhance integrated civilian-military planning throughout the crisis spectrum;

- develop the capability to train and develop local forces in crisis zones, so that local authorities are able, as quickly as possible, to maintain security without international assistance;
- identify and train civilian specialists from member states, made available for rapid deployment by Allies for selected missions, able to work alongside our military personnel and civilian specialists from partner countries and institutions;
- broaden and intensify the political consultations among Allies, and with partners, both on a regular basis and in dealing with all stages of a crisis before, during and after.

Promoting International Security through Cooperation
Arms Control, Disarmament, and Non-Proliferation

26. NATO seeks its security at the lowest possible level of forces. Arms control, disarmament and non-proliferation contribute to peace, security and stability, and should ensure undiminished security for all Alliance members. We will continue to play our part in reinforcing arms control and in promoting disarmament of both conventional weapons and weapons of mass destruction, as well as non-proliferation efforts:

- We are resolved to seek a safer world for all and to create the conditions for a world without nuclear weapons in accordance with the goals of the Nuclear Non-Proliferation Treaty, in a way that promotes international stability, and is based on the principle of undiminished security for all.
- With the changes in the security environment since the end of the Cold War, we have dramatically reduced the number of nuclear weapons stationed in Europe and our reliance on nuclear weapons in NATO strategy. We will seek to create the conditions for further reductions in the future.
- In any future reductions, our aim should be to seek Russian agreement to increase transparency on its nuclear weapons in Europe and relocate these weapons away from the territory of NATO members. Any further steps must take into account the disparity with the greater Russian stockpiles of short-range nuclear weapons.
- We are committed to conventional arms control, which provides predictability, transparency and a means to keep armaments at the lowest possible level for stability. We will work to strengthen the

conventional arms control regime in Europe on the basis of reciprocity, transparency and host-nation consent.

- We will explore ways for our political means and military capabilities to contribute to international efforts to fight proliferation.
- National decisions regarding arms control and disarmament may have an impact on the security of all Alliance members. We are committed to maintain, and develop as necessary, appropriate consultations among Allies on these issues.

Open Door

27. NATO's enlargement has contributed substantially to the security of Allies; the prospect of further enlargement and the spirit of cooperative security have advanced stability in Europe more broadly. Our goal of a Europe whole and free, and sharing common values, would be best served by the eventual integration of all European countries that so desire into Euro-Atlantic structures.

- The door to NATO membership remains fully open to all European democracies which share the values of our Alliance, which are willing and able to assume the responsibilities and obligations of membership, and whose inclusion can contribute to common security and stability.

Partnerships

28. The promotion of Euro-Atlantic security is best assured through a wide network of partner relationships with countries and organisations around the globe. These partnerships make a concrete and valued contribution to the success of NATO's fundamental tasks.

29. Dialogue and cooperation with partners can make a concrete contribution to enhancing international security, to defending the values on which our Alliance is based, to NATO's operations, and to preparing interested nations for membership of NATO. These relationships will be based on reciprocity, mutual benefit and mutual respect.

30. We will enhance our partnerships through flexible formats that bring NATO and partners together across and beyond existing frameworks:

- We are prepared to develop political dialogue and practical cooperation with any nations and relevant organisations across the globe that share our interest in peaceful international relations.

- We will be open to consultation with any partner country on security issues of common concern.
- We will give our operational partners a structural role in shaping strategy and decisions on NATO-led missions to which they contribute.
- We will further develop our existing partnerships while preserving their specificity.

31. Cooperation between NATO and the United Nations continues to make a substantial contribution to security in operations around the world. The Alliance aims to deepen political dialogue and practical cooperation with the UN, as set out in the UN–NATO Declaration signed in 2008, including through:

- enhanced liaison between the two Headquarters;
- more regular political consultation; and
- enhanced practical cooperation in managing crises where both organisations are engaged.

32. An active and effective European Union contributes to the overall security of the Euro-Atlantic area. Therefore the EU is a unique and essential partner for NATO. The two organisations share a majority of members, and all members of both organisations share common values. NATO recognizes the importance of a stronger and more capable European defence. We welcome the entry into force of the Lisbon Treaty, which provides a framework for strengthening the EU's capacities to address common security challenges. Non-EU Allies make a significant contribution to these efforts. For the strategic partnership between NATO and the EU, their fullest involvement in these efforts is essential. NATO and the EU can and should play complementary and mutually reinforcing roles in supporting international peace and security. We are determined to make our contribution to create more favourable circumstances through which we will:

- fully strengthen the strategic partnership with the EU, in the spirit of full mutual openness, transparency, complementarity and respect for the autonomy and institutional integrity of both organisations;
- enhance our practical cooperation in operations throughout the crisis spectrum, from coordinated planning to mutual support in the field;

- broaden our political consultations to include all issues of common concern, in order to share assessments and perspectives;
- cooperate more fully in capability development, to minimise duplication and maximise cost-effectiveness.

33. NATO–Russia cooperation is of strategic importance as it contributes to creating a common space of peace, stability and security. NATO poses no threat to Russia. On the contrary: we want to see a true strategic partnership between NATO and Russia, and we will act accordingly, with the expectation of reciprocity from Russia.

34. The NATO–Russia relationship is based upon the goals, principles and commitments of the NATO–Russia Founding Act and the Rome Declaration, especially regarding the respect of democratic principles and the sovereignty, independence and territorial integrity of all states in the Euro-Atlantic area. Notwithstanding differences on particular issues, we remain convinced that the security of NATO and Russia is intertwined and that a strong and constructive partnership based on mutual confidence, transparency and predictability can best serve our security. We are determined to:

- enhance the political consultations and practical cooperation with Russia in areas of shared interests, including missile defence, counter-terrorism, counter-narcotics, counter-piracy and the promotion of wider international security;
- use the full potential of the NATO–Russia Council for dialogue and joint action with Russia.

35. The Euro-Atlantic Partnership Council and Partnership for Peace are central to our vision of Europe whole, free and in peace. We are firmly committed to the development of friendly and cooperative relations with all countries of the Mediterranean, and we intend to further develop the Mediterranean Dialogue in the coming years. We attach great importance to peace and stability in the Gulf region, and we intend to strengthen our cooperation in the Istanbul Cooperation Initiative. We will aim to:

- enhance consultations and practical military cooperation with our partners in the Euro-Atlantic Partnership Council;
- continue and develop the partnerships with Ukraine and Georgia within the NATO–Ukraine and NATO–Georgia Commissions, based on

the NATO decision at the Bucharest summit 2008, and taking into account the Euro-Atlantic orientation or aspiration of each of the countries;
- facilitate the Euro-Atlantic integration of the Western Balkans, with the aim to ensure lasting peace and stability based on democratic values, regional cooperation and good neighbourly relations;
- deepen the cooperation with current members of the Mediterranean Dialogue and be open to the inclusion in the Mediterranean Dialogue of other countries of the region;
- develop a deeper security partnership with our Gulf partners and remain ready to welcome new partners in the Istanbul Cooperation Initiative.

Reform and Transformation

36. Unique in history, NATO is a security Alliance that fields military forces able to operate together in any environment; that can control operations anywhere through its integrated military command structure; and that has at its disposal core capabilities that few Allies could afford individually.

37. NATO must have sufficient resources financial, military and human to carry out its missions, which are essential to the security of Alliance populations and territory. Those resources must, however, be used in the most efficient and effective way possible. We will:

- maximise the deployability of our forces, and their capacity to sustain operations in the field, including by undertaking focused efforts to meet NATO's usability targets;
- ensure the maximum coherence in defence planning, to reduce unnecessary duplication, and to focus our capability development on modern requirements;
- develop and operate capabilities jointly, for reasons of cost effectiveness and as a manifestation of solidarity;
- preserve and strengthen the common capabilities, standards, structures and funding that bind us together;
- engage in a process of continual reform, to streamline structures, improve working methods and maximise efficiency.

An Alliance for the 21st Century

38. We, the political leaders of NATO, are determined to continue renewal of our Alliance so that it is fit for purpose in addressing the 21st Century security challenges. We are firmly committed to preserve its effectiveness as the globe's most successful political-military Alliance. Our Alliance thrives as a source of hope because it is based on common values of individual liberty, democracy, human rights and the rule of law, and because our common essential and enduring purpose is to safeguard the freedom and security of its members. These values and objectives are universal and perpetual, and we are determined to defend them through unity, solidarity, strength and resolve.

Part I

THE EVOLUTION OF THE ALLIANCE

Chapter 1

NATO's Radical Response to the Nuclear Revolution

Francis J. Gavin

In the seventh decade since the United States, Canada, and their West European allies negotiated and signed a peacetime military alliance, what is its historical legacy? Broadly speaking, there are two ways to think about the North Atlantic Treaty and the institution it engendered, the North Atlantic Treaty Organization (NATO).

The first view—the one I would suggest is the conventional wisdom—sees NATO as a fairly orthodox and benign organization. It emerged to deal with the looming specter of Soviet expansion that threatened a weak, disorganized, and embittered Western Europe struggling to find its bearings after World War II. Led but not dominated by the United States, NATO succeeded by creating a largely defensive strategy that deterred but did not threaten the Soviet Union. In the process, it served as a vehicle to lessen and eventually eliminate long-held intra-European tensions by focusing on cooperation and consensus. Its success in promoting European security led NATO, despite predictions to the contrary, not only to survive the end of the Cold War but to expand both its membership and its mission over the past three decades.[1]

There is much truth in this view. Building upon and expanding the March 1948 Brussels Treaty signed by Great Britain, France, Belgium, the Netherlands, and Luxembourg, the original signatories to the 1949 treaty, while recognizing its boldness, did not see it as a revolutionary act. Few if any believed NATO was more than a political association to help pool and coordinate their collective resources while generating a mechanism to distribute military aid from the United Sates. No one anticipated developing a fully integrated military organization and lasting after the original threat disappeared.

A second view recognizes that NATO developed into (and in some ways remains) a truly radical organization, unprecedented in the history of international politics. To give just a few examples: before NATO, alliances were fungible and ever-shifting, constantly changing members and measured in years, not decades. NATO developed into something altogether different: once you get in, it has been almost impossible (with the partial exception of France), to get out, even after the original geopolitical impetus for the alliance's formation disappeared. Furthermore, NATO became a vehicle to rehabilitate and exploit West German military power less than a decade after the horrors of Nazi Germany, a fact that alarmed not just Soviet adversaries but many members the alliance was set up to protect. At the same time, it successfully managed to restrain West Germany's political ambitions and prevent it from accessing the most powerful new weapons, all to reassure both NATO's enemies and its own members. When the Cold War ended, NATO was a key enabler of German reunification, despite deep reservations in Russia and throughout Europe. In the successful aftermath of reunification, NATO expanded eastward into territories long seen as part of Russia's sphere of influence. None of this was foreseen in 1949.[2]

Finally, NATO's relationship with the United States is especially puzzling and hard to square with the more conventional understanding of the organization. From our contemporary perspective, many see NATO as an instrument of American hegemony in and over Europe, reflecting the United States' imperial ambitions in the world. For more than a few American leaders, however, NATO was, from its earliest days, a resented and unloved burden. Before NATO, the United States was allergic to peacetime alliances and standing military deployments overseas. NATO's military strategy developed in ways completely at odds with the traditional American way of warfare, which was predicated upon exploiting the nation's geographic and economic advantages to mobilize slowly but massively to fight grinding wars of attrition.[3] NATO's military plans and deployments threatened the United States' long-held beliefs in strict civilian control of the military and congressional oversight in matters of war and peace. Most important, the notion that the US would not only permanently commit to such an entity, but forwardly deploy hundreds of thousands of troops, would have been dismissed as absurd when the treaty was first considered.

What factors transformed NATO's original, more modest ambitions in just a few years? One looms above all else: nuclear weapons. The revolution in military technology (especially thermonuclear weapons), the ability to deliver them rapidly and over great distances, and the near futility of defensive measures had a profound influence on geopolitics and military affairs during the postwar era, driving much of NATO's more radical orientation. In a non-nuclear world, or a world where the United States retained its atomic monopoly, NATO might have been a conventional alliance: an agreement among sovereign states to pool resources in the face of a common enemy, an arrangement that would loosen and disappear altogether as the shared threat changed or disappeared. But the unique challenges brought on by nuclear weapons demanded dramatic responses, which shaped NATO's choices from the 1950s onward and, in ways rarely stated, continue to do so to this day.

In this essay I will focus on two of the interrelated and radical strategic choices made by NATO and the challenges they presented. First, I will look at how and why NATO adopted an extraordinarily aggressive military strategy in the early and mid-1950s. First laid out in the strategy document MC-48 (see Documents section), NATO's strategy appeared to rely on the massive, preemptive use of nuclear weapons against Soviet military assets in the first hours of a war. Although the alliance began curtailing some aspects of this strategy in the 1960s, many of its aggressive features remained in place throughout the Cold War. The second NATO choice involved the organization's s role, driven largely by US preferences, as a vehicle to suppress the spread of nuclear weapons within (and outside of) the alliance. One of NATO's most important, yet unstated and largely unrecognized missions, was and remains nuclear nonproliferation.

These dual nuclear missions were often in conflict: a military strategy that relied so heavily on threatening early and massive use of nuclear weapons intensified the desire of NATO members to possess them. These contradictions, and the difficulties spawned by the political and military policies needed to carry out NATO's radical mission, were never fully resolved. The result was decades of tensions and even crisis, involving both alliance members and outside countries. Ironically, however, these same radical policies helped stabilize geopolitics in what was once the world's cauldron of war, Central Europe.

NATO NEEDS A STRATEGY

NATO's early efforts to develop a military strategy have been effectively laid out by several scholars, notably Robert Wampler, David Rosenberg, and especially Marc Trachtenberg.[4] But the narrative is worth repeating. Early postwar plans to defend Western Europe, which preceded NATO, were rather simplistic. They recognized an essential asymmetry between the East and the West: the Soviet Union had an overwhelming superiority in conventional military power, which might allow it to overrun and dominate the European Continent. The United States had a monopoly on atomic weapons. It did not, however, possess a large number of bombs, which were unassembled and not married to delivery capabilities. While the means to deliver the weapons and their destructive capacity were limited compared to what was to come, the United States believed, or rather hoped, that the threat of using the bomb was enough to deter a Russian attack while Western Europe recovered. Should deterrence fail and war ensue, the United States would unleash its stockpile of atomic bombs on Russia while mobilizing its industrial base to fight and win a longer war. Such a Soviet attack was not expected, however, given that Russia was itself recovering from the devastation of war.

The unexpected testing of a nuclear device by the Soviet Union in August 1949 upended those assumptions. If both superpowers had the bomb, wouldn't their weapons cancel each other out? In other words, could the United States be expected to launch an atomic assault on Russia if it would be hit by devastating attacks in return? And even if the United States were willing to take such risks, from where would it launch these attacks, and how would it return and liberate the Continent? The United States and its Western European allies faced a dire prospect: Europe quickly overrun by Soviet conventional military power, the United States held off by Soviet atomic power, and the enormous resources of the captured Continent exploited. Even without a war, this strategic reality was bound to cast a shadow over Europe, possibly leading to an unwelcome drift toward accommodation and neutrality vis-à-vis the Soviets. These disturbing scenarios seemed even more plausible after the North Korean invasion of South Korea in June 1950, and the People's Republic of China's subsequent intervention against UN forces led by the United States. The Sino-Soviet bloc appeared united, and atomic weapons seemed to make it more aggressive. Western Europe was exposed and vulnerable, and the Communist powers appeared on the move, all while a large portion of America's forces were pinned down on the Korean peninsula.

One possible response was to try to match Soviet conventional power. In fact, early NATO goals called for just that: a force of ninety divisions, just enough, it was hoped, to keep Western Europe from being overrun. But this goal proved out of reach for NATO members, for financial and political reasons.

NATO faced a profound strategic challenge: an alliance with weak, recovering states, led by a superpower an ocean away filled with deep ambivalence about any permanent military commitment to Europe. A further challenge was that the greatest reservoir of unexploited military power lay in West Germany, a divided and occupied country less than a decade removed from the end of World War II and the demise of nazism. Any effort to build up and exploit this unused power was bound to create political difficulties of the highest order, both vis-à-vis the Soviets and within NATO.

NATO's response was a military strategy eventually laid out in MC-48. This strategy was deeply intertwined with both complex negotiations over the political and military status of the Federal Republic of Germany (FRG) and the nuclear strategy of the United States.[5] It had several components. First, West Germany's untapped military power had to be exploited if NATO was to have any chance of stopping a Soviet onslaught. But this policy carried enormous risks. Would the FRG's neighbors, both allies and adversaries, accept West German rearmament so soon after the war? How would rearmament affect West German behavior and ambitions? The collapse of the European Defense Community negotiations in 1954 demonstrated how complicated and volatile the "German question" was. The issue was not just the recent memory of the horrors of World War II and the Holocaust. Even a truly reformed, repentant FRG was not a status-quo state. It was divided, and presumably one of its primary goals would be reunification. How might that square with the objectives of other European powers (and Russia) that were not displeased by the status quo?

The second issue was that rearmament would require limitations and controls on German power. The FRG could not have complete freedom to pursue whatever foreign policy it wanted, nor could it have its own nuclear weapons, restrictions that were enunciated in a series of political agreements reached in 1954. But how could the FRG's limited political and especially military status be maintained? The rest of NATO would demand a strong American presence to keep a lid on German ambitions. Would West Germany accept such discrimination, given the resentment that similar restrictions had produced in interwar Germany? Would the United States, long allergic to such obligations, be willing to commit forces to the Continent in large enough numbers, and for a sufficiently long term, to make its European allies (and again the Russians) comfortable with a semisovereign West German state and a revived army? And how might the Soviets, emboldened by their acquisition of atomic power, react to this new arrangement? None of these questions could be answered with confidence as the strategy was developed and implemented.

The military challenges for NATO were as daunting as the political issues. First, the alliance confronted a Soviet conventional superiority that it was not likely to match. Despite the loss of the nuclear monopoly, atomic weapons were bound to be part of any military strategy. How would they be employed? Second, to ensure West German participation, the FRG would have to be defended as best as possible at the intra-German border; West Germany was unlikely to participate in a plan that ceded its territory in the first days of the conflict. Better still, from the German perspective, would be to attack Warsaw Pact military assets before they even reached the border with the FRG.

The military strategy that ensued—both from MC-48 and from the US efforts (including President Dwight D. Eisenhower's Solarium exercise to explore different possible strategies) that produced the "New Look," or massive-retaliation, policy—was truly radical. It contained both preemptive and counterforce elements. In order to defeat a Soviet attack, nuclear weapons would have to be used early—even, it was hinted, when it was clear that the Soviets were invading but before any actual shots had been fired. The key, however, would be to incapacitate or blunt the USSR's ability to respond with its own nuclear weapons. This meant that Soviet nuclear assets would have to be targeted.[6] The United States would not simply react, slowly, as the war developed, biding its time and slowly mobilizing for a war of attrition. Instead, it would react as soon as possible, perhaps as soon as it became clear that war was imminent.

It is important to keep in mind what NATO's military strategy was not: it was not passive or reactive, nor did it rely on the concept of mutual assured destruction (MAD). Instead, it was a strategy that contemplated massive use of nuclear weapons against specific Soviet military targets at the start of a war. The number of weapons, the sophistication of the delivery systems, and the intelligence capabilities needed to implement such a strategy were extraordinary, far beyond what would be required if NATO had adopted a less ambitious strategy or if the United States was only defending itself. More worrisome, this strategy, and the military force needed to carry it out, would look highly threatening to the Soviets; it could even be interpreted as a first-strike, or preemptive, force.

The strategy was only possible because the United States implemented a massive military buildup, as called for in the April 1950 document NSC-68 and applied in the years after China's intervention in the Korean conflict. The US defense budget was almost quadrupled, and most of the funds went to building nuclear weapons and delivery systems. In 1952, the United States successfully tested thermonuclear weapons, leading to massive increases in the destructive capacity of the American stockpile. This military shield, it was hoped, would deter the Soviets while NATO developed and implemented its sweeping transformation. The strategy also required a complex set of political trade-offs and compromises developed in 1954: a significant American military commitment to allow West German rearmament to take place despite significant limitations on the political and military independence of the Federal Republic of Germany. The vision behind General Hastings Ismay's oft-cited comment—that the goal of NATO was to keep the Americans in, the Russians out, and the Germans down—was to be realized, though at considerable risk and cost.

The combination of massive retaliation and MC-48 was, by all measures, successful. Western Europe recovered politically, economically, and militarily, the Soviets were deterred, and the danger of war appeared to recede. By the mid-1950s, stability and confidence began to replace panic in Central Europe. NATO's military strategy, however, contained the seeds of its own demise. What would happen if and when the United States grew tired of its expensive military commitment to Western Europe? What if the West Germans resisted the political and military restrictions placed upon them? The most pressing short-term concern was the Soviet reaction to the strategy. What if the USSR responded with its own military buildup, developing the ability to strike quickly and decisively with nuclear weapons, not just in Western Europe but also in the continental United States? The launch of Russia's Sputnik satellite in 1957, and the ensuing fears of both a bomber and a missile gap between the two superpowers, highlighted the worrying fact that the preemptive nuclear strategy that was at the military and political heart of the NATO strategy would last only as long as the United States and its Strategic Air Command could credibly threaten a first strike.

Thus, the conventional wisdom, while acknowledging the aggressive nature of MC-48 and massive retaliation, argues that it was a short-lived strategy. Even by the end of the Eisenhower administration, and certainly by the

Kennedy/Johnson period, this aggressive strategy fell out of favor. Building on the work of many of its critics, NATO adopted a more nuanced, fine-tuned strategy that came to be called "flexible response." This strategy was first laid out by US Secretary of Defense Robert McNamara in a secret speech to NATO defense Ministers in Athens, Greece, in the spring of 1962. Formally embraced as NATO strategy in MC-14/3 in January 1968, it was supposed to be a dramatic break with the past. The US promise to defend Western Europe with its strategic nuclear weapons was seen as problematic. The confrontations with the Soviet Union in 1958 and 1961 over the status of West Berlin had revealed that there were crisis scenarios where employing military forces at a far lower level of the escalatory ladder might be appropriate. Flexible response was supposed to be a strategy that relied far more on conventional forces, that paused before using nuclear weapons, and that resisted rapid escalation. Furthermore, as the 1960s and 1970s progressed, there seemed to be at least a public embrace in certain strategic and policy circles of the idea of "mutual vulnerability," a condition of mutual assured destruction between the superpowers.

As I have written elsewhere, there is evidence that the differences between the older NATO strategy and the new one were overdrawn.[7] The strategic nuclear plans of the United States, which were the backbone of any NATO military strategy against the Soviet Union, still appeared to contain preemptive and counterforce elements. Despite lots of pressure, NATO never came close to embracing a "no-first-use" doctrine. Nor did the United States ever permanently forgo its efforts to achieve the nuclear primacy needed to make NATO's radical nuclear strategy plausible. For example, the United States spent hundreds of billions of dollars on nuclear forces, delivery capabilities, and targeting intelligence in the later years of the Cold War, well after it had achieved quantitative parity with the Soviet nuclear arsenal. These enormous resources weren't spent to increase the sheer numbers or destructive capabilities of the weapons, both of which were restricted by strategic arms limitation treaties with the Soviets (SALT I and SALT II). Instead, the money went into making US forces faster, more accurate, and better able to survive a Soviet nuclear attack. Furthermore, the United States increased its ability to locate, target, and destroy Soviet nuclear forces by developing such weapons as the Pershing II, Trident D5, and MX missiles, the B-1 bomber, and C3I (command, control, communication, and intelligence) procedures, as well as the ability to attack Soviet submarines with nuclear weapons (antisubmarine warfare, or ASW). These forces were the backbone of a counterforce strategy whose emphasis on intelligence, accuracy, speed, and hard-target capabilities seemed to indicate that it retained its preemptive qualities.[8] A strategy based on MAD which assumed that NATO and the United States would take action against enemy civilian targets after absorbing a nuclear first strike would not demand such technologically advanced, sophisticated, and expensive systems. Why build these forces, at such financial and political cost, if your strategy was based on mutual vulnerability?

NATO's strategy was not driven solely by aggressive or imperial instincts on the part of the United States; in fact, top American decision-makers often resented and tried to lessen or end the alliance's commitment to nuclear deterrence. Nor was the strategy the result of bureaucratic, organizational, or ideological factors alone. It was not, to cite one of our foremost scholars of nuclear strategy, "illogical."[9] Instead, the strategy was driven by the same political and military puzzle that was present at the start of the thermonuclear age and persisted for decades: how could NATO deter the Soviet Union and defend Western Europe by relying on West German economic and military power, without allowing it to develop its own nuclear weapons? If the strategy accepted nuclear parity, or MAD, as a "fact," there was little reason for the FRG to take seriously NATO's promise to defend it. If the FRG were to pursue the logical next step and acquire its own nuclear weapons, the consequences might be grave indeed.

WHAT IS GOOD FOR ME IS NOT GOOD FOR YOU

If NATO retained elements of a preemptive, nuclear-intensive strategy, why did the rhetoric of the alliance change in the 1960s and beyond? Why did both the United States and NATO try to distance themselves from the ideas they had embraced during the 1950s?

There is no doubt that some of the more aggressive elements of the early NATO strategy were reined in, in part because of the influence such a forward-leaning strategy had on nuclear proliferation. NATO's strategy prioritized nuclear weapons, making it clear they and not other types of armaments were what mattered in the modern world. Tanks, planes, and divisions were fine, but such assets were not decisive in conflict. States that didn't possess nuclear weapons would be relegated, almost by definition, to second-rate status. The centrality of nuclear weapons in NATO's plans made it hard to argue, as many advocates of nuclear nonproliferation contended, that such weapons were ugly, immoral, or irrelevant.

Another factor in NATO's rhetorical shift was the nature of the strategy itself: if nuclear weapons were to be used very early in any conflict, almost preemptively, then the decision about when and how to use them would have to be predelegated from the highest political levels down to commanders on the battlefield. There would be very little time for national legislatures to debate whether to go to war or not. Decisions would have to be made in hours, not days or weeks, and national leaders would have to rely on military officials on the scene. And NATO, as an integrated military organization, might find high-ranking military officials from any number of states, including West Germany, involved in these decisions.[10]

We now know that West German officials consciously sought not to foreclose the option of developing their own atomic bomb. They also pressured the United States to give them some say over nuclear decision-making within NATO, as well as access to and control over the weapons. This initiative—to which President Eisenhower was personally sympathetic—generated grave tensions with the Soviet Union and concern within the alliance itself. Even those who did not share Eisenhower's view that a nuclearized Bundeswehr was both inevitable and not disastrous, recognized that the question had to be handled carefully. There was a widespread fear of the consequences of blatantly treating West Germany's nuclear ambitions differently than, say, France's and Great Britain's.

As the 1960s progressed, broader concerns over the consequences of unchecked nuclear proliferation grew.[11] West Germany's potential nuclearization was, because of its history and geopolitical situation, in a category by itself. By the late 1950s, the Soviet Union made it clear that it would not accept a West Germany with the bomb. This was the driving issue behind the great crisis period of 1958–1962, and by 1963 the United States agreed. But the prospect of other nations acquiring the bomb, either within the NATO alliance (say, Italy) or outside (say, India, China, Japan, Sweden, or Australia), was a cause for concern. How long could NATO expect West Germany to remain non-nuclear if less important states like Sweden or Israel had atomic weapons? There was also a fear of nuclear "tipping points," or dominoes, whereby if one key state acquired the bomb, several others might as well.[12] Not only would this potentially make the world more dangerous, the United States in particular was worried that nuclear weapons would be used to *deter* it. As a result, nuclear nonproliferation became a far higher US strategic interest, and its policies in this area became more vigorous. By the end of the

1960s, after remarkable cooperation with its adversary, the Soviet Union, a Nuclear Non-Proliferation Treaty was signed.

The US nuclear nonproliferation policy was in some tension with NATO's forward-leaning nuclear strategy.[13] Various efforts were made to bridge this gap, such as the ill-fated Multilateral Force initiative and the Nuclear Planning Group. The strategy of flexible response, with its stated emphasis on the need for centralized control of nuclear decision-making, was also an effort to ease proliferation pressures within the alliance. The Kennedy and Johnson administrations were undoubtedly alarmed by the rather loose controls and predelegation orders they inherited in NATO's nuclear plans. But it was not lost on European observers such as the French and even the British that requiring centralized control was an argument against independent nuclear programs.

On the other hand, NATO's radical military strategy served a nonproliferation purpose. If West Germany and other non-nuclear NATO states were to eschew the bomb, they would have to be convinced that the strategy would deter an attack and protect them should war come. The credibility of America's nuclear umbrella, its extended deterrent guarantee, would be (and was) doubted in an age of nuclear parity, especially if the Soviet Union retained a significant edge in conventional capabilities.[14] To a certain extent, this was a problem that simply had to be accepted. But a strategy could be devised, and forces developed, that at least made a military defense of Europe against a Soviet invasion plausible. If the United States had hundreds of thousands of conventional forces on the front lines of any battle, it would be hard to disentangle them from the conflict. And if the US continued to build a force that made a counterforce, preemptive nuclear strike *plausible,* not to say wise, if all other options failed, this could enhance deterrence. West Germany first and foremost, but also others inside and outside the NATO alliance, might make the calculation that US security guarantees were, if not as effective a deterrent as their own nuclear weapons, good enough, and would come without all the complications, costs, and controversies that a national nuclear weapons program would bring.

This narrative, stressing both the continuing elements of NATO's radical strategy through the end of the Cold War and the linkage between this strategy and nuclear nonproliferation, is more speculative than one would like. We don't have as many documents for the 1970s and 1980s as for earlier periods, and most documents involving both nuclear weapons and the German question are likely to remain classified for the foreseeable future. Furthermore, the deep sensitivity surrounding these questions, and the treatment by the United States of its closest allies, often produced a euphemistic language to avoid hurt feelings (for instance, the phrase "European stability" became a cover for the German question). The argument for this later period is supported less by historical evidence than by an appreciation of the logic of nuclear weapons and their profound influence on international affairs. But the documents, once they become available, may well tell a different story.

CONSTANT CRISIS TO GENERATE STABILITY

Efforts were undertaken to make NATO's military plans more flexible and less frightening. The 1967 Harmel Report and the ensuing MC-14/3 document officially enshrined aspects of flexible response into NATO's war planning, though again the degree of change has often been overstated. In some ways, however, the specifics of the strategy are less important than the overall logic. Relying on the nuclear umbrella of the United States, NATO's embrace of extended deterrence was guaranteed to generate continual crisis, both within the alliance and vis-à-vis the Soviets.[15] This tension was felt between the United States and its European NATO partners, among NATO's European powers, between NATO and the Warsaw Pact, and within the United States itself.

In hindsight, it's clear that this sense of perpetual crisis was in the DNA of NATO's radical strategy. Consider the position of the Federal Republic of Germany within the alliance. The West Germans resented being discriminated against in the nuclear field, especially as Great Britain and France developed their own weapons. Why should they be singled out, especially when NATO's strategy emphasized nuclear weapons? American policymakers were keenly aware that the failure to impose military restrictions on Germany during the interwar period had played a role in the rise of the Third Reich. Nevertheless, any efforts by NATO or the United States to reassure the FRG on this point by giving them access to nuclear weapons produced complaints by the Russians and other European countries. To generate the reassurance necessary to keep West Germany content, the United States had to deploy large numbers of conventional forces.

NATO's strategy also generated tension within the United States. The expense of maintaining these conventional forces, in both budgetary and balance-of-payments terms, provoked constant complaints among American policymakers. Keeping several hundred thousand US troops and their families in West Germany, while the Vietnam War and other conflicts raged and

America's economic woes put pressure on budgets and currency reserves, tested the political capabilities of several administrations.[16] The whole NATO strategy of extended deterrence was predicated on meaningful United States nuclear superiority and a willingness to use nuclear weapons, if not first, at least early in a conflict. Such an aggressive and potentially dangerous strategy was alarming both to the Soviet Union and to many in the United States.

Many of the crises in NATO's history had one or more of these dynamics as their taproot. In the late 1950s, for example, NATO moved toward allowing West Germany greater access to and control over nuclear weapons. The Soviets responded by initiating the Berlin crises of 1958 and 1961, in part to indicate their great displeasure. By 1963, the United State recognized that NATO could not allow nuclear weapons to fall in the hands of the Federal Republic and, through the mechanism of the Partial Nuclear Test Ban Treaty negotiations in the summer of 1963, came to an agreement on this point with the Soviets. The West German government was deeply upset, and the United States responded by promising to station American troops in the country on a permanent basis. The costs of these troops, however, were onerous, and throughout the 1960s the United States made efforts to pull them out, to the anger of West Germany.[17]

The tensions of the 1970s turned around both these issues and the Soviet achievement of strategic nuclear parity with the United States. How could America's extended deterrent, its willingness to use nuclear weapons if Western Europe was attacked, be carried out if the promise to "trade Chicago for Hamburg" was not credible? As the USSR continued to upgrade its strategic nuclear forces, medium-range missiles, and conventional forces, the sense of crisis deepened. The so called Euromissile crisis generated by the Soviet deployment of massive, rapid SS-20s targeted at Western Europe caused deep anxiety, as did NATO's deployment of Pershing II missiles in response.[18]

Tellingly, NATO's perpetual sense of crisis abated but did not completely go away once the Cold War ended and the supposed target of the alliance's military strategy, the Soviet Union, disappeared. At least one part of NATO's radical strategy, nuclear nonproliferation, presumably remained. Consider the controversial subject of NATO expansion. From its earliest days, the policy was justified by the need to spread stability and democracy to the former Eastern bloc. But consider another (though complementary) logic. Given what we know about the extraordinary power of nuclear weapons to deter conventional invasions, such weapons must have been extraordinarily appealing to a newly independent Poland. Poland's history was scarred by brutal invasions and land grabs by both Germany and Russia, and the prospect of forever ending such a nightmare must have been very appealing. But a Poland with nuclear weapons, no matter how justified and understandable it would have been given its history and interests, would have upset the nuclear nonproliferation regime. More to the point, it would have opened up the awkward question of nuclear weapons in Central Europe, and in particular, a newly unified Germany. Could Germany long remain non-nuclear with nuclear-armed countries to both the east and west? Perhaps, but would anyone really want to risk finding out? Expanding NATO, and a credible US nuclear umbrella, to Poland and other Eastern European countries would arguably address these concerns, at least partially.

The irony of NATO's radical military strategy during the Cold War is that while it created constant crisis and generated both inter- and intra-alliance tension, it was ultimately stabilizing—certainly more so than the alternative strategies the alliance might have chosen. NATO could have attempted to match Soviet conventional capabilities, with potentially ruinous economic and political consequences. Or the United States could have left Western Europe to organize its own defense. As long as nuclear weapons existed, however, and as long as the Soviet Union possessed and demonstrated a willingness to use them, the temptation for Western Europe, and particularly the Federal Republic of Germany, to acquire them would have been enormous. A divided Germany—with nuclear weapons—would have been unacceptable not only to the Soviet Union, but to Great Britain and France as well. A Western alliance would have been difficult if not impossible to create under those circumstances. Eschewing the nuclear route, however, the FRG would have feared domination by the Russians. The drift toward neutrality may have been unavoidable, with all the geopolitical dangers that would bring. In the absence of NATO's radical nuclear strategy, where West Germany was both credibly protected and constrained by American power, the options were not appealing.

The constant crisis and tension produced by NATO's strategy, both within the alliance and with the Soviet Union and the Warsaw Pact, exacted a high price, but it was likely necessary to remedy the difficult and potentially explosive issues surrounding the German problem in a nuclear world.

CONCLUSION

To argue that NATO's nuclear strategy during the Cold War was radical is not necessarily to condemn it. On the one hand, a counterforce, preemptive strategy involved serious risks and dangers. A strategy focused on the utility of nuclear weapons made the bomb more appealing, and efforts to promote nuclear nonproliferation less convincing. In a crisis, NATO's strategy made the dangers of miscalculation or an accident far higher. Furthermore, any effort to establish credibility in a nuclear crisis could have led to dangerous brinkmanship and unthinkable disaster. Even absent such a cataclysm, NATO's radical nuclear strategy demanded extraordinary expenditures to improve targeting, speed, accuracy, survivability, and intelligence. This fueled an expensive and contentious *qualitative* arms race, ironically at the very time that SALT I and SALT II successfully limited the *quantitative* competition in strategic nuclear arms between the superpowers. NATO's strategy was expensive both economically and politically.

On the other hand, the strategy appeared to work. Historians are sensitive to the fact that correlation is not always (or even often) causation, but the Cold War ended on terms favorable to NATO. Germany did not acquire nuclear weapons, and there are far fewer nuclear weapons states around the world than anyone would have predicted or hoped for fifty years ago. Most important, nuclear weapons have never been used by or against NATO, or anyone else for that matter, since 1945. Would a less radical strategy—one based solely on conventional defense, or one that acknowledged and accepted mutual nuclear vulnerability—have produced similar results? We can't know, of course. But merely posing the question highlights how remarkable NATO's history has been.

Notes

1. The best version of this conventional wisdom can be found throughout John Lewis Gaddis, *Strategies of Containment: A Critical Appraisal of American National Security Policy during the Cold War* (New York: Oxford University Press, 2005). See also Robert J. Art, *A Grand Strategy for America* (Ithaca: Cornell University Press, 2003), pp. 214–16.

2. Much of this analysis is based on the pathbreaking work of Marc Trachtenberg. See especially "The Nuclearization of NATO and U.S.–West European Relations" and "The Berlin Crisis" in *History and Strategy* (Princeton: Princeton University Press, 1991), pp. 153–234; and *A Constructed Peace: The Making of the European Settlement, 1945–1963* (Princeton: Princeton University Press, 1997), especially pp. 95–145.

3. Russell F. Weigley, *The American Way of War: A History of United States Military Strategy and Policy* (Bloomington: Indiana University Press, 1960).

4. Robert Wampler, "Ambiguous Legacy: The United States, Great Britain, and the Formulation of NATO Strategy, 1948–1957" (Ph.D. dissertation, Harvard University, 1991); David Alan Rosenberg, "A Smoking Radiating Ruin at the End of Two Hours": Documents on American Plans for Nuclear War with the Soviet Union, 1954–1955," *International Security*, Volume 6, Number 3 (Winter 1981/1982), pp. 3–38; David Alan Rosenberg, "The Origins of Overkill: Nuclear Weapons and American Strategy, 1945–1960," *International Security*, Volume 7, Number 4 (Spring 1983), pp. 3–71.

5. Dr. Gregory W. Pedlow, chief, Historical Office Supreme Headquarters Allied Powers Europe, in collaboration with NATO International Staff Central Archives, NATO Strategy Documents, 1949–1969, available at http://www.nato.int/archives/strategy.htm.

6. Trachtenberg, "The Nuclearization of NATO."

7. Francis J. Gavin, *Nuclear Statecraft: History and Strategy in America's Atomic Age* (Ithaca: Cornell University Press, 2012), pp. 30–56.

8. Austin Long and Brendan Rittenhouse Green, "Stalking the Secure Second Strike: Intelligence, Counterforce, and Nuclear Strategy," *Journal of Strategic Studies*, Volume 38 (2015), pp. 1–2, 38–73, doi: 10.1080/01402390.2014.958150.

9. Robert Jervis, *The Illogic of American Nuclear Strategy* (Ithaca: Cornell University Press, 1984).

10. Trachtenberg, "The Nuclearization of NATO."

11. Francis J. Gavin, "Blasts from the Past: Proliferation Lessons from the 1960s," *International Security*, Volume 29, Number 3 (Winter 2004/2005), pp. 100–135. See also Shane J. Maddock, *Nuclear Apartheid: The Quest for American Atomic Supremacy from World War II to the Present* (Chapel Hill: University of North Carolina Press, 2010).

12. Nicholas L. Miller, "The Secret Success of Nonproliferation Sanctions. International Organization," available on CJO2014. doi:10.1017/S0020818314000216.

13. Susanna Schrafstetter and Stephen Twigge, *Avoiding Armageddon: Europe, the United States, and the Struggle for Nuclear Nonproliferation, 1945–1970* (Westport, CT: Praeger Press, 2004).

14. Many analysts overstated Soviet superiority in conventional capabilities throughout the Cold War, insisting that from the early 1960s on NATO forces could have likely withstood a Soviet invasion of Western Europe without immediate recourse to nuclear weapons. See, for example, John J. Mearsheimer, "Why the Soviets Can't Win Quickly in Central Europe," *International Security*, Volume 7, Number 1 (Summer 1982), pp. 3–39.

15. A Google search on "NATO" and "crisis" yields 26 million hits.

16. Francis J. Gavin, *Gold, Dollars, and Power: The Politics of International Monetary Relations, 1958–1971* (Chapel Hill: University of North Carolina Press, 2004).

17. These stories can be found in Gavin, *Gold, Dollars, and Power* and Trachtenberg, *A Constructed Peace*.

18. On the Euromissile crisis, see Leopoldo Nuti's excellent edited volume *The Euromissile Crisis and the End of the Cold War* (forthcoming).

Chapter 2

NATO and Nuclear Proliferation, 1949–1968

Alexandre Debs and Nuno P. Monteiro

Nuclear nonproliferation is among the foreign-policy objectives that Washington has pursued more consistently over the past few decades. Perhaps counterintuitively, US security alliances feature prominently among the tools Washington has used to contain the spread of nuclear weapons.

Recent US nonproliferation efforts have focused mostly on American allies in East Asia and the Middle East. In East Asia, the development of the North Korean nuclear weapons capability over the last decade has led to reinvigorated US security guarantees to South Korea in order to maintain its non-nuclear status. Likewise, Iranian progress toward a nuclear capability until the "Iran Deal"—the 2015 Joint Comprehensive Plan of Action— generated considerable worry that Saudi Arabia would follow suit, acquiring its own nuclear deterrent.[1]

In Europe, concerns over proliferation have remained milder. For decades now, no European country has actively attempted to develop nuclear weapons. Yet, NATO played a key role in deterring the further spread of nuclear weapons among Washington's European allies during the first two decades of the alliance, between 1949 and 1968. In the immediate aftermath of World War II, US desire to decrease its conventional forces in Europe led Washington to emphasize the role of atomic weapons in deterring Soviet aggression. With Moscow's acquisition of nuclear weapons in 1949, and its successful launch of Sputnik in 1957, however, concerns emerged over Washington's willingness to "go nuclear" in retaliation against a Soviet invasion of Western Europe. This new strategic situation, in turn, increased pressure on European NATO members to build their own independent nuclear arsenals.

Doubting US guarantees of protection and eager to maintain independent foreign policies, Great Britain and France acquired nuclear weapons in 1952 and 1960, respectively. Both the United States and the Soviet Union largely acquiesced to their nuclearization. In fact, through the mid-1960s Washington contemplated nuclear sharing agreements with its NATO allies in order to lower their willingness to build the bomb. But when the Soviets manifested staunch opposition to any nuclear sharing arrangements based on concerns that this would facilitate an independent German nuclear force, the United States dropped its sharing plans and coerced Bonn into abandoning its nuclear ambitions. The Nuclear Non-Proliferation Treaty (NPT) is at least partly the byproduct of these coordinated efforts by the two superpowers to coerce Germany into remaining non-nuclear.[2]

As the recently empowered Donald Trump administration devises its nuclear and alliance policies, these events remind us of the role played by US security guarantees in deterring the further spread of nuclear weapons. Without firm commitments from Washington to their security, US allies such as Germany, Japan, or South Korea are more likely to (re)initiate their nuclear development efforts. This, in turn, would lead our common adversaries to redouble their security efforts, including redoubling their own nuclear efforts. In the end, a policy that aims at decreasing US commitments to the security of others and the costs they entail might well have the opposite effect, requiring Washington to spend more in order to keep an effective deterrent.

In this chapter, we shed light on the motivations behind US nonproliferation efforts within NATO between 1949 and 1968, when negotiations for the NPT were concluded. Until the mid-1960s, American efforts to prevent the spread of the bomb were relatively mild. From then on, Washington followed a two-pronged nonproliferation approach within NATO. On the one hand, the United States reinforced its commitment to the security of any ally considering nuclear weapons. On the other hand, US policymakers emphasized how this commitment was conditional on the abandonment of their ally's nuclear ambitions. To understand NATO's role in stymieing proliferation among its members, we highlight these efforts describing their different intensity and, ultimately, their different degree of success in the French and West German cases. In our view, the United States acquiesced to French nuclear acquisition while strongly opposing German efforts to get the bomb because, whereas French nuclearization was of no great concern to Moscow, German nuclearization might result in a conflict with the Soviet Union. We then establish the role NATO had on the nuclear ambitions of other, non-NATO US allies by looking at two of these: Sweden and Israel. Whereas in the case of Sweden NATO dampened pressure for nuclear acquisition, in the case of Israel, it bolstered proliferation pressure.

NATO AND NUCLEAR PROLIFERATION, 1949–1968

Facing a conventionally superior Soviet Union in Europe, the United States relied on the threat of nuclear retaliation to deter aggression against its NATO allies. During President Dwight D. Eisenhower's administration, this led to the development of a doctrine of "massive retaliation," promising to react to any Soviet attack on Western Europe with a nuclear response en masse. At the same time, Eisenhower implemented an "Atoms for Peace" policy, sharing civilian nuclear technology with allies while demanding that they not use it for military goals. This approach raised a challenge for nuclear nonproliferation. The threat of US massive retaliation might not be deemed credible by NATO allies, who might take advantage of US cooperation with their civilian nuclear programs to acquire the bomb. Eisenhower, however, thought that industrially advanced NATO allies would inevitably develop their own nuclear weapons and share the burden of defending Western Europe, and so did not put much stock in nonproliferation efforts.[3] In fact, Eisenhower loosened the Atomic Energy Act of 1946, allowing NATO allies to access information on the "external characteristics of nuclear weapons," to train in their use, and to obtain fissionable materials and sensitive information.[4] By 1960, the year France acquired nuclear weapons, Eisenhower supported increased European control over NATO's nuclear forces, stating, "we should not deny to our allies what the enemies, what your potential enemy already has."[5] That year, the administration developed the concept of a multilateral force (MLF), a sea-based force armed with US nuclear warheads and operated by international NATO crews under joint NATO control with a US veto.[6]

The Kennedy administration put forth a different US nuclear policy. To counter proliferation, President John F. Kennedy pushed for the Partial Test Ban Treaty (PTBT), which was ratified in 1963, and laid the foundations for the NPT.[7] At the same time, Kennedy adopted a policy of "flexible response," promising to react to an eventual Soviet conventional attack on NATO allies by relying mostly on conventional weapons and only gradually introducing nuclear options. This doctrine attempted to improve the credibility of US threats of retaliation, alleviating pressures for nuclear proliferation among European NATO members.

In practice, however, the policies of the Kennedy administration retained important points of continuity with those of its predecessor. To begin with, Kennedy opposed the conventional buildup that flexible response required and instead attempted to reduce the number of US troops in Europe.[8] At the same time, attempting to centralize US nuclear decision-making with that of its European NATO allies, Kennedy endorsed the MLF.[9]

President Lyndon Johnson initially maintained this same approach, hoping the MLF would satiate appetite for the spread of nuclear weapons within NATO. Both the Soviet Union and other European US allies, however, having fought Germany in two world wars over the previous half-century, were concerned that the MLF would serve as a route to proliferation and, specifically, give Germany the ability to issue independent nuclear threats. This concern might lead to preventive Soviet action, which in turn might entrap the United States in a European conflict. To avoid this risk, the United States gradually turned away from the MLF between 1964 and 1966 and then pushed for a nonproliferation agreement with the Soviet Union, eventually resulting in the NPT, whereby nuclear powers agreed to renounce nuclear sharing, and non-nuclear-weapons states agreed to forgo any attempt to acquire their own nuclear arsenal, subject to inspections. Faced with US threats of abandonment if it insisted on its nuclear pursuit, West Germany relented, giving up its nuclear ambitions.

Taking stock, when NPT negotiations were concluded by the late 1960s, US nuclear nonproliferation policy within the NATO context had changed from a relatively benign view of the spread of nuclear weapons among its European allies to a strong effort to avoid proliferation within NATO, which went as far as colluding with the Soviet Union in the creation of the NPT in order to avoid nuclear acquisition by West Germany. By the end of the first two decades after the ratification of the North Atlantic Treaty, three of the alliance's most important European members had reached opposite outcomes in their paths to nuclearization. Whereas Britain and France had acquired independent nuclear arsenals, West Germany had been coerced by the United States to abandon its nuclear ambitions.

France

France's nuclear program, initiated at the end of World War II, culminated with the first test of a nuclear weapon in 1960. Its quick progress in the 1950s is inextricably connected to growing French skepticism about the reliability of US security guarantees in defending both global French interests and the French mainland itself.

On October 18, 1945, Charles de Gaulle, president of the provisional government, set up the Atomic Energy Commission (CEA). While the CEA was legally set up to oversee both the civilian and military applications of nuclear energy, it was initially committed to the peaceful uses of nuclear energy.[10] During the discussions over the international control of nuclear weapons at the United Nations in June 1946, French ambassador Alexandre Parodi claimed that the French nuclear program was purely for civilian uses.[11] In March 1950, the high commissioner of the CEA, Frédéric Joliot-Curie, signed the Stockholm Appeal calling for a ban on nuclear weapons.[12] Joliot-Curie, a member of the French Communist Party, declared at the party congress the following month that "[n]ever will progressive scientists and Communist scientists contribute one iota of their science to war against the Soviet Union."[13] Such actions caused a stir in French and American media, and by the end of April, Joliot-Curie was fired.

Political developments in the next few years, starting with a change in NATO policy, encouraged France to pursue the military applications of nuclear energy. In January 1954, US Secretary of State John Foster Dulles announced a new strategy for NATO, the "New Look," which promised an automatic massive atomic retaliation in response to a hypothetical Soviet invasion of Western Europe. Such a policy decreased the value of French conventional forces and boosted the case made that only nuclearization would reinstate France to the major-power club.[14] In a note to French Prime Minister Pierre Mendès France later that year, diplomat Jean-Marie Boegner explained that "national independence, and the autonomy of our diplomacy, on which the survival of the French union depends to a large extent, requires France to pursue its own efforts in the development of military applications of nuclear energy."[15]

French leaders were becoming increasingly anxious about their strategic dependency on the United States in light of the sharply different views on foreign policy priorities held in Washington and Paris. The French defeat at Dien Bien Phu was a particularly traumatic experience. In the spring of 1954, French troops were fighting to maintain control over Indochina. To counter a Viet Minh attack on Dien Bien Phu, they requested American air support. President Eisenhower, however, declined to support them, virtually guaranteeing a French defeat and exposing the inadequacy of alliances in protecting

French global interests.[16] French military leaders were convinced that tactical nuclear weapons might have prevented their loss at Dien Bien Phu.[17] Furthermore, defeat in Indochina exemplified how the Soviet threat might manifest itself through sponsored independence movements rather than an assault on Western Europe. This made nuclear weapons necessary both to deter Soviet support to these movements and to secure the French mainland if the country's conventional military were forced to fight them overseas.[18] Before the year was over, Prime Minister Mendès France made the key decision to advance toward building an atomic bomb.[19] On December 26, Mendès France convened a meeting at the Quai d'Orsay with all the relevant policymakers, about forty in total, to discuss the possibility of a nuclear weapons program. Mendès France approved such a program, and two days later a new division was created within the CEA, the Bureau d'études générales, to pursue the military applications of nuclear energy.[20] The French nuclear program was now clearly geared toward building a bomb.

Developments in the mid- to late 1950s only reinforced growing French skepticism toward US security guarantees. In the summer of 1956, Washington again undermined Paris's pursuit of its foreign policy aims. In July, Egyptian President Gamal Abdel Nasser nationalized the Suez Canal. France and Britain were determined to recapture the canal and devised a plan to do so, in alliance with Israel. In late October they launched their operation, but a week later the Soviets threatened nuclear attack on all three countries.[21] Washington threatened Moscow with retaliation against nuclear attacks on Britain or France, while at the same time coercing its allies to end hostilities. Soon they capitulated to US pressure.[22] For de Gaulle, the Suez Crisis showed that "American nuclear power does not necessarily and immediately meet all the eventualities concerning France and Europe."[23] The crisis thus clearly exemplified the divergence of interests between Washington and Paris and the lack of credibility of US guarantees that French decision-makers had earlier feared; it also shifted public preferences in favor of the bomb.[24] In November and December 1956, the administration of Guy Mollet intensified efforts to prepare for a nuclear test.[25]

By 1958, with Washington publicly supporting national independence movements, the Fourth Republic disintegrated over violence in Algeria. France felt diplomatically isolated.[26] Its possessions in North Africa, the Mediterranean, and the DOM-TOM (Départements et territoires d'outre mer) were considered vital interests, integral to the "metaphysical survival" of the nation.[27] Washington, however, considered that French overseas operations "seriously weakened the [NATO] alliance."[28] The United States therefore offered to protect only the French mainland from unprovoked attack, undermining French goals in Africa.[29]

US protection of the French mainland, however, was itself becoming increasingly dubious. In October 1957, Sputnik had demonstrated the Soviets' ability to target the United States with a nuclear warhead, leading to a reevaluation of NATO nuclear strategy, "whereby a massive retaliation against Soviet cities thereafter would be seen only as a last resort option."[30] As de Gaulle would later put it to President Kennedy, this meant "the United States would use nuclear weapons only if its own territory was directly threatened."[31]

In April 1958, Félix Gaillard, president of the Council of Ministers, signed a decision to test a nuclear device by the first trimester of 1960.[32] The program was on track for a nuclear test when de Gaulle took office in June 1958.[33] That same year, when faced with a French request for nuclear assistance, Secretary Dulles refused it, invoking the potential for strategic instability generated by proliferation among its allies.[34] In a June 30, 1958, meeting, Dulles added that Washington was committed to the defense of the "free world on terms that would deny nuclear power where it might be subject to possible irresponsible use."[35] Resenting the implication, France withdrew from NATO's military structure in 1959, and on February 13, 1960, France tested its first nuclear weapon.[36]

Overall, NATO played an important role in the initial motivation for the French nuclear weapons program.[37] NATO also affected the role that French policymakers assigned to an eventual nuclear arsenal. In the Fourth Republic, most of the French decision-makers were interested in developing a nuclear arsenal that would be integrated in NATO forces. For a brief period in 1957–1958, France considered developing nuclear weapons jointly with Italy and West Germany, sharing the cost of a program and allowing for a Continental voice within NATO.[38] Clearly, de Gaulle went further than his predecessors in pressing for French autonomy. Yet there was an important continuity between policymakers in the Fourth and Fifth Republics. All key policymakers concluded that nuclear weapons served the national interest.[39] The core issue was that France felt it needed greater freedom of action in deciding which security goals to pursue.

NATO also played an enabling role for France's nuclear weapons program, by providing a nuclear umbrella. As politicians in both Paris and Moscow were aware, French nuclearization did not increase the overall threat faced by the Soviets. It merely complicated Moscow's calculus when its actions impacted French interests not shared by Washington. As Soviet Premier Nikita Khrushchev would later say to the French: "Your atomic force is made to annoy the Americans."[40] In contrast, a counterproliferation attack on France would be extremely risky, possibly escalating into a nuclear exchange between the superpowers. Given the small consequences of French nuclearization, and the high cost of a preventive attack against France, Moscow adopted an accommodating posture toward French nuclear ambitions.[41]

In sum, France nuclearized to guarantee its ability to secure both its own homeland and its interests abroad. An independent *force de frappe* boosted Paris's ability to further its goals in at least three ways. First, it made clear to the Soviet Union that any threat of attack on the French homeland would be met with a nuclear retaliation. Second, it immunized Paris against nuclear coercion when pursuing its interests abroad. Finally, it freed up French conventional forces to pursue global goals while guaranteeing the mainland's security. As de Gaulle put it, the *force de frappe* was "the only effective way of ensuring [France's] territorial integrity and political independence."[42]

West Germany

West Germany considered the nuclear option in the 1950s and 1960s. As the frontline NATO state facing the Soviet Union, West Germany had good reason to value an autonomous nuclear deterrent. Yet, at the same time, West Germany's survival and its ability to develop a nuclear weapon without suffering a Soviet preventive attack depended on US protection. When Washington understood the potential that German proliferation had to provoke a Soviet military reaction, it coerced Bonn into forfeiting its nuclear ambitions.

Following its creation in 1949 and its recognition as a sovereign state six years later, the Federal Republic of Germany sought to reunify with East Germany. The East, however, remained within the orbit of the Soviet Union, a much stronger enemy that enjoyed a preponderance of conventional power in Central Europe. To ensure its survival, Bonn relied on Washington, pledging in the initial aftermath of acquiring full sovereignty in 1955 to remain non-nuclear.[43]

The United States saw the protection of West Germany and of Western Europe more generally as a key global interest, given the region's geographical proximity to Soviet territory and its economic potential. Consequently, the United States committed significant resources to the European theater with the Marshall Plan and the creation of NATO.[44] Yet doubts soon emerged about the reliability of US commitments. In 1955 the Carte Blanche war games estimated the number of German citizens who would be killed or injured in a superpower conflict at 5 million.[45] In July 1956, the Radford plan, which stated Washington's intentions to withdraw 800,000 troops from the Continent and rely more heavily on nuclear weapons, was leaked to the press.[46]

These developments caused great alarm in Bonn. Chancellor Konrad Adenauer declared to the press that he opposed a policy where "America is a fortress for itself, because that would mean that we would be outside that fortress."[47] He wrote to Secretary of State Dulles on July 22, 1956, that as a result of the Radford plan, "Europe, including Germany, has lost its confidence in the United States' reliability."[48] In September 1956, Adenauer declared that "Germany cannot remain a nuclear protectorate."[49] Consequently, he vowed to acquire "the most modern weapons" for West Germany.[50] The following month, Franz Josef Strauss was named minister of defense, and both men committed to acquiring nuclear weapons.

The Soviet Union's successful launch of Sputnik in October 1957 further exacerbated Bonn's security concerns. West Germany held bilateral talks with France and, in April 1958, signed an agreement with both the Paris and Rome governments for the development of a secret nuclear program.[51] Eventually, the program was discovered and heavily criticized by Washington and London, and ended up being canceled by French President de Gaulle in the fall of 1958.

Despite this official end to the West German nuclear weapons program, Bonn's willingness to acquire nuclear weapons did not dwindle. In December 1962, President Kennedy proposed the creation of a multilateral force, an idea initially conceived during the Eisenhower administration, to integrate national nuclear arsenals under a single command within NATO.[52] For the United States, the centralization of decision-making was an important tenet of Kennedy's foreign policy. Additionally, the MLF could satiate West Germany's appetite for nuclear weapons. In June 1964, Adrian Fisher, the deputy director of the US Arms Control and Disarmament Agency, wrote in a memo to Secretary of State Dean Rusk that the MLF "was intended to support our nonproliferation policy in the light of the growing nuclear ambitions of the Federal Republic."[53]

West Germany quickly saw the MLF as the best way to obtain control over nuclear weapons. After endorsing the MLF proposal in January 1963, Adenauer stated: "We must arrange within NATO so that a decision can be taken to use atomic weapons even before the [US] President is heard from."[54]

The Soviet Union was concerned about the proliferation risks presented by the MLF, however. Safeguards for a US veto over the use of MLF nuclear weapons might fail, and West Germany might also acquire useful information from its participation in the MLF to develop its own nuclear weapons.[55] When Kennedy described the MLF to the Soviets in April 1963, Khrushchev was amazed by his "attempt to convince me that neither the multinational nor multilateral nuclear forces being planned for NATO will increase the danger of the spreading of nuclear weapons." For Khrushchev, the MLF was "a crack" in nonproliferation efforts, and "once such a crack exists there will be found fingers which in this fashion will find their way to the control panels of these weapons."[56]

West German nuclearization was a frightening prospect for the Soviet Union. There is strong evidence that Khrushchev engineered the Berlin crisis of 1958–1962 to pressure the United States to keep West Germany nonnuclear.[57] In July 1962, at a meeting of the UN's Eighteen-Nation Committee on Disarmament, the Soviet representative stated that nonproliferation "cannot be discussed in an abstract fashion. It is primarily the question of the spread of nuclear weapons to West Germany."[58] During the negotiations for the NPT, a Soviet representative declared: "We primarily designed the whole treaty to close all doors and windows on the possibility of the Federal Republic of Germany having nuclear weapons."[59]

The Soviets were willing to consider a range of actions to ensure that West Germany would sign the treaty. In January 1966, Soviet Chairman Alexei Kosygin complained that NATO members seemed to be debating "how and to what extent to satisfy the growing nuclear demands of West Germany."[60] He stated that the Soviet Union would be "forced to take all measures which it, along with its allies and friends, would consider necessary for securing peace in Europe" in the event that West Germany "got access to nuclear weapons" in any form.[61]

Given Soviet concerns about West German nuclearization, and the risks of entrapment in a conflict with the Soviet Union, the United States gradually turned away from the MLF between 1964 and 1966.[62] Instead of trying to prevent West German nuclearization by removing its willingness to proliferate, Washington would now try to prevent West German nuclearization by removing its protégé's opportunity to proliferate. US Ambassador to West Germany George McGhee told Secretary of State Rusk that the Federal Republic of Germany should reassure Eastern European countries of its foreign ambitions, renouncing nuclear weapons and at least accept the Oder-Neisse line.[63] If the Federal Republic of Germany attempted to acquire a nuclear capability, the United States "would withdraw our forces and support for Germany first," the other NATO allies "would dissociate themselves from

Germany," and the Soviets would "make such efforts the subject of a preemptive attack." Ultimately, McGhee was convinced, West Germany could not acquire a national nuclear capability. This was not because of any inability to fulfill the necessary technical requirements, "but because neither the Soviets—or her allies including us, would permit her to do it."[64] With that goal in mind, the United States completed an agreement with the Soviet Union for the NPT, whereby nuclear powers agreed to renounce nuclear sharing, and non-nuclear weapons states agreed to forgo any attempt to acquire their own nuclear arsenals, subject to inspections. The two countries signed the treaty on July 1, 1968, along with sixty-two other countries.

West German leaders objected to US coercion.[65] In February 1967, West German Chancellor Kurt Kiesinger denounced the NPT as an act of superpower "atomic complicity."[66] He later went as far as declaring that the treaty was "part of a superpower conspiracy to split and denuclearize Germany forever."[67] Former West German Defense Minister Strauss called the NPT "a new Versailles, and one of cosmic dimensions." Adenauer called it a "Morgenthau Plan raised to the power of two" and a "death warrant" for West Germany.[68] Yet West German leaders had little choice. Facing a strong enemy in the Soviet Union, West Germany gave up its nuclear ambitions because it lacked the opportunity to proliferate. Under Chancellor Willy Brandt, West Germany signed the NPT on November 28, 1969, and worked for the improvement of relations with the Soviet Union, eventually leading to the signature of the Treaty of Moscow in 1970.[69]

NATO'S BROADER IMPACT ON NUCLEAR PROLIFERATION (1949–1968)

NATO's existence also influenced nuclear decision-making in non-NATO US allies. It did so in two ways. First, by providing protection against Soviet aggression, NATO dampened pressure for nuclearization among Western European countries that were not NATO members. This dynamic is most clear in the case of Sweden, culminating in its nuclear forbearance by the mid-1960s. Second, by providing a benchmark for US security commitments, NATO increased proliferation pressure on countries that were denied this same standard of protection. This dynamic underpinned Israeli nuclear efforts during the 1960s, culminating in its nuclear acquisition late that decade.

Sweden

In the early years of the Cold War, Sweden was interested in developing an independent nuclear deterrent. Its nuclear program was initiated in 1946[70] and in 1952, the Swedish military placed itself behind the nuclear effort.[71] Between 1954 and 1962, the program had the support of Sweden's political leadership, advancing steadily. In 1962, however, the Swedish military argued for shifting defense priorities back to conventional forces.[72] The following year, Prime Minister Tage Erlander informed US Ambassador J. Graham Parsons that, although Sweden "had the possibility of developing its own weapons rather quickly and quite easily," it now supported a test ban treaty and other proliferation-averting measures.[73] Funding for the nuclear program was cut, leading to its extinction in 1969.[74]

NATO policy played an important role in Sweden's nuclear pursuit and eventual abandonment. During the 1950s, Sweden was concerned about the superpowers' growing nuclear arsenals and lax nonproliferation policies.[75] Stockholm feared entrapment in a superpower conflict. By the early 1960s, however, progress in negotiations toward the Partial Test Ban Treaty of 1963 and reinvigorated discussions about the NPT suggested the overall likelihood of proliferation would go down. Most important, as a Defense Ministry report stated in 1965, Sweden became convinced that it "by and large is under the nuclear umbrella approximately in the same way that countries in our vicinity are, regardless which power bloc or great power sphere of interests they belong to."[76]

While the ambiguous language reflects its pledge of neutrality, Sweden nevertheless identified the Soviet Union as its only plausible potential enemy. Over the years, Sweden had prepared to receive NATO's assistance in the event of a conflict with the Soviet Union, in the form of bombing against Soviet air force and naval facilities plus the provision of supplies to Swedish forces.[77]

In pursuing these efforts, Swedish leaders assumed that "lending such assistance was in the interests of the Western Powers themselves."[78] They were correct. While opposing Swedish nuclearization, Washington believed it must help put Sweden "in the best possible position to resist Soviet pressure or aggression" even if that required that the United States "be prepared to come to the assistance of Sweden as part of a U.N. or NATO action."[79] Given the expected support of NATO in the event of a Soviet aggression, Sweden no longer needed an independent nuclear arsenal.

Israel

Immediately after achieving independence in 1948, Israel faced a severe security threat from neighboring Arab states. Not until 1957, however, would Israel receive any US security guarantees. That year, Eisenhower unveiled his Middle East doctrine, advocating military assistance to friendly states in the region.[80] The US gave Israel its first private security guarantee, with Eisenhower telling Prime Minister David Ben-Gurion that he "should have no doubt of deep U.S. interests in preservation [of] integrity and independence of Israel."[81] Israel finally had a nuclear ally.

Yet, US guarantees to Israel were markedly inferior to those Washington offered its NATO allies. This difference would be evident during the Suez Crisis of 1956. When the Soviet Union reacted to British, French, and Israeli military action around the Suez Canal by threatening nuclear retaliation against all three, President Eisenhower publicly pledged to retaliate against attacks on London or Paris, ignoring Israel, whom he warned "risked U.N. opprobrium, Soviet attack, and the termination of all U.S. aid."[82] The following year, Ben-Gurion requested a demonstration that Washington's "NATO commitment should be extended to the Middle East."[83] Secretary of State Dulles declined, asserting that US support had been made "quite clear to the Soviet Union."[84] Israel would have to make do with private security guarantees of dubious deterrent value.

At the same time, an Israeli bomb risked entrapping the United States. Therefore, Washington declined Israeli requests for nuclear technology and pressured France to do the same.[85] Moreover, Eisenhower demanded that Israel "declare unreservedly that she had no plans to manufacture atomic weapons,"[86] a request Ben-Gurion ignored.[87] The Kennedy administration reinforced this effort to connect US support to the abandonment of Israeli nuclear ambitions. Resisting any public security pledges, Kennedy made clear to Israeli Foreign Minister Golda Meir that "in case of an invasion the United States would come to the support of Israel," expecting that in return Israel "would give consideration to our problems on this atomic reactor."[88] Starting in 1961, Kennedy redoubled his efforts to make Israel abandon any nuclear aspirations, demanding that US inspectors be granted access to Israel's nuclear facilities.[89]

In early 1963, Israel's security outlook worsened. Unrest in Jordan, coups in Iraq and Syria, and a joint Egyptian, Iraqi, and Syrian declaration vowing to liberate Palestine prompted renewed fears of encirclement by Arab radicals.[90] Israel repeated its demand for an explicit American NATO-like guarantee. Unmoved, Kennedy reiterated his private assurances, avoided a public declaration, and noted that US commitment and support for Israel were conditional on Washington's ability to guarantee that Israel's nuclear program had no military aims.[91] In response, Ben-Gurion turned JFK's rationale on its head, framing his request for a formal US security pledge explicitly in terms of the need for Israel to have access to nuclear capabilities.[92] Kennedy remained obdurate, however, leading new Israeli Prime Minister Levi Eshkol to make the quid pro quo of public US support in exchange for the abandonment of Israel's military nuclear program even more explicit.[93]

The same dynamic continued during the Johnson years.[94] While in private Washington continued to pledge support for the security of Israel and to supply Israel with conventional weapons, it refused to make any public NATO-like commitments and threatened to withdraw any support in case Israel pursued atomic weapons. This led Israel to press on with nuclear development, acquiring the bomb in the late 1960s.

CONCLUSION

Since early in the nuclear age, NATO has been an important instrument in the effort to stymie the spread of nuclear weapons. By placing advanced Western European countries under the US nuclear umbrella, NATO has alleviated proliferation pressure among US allies in Europe. Among these, only Britain and France, which possess broader foreign policy goals than any other European NATO member, have acquired the bomb. West Germany was dubious about US security guarantees and aimed at reunifying with East Germany. Yet, its nuclearization was opposed by the Soviet Union. Faced with Soviet opposition to German nuclearization, Washington coerced West Germany into remaining non-nuclear. Eventually, German reunification was brought about peacefully with the end of the Cold War. Since then, no NATO member has ever explored the nuclear option. In fact, for as long as the US nuclear umbrella continues to cover European NATO countries, it is difficult to foresee a set of circumstances that would generate additional nuclear proliferation within NATO.

But Europe is not the only setting in which NATO plays a role in the politics of nuclear proliferation. By establishing a benchmark for what reliable US protection looks like, NATO may well contribute to proliferation in other regions of the globe. For example, as tensions between US allies and China continue to mount in East Asia, it is conceivable that NATO's alliance template will be invoked by these allies in an attempt to obtain more reliable US guarantees. Should Washington decline to provide these, proliferation in Asia is not out of the question as China continues to rise. Likewise, eventual Iranian nuclearization might lead US allies in the Middle East to demand NATO-like US guarantees. Should Washington withhold these, proliferation pressures in the region would mount. Overall, these dynamics highlight the important role that alliances play in the politics of nuclear proliferation.[95]

Notes

1. For analyses of the Iran Deal, see, e.g., George Perkovich, Mark Hibbs, James M. Acton, and Toby Dalton, *Parsing the Iran Deal: An Analysis of the Iran Deal from a Nonproliferation Perspective* (Washington, DC: Carnegie Endowment for International Peace, 2015); Gary Samore, *The Iran Nuclear Deal: A Definitive Guide* (Cambridge, MA: Harvard Kennedy School's Belfer Center for Science and International Affairs, 2015).

2. See Marc Trachtenberg, *A Constructed Peace: The Making of the European Settlement, 1945–1963* (Princeton, NJ: Princeton University Press, 1999); Andrew Coe and Jane Vaynman, "Collusion and the Nuclear Nonproliferation Regime," *Journal of Politics* 77(4) (2015), 983–97.

3. Trachtenberg, *A Constructed Peace*, 261, 262.

4. Joseph S. Nye, Jr., "The Superpowers and the Non-Proliferation Treaty," in Albert Carnesale and Richard N. Haass, eds., *Superpower Arms Control* (Cambridge, MA: Ballinger, 1987), 167.

5. Quoted in Catherine M. Kelleher, *Germany and the Politics of Nuclear Weapons* (New York: Columbia University Press, 1975), 139.

6. See Glenn T. Seaborg, *Stemming the Tide: Arms Control in the Johnson Years* (Lexington, MA: Lexington Books, 1987), 86; George Bunn, *Arms Control by Committee: Managing Negotiations with the Russians* (Stanford, CA: Stanford University Press, 1992), 64; Ronald J. Granieri, *The Ambivalent Alliance: Konrad Adenauer, the CDU/CSU, and the West, 1949–1966* (New York: Berghahn Books, 2004), 164–65; Hal Brands, "Non-Proliferation and the Dynamics of the Middle Cold War: The Superpowers, the MLF, and the NPT," *Cold War History* 7(3) (2007), 393–94.

7. See Bunn, *Arms Control by Committee*, 65–66.

8. Francis J. Gavin, *Nuclear Statecraft: History and Strategy in America's Atomic Age* (Ithaca: Cornell University Press, 2012), 42–43.

9. See Granieri, *The Ambivalent Alliance*, 164–65.

10. See, e.g., Maurice Vaisse, "La choix atomique de la France (1945–1958)," *Vingtième siècle. Revue d'histoire* 36 (1992), 21–30; Dominique Mongin, *La bombe atomique française, 1945–1958* (Brussels: Bruylant, 1997).

11. See, e.g., Mongin, *La bombe atomique française*, 56.

12. See ibid., 113.

13. See, e.g., Bertrand Goldschmidt, *Les rivalités atomiques, 1939–1966* (Paris: Fayard, 1967), trans. as *Atomic Rivals: A Candid Memoir of Rivalries among the Allies over the Bomb* (New Brunswick, NJ: Rutgers University Press, 1990), 346.

14. See, e.g., Georges-Henri Soutou, "La politique nucléaire de Pierre Mendès France," *Relations internationales* 59 (1989), 319; Mongin, *La bombe atomique française*, 310. For a dissenting view, see Jacques C. Hymans, *The Psychology of Nuclear Proliferation: Identity, Emotions, and Foreign Policy* (New York: Cambridge University Press, 2006), 95.

15. Quoted in Soutou, "La politique nucléaire de Pierre Mendès France," 320.

16. See George C. Herring and Richard H. Immerman, "Eisenhower, Dulles, and Dien Bien Phu," *Journal of American History* 71(2) (1984), 343–63; Avery Goldstein, *Deterrence and Security in the 21st Century: China, Britain, France, and the Enduring Legacy of the Nuclear Revolution* (Stanford, CA: Stanford University Press, 2000), 187–88.

17. See Wilfried Kohl, *French Nuclear Diplomacy* (Princeton, NJ: Princeton University Press, 1971), 21–22.

18. See ibid., 32–33.

19. See Soutou, "La politique nucléaire de Pierre Mendès France."

20. See ibid., 324–26; Mongin, *La bombe atomique française*, 328–34. The program was meant to remain secret. Years later, Mendès France minimized his role in the French nuclear weapons program (see Soutou, "La politique nucléaire de Pierre Mendès France").

21. See Avner Cohen, *Israel and the Bomb* (New York: Columbia University Press, 1998), 55; Goldstein, *Deterrence and Security in the 21st Century*, 164. On the Suez Crisis, see, e.g., Diane B. Kunz, *Economic*

Diplomacy in the Suez Crisis (Chapel Hill: University of North Carolina Press, 1991); Keith Kyle, Suez: Britain's End of Empire in the Middle East (London: I. B. Tauris, 2003).

22. See Goldstein, Deterrence and Security in the 21st Century, 164.
23. Quoted in Kohl, French Nuclear Diplomacy, 191.
24. See Mongin, La bombe atomique française, 442.
25. See ibid., 436–38.
26. See, e.g., ibid., 36.
27. See Beatrice Heuser, Nuclear Mentalities? Strategies and Beliefs in Britain, France, and the FRG (London: Macmillan, 1998), 97–98.
28. Alfred Grosser, "France and Germany in the Atlantic Community," International Organization 17(3) (1963), 558.
29. See ibid.
30. Bruno Tertrais, "Destruction assurée: The Origins and Development of French Nuclear Strategy, 1945–1982," Getting MAD: Nuclear Mutual Assured Destruction, Its Origins and Practice, Henry D. Sokolski, ed. (Carlisle, PA: Strategic Studies Institute, 2004), 57.
31. Paraphrased in Pierre Gallois, "French Defense Planning—The Future in the Past," International Security 1(2) (1976), 17.
32. See Mongin, La bombe atomique française, 453.
33. See Goldschmidt, Les rivalités atomiques, 357.
34. Dulles Papers, Category IX, Conference Dossiers, Special Subject, June 30, 1958, quoted in Kohl, French Nuclear Diplomacy, 65–66.
35. Ibid., 65–66.
36. See George A. Kelly, "The Political Background of the French A-Bomb," Orbis 4(3) (1960), 284.
37. For the role of Pierre Gallois, member of the NATO New Approach Group, in explaining nuclear strategy to French decision-makers in 1956, see, e.g., Mongin, La bombe atomique française, 404–08, 418–20.
38. See Georges-Henri Soutou, "Les accords de 1957 et 1958: Vers une communauté stratégique et nucléaire entre la France, l'Allemagne et l'Italie?" Matériaux pour l'histoire de notre temps 31 (1993), 1–12; Leopoldo Nuti, "The F-I-G Story Revisited," Storia delle relazioni internazionali 13(1) (1998), 69–100.
39. See Mongin, La bombe atomique française, 456–57.
40. Heuser, Nuclear Mentalities?, 119–20.
41. Philip Gordon, A Certain Idea of France: French Security Policy and the Gaullist Legacy (Princeton, NJ: Princeton University Press, 1993), 60.
42. Quoted in Goldstein, Deterrence and Security in the 21st Century, 181. Some authors argue that France nuclearized in order to boost its prestige and status (see, e.g., Heuser, Nuclear Mentalities, 100–101). In our view, Paris tied French status to specific strategic goals, the pursuit of which, in the absence of specific US support and given the Soviet threat, required a nuclear arsenal. This explains why, unlike most other (presumably also status-seeking) countries, France nuclearized.
43. See Memorandum of Conversation, June 22, 1962, Foreign Relations of the United States [FRUS], 1961–1963, Vol. 13: Western Europe and Canada (Washington, DC: Government Printing Office [GPO], 1994), 422; Hans-Peter Schwarz, Konrad Adenauer: A German Politician and Statesman in a Period of War, Revolution, and Reconstruction (Providence, RI: Berghahn, 1997), 123; and Granieri, The Ambivalent Alliance, 83.
44. On the Marshall Plan, see, e.g., Michael J. Hogan, The Marshall Plan: America, Britain and the Reconstruction of Western Europe, 1947–1952 (New York: Cambridge University Press, 1989).
45. See Jeffrey Boutwell, The German Nuclear Dilemma (Ithaca, NY: Cornell University Press, 1990), 18.
46. See Schwarz, Konrad Adenauer, 235; and Granieri, The Ambivalent Alliance, 88.
47. Ibid.
48. Schwarz, Konrad Adenauer, 235.

49. Ibid., 239–40; and Granieri, *The Ambivalent Alliance*, 99.
50. Boutwell, *The German Nuclear Dilemma*, 19.
51. See Kelleher, *Germany and the Politics of Nuclear Weapons*, 149; Pertti Ahonen, "Franz-Josef Strauss and the German Nuclear Question, 1956–1962," *Journal of Strategic Studies* 18(1) (1995), 32–33; and Harald Müller, "Germany and WMD Proliferation," *Nonproliferation Review* 10(2) (2003), 2.
52. See Granieri, *The Ambivalent Alliance*, 164.
53. Seaborg, *Stemming the Tide*, 131.
54. Jenifer Mackby and Walter B. Slocombe, "Germany: The Model Case, a Historical Imperative," in Kurt M. Campbell, Robert J. Einhorn, and Mitchell B. Reiss, eds., *The Nuclear Tipping Point: Why States Reconsider Their Nuclear Choices* (Washington, DC: Brookings Institution Press, 2004), 191.
55. US allies were also concerned. In October 1964, recently elected British Prime Minister Harold Wilson famously objected to the MLF in the following terms: "If you have a boy and wish to sublimate his sex appetite, it is unwise to take him to a strip-tease show." See Kelleher, *Germany and the Politics of Nuclear Weapons*, 252.
56. Message from Chairman Khrushchev to President Kennedy, undated, FRUS, 1961–1963, Vol. 6: *Kennedy-Khrushchev Exchanges* (Washington, DC: GPO, 1996), 274.
57. According to Joseph S. Nye, Jr., Khrushchev believed "Berlin was a 'blister' that he could step on to make the Americans feel pain. He could trade stability in the status of Berlin for Western assurances that the Federal Republic of Germany would not get nuclear weapons." See Nye, "The Superpowers and the Non-Proliferation Treaty," in Albert Carnesale and Richard N. Haass, eds., *Superpower Arms Control: Setting the Record Straight* (Cambridge, MA: Ballinger, 1987), 169. According to Marc Trachtenberg, "[t]he German nuclear question thus lay at the heart of Soviet policy during the Berlin Crisis." See Trachtenberg, *A Constructed Peace*, 253.
58. Nye, "The Superpowers and the Non-Proliferation Treaty," 169.
59. Matthias Küntzel, *Bonn and the Bomb: German Politics and the Nuclear Option* (London: Pluto, 1995), 20.
60. Message from Chairman Kosygin to President Johnson, Moscow, February 1, 1965, FRUS, 1964–1968, Vol. 11: *Arms Control and Disarmament* (Washington, DC: GPO, 1997), 186–88; Translation of Message Handed Acting Secretary of State by Soviet Ambassador Dobrynin, January 11, 1966, FRUS, 1964–1968, Vol. 11: *Arms Control and Disarmament*, 279.
61. Ibid., 280. See also Kosygin's press conference in London in February 1967, quoted in Seaborg, *Stemming the Tide*, 359.
62. Kelleher argues that the MLF was effectively killed in December 1964, when it was put on hold by President Johnson. See Kelleher, *Germany and the Politics of Nuclear Weapons*, 254. Negotiations about the NPT continued for more than a year afterward. McGeorge Bundy argues that the MLF was dropped at end of 1965; see Bundy, *Danger and Survival: Choices about the Bomb in the First Fifty Years* (New York: Random House, 1988), 494. Frank Costigliola argues that it "faded away" in 1966; see Costigliola, "Lyndon B. Johnson, Germany, and 'the End of the Cold War,'" in Warren I. Cohen and Nancy Bernkopf Tucker, eds., *Lyndon Johnson Confronts the World: American Foreign Policy, 1963–1968* (New York: Cambridge University Press, 1994), 180. Mathias Küntzel says that it ended in November 1966, with the resignation of Ludwig Erhard's government; see Küntzel, *Bonn and the Bomb*, 54.
63. The Oder-Neisse line, formed by the Oder and Lusatian Neisse rivers, was established as the border between the German Democratic Republic (East Germany) and Poland after World War II, leading to a net loss of "German" territory relative to the prewar border.
64. Letter from the Ambassador to Germany (McGhee) to Secretary of State Rusk, August 25, 1966, FRUS, 1964–1968, Vol. 15: *Germany and Berlin* (Washington, DC: GPO, 1999), 395.
65. Although not all West German leaders were in favor of nuclear acquisition, those opposed to it were unable to persuade the majority of the decision-making elite in Bonn to forfeit its nuclear ambitions before the exercise of strong US nonproliferation pressure. On the different positions of German elites vis-à-vis the nuclear question and their role in German nuclear forbearance, see Jonas Schneider,

"Nuclear Nonproliferation within the Context of U.S. Alliances: Protection, Status, and the Psychology of West Germany's Nuclear Reversal," paper presented at the 2014 annual convention of the International Studies Association.

66. Küntzel, *Bonn and the Bomb*, 96.

67. Shane J. Maddock, *Nuclear Apartheid: The Quest for American Atomic Supremacy from World War II to the Present* (Chapel Hill: University of North Carolina Press, 2010), 276.

68. Küntzel, *Bonn and the Bomb*, 90. See also Mackby and Slocombe, "Germany," 180, 196–97. The Morgenthau Plan, named after US Secretary of the Treasury Henry Morgenthau, Jr. (1934–1945), meant to eliminate Germany's industrial power after World War II, so as to prevent the resurgence of its military power.

69. West Germany ratified the NPT in 1975. When it was reunited, Germany reiterated its renunciation of nuclear weapons and in 1994 voted to extend the NPT indefinitely.

70. See Wilhelm Agrell, "The Bomb that Never Was: The Rise and Fall of the Swedish Nuclear Weapons Programme," in *Arms Races: Technological and Political Dynamics*, ed. Nils Peter Gleditsch and Olav Njølstad (London: Sage, 1990), 54.

71. See ibid, 160–65; Lars Wallin, "Sweden," in Regina Cowen Karp, ed., *Security with Nuclear Weapons?: Different Perspectives on National Security* (Oxford: Oxford University Press, 1991), 368.

72. See Agrell, "The Bomb that Never Was," 166–67.

73. See Paul M. Cole, "Atomic Bombast: Nuclear Weapon Decision-Making in Sweden, 1946–72," *Washington Quarterly* 20(2) (1997), 243. Some argue that Swedish forbearance was due to a strong commitment to international norms, a high level of trust in international treaties, and a desire not to harm NPT negotiations; see, e.g., Maria Rost Rublee, *Nonproliferation Norms: Why States Choose Nuclear Restraint* (Athens: University of Georgia Press, 2009), 180. The evidence against such a normative argument is strong, however. A 1959 report by the Swedish ruling party at the time (SAP) asserted that "Sweden will not give up nuclear weapons due to ethical reasons, if other countries equip their forces with such weapons" (Sveriges socialdemokratiska arbetareparti, *Neutralitet, Försvar, Atomvapen* [Stockholm: Tiden, 1960], 110). In 1965, the Swedish Ministry of Defense argued that if "nuclear weapons become a normal part of small nations' armed forces, the question of Swedish nuclear weapons could come again at this time" (Försvarsdepartementet, *Säkerhetspolitik och Försvarsutgifter: Förslag om Försvarsutgifterna 1968/72* [Stockholm: Statent offentliga utredningar, 1965], 73–74). Tellingly, the dual-purpose Ågesta nuclear reactor, shut down in 1974, remains ready for reactivation within months; see Steve Coll, "Neutral Sweden Quietly Keeps Nuclear Option Open," *Washington Post*, November 24, 1994, 1 and A-42.

74. See Wallin, "Sweden," 365.

75. See ÖB-utredningarna 1957, *Kontakt med Krigsmakten* (1957), 282, 290.

76. Försvarsdepartementet, *Säkerhetspolitik och Försvarsutgifter*, 138.

77. See Gösta Gunnarsson, Wilhelm Carlgren, Leif Leifland, Yngve Möller, Olof Ruin, and Göran Rystad, *Had There Been a War: Preparations for the Reception of Military Assistance 1949–1969*, Report of the Commission on Neutrality Policy (Stockholm: National Defense Research Establishment, 1994), 9–10.

78. Ibid., 34; see also ibid., 11.

79. Ibid., 13.

80. See Warren Bass, *Support Any Friend: Kennedy's Middle East and the Making of the U.S.–Israel Alliance* (Oxford: Oxford University Press, 2003), 45–46.

81. Quoted in Douglas Little, "The Making of a Special Relationship," *International Journal of Middle East Studies* 25(4) (1993), 565.

82. Bass, *Support Any Friend*, 44.

83. Bergus, "Israel," October 28, 1957, quoted in Little, "The Making of a Special Relationship," 565.

84. State Department memcon, "Israel's Need for Security Guarantee," October 31, 1957, quoted in ibid., 565.

85. See Matthew Kroenig, *Exporting the Bomb: Technology Transfer and the Spread of Nuclear Weapons* (Ithaca, NY: Cornell University Press, 2010), 69, 74–75.
86. Little, "The Making of a Special Relationship," 567.
87. See ibid., 567.
88. Ibid., 569; Bass, *Support Any Friend*, 206–07.
89. See Bass, *Support Any Friend*, 199–206.
90. See Little, "The Making of a Special Relationship," 569; Bass, *Support Any Friend*, 211–12.
91. See Little, "The Making of a Special Relationship," 569–70; Bass, *Support Any Friend*, 211–16.
92. See Bass, *Support Any Friend*, 213.
93. See ibid., 236.
94. See Little, "The Making of a Special Relationship," 575.
95. See Nuno P. Monteiro and Alexandre Debs, "The Strategic Logic of Nuclear Proliferation," *International Security* 39(2) (2014), 7–51; Alexandre Debs and Nuno P. Monteiro, *Nuclear Politics: The Strategic Causes of Proliferation* (New York: Cambridge University Press, 2017).

Chapter 3

The Contest over NATO's Future:
The US, France, and the Concept of Pan-Europeanism after the Fall of the Berlin Wall, 1989–1990

Mary Elise Sarotte

This edited volume centers on the way that NATO has affected, and been affected by, transatlantic politics and relationships during and since the Cold War. My essay contributes to this endeavor by examining the contest over NATO that erupted immediately after the unexpected opening of the Berlin Wall and the crumbling of the Cold War political order in 1989–1990.[1] As a result of the stunningly swift disappearance of the barriers between the two parts of Berlin and of Germany, pressing questions about the future of the transatlantic relationship and of NATO's role in it suddenly rose to the tops of agendas in capitals on both sides of the Atlantic Ocean.

The George H. W. Bush administration, in office only since January 1989, abruptly found itself confronted by the need to define the alliance's purpose under rapidly changing political circumstances. As wits had often remarked, the alliance's purpose during the decades-long Cold War had been threefold: to keep the Americans in, the Russians out, and the Germans down. With the Soviet bloc and soon the Soviet Union itself in a process of collapse, the Cold War mission of keeping the Soviets out of Western Europe was clearly drawing to a close. But what would post–Cold War relations with Moscow bring? Did NATO need to continue to pursue its other two goals, namely, keeping the Americans in and the Germans down? In other words, would

Germans and Europeans try to hand the Americans their hats and send them back across the Atlantic?

Alternatively, might Washington use the crisis of 1989–1990 to take a long, hard look at the costs of serving as the dominant power in an alliance of military unequals, reconsider its role, and perhaps retrench homeward? Or would the Bush administration choose to "double-down" on NATO as the preeminent post–Cold War security organization, thereby holding on to a successful institution but also potentially to a conflict with Moscow? In late 1989 and early 1990 it rapidly became apparent that President Bush preferred the latter strategy. He, along with the leader of West Germany, Chancellor Helmut Kohl, felt strongly that it was necessary to keep NATO at the heart of transatlantic and European security in the post–Cold War era. As I have published in detail elsewhere, the two men believed that the Cold War strategy of tightly integrating West Germany into NATO had paid handsome dividends, and that perpetuating the practice was necessary. It would, they felt, have the double benefit of, first, ensuring European security during a volatile time of global transition, and, second, of blocking the rise of alternative visions for new structures that might, in their view, be less congenial.[2]

In particular, Washington felt it was essential—after it became clear in the course of 1990 that the unexpected opening of the Wall on November 9, 1989, would lead to rapid German reunification, perhaps by the end of that year—that not just western Germany but all of a reuniting Germany needed either to remain or to become NATO territory. There was even some speculative discussion as early as 1990 about expanding NATO into Eastern Europe, speculation that made little progress at the time but would later become a reality under Bush's successor, President Bill Clinton.[3]

A shared internal strategy thus arose in consultation between Bonn and Washington in the course of repeated conversations and meetings throughout 1990. That strategy was, in the words of Robert Gates, later defense secretary but at the time a deputy national security adviser, to "bribe the Soviets out." The full sequence of events (which I have described elsewhere in detail) is too lengthy to recapitulate here; summarized bluntly, this strategy worked. The Soviet leader, Mikhail Gorbachev, was facing too many problems both at home and abroad to counter this strategy effectively. He ended up taking what Gates called the "bribe." It was paid, in the end, by Bonn, in the interest of securing unification as quickly as possible.[4]

THE SIGNIFICANCE OF FRANCO-AMERICAN RELATIONS

One of the most effective ways to understand these developments in 1989–1990 is by focusing on Franco-American relations. Why are the contacts between Paris and Washington important in this context, when the story seems to be largely a German and superpower one? Because it was apparent to all leaders involved that Bonn, Moscow, and Washington could not implement German unification on their own, for a number of reasons.

When Nazi Germany surrendered unconditionally in 1945, four powers gained occupation rights: the US, the Soviet Union, France, and Great Britain. Although somewhat altered in the intervening decades, not least by the creation of NATO and the Warsaw Pact, the four powers still had both (1) far-reaching legal authority in divided Germany, particularly in divided Berlin, and (2) large numbers of their nationals stationed as troops there under varying alliance and occupation accords. As a result, in 1990 all four had to be involved in the legal process of reunification, not just Moscow and Washington in consultation with East Berlin and Bonn (at the time the capitals of East Germany and West Germany, respectively).

Hence the superpowers and the Germans had to take French and British views into account. But, while Franco-American and Franco-West German contacts were frequent and significant, the parallel claim does not hold: British contacts with the other powers were not similarly significant in 1989–1990. The earlier close working relationship between President Ronald Reagan and Prime Minister Margaret Thatcher had, of course, disappeared once Reagan left office at the end of his second term. The new Bush team, though avoiding overt criticism of Reagan, came into office determined to chart its own course and to put its own stamp on foreign affairs. Thus, when Bush traveled to West Germany early in his presidency and announced in a major speech in Mainz in May 1989 that Bonn and Washington were partners in leadership, London abruptly felt itself being publicly downgraded.[5]

The unexpected opening of the Berlin Wall in November then worsened matters for Great Britain. Thatcher's categorical, visceral opposition to the possibility of rapid German unification after the Wall's opening meant that she marginalized herself among other European leaders and with Washington once such a possibility became, first, a likelihood and then, rapidly, an inevitability. The British Foreign and Commonwealth Office realized that Thatcher was increasingly out of step with developing realities, but efforts to influence policy only resulted in counterproductive friction with 10 Downing Street at a critical time.⁶ Even worse, the prime minister was on the verge of losing office. Challenges from within her own party would ultimately result in her ouster in 1990. In short, the turmoil at the top of British politics at the critical time of transition from the Cold War to the post–Cold War era meant that London played only a marginal role in the process of defining security for Europe's post-Wall future.

In contrast, the leader of France was secure in his role in 1990. President François Mitterrand not only maintained his dominance over French foreign policy but also, in the second half of 1989, even held the rotating presidency of the European Community (EC). In stark contrast to Thatcher, he had established a close, productive working relationship with Kohl in the course of the 1980s. One might have expected the opposite to be the case, given that Thatcher and Kohl both represented right-of-center parties, while Mitterrand was a leader of the left. The evidentiary record, however, shows close policy coordination throughout this period between Mitterrand and Kohl, but little between Thatcher and Kohl personally. Finally, France additionally mattered because, of the four occupying powers, the French president was the one major head of state to espouse a different post-Wall view of European security from that of Bonn and Washington. He argued for creating or expanding pan-European security institutions, such as the Conference on Security and Cooperation in Europe (CSCE), in the new post-Wall era.⁷

There appear to have been multiple motives behind his interest in pan-Europeanism. As one of Mitterrand's aides, Jean Musitelli, later put it, the French president was thereby trying to ensure that the unification of Germany and the collapse of the Soviet Union did not have the paradoxical effect of weakening European integration.⁸ In the more skeptical words of political scientist Julie Newton, Mitterrand hoped to use pan-Europeanism "as a tool for furthering his own, narrower objectives, which included achieving peaceful Soviet agreement to German reunification, maintaining stability in the East, and avoiding handing 'excessive powers' to NATO and the US in the new Europe."⁹

Whatever Mitterrand's true motives were, it became apparent to President Bush in 1990 that he needed to deal personally with Mitterrand and his views as a key part of the process of unifying Germany. The US president thus faced the challenge of either isolating Mitterrand or bringing the French president over to the policy that Bush and Kohl wished to follow. He and Kohl chose the latter, which is fortunate for historians. By looking at the documents produced by this process, that is, the archival sources that have largely become available in French and German archives (the matching US sources are often, though not always, still classified), it is possible to see the outlines of the competition over NATO's future in a particularly clear way. NATO's significance to Washington—both the alliance as a whole and its nuclear posture—emerges plainly from the confidential contacts between the two leaders and their foreign policy teams.

"NO NUKES, NO TROOPS"

Writing in April 1990, a senior adviser to the president of France, Loïc Hennekine, spoke of the "paradox of Franco-American relations in the current phase."[10] On the one hand, there was a strong personal connection between Bush and Mitterrand. The US president even invited his French counterpart to his private summer compound in Kennebunkport, Maine, a rare honor. And, during the time that both men were in office, Bush would close his communications to Mitterrand with phrases such as "François, there is no leader in Europe today whom I respect more."[11]

The cooperative nature of the Paris–Washington relationship did not preclude, on the other hand, differences of opinion about the future of European security.[12] Even the preliminary question of who should be involved in defining the future of European security was proving difficult in early 1990. Should it be just the four powers that still held legal rights over Germany as a result of World War II? Or should the two Germanies be involved as well, meaning some kind of "two plus four" talks? Or should it be the members of the EC, in other words, "the twelve?" Or should it be the members of NATO, "the sixteen?" Or should it be the members of the CSCE, the "thirty-five," which included Eastern European countries? The French president felt strongly that inclusivity was important and would in particular advocate a large role for the Poles, something that Kohl would resist. Mitterrand's opinions carried extra weight in late 1989, given that (as mentioned above) France held the rotating presidency of the EC at the time.

Washington felt it necessary to keep the number of entities involved in decision-making about post–Cold War Europe to as small a number as possible. An early, abortive effort to use the minimum possible number, "the four," in December 1989 produced so much outrage in Bonn that Washington backtracked and switched to the idea of a "four-plus-two" format, that is, including the two Germanies. West Germans pointedly referred to the talks as the "two-plus-four," and eventually this became the most commonly used name for them. The US thereby avoided a forum with the twelve, the sixteen, or the thirty-five, but France retained significant influence in the process as one of the four.

In the course of contacts with Paris about the conduct of the two-plus-four talks, both Bush and Kohl made clear to Mitterrand and his advisers that they felt the only organization that could secure Europe in the future was NATO. As Mitterrand's aide Hubert Védrine remarked, NATO's survival and continued preeminence was, in 1990, "the only issue" that truly concerned Bush.[13] NATO mattered because it was the organization that ensured that the US would have a permanent say in post–Cold War European security, and that say would ultimately continue to be guaranteed by its thermonuclear arsenal. Another of Mitterrand's aides, Caroline de Margerie, reported to her boss that Washington spoke very bluntly when it came to this issue. NATO troops would stay and so would their nuclear weapons: "The real sticking point" for Washington, she reported, was "the denuclearization of Germany. As Bush said to Kohl: 'No nukes, no troops.'"[14]

AVOIDING A "GLOBAL GREEN LIGHT"?

In contrast, while still viewing NATO as important, Mitterrand and his allies hoped that the end of the Cold War might provide an opportunity to extend or create pan-European institutions, not just in the realm of security but also in other areas. Mitterrand and his aides felt more generally that they should seize the 1989–1990 moment to promote a more "European Europe." A "French conundrum" thus arose, in the words of historian Frédéric Bozo; France wanted to keep a united Germany in NATO, but it did not want simply to perpetuate the Cold War status quo full stop. Developing parallel pan-European institutions seemed like a potential way of resolving this conundrum.[15]

Mitterrand's aides also believed strongly that the Soviets needed to be permitted "to save face" in the interest of future harmony in undivided Europe. De Margerie summarized this view as follows: "It is necessary to propose to the Soviets an overall package [un paquet global] that *compensates* for the retention of NATO and permits them to save face, all while maintaining the elements of safety that are important for the alliance" (emphasis in original).[16] Mitterrand felt that pan-Europeanism could serve that purpose. Renewing earlier Gaullist notions, he hoped in the longer run to make progress on the goal of creating a "European Europe," or a Greater Europe (*Grande Europe*), crossing the former Cold War divide and stretching from France to the Soviet Union.[17]

Mitterrand was in this regard thinking similarly to the West German foreign minister, Hans-Dietrich Genscher. Genscher was the leading politician in the West German Liberal Party, or FDP by its German initials. The Liberals' decision to enter into a governing coalition with Kohl's Christian Democratic Union was what had enabled Kohl to become chancellor in the first place; hence, since Genscher and his small party were, in essence, kingmakers, they could allow themselves luxuries such as views that differed from those of the chancellor.

Genscher had starting saying publicly in early 1990 that, if NATO were indeed to remain as the predominant post–Cold War security organization, it could not extend to the east, for that would be too threatening to the Soviet Union. He even told the bestselling German newspaper *Bild am Sonntag* in an interview that putting East Germany into NATO would be the end of the dream of unity.[18] In private remarks in 1990, Genscher further noted that he found the concept of potentially extending NATO to East European countries, not just to eastern Germany, to be inadvisable because of the difficulties that it would cause Gorbachev.[19]

Genscher was, however, overruled by Kohl, who discussed the matter at length with Bush at Camp David in February 1990. Kohl had intentionally chosen not to bring Genscher to this meeting, despite the demands of protocol that Genscher come, since his US equivalent, Secretary of State James Baker, was in attendance. Presumably Kohl left Genscher by the side of the road due to their differences on this critical issue.

In private talks at Camp David, Bush made his feelings clear. Moscow could not make demands about the alliance's future. "To hell with that! We prevailed, they didn't. We can't let the Soviets clutch victory from the jaws of defeat."[20] Bush would not allow the Soviet Union to determine issues such as a united Germany's role in a future NATO.

Bush persuaded Kohl to abandon an idea that the German chancellor had been considering. According to this idea, a united Germany might remain in NATO, but leave its integrated military command, as France itself had once done. Yet, in the course of the Camp David meeting, Kohl came to agree with Bush that Bonn and Washington should push for full NATO membership for united Germany. Moscow would eventually accept it, they guessed, but Kohl was also certain that the Soviets "will want to be paid for it." It was clear who would be paying that price: Bush noted that Kohl had "deep pockets."[21]

It soon became apparent to other members of the two-plus-four that Genscher's earlier remarks no longer represented West German policy. By March 1990, the Soviet foreign minister, Eduard Shevardnadze, was complaining to the French that Genscher's ideas clearly were out of date. Shevardnadze noted that Genscher's formula, "according to which the territory of NATO and the troops stationed would not be extended to the East," was not current.[22] He was right, and soon others noticed as well.

Critics also attacked the related idea of a potential special status within the alliance for former East Germany as unworkable. NATO's secretary general, Manfred Woerner, highlighted the difficulties if the western part of Germany remained a full member of NATO, in contrast to the new eastern part. How could NATO offer the citizens of the same country two different levels of protection?[23] And what would that mean for nuclear deployments? Washington found these questions unsettling and began to maneuver to prevent such outcomes.

Another open question was the nature of the relationship between NATO and any potential home-grown European security organization. As Védrine advised Mitterrand, "in order to continue to equilibrate Soviet military power and to enclose Germany, a true European defense allied with the United States is necessary."[24] But French notions of a "complementary alliance" arising from either the EC or the CSCE were not popular in Washington. Védrine argued France should continue to make such counterproposals, however, because otherwise Washington would think that it had a "global green light for a 'new Atlanticism,'" with all that that could imply about a desire for a limited European role."[25]

BUSH MAKES HIS PREFERENCES KNOWN

Mitterrand's efforts to have his representatives in the two-plus-four talks broach such topics, however, met with resistance in both Bonn and Washington. President Bush simply did not want the two-plus-four forum to attempt to address major issues for the simple reason that the Soviets had a veto in that forum. Additionally, disputes might become stumbling blocks and delay the process toward German unification.

By April 1990, Bush was deeply concerned about this French effort to widen the scope of the two-plus-four talks. The US president felt it necessary to spell out his thinking in an extensive, detailed telegram to Mitterrand directly. It is worth quoting from this telegram at some length, because it provides an unusually clear window on US strategic thinking at that time.

Bush began by saying to Mitterrand that "I am deeply committed to the US political, economic and military role in maintaining European stability. And it is absolutely clear that in the period ahead a strong US–French relationship is essential to that stability." He spelled out his top priorities to

Mitterrand: (1) that Germany should have full membership of NATO, including of Article 5; (2) that allied forces should remain in Germany; and (3) that NATO should continue to deploy both nuclear and conventional weapons.

In Bush's opinion, these three issues were not, and should never be, up for discussion in the two-plus-four talks. As the US president put it, we need to "be very clear about the objectives of the two plus four. The main purpose of the two plus four process should be to restore full sovereignty to a peaceful, democratic, and united German state." He was

> delighted that the Western officials in the one plus three meeting [a Western preparatory session for a full two-plus-four session] on April 10 agreed that the two plus four should not negotiate over Germany's right to remain a full member of NATO; should not decide the fate of allied conventional or nuclear forces on the territory of the current FRG; should not agree on the future size of a united Germany's armed forces; and should not replace the old four power rights with new discriminatory limits on German sovereignty a prescription for future instability.

The problem was that the USSR "may well want the two plus four to decide all of these matters, to use the two plus four forum to undermine German security ties to the West and the coherence of NATO's deterrent posture." He warned Mitterrand that they should "in no event allow Moscow to manipulate the two plus four mechanism in ways that could fracture Western defense and Germany's irreplaceable part in it." Nor did Bush see the CSCE as the way forward. As he put it, "I hope that you agree that the North Atlantic Alliance is an essential component of Europe's future. I do not foresee that the CSCE can replace NATO as the guarantor of Western security and stability. Indeed, it is difficult to visualize how a European collective security arrangement including Eastern Europe, and perhaps even the Soviet Union, would have the capability to deter threats to Western Europe." He concluded: "NATO is the only plausible justification in my country for the American military presence in Europe. If NATO is allowed to wither because it has no meaningful political place in the new Europe, the basis for a long-term US military commitment can die with it."[26]

In short, Bush was making clear to Mitterrand that the two-plus-four should limit itself to completing only the minimum necessary steps needed to dissolve four power legal rights in Germany. Decisions about the future of NATO and its nuclear arsenal were not, in the view of the US, necessary to accomplish that goal, and thus should not up for debate in the two-plus-four forum.²⁷ Moreover, Washington was also not interested in debating alternative, pan-European collective security organizations, either in the two-plus-four talks or indeed at all.²⁸

MITTERRAND MOVES TOO SLOWLY

Over the Fourth of July holiday in 1990, Bush and his advisers met at his vacation home in Kennebunkport, where Bush had received Mitterrand in May 1989. Bush and his subordinates defined their primary goal: to get a unified Germany into NATO as soon as possible.²⁹ The secretary of state, Baker, suggested that the real future risk to NATO might come from CSCE, or, more precisely, French notions of building a new security structure around it. Baker's comments were meant to suggest that decisive leadership would ensure that the US-led security organization would maintain its significance in the post–Cold War world.³⁰ Bush asked, "do [the] French really want to see us out of there?" Baker replied that the French did not exactly want the Americans to disappear entirely, but would prefer them to become mercenaries, available for hire only when needed. Robert Zoellick, at the time a senior State Department official and also in attendance, additionally pointed out that Mitterrand was seeking assurances that NATO would not go "out-of-area."³¹ In other words, although he did not use this phrase at the time according to surviving notes, the French felt that the US should not think that it had a "global green light" (in the words of Védrine).

The French president did not give up on his vision of a pan-European structure, however, even as Bonn and Washington increasingly succeeded in their efforts to "bribe" Gorbachev into accepting NATO membership of all of a united Germany. Mitterrand failed to realize how much speed was of the essence, however. In the longer term, he still hoped for nothing less than to create a greater Europe "from the Atlantic to the Urals."³² Mitterrand would even organize a summit to this effect in Prague in June 1991.

But by then Bonn and Washington had long since convinced Gorbachev to accept their vision of NATO. That breakthrough had come partly in May and June 1990, at the Washington summit between Bush and Gorbachev, and partly in July 1990, when Kohl and Gorbachev met in the Soviet Union to discuss practical details of German unification. Here, too, Mitterrand had played a role; meeting with Gorbachev just before the Washington summit, he acknowledged to the Soviet leader that, while they both might still wish to consider alternatives, Bonn and Washington's vision was clearly winning out and they needed to acknowledge that. The bottom line was that Paris, while it might wish for changes to NATO, was not willing to risk a rupture with Bonn and Washington.[33]

The one major, still-open question in autumn 1990, however, was exactly what an extension of NATO to former East Germany would mean, not least in nuclear terms. Gorbachev and his aides reasoned that letting NATO expand into soon-to-be former East Germany, but without nuclear weapons, would not change the balance of power that mattered, namely, the overall nuclear balance in Europe and the world. Unfortunately for Moscow, Soviet leaders did not realize that, behind the scenes, Bonn and Washington had begun to speculate on the future role of NATO in Eastern Europe as well (although such speculation would end once the invasion of Kuwait by Saddam Hussein moved the Gulf to the top of the US security agenda; the issue would only come to the fore once again in subsequent administrations).[34]

Gorbachev ultimately agreed to a reunited Germany wholly in NATO, but with restrictions on the kinds of troops that could be deployed to former East German territory, and prohibitions against nuclear weapons. All of these restrictions persist to this day. Washington and Bonn agreed, but made sure that in the written documents emerging from the talks, namely the final two-plus-four treaty of September 1990, such restrictions applied only to eastern Germany and did not set a precedent for other areas. In other words, the door for further eastward movement of NATO stayed open. Zoellick, one of the lead negotiators in this matter, said in later interviews that he was thinking of Poland as he finalized the wording in the accords but did not, of course, tip his hand to his Soviet negotiation partners.[35]

Thus, by the time Mitterrand was able to begin serious consultations with Eastern European leaders on alternative security organizations in 1990 and 1991, it was too late for his purposes to succeed. The former Warsaw Pact countries had by that point realized that the post–Cold War security order was going to look very much like the Cold War security order. In the immediate wake of the collapse of the Wall, they had briefly worried more about revived German nationalism than about the Soviet Union under Gorbachev as a security threat and, in part, showed interest in pan-European security projects and even security cooperation with Moscow for that reason. However, that interest dissipated once it became clear that post–Cold War security would, just like Cold War security, rest upon NATO.

That being the case, East Europeans wanted to be on the Western side of any future NATO/non-NATO line. In other words, they had become more interested in membership of NATO—which, by 1990, was clearly going to remain the dominant institution in post-Wall European security—and less interested in some kind of intermediate organization such as Mitterrand was proposing. It was simply too indefinite a concept and, in addition, a creeping suspicion emerged among Eastern European capitals about it. The French president's pan-European *security* project might be a kind of delaying tactic, or halfway house, designed to replace or stall the potential pan-European *economic* project of EC expansion. Mitterrand seemed interested in completing the project only at some indefinite point in the future, whereas East Europeans wanted pressing concerns resolved as soon as possible.[36] And there were concerns about the idea of a security structure that might include Moscow but exclude Washington. As a result of all of these issues, the project of a pan-European security institution soon died.

EPILOGUE: FROM 1990 TO TODAY

The extent of Zoellick's success in phrasing the two-plus-four accord in such a way that future expansion remained possible became clear in the course of the 1990s. NATO expanded to twelve Eastern European countries in three rounds of enlargement, a process initiated during the tenure of Bush's successor, President Bill Clinton. As the expansion process unfolded, the Russian (no longer Soviet) leader Boris Yeltsin began to complain that the two-plus-four accord of 1990 ought to have precluded such expansion.

Thanks to the work of the Western two-plus-four negotiators, however, State Department officials could confidently reply in 1996 that the text of the accord did no such thing. As summarized in a confidential internal analysis prepared for Strobe Talbott, at the time acting secretary of state, the department's considered view was that Yeltsin's objection was "a specious argument which we should refute definitively." John Kornblum and John Herbst, the two State Department officials who submitted this internal analysis to Talbott, held that the terms of the two-plus-four treaty simply did "not apply to territory outside Germany." Kornblum and Herbst noted that, while the treaty did prohibit "stationing or deployment of foreign troops and nuclear weapons systems in the eastern Länder [states]" of united Germany, it had no bearing on Eastern Europe. As a result, Russian claims that any eastward movement beyond eastern Germany would "'violate the spirit of the two-plus-four agreement' are completely unfounded." Moscow's view that "the extension of NATO 'infrastructure' into central and Eastern Europe would be impossible for Russia ever to accept and would doom our efforts to create a comprehensive European security system" were, in the authors' view, equally unfounded.[37]

In understanding today's renewed tensions between Russia and the US, knowledge of the narrative summarized above is essential. It shows Washington's conviction in 1989–1990 that NATO, as a proven, successful organization, should continue to dominate European security, and that the continued presence of NATO troops in Europe necessarily meant that of their nuclear weapons as well. In contrast, Mitterrand felt that the opportunity of the end of the Cold War should be seized as a means of overcoming longstanding European divisions, some going back much further than the Cold War itself. By contrasting Mitterrand's vision with the actual outcome, we are thus better able to understand that NATO's perpetuation into the post–Cold War era was hardly a given, but rather the active result of US and West German efforts in the contest over NATO's future beyond the end of the Cold War.

The twenty-fifth anniversary of these events coincided, tragically, with the renewal of violent alterations to European borders. President Vladimir Putin of Russia annexed Crimea in the wake of the 2014 political upheaval in Kiev. The Russian leader was also behind the 2014–2015 larger land invasion of other regions of Ukraine as well. Putin thereby slammed shut the already closing window of opportunity for creating pan-European security as defined by Mitterrand, meaning from France to the Soviet Union/Russia.

While the historical events described in this essay in no way excuse or legitimate Putin's actions, we must keep them in mind if we want to understand the decay in post–Cold War relations between the West and Russia. At the time of writing of this chapter (2015), relations with Moscow are at a post–Cold War low. Russia under Putin has experienced de-democratization, censorship, and rising homophobia and xenophobia. Its neighbors have endured aggression, energy shutoffs, and armed incursions. Journalists and human rights activists attempting to call attention to these events, such as Anna Politkovskaya, have died mysteriously.

Dealing with Russia in its current aggressive and hostile incarnation is thus already difficult enough. Now that evidence about one of the most contentious issues in US–Russian relations has become abundantly available, in large part thanks to French archives, neither Moscow nor the West should complicate matters further by misstating what happened at the close of the Cold War. This evidence documents the debate over the future of European security. Bonn and Washington ultimately succeeded with a vision of European security that perpetuated the classic Cold War institution, NATO. This solution enabled a swift and peaceful reunification process to unfold. Mitterrand's alternative, by comparison, remained vague, under-conceptualized, and had no convincing roadmap or timeline toward completion. The motives behind his calls for pan-Europeanism were many, not always in accord with the goals of his allies.

Nonetheless, it is worth noting in closing that the Franco-American correspondence carries the scent of a lost opportunity. The French understood the need to "compensate" the Soviets in some way for the loss of East European territory; not so much because Moscow was strong enough to demand compensation in 1990—it was not—but rather as a kind of insurance or hedge against future Russian bitterness and future crises in Europe. Paris ultimately deferred to the wishes of Bonn and Washington, but, in hindsight, perhaps the subsequent history of post–Cold War Western–Russian relations would have taken a less tragic turn had Mitterrand enjoyed more success.

Notes

1. For more on this topic, see Mary Elise Sarotte, *The Collapse: The Accidental Opening of the Berlin Wall* (New York: Basic Books, 2014). Due to space constraints in this edited volume, it is not feasible to provide a lengthy list of the large number of significant works on this subject here, so readers are invited to peruse the endnotes to *The Collapse* for references to additional writings on this subject.

2. See my *1989: The Struggle to Create Post–Cold War Europe* (Princeton, NJ: Princeton University Press, 2009; new and updated edition, 2014). See also my articles "Perpetuating U.S. Preeminence: The 1990 Deals to 'Bribe the Soviets Out' and Move NATO In," *International Security* 35 (July 2010): 110–37; and "A Broken Promise?" *Foreign Affairs*, Sept.–Oct. 2014: 90–97. Again, the footnotes to these items provide citations to more of the important literature on this subject than it is possible to cite here.

3. This speculation is discussed in the new afterword to the updated edition of *1989*, 215–29. For more on the process of NATO expansion in the Clinton era, see Ronald D. Asmus, *Opening NATO's Door: How the Alliance Remade Itself for a New Era* (New York: Columbia University Press, 2002).

4. Robert M. Gates, *From the Shadows* (New York: Touchstone, 1996), 492. See also my article "In Victory, Magnanimity," *International Politics* 48 (August 2011): 482–95.

5. For the original text of Bush's Mainz speech, see "A Europe Whole and Free, Remarks to the Citizens in Mainz. President George Bush. Rheingoldhalle. Mainz, Federal Republic of Germany, May 31, 1989," on the website of the U.S. Diplomatic Mission to Germany, available at http://usa.usembassy.de/etexts/ga6-890531.htm. For more about Thatcher on the periphery in 1989–1990, see Rodric Braithwaite, "Gorbachev and Thatcher," *Journal of European Integration History* 16, no. 1 (2010): 31.

6. For more on the conflict between the Foreign and Commonwealth Office and No. 10 Downing Street over this topic, see Patrick Salmon, Keith Hamilton, and Stephen Twigge, eds., *Documents on British Policy Overseas*, Series III, Vol. VII, *German Unification, 1989–1990* (London: Routledge, 2009).

7. For more on the interaction between European integration and developments in European security, see Kiran Klaus Patel and Kenneth Weisbrode, eds., *European Integration and the Atlantic Community in the 1980s* (Cambridge: Cambridge University Press, 2013).

8. Jean Musitelli, "François Mitterrand, l'européen: Point de vue," June 2, 2004, posted on the website of the Mitterrand Institute, www.mitterrand.org/François-Mitterrand-l-europeen.html.

9. Julie Newton, "Gorbachev, Mitterrand, and the Emergence of the Post–Cold War Order in Europe," *Europe-Asia Studies* 65, no. 2 (March 2013): 294.

10. Archives nationales (AN), Archives d'Elisabeth Guigou (EG), 5 AG 4 EG 170, Entretiens officiels de François Mitterrand notamment avec Margaret Thatcher, Felipe Gonzalez et Helmut Kohl, préparation notes internes, notes manuscrites, télégrammes, discours, mémorandum, comptes rendus, 1987–1990; "Loïc Hennekine, Présidence de la République, Le Conseiller Diplomatique, Paris, le 18 avril 1990, NOTE POUR LE PRESIDENT DE LA REPUBLIQUE," 1. This and all other AN documents released per my dérogation, June 4, 2008. The author wishes to thank Frédéric Bozo and Georges Saunier for their assistance in filing this dérogation, and Bozo for comments on an earlier draft of this chapter.

11. AN, 5 AG 4 EG 170, Entretiens officiels, "O 171642Z APR 90m Fm White House, To Elysée Palace, Antenne Spéciale de Transmissions de l'Élysée, Télétype Bleu."

12. The pathbreaking work of Frédéric Bozo has convincingly challenged the previously inaccurate view that Franco-American relations at the end of the Cold War were unremittingly hostile; rather, as he has shown, there was disagreement, but within a larger context of cooperation. See, to cite five examples in chronological order, (1) Frédéric Bozo, *Mitterrand, la fin de la guerre froide et l'unification allemande: De Yalta à Maastricht* (Paris: Odile Jacob, 2005), available in English as *Mitterrand, the End of the Cold War, and German Unification* (New York: Berghahn, 2009); (2) Bozo, "Mitterrand's France, the End of the Cold War, and German Unification: A Reappraisal," *Cold War History* 7, no. 4 (2007): 455–78; (3) Bozo, "France, German Unification, and European Integration," in *Europe and the End of the Cold War*, ed. Frédéric Bozo, Marie-Pierre Rey, N. Piers Ludlow, and Leopoldo Nuti (London: Routledge, 2008); (4) Bozo, "'Winners' and 'Losers': France, the United States, and the End of the Cold War," *Diplomatic History* 33 (November 2009): 927–56; and (5) Bozo, "'I Feel More Comfortable with You': France, the Soviet Union, and German Unification," *Journal of Cold War Studies*, in press. The author thanks Bozo for providing an advance copy of the latter article.

13. On this issue, see Hubert Védrine, *Les mondes de François Mitterrand* (Paris: Fayard, 1996), 443; and James M. Goldgeier, *Not Whether but When: The US Decision to Enlarge NATO* (Washington, DC: Brookings Institution Press, 1999), chapter 2.

14. AN, 5 AG 4 Archives de Caroline de Margerie (CDM) 33, dossier 1, République fédérale d'Allemagne (RFA) et République démocratique allemande (RDA), "Présidence de la République, Le Chargé de Mission, Paris, le 15 mars 1990, COMPTE RENDU DU DEJEUNER DE JACQUES ATTALI AVEC HORST TELTSCHIK (jeudi 15 mars 1990)," 1. "BUSH a dit à KOHL 'No nukes, no troops.'"

15. Bozo, "'I Feel More Comfortable with You.'"

16. "COMPTE RENDU DU DEJEUNER DE JACQUES ATTALI AVEC HORST TELTSCHIK," 1–2. The original full quotation is as follows: "Il faut donc proposer aux Soviétiques un paquet global qui compense le maintien dans l'OTAN et leur permette de sauver la face, tout en maintenant des éléments de sécurité importants pour l'alliance."

17. Frédéric Bozo, "The Failure of a Grand Design: Mitterrand's European Confederation, 1989–1991," *Contemporary European History* 17, no. 3 (2008): 393–95.

18. French Foreign Ministry (MAE), 6125, telegram, January 31, 1990.

19. Sarotte, "Perpetuating U.S. Preeminence: The 1990 Deals to 'Bribe the Soviets Out' and Move NATO In," 116–17; and Sarotte, "A Broken Promise?"

20. Memorandum of Conversation, "Meeting with Chancellor Helmut Kohl," Feb. 24, 1990, GHWBPL, released due to the author's request, MR-2008–0651 of May 21, 2008; see also George H. W. Bush and Brent Scowcroft, *A World Transformed* (New York: Knopf, 1998), 253. For more on Bush's motivations generally, see Jeffrey Engel, *When the World Seemed New* (New York: Houghton Mifflin Harcourt, forthcoming).

THE CONTEST OVER NATO'S FUTURE 227

21. "Gespräch des Bundeskanzlers Kohl mit Präsident Bush, Camp David, 24. Feb. 1990," document 192, in Hanns Jürgen Küsters and Daniel Hoffman, eds., *Dokumente zur Deutschlandpolitik: Deutsche Einheit, Sonderedition aus den Akten des Bundeskanzleramtes 1989/90* (hereafter DESE) (Munich: Oldenbourg Verlag, 1998), 868–69. See also Philip Zelikow and Condoleezza Rice, *Germany Unified and Europe Transformed: A Study in Statecraft* (Cambridge, MA: Harvard University Press, 1995), 215; and the multivolume study produced by a group of German professors who received early access to West German documents, *Geschichte der deutschen Einheit* (Stuttgart: Deutsche Verlags-Anstalt, 1998), in particular vol. 4, Werner Weidenfeld, Peter M. Wagner, and Elke Bruck, *Außenpolitik für die deutsche Einheit: Die Entscheidungsjahre 1989/90*, 269, 466.

22. AN, 5 AG 4 CDM 36, dossier 2, télégramme, Boidevaix to M. Bianco, M. Hennekine, Mme. de Margerie, Le Ministre d'Etat, M. Kesedjin, M. Danon, le 28 mars 1990, "OBJET: COMMUNICATION AUX AMBASSADEURS DES TROIS PUISSANCES (1/2)."

23. MAE, Direction d'Europe, 6125, 1986–1990, DIRECTION DE L'EUROPE CONTINENTALE, Série ALL, Sous Série 1, Dossier 2, UNIFICATION ALLEMANDE, POSITION DE L'OTAN, télégramme, le 27 février 1990.

24. AN, 5 AG 4 EG 170, Entretiens officiels de François Mitterrand, Folder 16, Entretien de François Mitterrand avec GEORGE BUSH, président des Etats-Unis d'Amérique, KEY LARGO 19 avril 1990, "Présidence de la République, Paris, le 10 avril 1990, NOTE POUR LE PRESIDENT DE LA REPUBLIQUE, A/s une proposition de défense européenne." Mitterrand wrote by hand on the top: "*Note à garde FM.*"

25. AN, 5 AG 4 EG 170, Entretiens officiels de François Mitterrand, "Le Conseiller à la Présidence de la République, Paris, le 11 avril 1990, NOTE POUR LE PRESIDENT DE LA REPUBLIQUE, A/s votre rencontre avec le Président BUSH; le rôle de l'OTAN," signed Hubert Védrine.

26. AN, 5 AG 4 EG 170, Entretiens officiels, "O 171642Z APR 90m Fm White House, To Elysée Palace, Antenne Spéciale de Transmissions de l'Élysée, Télétype Bleu." Original in English in the French archives.

27. AN, 5 AG 4 CDM 36, dossier 2, Réunification allemande, "DRAFT PREPARATORY PAPER: OPTIONS FOR A SETTLEMENT ON GERMANY," no date, but from context on or around April 17, 1990.

28. AN, 5 AG 4 EG 170, Entretiens officiels de François Mitterrand, Loïc Hennekine, Présidence de la République, Le Conseiller Diplomatique, "Paris, le 18 avril 1990, NOTE POUR LE PRESIDENT DE LA REPUBLIQUE, *Objet* Les Etats-Unis et la CSCE." Summarizing Washington's view, this report concludes that "elle [the Bush administration] ne croit pas à un arrangement de sécurité collective englobant les pays de l'Est et l'URSS."

29. "Notes from Jim Cicconi [note taker] re: 7/3/90 pre-NATO Summit briefing at Kennebunkport," folder 3, box 109, 8c monthly files, Papers of James Baker, Mudd Library, Princeton University. In their account, Zelikow and Rice say that no formal transcript of this meeting survived (fortunately, the Cicconi notes did), but they agree that Zoellick's briefing was one of the most important ones. Zelikow and Rice, *Germany Unified*, 321.

30. For discussion of the relative weights of CSCE and NATO in US foreign policy at this time, see Raymond Garthoff, *The Great Transition: American–Soviet Relations and the End of the Cold War* (Washington: Brookings Institution Press, 1994), 427.

31. Mitterrand would also indicate frustration around this time by pulling 50,000 troops out of Germany ahead of the other allies and resisting the formation of multinational units. "56. Deutschfranzösische Konsultationen, München, 17./18. September 1990," document 424, DESE, 1544–46; see also Zelikow and Rice, *Germany Unified*, 323.

32. Bozo, "The Failure of a Grand Design," 393.
33. Bozo, "'I Feel More Comfortable with You.'"
34. See the new afterword to the updated edition of my *1989*.
35. Sarotte, *1989*, 192.
36. Newton, "Gorbachev, Mitterrand," 294.

37. I spent seven years filing repeated requests with the State Department in order to get this document declassified via a Freedom of Information Act request. (I filed my request, Case No. F2008–02356, in 2008; I received the document in 2015.) I am grateful to John Hackett and James Graham Wilson for their help in securing this document. See Wilson's own insightful study, *The Triumph of Improvisation: Gorbachev's Adaptability, Reagan's Engagement, and the End of the Cold War* (Ithaca, NY: Cornell University Press, 2014).

Part II

CURRENT CHALLENGES

Chapter 4

Toward an Open and Accountable NATO

Ian Davis

While transparency has been one of the burning issues in public policy over the last decade or so, it has not historically been a natural inclination for defense institutions or intergovernmental organizations. Bodies tasked with securing national or international security have been instinctively wary of greater openness of information about institutional activities and actions.

At a swearing-in ceremony for senior US officials in January 2009, President Barack Obama said, "For a long time now there's been too much secrecy in this city," adding, "Transparency and rule of law will be the touchstones of this presidency." "Starting today, every agency and department should know that this administration stands on the side not of those who seek to withhold information, but those who seek to make it known."

While President Obama was talking about Washington, DC—and a country with a longstanding Freedom of Information Act (signed by President Lyndon Johnson in 1966) and C-SPAN coverage of parts of the US federal government since 1979—he could equally have been referring to Brussels. And while most people equate a lack of transparency in that city with the institutions of the European Union, in many respects there is an even greater democratic deficit at the heart of NATO. This deficit can be seen to exist at four levels: within the closed inner workings of the alliance; as a result of Cold War legacy secrecy and classification rules; through poor budgetary controls and nonexistent performance metrics; and weak parliamentary and public oversight, including sluggish mechanisms of engagement and outreach by NATO itself. Each of these issues is discussed in more detail below.

NATO is one of the few major intergovernmental bodies not to have even a basic information disclosure policy. There have been a number of interesting developments in the "right to know" field in recent years, including an information disclosure policy adopted by the World Bank and interagency task force reviews of national security classification policy in the United States.[1] NATO, however, continues to be a closed and secretive organization distant from the general public.

A comparison between the World Bank and NATO is illustrative.[2] In 2010, the bank revised its Access to Information Disclosure Policy to assume that all its information is publicly available unless it is specifically exempted. The new policy also affords an appeals process for stakeholders who are denied information. The bank has also launched an Open Data Initiative that provides the public with free access to its vast database of development indicators. And most recently, the bank has made its audited financial statements and its Sanction Board decisions on contractor-corruption cases available for public scrutiny.

Yet within NATO, even finding information on something as basic as running costs remains problematic. NATO does not publish an annual budget or financial report, as is routinely done by a growing number of other intergovernmental bodies, such as the EU and World Bank. Before examining NATO's record in more detail, however, it is worth pausing to consider the issue of secrecy and transparency in modern governance in general, and in foreign and defense affairs in particular.

UNLOCKING THE SECURITY STATE: A SHORT HISTORY

The last two decades have seen an explosion in the measurement of government openness and the accessibility of information to the public. This is due largely to the developing awareness worldwide in the usefulness of transparency as a tool for promoting reform, and to the emergence since the 1990s of a global right-to-information movement.

Today, over 110 countries have information access laws, with the majority passing them only since 2000.[3] Many of these laws were enacted during periods of democratic transition or regime change. In many countries, they were also the result of popular protest for more open government. In others, laws were passed to meet aid or other requirements, like EU accession. The first enactment of a freedom of information (FOI) law in a NATO member state occurred in 1966 (in the United States), and all bar two have had FOI laws in force since at least 2006. Spain finally adopted an FOI law in 2014, leaving Luxembourg as the only alliance member without such legislation.

However, defense institutions and armed forces within NATO member states have tended to resist such changes. National security and the public's right to know are often viewed as pulling in opposite directions, and national security is usually well insulated from FOI requests by exemptions in the legislation. In the UK, for example, it is not possible to send a request to any of the official national security agencies such as MI5, MI6, and GCHQ, and any information "required for the purpose of safeguarding national security" is also exempt.

The question of how to ensure public access to government information without jeopardizing legitimate efforts to protect people from national security threats was the focus of a new set of global principles unveiled in June 2013. The Global Principles on National Security and the Right to Information (Tshwane Principles)[4] were the result of over two years of consultation around the world, facilitated by the Open Society Justice Initiative and involving governments, former security officials, civil society groups, and academics. In addition to addressing what government-held information may legitimately be kept secret and what information should be disclosed, they outline standards for the treatment of whistleblowers who act in the public interest, as well as issues related to classification and declassification. However, no government has so far adopted the principles as a national standard.

Within the EU, the right of access to documents is a fundamental right of all citizens as enshrined in the Treaty on the Functioning of the European Union (Article 15) and the Charter of Fundamental Rights of the European Union (Article 42). The mechanisms for making documents requests and the rules on exceptions are developed in Regulation 1049/2001 and apply to the European Commission, the European Parliament, and the Council of the European Union—as well as to other offices, bodies, and agencies. These transparency rules are the EU's equivalent of an access to information or freedom of information law. Within NATO, however, the picture is very different. Most of the alliance's work takes place away from the glare of publicity in an assortment of projects involving numerous specialized agencies, centers, committees, groups, and panels.

THE VEILED INNER WORKINGS OF THE ALLIANCE

Each member state sends a permanent diplomatic delegation to NATO's Brussels headquarters. The North Atlantic Council (NAC) of permanent delegations meets at least once a week and has effective control of NATO policymaking. The NAC also meets at higher levels of foreign ministers, defense ministers, or heads of government where major decisions are made. It is the only decision-making body within NATO that was established by the founding treaty. All decisions have the same status at whatever level they are made. Decisions are made by consensus and there is no scope for majority decisions within the NAC. The NAC is chaired by the NATO secretary general. The alliance works through a number of committees and subcommittees, the most important of which are chaired by the secretary general.

NATO's extensive network of committees covers everything from political issues, to improving capabilities, to technical issues related to the alliance's military interoperability. The principal NATO committees are the Nuclear Planning Group (NPG) and the Military Committee. Many committees report directly to the NAC, including: Deputies Committee; Political and Partnerships Committee; Defence Policy and Planning Committee; Committee on Proliferation; Consultation, Command and Control Board (C3B); Operations Policy Committee; High Level Task Force on Conventional Arms Control; Verification Coordinating Committee; Conference of National Armaments Directors (CNAD); Committee for Standardization; Logistics Committee; Resource Policy and Planning Board; Air and Missile Defence Committee; Air Traffic Management Committee; Civil Emergency Planning Committee; Committee on Public Diplomacy; Council Operations and Exercises Committee; Security Committee; Civilian Intelligence Committee; and Archives Committee. Within many of these committees there are also working groups and subcommittees. Very few of these committees would be recognizable to the public, and their work rarely features in the media.

The CNAD, for example, has been going since 1966 and is the senior NATO body responsible for collaboration between member countries on equipment and research projects. One national armaments director (NAD) is appointed from each member state and is usually a senior official from the state's ministry of defense.

The pinnacle NATO event is the summit with heads of government. These confidential face-to-face meetings among the twenty-nine allied leaders take place about once every two years and are considered the NATO crown jewels. More regular meetings (about three or four times per annum) also take place between foreign and defense ministers. The processes of developing the policies those NATO leaders endorse at summits or ministerial meetings largely fly under the public radar, and participation by nonofficial interested parties is limited. Decisions of the NAC are expressed in communiqués, but these are often bland and much other committee work goes unreported. While the names of these committees may be known (if you know where to look), the names of their members usually are not made public. Nor are agendas, background papers, or draft documents. Generally they work in private and do not provide minutes. The standard litany of transparency weaknesses includes:

- a lack of basic organizational information, making it hard to know even who's involved;
- a lack of information about what the intergovernmental working groups are doing as they develop the commitments for the leaders to endorse; and
- weak measurement about how the member states are doing in fulfilling their commitments.

In general, the process of policy formulation—the discussions, debates, arguments, meetings, research, back-and-forth—largely remains out of view and behind closed doors. Even when the NATO policy development process moves to an agreed course of action across the alliance, the default position remains to withhold information. It doesn't have to be like this. In September 2011, the alliance authorized the declassification and release of the NATO political guidance on ways to improve its involvement in stabilization and reconstruction. The guidance had been officially approved by NATO defense ministers a year earlier and sets out the principles on which NATO can plan for, employ, and coordinate civilian and military crisis management capabilities that nations provide for alliance missions. Given that the document's core rationale was to coordinate activities with external actors, it should have been afforded "open access" status from the outset. NATO's longstanding secrecy and classification rules, however, work against such "commonsense" judgments.

NATO'S SECRECY AND CLASSIFICATION RULES

NATO's classification system is worse than opaque. According to Transparency International, "little is known about the information standards within NATO since not many documents on the subject are made public.

However, from the few that are, a number of weaknesses in the system are highlighted. These include not defining rules of protection and thus making the system prone to arbitrary classifications, not listing the subjects which may require classification, and not developing an expiry of classification periods."[5]

Throughout most of NATO's history, its secrecy policy was contained in a document referred to as C-M(55)15(Final). Although this document was unclassified, for decades NATO refused to make it publicly available. Research by Alasdair Roberts suggests that the document established a very conservative classification system "excessively tilted towards secrecy" at the outset and remained relatively constant over the next four decades. He identified "five basic features"—breadth, depth, centralization, and controlled distribution and personnel controls—"each of which has been adopted with the aim of ensuring a high level of security for information."[6] And rather than revisiting these rules after the end of the Cold War, they simply became a requirement for those states in Central and Eastern Europe seeking accession to NATO.[7]

While some of the main contemporary documents regulating NATO's classification regime are now in the public domain,[8] there is very little information on their practice, nor much to suggest any significant changes in the last decade. These classification rules also extend to partner nations through agreements reached within such frameworks as Partnership for Peace (PfP), Euro-Atlantic Partnership Council, and Mediterranean Dialogue. Even the EU's classification system was altered in line with NATO standards, and both comprise four levels of classification: top secret, secret, confidential, and restricted.[9] Both NATO and the EU require the establishment of a national security authority for the protection of NATO and EU classified information. National security authorities have to be set up not only by the member states but also by other countries cooperating with NATO or the EU and holding their classified information.

Given the scale and importance of the NATO security apparatus, it ought to be subjected to close scrutiny. The only way that external observers can really understand what is happening in NATO is to read the documents it produces and then put those documents in a historical context. Only with this full picture is it possible to grasp the significance of what is being proposed or implemented. But under existing classification rules, many important documents are not released.

The development of missile defenses within NATO offers one important example. A 10,000-page feasibility study funded by NATO (i.e., by European and US taxpayers) on the missile threat to Europe and how to defend against it was completed in May 2006. The classified study was developed by an international consortium of industries, led by the US firm Science Applications International Corporation (SAIC). Based in McLean, Virginia, SAIC is comprised of the following companies: Raytheon (US), EADS Astrium (Europe), Thales (France), Thales Raytheon System Company (France/US); IABG (Germany), TNO (Netherlands), Qinetiq (UK), DATAMAT (Italy), and Diehl (German). SAIC not only carried out the feasibility study, it was also the successful bidder for the NATO missile defense contract worth 75 million euros over a period of six years. This contract was agreed behind closed doors at the Riga summit in November 2006, with no prior independent scrutiny of the feasibility study or debate in the elected chambers of the then twenty-six member states. None of the NATO-funded feasibility studies and missile proliferation threat assessments over the past fifteen years that have been used to justify deployment of territorial missile defenses have been declassified and openly published.

Despite NATO's almost daily bombardment of Facebook, Twitter, and YouTube with press statements, news stories, and background videos, the "diplomatic brick walls" remain intact. Copies of the documentation that might allow independent evaluation of what NATO officials are thinking and with whom they are doing business are rarely if ever set out in the public domain. NATO defense ministers at their October 2011 meeting, for example, discussed the initial findings of a task force to promote Smart Defense, one of the key initiatives later unveiled at the 2012 Chicago summit. A request for a list of task force members, its terms of reference, and a copy of the initial findings met with the curt response that this was an "internal task force" operating at the "working level": in other words, outside of the public purview. But this information would normally be available for a national-level task force, either as a matter of course or following an FOI request.

WHO PAYS THE NATO PIPER AND ARE ALLIES PLAYING THE RIGHT TUNE?

One of the longest-running fault lines within NATO has been the "burden sharing" debate, with accusations that Europe spends too little on defense and is being protected at American taxpayer expense.[10] However, large parts of the US military budget have nothing whatsoever to do with NATO or European security, while in Europe, NATO is seen by its member states as the cornerstone of their defense policies. Thus, while Americans do pick up a disproportionate share of the NATO tab, this is nowhere near the level that is widely accepted as "common currency" in the debate.

Moreover, claims that the disparity between the US and Europe is at a historic high are misplaced.[11] NATO defense spending was at its most disproportionate in 1952, when the US share constituted almost 77 percent of the alliance total. Conversely, NATO military spending was closest to parity in 1999, when the US share constituted 55 percent of the total and when Europeans were making major contributions to NATO stability operations in the Balkans.[12]

The costs of running NATO and implementing its policies and activities are officially met in two ways—contributions to a common funding pool and participation in NATO-led operations. A third way of looking at the issue is to assess the extent to which nationally procured military forces also contribute to NATO's deterrence posture and Article 5 (collective defense) commitments. As regards the officially recognized budgetary process, direct contributions to the NATO common funding pool are made by members in accordance with an agreed cost-sharing formula based on relative gross national income. There are three budgets within the common funding arrangements: a civil budget, a military budget, and the Security Investment Program, which pays for NATO installations and facilities.

Prior to 2015, the NATO website only provided some background on the budgetary process, but the actual budget amounts and respective member state contributions were not available. This changed in 2015, however, and both the NATO website and the latest annual reports by the NATO secretary general (see below) provide headline figures for the three NATO budgets. This data confirms the NATO annual budget as 2.1 billion euros in both 2015 and 2016. Of course, these direct contributions to NATO represent a very small percentage of each member's overall defense budget. It is in contributing to NATO-led operations that the serious money begins to get spent, since member countries incur all their own deployment costs whenever they volunteer forces for such operations. With a few exceptions, it is nationally procured military forces and military assets such as ships, submarines, aircraft, tanks, artillery, or weapons systems that are or have been deployed in NATO missions in Kosovo, Afghanistan, and Libya. But there has been no official attempt to provide a detailed breakdown of how the costs stack up for each of these missions, although the US is widely perceived as the largest contributor to the first two.

In January 2012, then-NATO Secretary General Anders Fogh Rasmussen published for the first time an annual report, a practice that he repeated in 2013 and 2014. The current NATO secretary general, Jens Stoltenberg, has continued this practice and published his third annual report in March 2017.[13] While a welcome development, the reports are little more than public relations devices to illustrate NATO's achievements while remaining mute on negative features. There is no explanation given as to the purpose of the reports, although they remain in keeping with Rasmussen's view (presumably now shared by Stoltenberg) of the secretary general's office as an independent agency for promoting NATO's strategic vision. Having said this, the last two annual reports published by Stoltenberg, at over 120 pages (previously the reports were under thirty pages), do provide a wealth of more detail on everything that NATO does, from general developments in capabilities and defense, to operations and missions, partnerships, and organizational matters. A chapter on the latter also includes a three-paragraph discussion on how NATO is attempting to address access to information issues.

The main thrust of Rasmussen's 2013 Annual Report, however, was to warn of the negative impact of national austerity measures on defense capabilities within the alliance, a recurring theme in the speeches of the then secretary general.[14] The report argues that current defense spending trends may lead to a widening of three perceived capabilities gaps: an intra-European gap; a transatlantic gap; and, most astonishing of all, a gap between the alliance and emerging powers that "could create a growing gap between their capacity to act and exert influence on the international stage and our ability to do so."

In a multipolar world, it is surely a given that NATO's capacity to exert influence on the international stage is constrained, and Rasmussen's claim that NATO might end up with a "growing" capabilities gap with emerging powers has about as much veracity as the mythical "missile gap" of the Cold War. While acknowledging that NATO's "accumulated defence spending continues to be the highest in the world" (60 percent of the global total in 2011, to be exact), he bemoans the "steadily downward" trend from 69 percent in 2003 to a projected 56 percent in 2014. However, this selective use of statistics is misleading.

First, the longer linear trend in NATO defense spending is upward[15] and not "steadily downward," although it does contain periods of rise and fall. Indeed, NATO's defense spending has doubled in real terms since the 1950s, although of course NATO membership has also risen from twelve to twenty-nine members over that time. One recent analysis shows that, in constant 2011 dollars, the total military spending of NATO nations in 2010 was greater than at any other point in the alliance's history.[16] This includes at any point during the Cold War. The bottom line, therefore, is that NATO is hardly on a downward spending curve, as suggested in the secretary general's 2013 report.

Second, the recent growth in defense spending in "emerging powers" only fractionally begins to close the huge capabilities gap that currently exists in NATO's favor. Third, no allowance is made for the contributions of partner countries to the alliance, even though, as the report says, "many NATO partners have made particular political, operational and financial contributions to NATO-led operations." If the military budgets of just four of NATO's partners—Japan, South Korea, Israel, and Saudi Arabia—are added to the analysis, NATO and these allies accounted for over 70 percent of global military spending in 2010. Add in other key partner countries, such as Australia, Austria, Finland, Georgia, Jordan, Morocco, New Zealand, Qatar, Sweden, Switzerland, and the United Arab Emirates, and it brings the total close to 80 percent. Having developed a network of structured partnerships with countries across the Euro-Atlantic area, the Mediterranean, and the Gulf region over the past two decades, what exactly is it that NATO has to fear from "emerging powers"?

NATO leaders also made a commitment at the 2014 summit in Wales to reverse the trend of declining defense budgets and raise them over the coming decade. During the Cold War the political (nonbinding) benchmark was 3 percent of GDP. In 2006 NATO defense ministers agreed that "Allies who currently devote to defence a proportion of GDP which is at or above 2% should aim to maintain the current proportion. Nations whose current proportion of GDP devoted to defence is below this level should halt any decline in defence expenditures and aim to increase defence spending in real terms within the planning period."

At the time of the new Defense Investment Pledge in 2014, only four member states—the US, UK, Greece, and Estonia—hit that 2006 target. At the Warsaw summit in July 2016, NATO was able to report a collective increase in year-on-year defense expenditure, the first since 2009, and the news that five member states spent a minimum of 2 percent of GDP on defense (the fifth country being Poland). However, several of NATO's major powers remained well below this figure (e.g., Germany at 1.19 percent, Italy at 1.1 percent, and Canada at 0.99 percent).

This spending commitment is unlikely to have much impact in the short term, and certainly not across the entire alliance. Indeed, on the day the new spending pledges were announced, a report suggested that the UK would soon drop below those spending goals,[17] while German Defense Minister Ursula von der Leyen went on record after the Wales summit as saying that she did not believe Berlin should dramatically increase its defense budget (and also questioned the validity of the 2 percent of GDP benchmark).[18]

At the latest Brussels Summit in May 2017, under pressure from new US President Donald Trump, NATO leaders agreed to develop annual national plans, setting out how member states intend to meet the 2014 Defense Investment Pledge. The national plans will cover three major areas: cash (how nations intend to meet their 2 percent commitment), capabilities (how to invest additional funding in key military capabilities), and contributions (how nations intend to contribute to NATO missions, operations, and other engagements).

Of course, defense spending is only one determinant of overall military ability, albeit a significant one. With greater transparency, it should be possible to unpack the NATO-specific commitments of each country and thereby provide a more comprehensive picture of NATO's military commitments and capabilities. Others have also suggested capability mapping to complement the 2 percent benchmark.[19]

The bottom line is that NATO's limited financial (and other) transparency makes it difficult to ensure that NATO-related spending (by both member states and collectively) is efficient and effective. Financial management information is routinely provided by intergovernmental bodies such as the EU and World Bank. But NATO does not yet provide basic information about its income, expenditure, or performance evaluations to the general public.

Public information about NATO's budgets and results is sparse because most of the information is classified. Thus, there is no way of knowing whether NATO is delivering value for the taxpayers' money. Consequently, citizens and parliaments of member countries are unable to monitor whether their contributions to NATO result in an efficient international organization. Concerns about the financial management of NATO even stretch to several of the international auditors responsible for auditing NATO expenditures. The International Board of Auditors for NATO (IBAN) consists of six NATO member states, operating on a three-year rotation, and has a staff of twenty. In 2014, one of its members, the Netherlands Court of Audit (NCA)—the official auditing body of the Dutch government—took the unprecedented step of launching a website that aims to stimulate further debate and progress on this important issue.[20] The NCA website shows NATO funding flows on an interactive world map. The (limited) data underlying the map are derived from public sources. The main conclusion on the NCA website is that:

> NATO is funded with taxpayers' money. However, it does not yet provide comprehensive information about its annual revenues, expenditures, and achievements to the taxpayer. NATO is also not yet transparent and public[ly] accountable for its financial management. It is not clear what NATO entities achieve or whether they give value for money. This is because most of NATO's financial and organisational information is undisclosed. Some of this information is considered too sensitive to disclose to the public; but there is also information, which is not deemed sensitive, but is simply not disclosed.

For a public auditing body to go on record in these terms is remarkable. The launch of the website resulted in media and political attention, especially in the Netherlands and Belgium (the leading political party in the latter asked for a full investigation). It has also resulted in significant policy movement within NATO itself. In a press release in July 2014, the NATO secretary general stressed the importance of accountability and financial transparency, and described measures taken to restructure and strengthen IBAN. But most significant of all, at the NATO summit in Wales, for the first time ever, the Summit Declaration (paragraph 112) contained a commitment to "further work in the areas of delivery of common funded capabilities, *reform governance and transparency and accountability, especially in the management of NATO's financial resources*" (emphasis added) and to report back progress at the next summit. One small but tangible change as part of this commitment is that NATO's Resource Policy and Planning Board (RPPB)—a subsidiary body of the NAC—for the first time publicly released a five-page executive summary of its 2015 Annual Report. This report assesses the performance of military common funding within NATO, and reviews the financial situation of the NATO Security Investment Program and the civil and military budgets.[21]

However, there appeared to be little, if any, reporting back on this issue at the Warsaw summit, which in an even longer Summit Declaration (in paragraph 137) effectively restated the earlier commitment to "continue improving accountability, governance and transparency," tasking the NAC to pursue these efforts and "report on progress by our next Summit." The Brussels Summit in 2017 did not even provide a closing declaration and, having been dominated by the agenda of President Trump, failed to provide any progress report in this area. How then will parliaments in member states hold NATO to this commitment?

WEAK PARLIAMENTARY AND PUBLIC OVERSIGHT

Scrutiny certainly exists in national legislatures and parliamentary committees, and some very effective investigation has occurred of NATO action (on Bosnia, Kosovo, and Afghanistan, for instance). This, however, has often been constrained by difficulties of accessing relevant information. For example, an eight-year delay in NATO telling the Serbian government where thousands of cluster bombs were dropped during the 1999 Kosovo campaign was described by Baroness Royall of Blaisdon in the UK House of Lords as "rather shameful."[22]

Another example is the UN commission investigating war crimes and human rights violations in Libya, which reported in March 2012. The commission states that it did not receive enough information from NATO to determine whether the alliance had followed its own guidelines for avoiding civilian casualties when it processed the intelligence related to those sites before bombing them. "The commission is unable to determine, for lack of sufficient information, whether these strikes were based on incorrect or outdated intelligence and, therefore, whether they were consistent with NATO's objective to take all necessary precaution to avoid civilian casualties entirely," the report said. It called upon NATO to conduct its own investigation "to determine the level of civilian casualties, and review how their procedures operated during Operation Unified Protector."

The role of national parliaments (including other national elected legislatures) in their arguably most important function—assenting to policy—is particularly underdeveloped. Many parliaments simply lack the power of prior authorization of national involvement in NATO military operations or of determining the length of any such deployment. Given the proliferation of NATO missions, this is a significant failing. Further, because NATO lacks a dynamic treaty base (the North Atlantic Treaty remains essentially unaltered since its adoption in 1949) and legal system (akin to that of the EU), parliaments are rarely afforded the opportunity to debate and decide upon major initiatives within the alliance. Executive prerogative often renders the positions of NATO members (and thus the decisions eventually arrived at within the alliance) out of reach of parliamentary oversight. Finally, while many countries have held referenda on EU membership, few have held parallel votes on accession to the alliance.

This state of affairs has its roots in the Vienna Convention on the Law of Treaties, which draws a distinction between an "ordinary agreement" and a treaty: an ordinary agreement (such as NATO's new Strategic Concept agreed at the Lisbon summit in 2010) goes into effect by force of the signature by the representatives of the states that are party to the agreement, while a treaty (such as the 1968 Nuclear Non-Proliferation Treaty) goes into force only after being ratified. This distinction is intended to facilitate the task of the executive branch in its international contacts and, depending on the specific constitutional arrangements within each state, usually frees it from the requirement to ask for the approval of parliament for every agreement.

Indeed, across the NATO alliance, foreign policy and the signing of international treaties and agreements are almost exclusively the responsibility of the executive branch. The role of parliaments in the approval of international agreements and treaties is negligible: in some NATO states (such as the Czech Republic, Denmark, France, Germany and Italy) there is an obligation of approval by the parliament of some treaties and agreements, although this may often be no more than a rubber-stamping exercise; in a minority of cases (such as the Netherlands and the United States) the approval of parliament is required for every treaty or agreement, with only a few exceptions; and in others (such as the UK) the treaty or agreement is only required to be laid on the parliament's table, by force of law or custom.

However, this situation of executive exclusivity is fast becoming untenable, given that in the contemporary world many public matters are settled by means of international law and the status of international security bodies such as NATO is becoming progressively stronger. These processes create the need for parliaments to be more involved in foreign policy and the ratification of treaties.

One such parliamentary body that could play a more significant role is the NATO Parliamentary Assembly (NATO PA). Founded in 1955, the NATO PA is an "unelected body of elected representatives" and, despite its title, lacks a formal connection to the alliance. The assembly consists of 260 parliamentary delegates who are selected from the members of the national parliaments of member countries "by the procedure best suited to each country."[23] The aim is to ensure that the composition of the delegation represents the political balance within the national parliament (and a member of government cannot be a delegate to the assembly). Delegates from fourteen associate countries, the European Parliament, four regional partner and Mediterranean associate member countries, as well as parliamentary observers from seven other countries and three interparliamentary assemblies also take part in its activities.

Through its discussions and meetings, the assembly helps to promote a common feeling of Atlantic solidarity in the various legislative assemblies and to further the aims and values of NATO. The various NATO PA committees and subcommittees produce reports, which are discussed in draft form at the assembly's annual spring session. The reports are then revised and updated for discussion, amendment, and adoption at the assembly's annual autumn session. At this latter session, the committees also produce policy recommendations, which are voted on by the full assembly and forwarded to the NAC. These recommendations have little more than an advisory status within NATO, however, and little attention is given to them outside of NATO circles. Finally, the committees and subcommittees also meet several times a year in member and associate nations, where they receive briefings from leading government and parliamentary representatives, as well as senior academics and experts.

The assembly website describes one of its aims as "to provide greater transparency of NATO policies, and thereby a degree of collective accountability." But this vague statement is neither an articulation of openness and accountability principles, nor something that is much seen in practice. In short, the assembly lacks formal power and can only hold NATO accountable by seeking to influence and encourage. There is not even any formal procedure for members of the assembly to report back to their respective parliaments on their activities.

These limitations in the NATO PA are symptomatic of the alliance's weak mechanisms of engagement with the public and civil society more generally. Its public diplomacy is more a means of transmitting policy than involving scholars, nongovernmental organizations (NGOs), and other stakeholders. NATO has also worked in the field with NGOs (e.g., in Kosovo and Afghanistan), but these bodies have no lobbying or policy-shaping roles.

WHY TRANSPARENCY AND ACCOUNTABILITY IN NATO MATTER

The democratic deficit outlined above matters for a whole host of reasons. It could be disguising mistakes and inefficiencies, and certainly encourages "business as usual" or "group think." Root causes of ineffectiveness within secretive bureaucracies include:

- aversion to self-criticism;
- vulnerability to partisan political or "special interest" capture; and

- the tendency of public officials (like all of us) to behave irresponsibly when unwatched, a situation that is exacerbated when national security is at stake, for the simple reason that insecurity is highly emotional, subjective, variable, and easy to manipulate for strategic ends.

The democratic deficit also increases the vulnerability and malleability of public opinion in foreign affairs at a time when current security threats, from Afghanistan to countering Islamic militants in the Middle East, are a matter of perception and judgment rather than fact. Moreover, current NATO operations involve real and growing risks and costs that need to be adequately explored and debated.

This democratic deficit is by no means all of NATO's doing. NATO's public affairs and diplomacy division has attempted to bring the alliance closer to the people and often uses creative forms of communication to do so. But it does so within the limitations of NATO's own disclosure mandate and with a clear public relations remit.

Then-Secretary General Rasmussen also placed a welcome emphasis on public consultation in the strategic concept review process that was concluded in Lisbon in November 2010, which he correctly described as "by far the most open and the most inclusive process of policy development NATO has ever conducted." But in this regard NATO was starting from a historically low point of almost no consultation on earlier strategic concepts. This time around, the early series of Harmel-plus type consultations,[24] with the eminent persons group headed by Madeleine Albright at its heart, generally surpassed expectations. However, after the expert group's analysis and recommendations were published, the transparency door slammed shut during the drafting and negotiation phase. Moreover, only the German parliament scheduled a prior committee hearing, and no formal parliamentary debate or vote on the concept took place in any member state.

While there may be a case for allowing governments to discuss finer points in private, not least to enable consensus building around some of the more contentious issues, the lack of time set aside for substantive prior parliamentary discussion of key documents such as the strategic concept represents woefully inadequate executive oversight.

Another major problem is the dearth of what might be described as "the journalism of verification": that is, discovering information, examining it for its truth, and narrating it in a comprehensible way. Without such investigative journalism, there is a real danger of the official version of events becoming the only version. This is especially true when the media reproduce press releases from NATO or from the defense ministries of member states unchecked and unchallenged as the cheapest way to acknowledge new information. The contesting of official versions of civilian casualties arising from drone strikes in Afghanistan and Pakistan is just one example of the important but diminishing role of good journalism.[25]

The bottom line is that the vital habits of democracy are based on the availability of reliable sources of information, followed by deliberation and debate. NATO's purpose has to be clear to all citizens, and only then will they be able to better hold it to account. So what needs to be done?

A MENU OF POTENTIAL REFORMS

Clearly, not everything NATO does should be open to public view or scrutiny. In the national security field, it is appropriate for some information shared by and with government agencies to remain confidential. There is a balance to be struck between openness and secrecy, but NATO is nowhere near getting that balance right. It is also worth asking why NATO chooses to continue to operate in this way. The answer lies in a combination of institutional inertia and a lack of sufficient political will to make the necessary changes. Within government national security circles transparency principles are often viewed with suspicion, and within parliaments, political parties, and opinion-shaping circles transparency is rarely seen as a priority issue worthy of expending political capital on. "Good governance" and "security sector" reforms are invariably targeted at other countries but ignored closer to home.

Irrespective of the absence of political will for change, a number of reforms are urgently required:

First, national parliaments in member states need to sharpen their scrutiny of NATO affairs. At a minimum, this means establishing a permanent standing parliamentary committee dedicated to NATO. Outside of the US, NATO remains the cornerstone of every other member state's defense policy. In the UK, for example, there is a parliamentary European Scrutiny Committee, made up of MPs who assess the legal and/or political importance of each EU document, decide which EU documents are debated, monitor the activities of UK ministers in the Council of the European Union, and keep legal, procedural, and institutional developments in the EU under review. There is also a Foreign Affairs Committee and a Defence Committee, both of which cast their gaze on NATO from time to time, as might one or two of the other thirty or so

UK parliamentary committees. There is also a nonparliamentary Intelligence and Security Committee, which reports to the prime minister and is staffed by officials from the Cabinet Office, and no doubt this also touches on intelligence sharing within the alliance. But if NATO is the cornerstone of British defense policy—at a great cost in both "blood and treasure" in Afghanistan—why is there no permanent standing committee dedicated to NATO?

Involving parliaments more in NATO policy would not be without its downsides, of course, especially in politically divided polities. In the US, for example, the requirement for Senate advice and consent to treaty ratification (but not for NATO-related agreements) makes it difficult to rally enough political support. But without it, measures agreed at NATO summits have very little legitimacy and may simply be revoked or renegotiated by the next administration.

In the second decade of the twenty-first century, surely it should be a NATO-wide norm for any significant international treaty or agreement—that is, one that impinges on human rights and fundamental freedoms, transfers sovereignty, requires the passing of a law, or carries the possibility of the deployment of armed force abroad—to always require consent from parliament, thereby giving the people a direct say in the external activities of the state. Parliaments should have a role in examining all decisions about the negotiation of treaties and multilateral accords, including determination of objectives, negotiating positions, the parameters within which the national delegation can operate, and the final decision as to whether to sign and ratify. This certainty of process would enable governments to negotiate with their overseas counterparts with authority and credibility. At a minimum, this should involve a parliamentary mechanism for considering tabled treaties or international instruments, such as the Joint Standing Committee on Treaties established by the Australian Parliament in September 2010.

Second, the democratic mandate of the NATO Parliamentary Assembly needs to be strengthened. In particular, there needs to be greater accountability and openness about how members are selected. The assembly needs candidates of independent mind, who enjoy cross-party support, and who have command of their briefs. At a minimum, the NATO PA representatives should be on fixed-term appointments and subject to some form of intraparliamentary election process (similar to that which was introduced in the UK for select committee chairs).

Third, NATO should adopt an information openness policy consistent with the access to information laws already in place in the alliance's twenty-nine member countries. Such a policy should include guidelines for proactive publication of core information, a mechanism by which the public can file requests for information, and an independent review body for hearing appeals against refusals or failures to make information public within a short time-frame. Access to documents in NATO should not be a "gift" from on high to be packaged, sanitized, and manipulated. The right of access to information is firmly established in international and national law as a human right and is essential for upholding the values that NATO was created to protect. It therefore applies to all national and international public bodies and should also apply to NATO.

Another option might be to introduce a system that would allow the public to view some of the internal NATO policy dialogues taking place, such as those between ministers and heads of state at summits or at ambassadorial level within the NAC. Live and unedited television coverage of parliamentary debates and many committee meetings is now commonplace in several member states (e.g., C-SPAN in the United States and BBC Parliament in the United Kingdom) and has expanded to cover other national agencies and bodies. Another potential model is B-SPAN, an unedited webcast launched by the World Bank in 2000. Although funding for B-SPAN was cut in 2005, during its initial five years of operation it produced more than 700 webcasts and had 250,000 viewers, mostly stakeholders (government officials, economists, academics, and development practitioners) wanting or needing to be immersed in the finer points of the subject.[26] A new N-SPAN service within NATO might allow the public to better understand why decisions are made, to the benefit of both alliance decision-making and a more informed public.

Fourth, a broader debate within NATO is needed as to the purpose of the secretary general's annual report and what goes in it. More needs to be done to link forecast performance and actual performance. This requires that NATO have a set of appropriate measures and robust systems to collect the results, followed by independent (as well as in-house) analysis, interpretation, and evaluation of the information. It also requires greater public access to information. The secretary general's annual report is not an end in itself, but should be the starting point for reporting NATO's performance story. As former US Senator Sam Nunn says,

> NATO should commit to publicly scoring the contributions and improved military capabilities of its members, as they implement their Wales summit commitments. Then, NATO should review progress every six months. NATO members have an historic pattern where pledges and promises on necessary

military improvements vastly exceed implementation. NATO member states must be held accountable for meeting their commitments.[27]

To this end, the annual national defence investment plans agreed at the 2017 Brussels NATO Summit are a step in the right direction. However, one thing is abundantly clear: NATO needs to become closer to its more than 1 billion citizen stakeholders. NATO is the sum not only of its intergovernmental political and military parts, but also of the 900 million citizens living in its twenty-nine member states and the more than 532 million additional citizens in states with partnership or contact agreements with the alliance. These citizens, rather than military forces, police, and other means of law enforcement, are at the heart of alliance security.

Addressing reporters in Downing Street during a visit to London in June 2011, the then head of NATO, Anders Fogh Rasmussen, declared that "NATO is more needed and wanted than ever, from Afghanistan to Kosovo, from the coast of Somalia to Libya. We are busier than ever before." This frenzied activity on the international stage also means that the amount of sensitive information held within NATO and the national security apparatus of member states is immensely larger than it was a generation ago. Technological change has caused an explosion in the rate of information production within NATO, as everywhere else. Unlike everywhere else, however, much of the information generated within NATO never sees the light of day.

There is a clear contradiction between the distinctive status of NATO as a "democratic" alliance and its lack of democratic legitimacy. This situation is also increasingly NATO-specific, as other intergovernmental organizations begin to embrace and grapple with greater transparency. In short, to deepen and extend NATO's shared values base requires an updated, more open, transparent, and accountable alliance, appropriate to twenty-first-century expectations. Parliamentary accountability within NATO requires clear and adequate mechanisms, and a relaxation of secrecy rules.

Notes

1. See, for example, *Transforming the Security Classification System: Report to the President from the Public Interest Declassification Board* (Washington, DC: Public Interest Declassification Board, November 2012), at: http://www.immagic.com/eLibrary/ARCHIVES/GENERAL/WHITEHSE/W121127P.pdf.

2. For an insider's account of transparency issues within the world's largest international financial institution, see David Shaman, *The World Bank Unveiled: Inside the Revolutionary Struggle for Transparency* (Parkhurst Brothers, October 2009).

3. For a list of countries with freedom of information regimes, see http://www.freedominfo.org/?p=18223.

4. *The Global Principles on National Security and the Right to Information* (Tshwane Principles), June 12, 2013 (Open Society Foundations, June 12, 2013), at: https://www.opensocietyfoundations.org/sites/default/files/global-principles-national-security-10232013.pdf.

5. *Classified Information: A Review of Current Legislation across Fifteen Countries and the EU*, Transparency International UK, April 2014, at: http://ti-defence.org/wp-content/uploads/2016/03/140911-Classified-Information.pdf. The report contains a short discussion of NATO information standards as an annex.

6. Alasdair Roberts, "Entangling Alliances: Nato's Security Policy and the Entrenchment of State Secrecy," *Cornell International Law Journal* 36, no. 2 (2003), Article 4.

7. Alasdair Roberts, "NATO, Secrecy, and the Right to Information," *East European Constitutional Review* (Fall 2002–Winter 2003): 86–94.

8. The main documents regulating the NATO classification regime are C-M(2002)49, *Security within the North Atlantic Treaty Organization*, June 17, 2002, supported by six directives on personnel security, physical security, security of information, industrial security, a primary directive on "INFOSEC," and an "INFOSEC Management Directive for CIS"; C-M(2002)50, *Protection Measures for NATO Civil and Military Bodies, Deployed NATO Forces and Installations (Assets) against Terrorist Threats*; C-M(2002)60, *The Management of Non-classified NATO Information*, July 11, 2002, which supports the NATO Information Management Policy (NIMP) (PO(99)47); and C-M(2008)0116, *Policy on the Public Disclosure of NATO Information*, November 12, 2008. See Roberts, "NATO, Secrecy, and the Right to Information."

9. For a discussion of how NATO's secretive measures were forced through EU institutions by circumventing the European Parliament, as well as the parliaments of the member states, and the struggle of the European Parliament and civil society for democratic access to information rules in the EU institutions, see Tony Bunyan, *Case Study: Secrecy and Openness in the European Union: The Ongoing Struggle for Freedom of Information*, at: http://freedominfo.org/features/20020930.htm. Also see the discussion on this issue in Martin Reichard, *The EU–NATO Relationship: A Legal and Political Perspective* (Ashgate, 2006), 311–52.

10. For a recent iteration of this debate, see "Donald Trump's Remarks Rattle NATO Allies and Stoke Debate on Cost Sharing," *New York Times*, July 21, 2016. For a historical perspective, see Keith Hartley and Todd Sandler, "NATO Burden-sharing: Past and Future," *Journal of Peace Research* 36, no. 6 (November 1999): 665–80.

11. Gideon Rachman, "Division and Crisis Risk Sapping the West's Power," *Financial Times*, September 1, 2014.

12. Janine Davidson, "Explainer: This Graph Shows How NATO's Military Capability Has Evolved Since 1949," Defense in Depth blog, Council on Foreign Relations, September 4, 2014, at: http://www.defenseone.com/politics/2014/09/graph-shows-how-natos-military-capability-has-evolved-1949/93257/.

13. *The Secretary General's Annual Report, 2016*, NATO Public Diplomacy Division, 2017, at: http://www.nato.int/nato_static_fl2014/assets/pdf/pdf_2017_03/20170313_SG_AnnualReport_2016_en.pdf.

14. See, for example, "NATO and Russia: Time to Engage," Remarks by NATO Secretary General Anders Fogh Rasmussen at the Munich Security Conference, NATO press release, February 1, 2014, available at: http://www.nato.int/cps/en/natohq/opinions_106788.htm?selectedLocale=en.

15. See, for example, the time-series data on military expenditure in the Stockholm International Peace Research Institute yearbook, published by Oxford University Press. The forty-seventh edition is *SIPRI Yearbook 2016: Armaments, Disarmament and International Security* (Oxford University Press/SIPRI, 2016).

16. Davidson, "Explainer: This Graph Shows How NATO's Military Capability Has Evolved Since 1949."

17. Ben Farmer, "British Defence Spending to Fall below Nato Benchmark,'" *Telegraph*, September 5, 2014.

18. "Von der Leyen Dubious about NATO's 2-percent Rule," *Deutsche Welle*, September 7, 2014.

19. Christian Mölling, *NATO's Two-Percent Illusion: Germany Needs to Encourage Greater Efficiency Within the Alliance*, SWP Comments, August 2014, available at: https://www.swp-berlin.org/fileadmin/contents/products/comments/2014C36_mlg.pdf.

20. The website URL is http://www.rekenkamer.nl/english/nato-transparency.

21. Resource Policy and Planning Board, RPPB Annual Report 2015, Executive Summary, AC/335-N(2016)0067 (INV), 3 August 2015, http://www.nato.int/nato_static_fl2014/assets/pdf/pdf_2016_09/20160909_1609-rppb-ann-rep-2015-eng.pdf.

22. *Hansard*, House of Lords Debate, 9 July 2007, c1229.

23. NATO Parliamentary Assembly, Rules of Procedure, Oslo, Norway, May 2009.

24. The 1967 "Report of the Council on the Future Tasks of the Alliance," also known as the Harmel Report (since it was initiated by Belgian Foreign Minister Pierre Harmel), was a seminal document in NATO's history. It evolved in two key stages: first with the setting up of special groups of high-level experts in February 1967, and second with a consultation and negotiation phase when the findings of each group were compared. The report set the scene for NATO's first steps toward a more cooperative approach to security issues that would emerge in 1991.

25. See, for example, the work of the Bureau of Investigative Journalism in tracking CIA drone strikes and other US covert actions in Pakistan, Yemen, and Somalia, available at: https://www.thebureauinvestigates.com/projects/drone-war.

26. David Shaman, "The Transparency Process," AidInfo blog, March 30, 2012, available at: https://theworldbankunveiled.wordpress.com/2012/05/18/the-transparency-of-process-as-reprinted-from-aidinfo-org/.

27. Sam Nunn, "Commentary: Nunn on the NATO Summit, Russia and Ukraine," NTI website, September 4, 2014, available at: http://www.nti.org/analysis/opinions/former-senator-sam-nunns-perspective-nato-summit-russia-ukraine/.

Chapter 5

The North Atlantic Treaty Organization: Is NATO a Force Fit for a New Century?

General Sir Graeme Lamb

> "The bonds of words are too weak to bridle men's ambition, avarice, anger, and other passions, without the fear of some coercive power."
>
> —Thomas Hobbes (*Leviathan*)

Hugo Grotius, considered by many to be the intellectual father of the Peace of Westphalia in 1648, wrestled rather eloquently in his earlier-seventeenth-century work *De jure* (On law) to find a legal case to encapsulate and enforce the desire to bring order out of the chaos of international conflict. Some three and a half centuries later NATO, with an absolute clarity of purpose underpinned by legally binding articles, did just that in Europe and North America. The question now arises: Is NATO, as structured and authorized, still fit today, and if so, for what mighty purpose?

Now, you might find Hugo Grotius a peculiar bedfellow in my opening argument, but unless one can make a compelling case—ideally, a legally enforceable one—for NATO's existence, then just as Alfred, Lord Tennyson in December 1854 put forward in his literary defense of the Light Brigade, NATO deserves no more than "to do or die." To bring order to the prospect of international conflict requires clarity of purpose to corral it, a steadfast commitment to set the conditions accepted by all to contain it, and laws beyond recourse to bind it. Only by the threat of coercion, as Thomas Hobbes suggested in *Leviathan*, and enforced through law, as Hugo Grotius sought in *De jure*, can sovereign states, by word and by deed, act and together hold firm against the possibility of an intended or unintended war.

Drawn up and enacted into law in 1949, NATO's Article 5 was the collective sword of Damocles that had been omitted from previous global policing efforts such as the Inter-Parliamentary Union (IPU) and the League of Nations. The IPU, established in 1889 by the great European parliamentarians, set out with the worthy intention of restraining the use of force by the voice of reason. For all its intellectual power, however, the union failed to arrest Europe's rapid slide to World War I in 1914. This missing muscle, recognized in Article 10 of an early draft of the Covenant of the League of Nations, caused the very public "treaty fight" of 1919, which saw President Woodrow Wilson's proposed treaty defeated by Senator Henry Cabot Lodge's spirited counterproposition that the United States could do more for the world by being American and not part of some international policing alliance. The result of this spat was the withdrawal of the United States from the league and the removal of the offending draft article from the treaty, without which the well-meaning and best efforts of the founding forty-two (eventually fifty-eight) signatories failed to curb Germany's growing military power and influence in the 1920s and 1930s. This collective unwisdom, carelessness, and good nature (as Winston Churchill recorded in his prologue to *The Gathering Storm*) blinded Europe to the rapid approach of World War II. The upshot of two catastrophic world wars was the harsh realization that good intentions, principles, and heartfelt desire alone cannot save the world from political and military recklessness. Germany's second assault on Europe forced the international community—reluctant before the 1940s to challenge open aggression—to bite the bullet and create a military force underpinned by an uncompromising legal and political framework fit for a resolute, meaningful, and collective European defense.

So, from these smouldering ashes and two world wars in Europe, NATO cemented at last a "grand alliance," and in doing so created a military monolithic amalgamation of Western forces prepared to contest armed aggression in Europe and North America. NATO was quite literally a military colossus, underpinned by a fierce and equally comprehensive collective political will that intended to bring order to curb the hint of an international conflict in Europe. This modern goliath, led by the United States, was prepared to provide guaranteed protection to those now-threatened weaker European nations bordering the Soviet Union. Under Article 5 of the Washington Treaty, the collective response to armed intervention by the USSR would be predetermined and decisive. Furthermore, this response was, during the period 1949–1989, seemingly without limits.

The NATO doctrine of MAD (mutual assured destruction) was within those limits. It was quite simply assured destruction, and to many it seemed quite mad, but it formed the basis for forty years of effective nuclear deterrence. Drawn from the likes of John Von Neumann's minimax theorem and the Nash Equilibrium, this deterrent posture, based on game theory, established that in a zero-sum contest with perfect information (each player knowing at each time all moves that have taken place so far), there exists a pair of strategies that allows each player to minimize his maximum losses. In blending this theorem into the Nash Equilibrium, where no player has anything to gain by changing their own strategic position, and since they are unable to change but know the opposition's position, a state of logical and semipermanent stalemate exists—a self-regulating standoff, so to speak. By guaranteeing a credible second-strike capability, any initial advantage by either side would be offset by an equally devastating disadvantage. The outcome was a form of calculated demonic order. Both parties set the conditions and were prepared to suffer near or total annihilation in the defense of their ideology and their member states, with the general public having little or no say in their certain, untimely, and unpleasant deaths.

As a result, NATO's almost unprecedented commitment to the collective security of its members legally, politically, and militarily provided depth and resilience to this twentieth-century treaty, unlike the previous well-intentioned but inconclusive international arrangements. The commitment was bound in place on April 4, 1949 with the Washington Treaty to specifically challenge and check armed aggression in Europe and North America. The treaty ensured an immediate armed response—not the well-meaning threat of words alone, but a near-automatic, credible, capable, and measurable military action. Once set in stone, NATO's forces, including nuclear arsenals, could be calculated and assessed, and their capability accurately judged by the Soviet Union. The success of the alliance, and its armed forces, fit for the purpose of securing Europe and North America, was to gall the USSR into action—first in completing its own matching set of incredibly destructive thermonuclear capabilities, and then, in 1955, in forming the Warsaw Pact, a Communist military conventional-force counterbalance to NATO. This period was defined not only by an arms race but by a battle of ideological commitment—Sputnik, manned spaceflight, "Reds under the beds," and an aggressive global expansion of superpower spheres of interest that allowed national resolve to be tested away from the European tripwire of the inner German border. Thus the battle was joined for one of the world's greatest tests of wills, the constant threat of large-scale conventional and tactical nuclear conflict in Europe, and the possibility of strategic nuclear global conflict.

Yet as dangerous as the Cold War was, it was strictly bounded by the geographical limits established from the outset by the Washington Treaty. NATO's military response was firmly tethered to its member states and specifically restricted to an armed attack in Europe or North America; the relatively small Article 6 (1), expanding the geographical limits of the treaty area beyond Europe and North America, was later inserted to accommodate French interests. This unequivocal, legally binding commitment of force would have stirred the heart of Thucydides in offering, albeit in the distant future of the twentieth century, proof of his interpretation of the Melian Dialogue in the History of the Peloponnesian War. Such a terrifying undertaking as outlined in Article 5 of the North Atlantic Treaty, defining an attack on one as an attack on all, was truly historic, but it had been conditioned by the tragic events of the twentieth century and the threat of another world war. The wider commitment of NATO to the United States, included in the treaty for such duties as peacekeeping, did not carry in any way the same legal commitment as Article 5 did for responding to an armed attack against any one of its member states. The treaty made clear that other activities were not legally binding but undertaken on the subjective test of faith, desire, and a willingness to uphold UN principles; it carried no greater assurance than for individual nations to choose, a choice that could be revoked at any time. This part of the treaty mirrored the earlier nineteenth- and twentieth-century efforts to enforce commonsense in international behavior through rational reasoning. For NATO, the use of its armed force remained strictly geographically confined and specifically targeted to its members' sovereign territorial borders, and not one yard beyond.

These conditions provided for both the superpowers a fixed point in Europe to judge each other's seriousness and resolve, while leaving them free to engage in regional third-party small wars, bitter diplomacy, and counter-influence operations elsewhere. The US and USSR contested the two great ideologies of the time, democracy and communism, while sitting atop two highly contested global spheres of interest in which the maxim "the enemy of my enemy is my friend" prevailed. Thus, the twentieth century closed with a titanic clash of cultures, and yet it was, for all its potential destructiveness, an end to a century in which, in spite of things, order prevailed. The stakes involved were quite literally off the charts, but they fitted into a set of global rules that were recognized and broadly respected by all. Spies operated under them, small regional wars were fought and shaped by them, global economies conformed to them, and political alliances bowed to them. The end result was global strategic certainty in Europe, underscored with acceptable and manageable regional uncertainty beyond.

The choice for each of the member states of NATO and the Warsaw Pact was: "Together we stand or divided we will fall." It was a compelling one. The core NATO and Warsaw Pact forces were fixed in this modern European "Great Game"—truly a tournament of shadows—but the superpowers' wider global interests were not. This allowed for regional conflicts such as Korea, Malaya, Vietnam, and a multiplicity of small wars to continue unabated, undisturbed, untouched by the rules of the European standoff. That was the Cold War that was never fought. Beyond North America and Europe, NATO did not contest those rules. It remained clean, uncluttered, true to its founders' ideals of ensuring and safeguarding the sovereign integrity of the signature nations, and those alone. This was the accepted way in which NATO functioned, a force for a very defined and specific role, legally bounded, politically restrained, and geographically restricted. NATO was fit for this purpose, and it worked while the vivid memories of two world wars and one Cold War had not yet dimmed. This was Lord Tennyson's why, the context on which NATO was built—why its forces were so structured, its political alliances forged, and its unwavering cohesion generated.

But all of this has changed. The twenty-first century is very different from the last one. The Cold War and the age of superpowers have disappeared as we knew them. Increasingly, "grand alliances" led by or under the umbrella of the United States or Russia, and made up of concerned and threatened nations, are no longer the accepted norms or seen as the solution by which governments can meet their responsibilities to provide safety for their people, security for their national prosperity, and a defense of their way of life. The need for a meaningful collective defense has, in many ways, departed with the demise of a bipolar world and an "in your face" daily diet of a great and fearful monolithic threat. The Warsaw Pact, so very credible and militarily capable for thirty-six years, disbanded simply because the USSR no longer had the money to sustain it, and because there was no longer any socialist alliance to defend. The much-lauded US victory over the USSR, captured in the iconic image of the Berlin Wall being breached and then pulled down, had far-reaching and unforeseen consequences. Russia's fall from superpower status released the forty-year-old deterrence lock on order in Europe, undermining the strategic certainty of the Cold War. Beyond Europe, regional uncertainty just became more uncertain.

Over the last two decades, the United States has gradually lost interest in global leadership. The self-interests of other countries, having been freed from direct Soviet influence and US interest, have flourished, leading to increasing global instability. In this ungoverned space, stateless transnational and subnational threats have spawned. The global controls, both explicit and implicit, of five decades of superpower oversight and "order" have gradually vaporized, leaving the rest of the world's nation-states (the United States and Russia obviously excluded) increasingly alone. The demise of this global leadership has pushed the twenty-first century toward a new abyss of widespread disorder. The end of the Cold War has, in my view, simply unhinged global balance, and we have been left with a great deal of yin (the shady side), but very little yang (the sunny side). Strategic certainty in Europe has been downgraded, and with it an unflinching defense. The words used today are stronger than ever, but the intent and the underlying confidence that nations will act collectively to defend up to and including the use of nuclear force is very doubtful. It is, I suspect, increasingly unlikely that the twenty-nine member states of NATO, in facing a diverse set of conflicting pressures on their individual nations, will act as one. When core national interests converge, it is still possible to briefly bring collective and forceful focus, as we saw following 9/11. But without an obvious and agreed global threat, a hard-wired organization capable of a robust collective defense with all its obligations, as NATO was structured in 1949, becomes a vehicle of choice rather than necessity. The alliance is no longer a unified force operating with a single will, and one to which Von Neumann and the Nash Equilibrium game theory can be accurately calculated as a zero-sum competition with perfect information. It is rather a plethora of seams and divergences into which an opposing force—be it terrorism, the Taliban, ISIS, or an increasingly assertive Russia—can penetrate to divide and generate dissent among alliance members. With the demise of the USSR and the proliferation of new threats, the operating concept "all for one and one for all" has to be challenged, and the need for a single alliance to contest a single massive and measurable threat questioned. After 1989, the nine new members of the alliance joined under significantly different circumstances than those that faced NATO in 1949. So if the original motivation to gather under a collective NATO alliance has changed, why would the twenty-nine member states reaffirm their commitment to the Washington Treaty sixty-eight years later?

The Russian military threat has, as we have seen in Georgia, Ukraine, and Syria, not entirely gone away, but it is at best a shadow of its former self. The question is, what might fill the considerable hole left by the disappearance of the Soviet Union and Warsaw Pact? The range of modern threats to national stability and security—for instance, cyber-terrorism and space security—is relatively small. The other issues that confront the international community—such as immigration, refugees, organized crime, WMD and nuclear proliferation, pandemics, civil nuclear disaster, climate instability, terrorism, failing states, piracy, and narcotics—are old threats, albeit today they carry significantly greater weight. The proliferation of technology, the global reach of handheld communications capable of influencing millions of multifaith and multicultural communities, and the ability for unreasonable men and women to export their ideas and violence, have vastly increased, and so has instability. These threats are, though, predominately dealt with by intelligence, special forces, police, immigration, homeland security, and the scientific community; few require multinational armed conventional forces, which may have a supporting but not a leading role. These modern threats demand a subtly different blend of forces. They are the same old doctrinal players of diplomatic, intelligence, military, political, economic, social, infrastructure, and information systems (DIME-PMESII), but with the military no longer in the lead or seen as the leading function. This reality challenges the simple dual-track NATO military and political structure to move toward a new, more inclusive, flattened organization looking for unity of effect, rather than the old Brussels bipolar unity of command structure.

If the threats facing the alliance are, as I suspect, of a new order of magnitude, then the threats facing an enlarged NATO are even greater. This new European and global uncertainty is further destabilized by the specter of an increasing number of failing states. Some 126 out of the 178 nation-states on the Fragile States Index (FSI) are rated as at potential or immediate risk of failing, based on social, economic, and political assessment. The capability mix required to correct weak and ineffective government, to be able to challenge organized crime, corruption, and cronyism, to redress and reinstate good governance and the rule of law, and to expose and ease social tensions is very different. The accumulated effect of an increasing number of semi-functional states weakens globalization, generates worldwide disorder, and presents a very real and present danger. Place into this social tension the conditions for unrest—be they poverty, failed expectations, high unemployment, or a general state of hopelessness—and radical movements promising all can make hay. Sectarian hatred, blind retribution, revenge, and retaliation allow for mindless brutality against humanity, accelerating the destabilization of government controls and breaking the fragile order of the nation-state. And breaking the nation-state is exactly what many intoxicated radicals intend. Lewis 'Atiyat Allah, who claimed to represent the terrorist network al-Qaeda after the Milan train bombings in 2004, declared that "the international system built up by the West since the Treaty of Westphalia will collapse; and a new international system will rise under the leadership of a mighty Islamic state." The creation of an Islamic caliphate governed under sharia law in Iraq and Syria draws from Sayyd Qutb's extreme interpretation of the Qur'an in his polemic *Social Justice in Islam*, written in 1953. This increasingly troubled world of ever more complex threats requires complex responses—no longer simply defense forces but a wide range of international and national security capabilities. In short, we need collective stability more than we need conventional collective defense.

Place this international and national instability, its tensions and stresses, inside Pandora's global twenty-first-century box and connect those who live within these failing states through the rise in the ownership of iPhones, Androids, iPads, and other simple and readily available technologies, and trouble will follow. With instant access to an open web, the Internet allows people to be connected, though not necessarily informed. Among its many benefits, it creates a breeding ground for propaganda and misinformation. This enables those who wish to terrorize, intimidate, force change, and create widespread fear. Terrorist organizations are increasingly able to operate alongside organized crime networks, to reach into and exploit disenfranchised communities, and to coerce local resistance, wreck progress, and create widespread dissent. As our day-to-day dependency on these widespread interconnected technologies mushrooms, they are both a blessing and curse. All are susceptible to cyber-attack or malware viruses capable of disrupting or deleting our control of personal, commercial, financial, or government data and threatening essential services. These modern threats do not look like force-on-force capabilities; they do not operate under a national banner or as part of a military "grand alliance"; they are complex, obscure at best, and invisible at worst, and are unlikely to be challenged by the collective defense of NATO forces from which we draw false comfort. Today's plethora of old and emerging diverse threats is no longer simply met by large standing conventional navies, armies, air forces, and marines, be they part of a nation's armed forces or a standing alliance or coalition. NATO is such a force and probably knows it.

In 2010 NATO took stock and agreed upon a new strategic concept (see Documents section) setting out broad roles and missions to take the alliance forward. Unlike in 1949, however, the document was so general that it provided little guidance and even less clarity. This exercise in the rhetoric of bold and meaningful change did little more than fine-tune the status quo, but was unable to rationalize the widespread differences that were increasingly self-evident within the alliance. All of this was a mere shadow of the heady clarity and grim commitment in which the NATO alliance was forged in 1949. In preparation for the September 2014 NATO summit, Chatham House commissioned an insightful research paper titled *NATO: Charting the Way Forward*. It reviewed the national security and defense statements of ten different NATO members, which set out a list of national security priorities. The resulting analysis, which is not pejorative but is most certainly instructive, lays out a widely differing threat perspective—the world as each individual member nation sees it. These differences among NATO members are crucial to the alliance's future and its failure to engender a fierce collective-defense identity. Today the numerous and multifaceted global interests of the United States are, unsurprisingly, wildly different from those of Norway, Poland, or Germany. The multiple threats that do affect all member states—from cyber to immigration, WMD proliferation, and organized crime—are not the same when viewed from Berlin or London. Likewise, each nation's resources—be they measured in manpower, money, or national defense architecture—accrue different weightings when set against one another. There is even greater disparity in the political will that member states are prepared to expend in pursuit of any one of these challenges. The body may be eager, but the mind is no longer willing.

This is the operating space that NATO now occupies. The question is, can the old structures and organization, eager as they might be, match up to the new and diverse threats? New threats demand new equipment and new or adapted organizations. With respect to the former, the defense-spending profile of NATO since the 1990s has been, at best, disappointing. There have been systematic reductions in real terms of defense spending, starting with the end of the Cold War and, more recently, following the financial crisis of 2008. The target agreed in 2006 of a minimum of 2 percent of GDP was met by only four of the member nations—the US, UK, Greece, and Estonia—in

2014, at the time of the new Defense Investment Pledge. At the 2016 Warsaw summit, NATO reported a collective increase in year-on-year expenditure for the first time since 2009. Although five members (the fifth being Poland) were now spending a minimum of 2 percent of GDP on defense, several of NATO's major powers still lagged behind.

Research and development constitutes, along with defense procurement and investment, around 15 percent of the defense budget, with the majority of defense spending devoted to fixed manpower costs. Without new money, NATO will be able neither to adapt existing structures nor to build new organizations. Based on current and previous trends, the promise of greater defense department efficiencies that would allow any of the twenty-nine member states to release existing money is highly unlikely, and the probability of politically sensitive major defense procurement projects being shelved to free up budgets even less so. Without new money, NATO will be able to shift priorities but not to change them. So fine words reinforcing NATO's role, firm commitments to its founding goals, and unanimously agreed training and funding targets will quietly fall by the wayside. The danger will be that change is talked about and believed but will be little more than a false promise. The result of no new money will be a decaying institution that is unable at present, and unlikely in the future, to significantly adjust to the new challenges; an institution that is politically useful, but militarily less so.

To find a compelling argument that will convince sovereign parliaments to spend more on conventional national and collective defense, and to convince their respective populations to support such a proposition, is as challenging as the threats themselves. Without a demonstrative clear and present danger requiring the need to retain large conventional military forces, the likelihood of falling budgets becomes increasingly real. It is only where occasional overseas intervention is necessary, following a UN Security Council resolution where the use of force is judged necessary to enforce international order for humanitarian reasons or under the somewhat damaged UN policy of the responsibility to protect (R2P) following the events in Libya, that conventional intervention makes political and public sense. While the use of conventional forces to support UN operations for NATO is within the alliance's charter, it is set only as an intention, a desire, a choice nations easily take when the going is good, but are less enthusiastic about if the situation is dangerously uncertain. Furthermore, the majority of UN deployments are supported by less well equipped or trained non-NATO forces, suggesting to the

NATO members that a lower capability, and therefore cheaper forces, can successfully undertake these missions. Nations will need to retain a pool of agile, very flexible, and discrete national capabilities to conduct relatively small-scale force deployments, including special forces operations, to assist struggling nations with counterterrorism, internal security, and counterinsurgency in order to arrest the fall of their failing states. Few of these situations require large-scale interoperable forces able to wage war. But war is what NATO stood for forty years ready to execute, not counterinsurgency, counterterrorist, peacekeeping, or small-scale internal security operations. For instance, Northern Ireland, an internal conflict, was seen for over four decades as a distraction to the UK preparation for the war in support of NATO in defending West Germany. The structure and organization of NATO were framed for this, trained for this, and fit for that very specific purpose. A force predominately focused on high-intensity general and nuclear war will look and operate very differently from one designed for peacekeeping and the complex twenty-first-century threats I have suggested.

The news is, of course, not all bad. NATO does engender interoperability and friendships, and sets and maintains standard operating procedures, common logistic and support capabilities, and many other attractive force enablers. As a force capability pool from which coalitions of the willing can be brought together rapidly on a case-by-case basis, it is a formidable, albeit extraordinarily expensive, consortium. The need to assess each threat outside the geographical boundaries of NATO on its individual merits increases the number of decision-makers from what was an immediate single NATO response during the Cold War. This was a well-oiled process ready to react, deploy, and fight at the tactical and operational level with the minimum of recourse and the maximum delegation of responsibility to act. Decision-making was well practiced and encapsulated in a unified chain of command, while the alliance's political and military committees sought to enable action, not to discuss it. Political maneuvering at the highest level focused on averting a tactical or strategic nuclear exchange, while at the lower level warning, moving, and, where possible, safeguarding the population. With the end of the Cold War, a consensus of twenty-nine members now requires over fifty separate political and military decision assessments to be made, with the result that the system is slow and unwieldy.

My premise is not to question the wider utility of NATO, nor to challenge what has been achieved since the end of the Cold War, but to ask: For what purpose and under which precise and binding legal authority does NATO operate today? The question should not be whether NATO can adapt. Of course it can, and in numerous ways it already has. The question is, should and can we afford it? The terrible harmony that underpinned the alliance's unwavering military capabilities and its cast-iron political will to execute has simply gone. On December 5, 1956, the Labour politician Aneurin Bevan gave a speech before the British House of Commons on the Suez Crisis and the need for clarity when going into or preparing for war. "I have been looking through the various objectives and reasons that the government have given to the House of Commons for making war on Egypt," Bevan said, "and it really is desirable that when a nation makes war upon another nation it should be quite clear why it does so. It should not keep changing the reasons as time goes on." NATO did just that for forty years. Since the fall of the USSR in 1991, it has been, at best, just muddling through. The reasons for its continued existence are not driven by the earlier-twentieth-century grim political and military determination that attended its birth. As such, the alliance lacks the clarity of purpose, the simple stoic nature of the mission to stand and fight to the death against all odds. NATO in my opinion is no longer, and has not been for the last twenty-seven years, fit for a clear and determined purpose.

My intention is not to dismiss NATO as a spent force that is no longer relevant. The range of threats we now face are both different and deadly, capable of killing on an industrial scale and changing our way of life. The possibility of major large-scale war is ever-present, but seemingly not imminent. NATO in its present declining form is affordable, but it does not attend to the real and potentially devastating modern threats. Without substantial new money, NATO cannot adapt to these with the flexibility necessary to remain a step or two ahead of them. The choice is not to dumb NATO down, nor to attempt to do considerably more with even less. It is to fundamentally restructure the alliance or disband it. A less-than-halfway house, promising much but able to deliver little, attacked by complex, multifaceted, adapting threats, will see our money badly spent and our hopes placed on a NATO based on Cold War battle modeling and preparations already fought. We technically won the Cold War but, as so often in history, are preparing to refight the next great series of battles with rules, equipment, manpower, doctrine, and defense capabilities that have already irreversibly, and forever, changed.

Chapter 6

Organizational Survival: NATO's Pragmatic Functionalism

Joanna Spear

When I first went to NATO headquarters in Brussels as a student in 1982, the briefings we received made it clear that the organization was in a "crisis": burdens were not being shared, tempers were getting short, military capabilities were inadequate, and therefore NATO's survival was not assured. It did survive, but the same refrain of crisis has echoed down the years and can be heard in discussions about NATO today. *Plus ça change, plus c'est la même chose?*

Over the ensuing decades when I had occasion to re-engage with the debates and literature on NATO, the same reprise was always there: NATO was in political trouble. The controversies often centered around "burden sharing," but they also related to geostrategic issues. At other times the disputes were about what the organization should or should not be doing. Always, however, the language was of political wrangling and lurching from crisis to crisis. Among the problems we can identify today are concerns that NATO will lose its cohesion now that the International Security Assistance Force (ISAF) mission in Afghanistan is over (replacing the previous angst about the underperformance of the organization in Afghanistan), doubts about the outcomes of the NATO mission in Libya (replacing the initial euphoria about the ousting of the Gaddafi regime), fears about a resurgent Russia's activities in Ukraine and Estonia, and its meddling in the elections of NATO member

265

states, and President Donald Trump's destabilizing early statement that NATO was obsolete, now replaced by an aggressive approach to the issue of greater European burden sharing.[1] Clearly, angst about NATO is not only historic but a current concern.

But if NATO was and is so crisis-ridden, why is the alliance still around? Its longevity is a particular puzzle given that the sole problem NATO was invented to confront, the Soviet colossus, is gone, and therefore the central *raison d'être* for NATO's existence disappeared nearly three decades ago. Why was NATO not wound up when the Soviet Union and the Warsaw Pact collapsed? Obviously the answer is that member states still want NATO to exist.[2] NATO is an intergovernmental organization, and if there were no state interest in it, the alliance would have formally disbanded, as the Southeast Asia Treaty Organization (SEATO) did, or just withered away, starved of money and talent.[3] As neither has happened, we know that NATO is considered useful. Nevertheless, ever since the alliance weathered the collapse of the Soviet empire, there has been almost constant debate over whether NATO is fit for purpose and what that purpose is.

This chapter examines NATO's fraught history and also seeks to show that, since the end of the Cold War, the organization's identity has been changing on a regular (nay, too regular) basis. Rather than being an institution with clear goals and objectives, as it was during the Cold War, NATO has become a pragmatic functionalist organization, taking on issues that help to perpetuate its role in the Western security architecture. In the last twenty-seven years NATO members have been more consistently and actively involved in military activities than during the first forty years of the alliance's existence, when not one military operation was undertaken.

I will consider several aspects of NATO's impressive survival in the face of persistent rumors of crises and its predicted demise. I will first discuss the Cold War years when, despite geostrategic issues that brought the alliance together, severe political tests nearly pulled it apart. Another feature of the era were the near-constant squabbles about funding NATO. The next section will chart the post–Cold War evolution of the alliance, both in terms of the many summit declarations and initiatives since 1990, and in terms of the operations it has undertaken. The chapter will conclude by considering NATO's future.

Many commentaries on NATO written during the post–Cold War period have reflected concerns about the organization losing its coherence, common purpose, and collegiality, generally through either loss of strategic focus, too much expansion, or the undertaking of disputed missions.[4] The implication is that NATO during the Cold War years was unified, organized, and congenial. But this was not true, as I will show below.

THE COLD WAR PERIOD

Despite being held together by the geostrategic "glue" of opposition to communism during the Cold War, NATO nevertheless lurched from crisis to crisis, with concerns about money expressed by the Americans as "burden sharing" being a constant subject of dispute. I will briefly discuss a number of the more significant geopolitical crises in the organization's history before turning to the long-running budgetary crisis.

In 1956 NATO faced two crises concurrently. The first was the violent Soviet suppression of the Hungarian Revolution, which in the context of the Cold War confrontation was potentially explosive. The second, concerning Egypt, had implications for how NATO could react to the Soviet intervention, but also threatened alliance cohesion as it pitted member states against each other. To consider first the crisis over Hungary, according to an aide-mémoire from a private meeting of the North Atlantic Council held soon after the Soviets intervened, "There was a general agreement that any action should be undertaken by member countries individually and not by NATO collectively. Although the Council should follow developments very closely and examine possible courses of action by member countries, nothing should be done which might provoke a more repressive policy by the Soviets in Hungary."[5] In responding to the crisis, NATO members acted through the United Nations to put pressure on the Soviet Union while coordinating their activities concerning humanitarian aid, dealing with Hungarian students stranded in Western Europe, and accepting refugees.[6] This response is early evidence of NATO's pragmatism, recognizing that this was not an issue over which the alliance wanted to provoke a "hot war" (though giving individual states room to make unilateral responses), but also wanting to condemn Soviet activities through the ultimate court of international opinion, the United Nations.

The second crisis was a significant challenge to NATO's internal cohesion: a dispute between member states over the Suez intervention. Britain and France, assisted by nonmember Israel, intervened in Egypt in an attempt to unseat President Gamal Abdel Nasser, whose anticolonialist, pronationalist (and anti-Israeli) activities were causing serious concern. Egypt's nationalization of the Suez Canal was perceived by these European powers as an economic and political threat. Britain and France intended to secure the canal using the excuse of entering as "peacekeepers" to keep Israel and Egypt apart (somewhat undermined by the fact that the Egyptian forces were already disengaging).

President Dwight D. Eisenhower, though no fan of Nasser, was opposed to the military intervention, on the grounds that "[t]he use of force would, it seems to me, vastly increase the area of jeopardy."[7] Moreover, CIA Director Allen Dulles asked: "How can anything be done about the Russians even if they suppress the revolt, when our own allies are guilty of exactly similar acts of aggression?"[8] Subsequently, the United States used its economic power to ensure that fellow NATO members Britain and France were forced into a humiliating withdrawal.[9] While the Suez debacle was not a NATO crisis per se, the fact that it involved member states, had economic and political implications for member states' access to oil, and threatened to circumscribe reactions to the Soviet suppression of the independence movement in Hungary made it a NATO issue.[10] According to a contemporary document, "With reference to [the] difference of views within NATO, the Turkish Government thought they were of a transitory character and that all efforts should be devoted to the restoration of unity and solidarity within the Alliance."[11] This glossing over of differences and recommittal to the organization would become a consistent feature of the aftermath of crises in NATO.

In the late 1950s and throughout the 1960s there were deep divisions between France and the other member states, particularly the United States, over the direction and leadership of NATO. French President Charles de Gaulle was extremely unhappy about what he regarded as "Anglo-Saxon" dominance, particularly American dominance, of the organization. When his demands for a greater French role were not (in his eyes) adequately met, de Gaulle began to independently redesign French military strategy and deployments. This led to a number of escalating internal crises, including that of 1959, when he withdrew French forces from the NATO Mediterranean fleet; a subsequent decision to disallow the placing of foreign nuclear forces on French soil (affecting NATO's massive retaliation strategy); and the 1962 decision to pull France's Atlantic and Channel naval fleets out of NATO command.[12] These moves culminated in the 1966 decision to withdraw all French armed forces from NATO's integrated military command and the demand that all NATO troops leave France. This involved relocating the Supreme Headquarters Allied Powers Europe (SHAPE) military command to Belgium and publicly acknowledging the significant disputes within NATO. While there were secret plans to ensure French reintegration with NATO's military command in the event that war broke out with the Soviet Union, it seemed that only global conflict would heal this rift within NATO.

From the late 1960s NATO's cohesion was also challenged by West Germany's policy of *Ostpolitik*, championed by German Social Democratic Party politician Willy Brandt (first when he was foreign minister and later as chancellor).[13] *Ostpolitik* involved West Germany seeking to improve relations with the East at a time when NATO was seriously preparing for all-out war with the Soviet bloc. West Germany had always had policies toward the East, but *Ostpolitik* was "distinguished from earlier experiments by the idealistic rhetoric and the flair for theater of its chief spokesman, who captured the imagination of the world, winning the Nobel peace prize in 1971."[14] Though primarily a diplomatic and economic policy (including treaties on steel, banking, and natural gas), it did not fit well with NATO policies and led to questions over whether West Germany could be trusted as a partner.[15]

Ironically, the same question arose in 1972, but now about the United States after President Richard Nixon and National Security Adviser Henry Kissinger's establishment of relations with Communist China and the signing of the "Basic Principles of Relations" with the Soviet Union. The European NATO allies had no inkling that these changes were coming. The US had withheld from them documents, then presented the outcome as a fait accompli, aggravating relations.[16]

Another unprecedented crisis arose in 1974: war between two NATO members, Greece and Turkey. The conflict concerned Cyprus, and the trigger was the Turkish invasion of the disputed island. "It is believed that the passive US attitude towards Cyprus can be explained by the fact that the US concern was not the rights or wrongs of either side or the fate of the two communities on the island, but rather a way to limit the potential damage to NATO and to the US strategic position in the Mediterranean."[17] Part of Greece's response to this American passivity was to withdraw its forces from the NATO command structure in protest. The invasion also led Greece to reevaluate the threats it faced, downgrading the Soviet threat and upgrading the strategic challenges posed by an assertive Turkey.[18] It was six years before Greece reintegrated into NATO's military command, and this was done with Turkish support in 1980.

A major crisis of the 1980s concerned nuclear force structures. The United States under President Ronald Reagan pursued "twin-track" diplomacy intended to bring the Soviet Union into nuclear arms control agreements by planning to station US nuclear cruise and Pershing missiles in Europe. When this did not immediately work, the US moved to place the missiles in the territories of her NATO allies West Germany and Great Britain. This met with European civil society opposition (despite government acquiescence), which was later spun around when during the 1986 Reykjavik summit the US was prepared to bargain away British and French independent nuclear forces as part of a bold deal for deep cuts in global nuclear weapons arsenals. As British Prime Minister Margaret Thatcher later wrote, "Hearing how far the Americans had been prepared to go was as if there had been an earthquake beneath my feet."[19] The deal with the Soviets ultimately failed because Reagan was unwilling to bargain away America's Strategic Defense Initiative (SDI), but the effect on the NATO allies was to raise serious questions about American commitment to NATO and to the sovereignty of NATO members.

In addition to these political crises, which tore at the coherence of NATO, there was a near-constant concern about funding. The issue of economics and how burdens should be shared was front and center in NATO's first-ever new "strategic concept" issued on January 6, 1950. This stated that contributions to NATO should be proportionate to a nation's geographical position, its industrial capacity, population, and military capabilities. However, the document also noted that the allies considering the military strength necessary to fulfill NATO plans "should bear in mind that economic recovery and the attainment of economic stability constitute important elements of their security." The aim was to defend the North Atlantic Treaty nations "through maximum efficiency of their armed forces with the minimum necessary expenditures of manpower, money and materials."[20] Over the next decades the issue of funding remained contentious. The European members tended to put emphasis on their economic recovery as an element of contributing to defense for a longer time than was either strictly justified or seemly.

Budget issues were important enough to drive strategic developments in the alliance. In 1956 NATO officially ended reliance upon high levels of conventional forces (set out in the NATO Medium Term Plan adopted on April 1, 1950) and shifted to a strategy of massive retaliation "primarily because maintaining high levels of conventional forces was viewed as being both economically and politically unfeasible."[21] In the new scenario lower levels of conventional forces would merely act as a "tripwire" triggering a nuclear response. However, the NATO budget once again became contentious when the alliance moved away from the nuclear doctrine of massive retaliation to a strategy of flexible response in 1967. When NATO was reliant upon nuclear weapons for its defense, the budgetary burden fell most heavily upon the United States (and to a much lesser extent Great Britain) as nuclear powers. However, NATO strategy now required a considerable increase in conventional forces to operationalize flexible response, and the US looked to its European allies to increase their defense spending on procurement accordingly, something that many were unwilling or unable to do. This generated considerable friction among NATO members. This debate intensified in the late 1970s and early 1980s as détente with the Soviet Union began to falter and the new Reagan administration in the US called on its NATO allies to significantly increase military spending to meet the exigencies of a "Second Cold War."[22] This was when I received my first NATO briefing on the failure of the Europeans (all of our group were British) to pull their weight in the alliance. Not surprisingly, the speaker at that meeting was American. "Burden sharing" issues were not solved to anyone's satisfaction by the end of the Cold War; each side trotted out the same arguments, but little progress was made. As will be shown in the next section, the disputes gained new energy with the end of the Cold War.

A contestable argument made about NATO is that it has only ever been about Europe. Certainly, concern about Europe was central to the founding and operation of the organization during the Cold War years. However, if one examines the Cold War history of the organization there are several signals of a wider geographical application of NATO. First, the North Atlantic Treaty, particularly following the accession of Turkey to the organization, actually denotes a somewhat broader geographical focus than just Europe:

> For the purpose of Article 5, an armed attack on one or more of the Parties is deemed to include an armed attack:
>
> - on the territory of any of the Parties in Europe or North America, on the Algerian Departments of France, on the territory of Turkey or on the islands under the jurisdiction of any of the Parties in the North Atlantic area north of the Tropic of Cancer;
> - on the forces, vessels, or aircraft of any of the Parties, when in or over these territories or any other area in Europe in which occupation forces of any of the Parties were stationed on the date when the Treaty entered into force or the Mediterranean Sea or the North Atlantic area north of the Tropic of Cancer.[23]

Second, Turkey's accession meant that the organization had an increased interest in Iraq as the southeastern flank of NATO.[24] Third, the inclusion of "the Algerian Departments of France," reflecting the fact that they were regarded as French sovereign territory, also pushed NATO's interest in North Africa. Fourth, there was recognition within the organization of its dependence on the flow of oil from the Middle East, giving it a stake in stability in that region; the issue was defined primarily as keeping the Soviets out.[25] Finally, there were arguments made during the era of apartheid in South Africa that NATO was dependent on the country for strategic minerals and might need to defend the trade routes from there to Europe. It was also argued that NATO had a stake in the country's stability, meaning that it should not intervene in the domestic politics of the state (the Afrikaans government particularly liked this argument).[26] Thus, these five points suggest that when NATO turned to consider a post–Cold War role, moving "out of area" was not such a shift as some colleagues, including James Goldgeier in this volume, present it as.

To sum up this discussion of intra-NATO discord during the Cold War period, as Michael Cox wrote in 1995: "although the Cold War may have been a great unifier, we should not forget how often it led to misunderstandings and differences between the United States and Europe. Nor should we forget the cruder varieties of anti-Americanism that had once been a feature of the intellectual landscape in Europe during the Cold War. It was not all plain sailing in the good old days."[27]

POST–COLD WAR NATO

In looking at NATO in the post–Cold War period, we can identify much greater activism compared to during the Cold War period. Particularly in the early post–Cold War period, new initiatives from NATO came quick and fast. NATO also evolved from an exclusively defensive alliance to one that was increasingly proactive on security issues. Since the end of the Cold War NATO has become an "expeditionary" military organization, explicitly expanding its remit and activity to more areas of the world and taking on new sorts of issues beyond traditional security. The period after the end of the Cold War but before the terrorist attacks on the United States on September 11, 2001 was a particularly fertile time in terms of NATO taking on new functions. This will be demonstrated by briefly reviewing the outcomes of NATO summit meetings, doctrinal developments, and operational deployments. This new activity was partially a result of the need to respond to international conditions, but was also partially due to NATO being what I would call a "pragmatic functionalist"; seeking to perpetuate the organization by appearing and ideally being useful. Since the end of the Cold War, the NATO Charter has been seen not so much as a ceiling limiting NATO actions, but as a floor for NATO's evolution.

During the period 1989–1990 there was debate over whether the newly unified Germany was to be admitted as a full NATO member, something that the Russians were strongly opposed to. In the end a compromise was reached with President Mikhail Gorbachev, although what exactly he was promised in return for acquiescing is debated.[28] At the same time as the issue of Germany was being considered, there was discussion of whether NATO had any role now that the Soviet Union had collapsed. Several arguments were made in favor of keeping NATO. One argument made was that NATO should be retained as a "hedge" against Russian resurgence (there were many policymakers who could not believe that the Cold War was really over). Others argued that the habits of cooperation developed in NATO during the Cold War should be continued, rather than starting anew with new security architectures such as a more powerful European Community, or relying on ill-equipped existing institutions such as the United Nations. In addition, the diplomats and career officials working at NATO were generally anxious to perpetuate the organization, and an important way to do that was to keep it relevant to the security challenges of the new era. Therefore a ministerial meeting at Turnberry in June 1990 (see Documents section) issued the "charge" to the NATO staff to begin the review of NATO strategy as the background for the development of a new strategic concept. In July at the London summit the members formally agreed to keep but transform NATO to reflect the more promising strategic environment. The "Declaration on a Transformed North Atlantic Alliance" (see Documents section) reflected this positive outlook: "Yet our Alliance must be even more an agent of change. It can help build the structures of a more united continent, supporting security and stability with the strength of our shared faith in democracy, the rights of the individual, and the peaceful resolution of disputes."[29]

However, even before NATO strategy had been revised NATO became engaged in military operations, something it had never done before. Eight days after the Iraqi invasion of Kuwait, NATO launched Operation Anchor Guard, deploying AWACS (Airborne Warning and Control Systems) aircraft to Turkey to monitor the southeast of the country in case of an Iraqi attack against the NATO member. The operation lasted for seven months and was overlapped by Operation Ace Guard, which deployed NATO ACE Mobile Force and air defenses to Turkey for three months, with both operations concluding in

March 1991. In some senses these operations set a precedent of activism for the "new NATO," and some of this thinking was reflected in the ideas presented by NATO staffs for the new strategic concept. The process of developing the concept was extensive:

> The review of NATO's strategy was a thorough three-track bureaucratic process which involved both civilian and military staffs. Three separate documents were produced: a political declaration drawn up by the NATO ambassadors, the new Strategic Concept negotiated by the International Staff's Strategy Review Group, and the Directive for the military implementation of the Strategic Concept prepared by the permanent military delegations, the International Military Staff and SHAPE.[30]

There was, however, no internal agreement about what the new strategic concept should be, and the documents prepared for consideration at the North Atlantic Council meeting reflected the divisions within the permanent staff at NATO headquarters. While a lot of the "legwork" for the concept had been completed prior to the summit, unusually for NATO a lot of negotiation and decision-making went on between ministers in the North Atlantic Council meeting because there was no consensus at the start of the meeting. The outcome of these negotiations was a fifty-nine-paragraph New Strategic Concept (see Documents section).[31]

The New Strategic Concept, released during the 1991 Rome summit, noted that: "In contrast with the predominant threat of the past, the risks to Allied security that remain are multi-faceted in nature and multi-directional, which makes them hard to predict and assess. NATO must be capable of responding to such risks if stability in Europe and the security of Alliance members are to be preserved."[32] Reflecting the new strategic environment, the New Strategic Concept declared that while the defense dimension was "indispensable," more attention could now be paid to economic, social, and environmental issues as ways of promoting security and stability in the Euro-Atlantic area. The concept also emphasized a broader approach to security (Part III: 23). This included stress on crisis management (Part III: 31–33) as an important NATO activity and was a significant departure from past language and approaches.[33] Importance was placed on conflict avoidance and, reflecting the European sense of the success of the Conference on Security and Cooperation in Europe (aka the Helsinki Process) in peacefully ending the Cold War, discussed increasing mutual understanding and confidence building between states, and even talked of expanding opportunities for partnerships (beyond the NATO membership) to deal with common security problems. The Rome summit's closing statement also reflected the broader approach now being taken by NATO:

> Our Strategic Concept underlines that Alliance security must take account of the global context. It points out risks of a wider nature, including proliferation of weapons of mass destruction, disruption of the flow of vital resources and actions of terrorism and sabotage, which can affect Alliance security interests.[34]

The Rome summit was the first to consider the deteriorating security situation in Yugoslavia, calling for a cessation of hostilities and expressing support for the European Community's efforts to implement a ceasefire and to facilitate peace negotiations.[35] As these calls went unheeded, the fate of the Balkans would play an important part in pushing NATO operations and strategy going forward. Indeed, some trenchant critics of NATO have asserted that the intervention in Yugoslavia was motivated less by concerns about human rights abuses than by the need to fashion a compelling new role for NATO.[36]

The next NATO operations reflected the new strategic environment; Operation Allied Goodwill I and II involved using NATO AWACS to fly humanitarian assistance experts and medical staff to Russia and other former Soviet states as part of an international relief effort to deal with the consequences of the total collapse of the centrally planned Communist economic system. Interestingly, after 1991 NATO began to use the nomenclature "crisis response operations," signaling that they were reactionary rather than proactive alliance activities, possibly to deflect criticisms of the new NATO. In May 1992 NATO launched Operation Fragile Genie to provide increased AWACS coverage of the central Mediterranean and North Africa during a period of heightened tension when Libya refused to hand over the Lockerbie bombing suspects and the UN-imposed sanctions on the country.[37]

At the Oslo ministerial meeting in 1992, peacekeeping became an official NATO mission. As the ministerial communiqué stated: "We support the valuable contribution of the United Nations to conflict settlement and peacekeeping in the Euro-Atlantic region. We reiterate our commitment to strengthening that organization's ability to carry out its larger endeavors for world peace. We welcome the fact that Allies participate in and contribute to United Nations peacekeeping and other efforts."[38]

The situation in the former Yugoslavia was becoming increasingly grave, with European Community efforts ineffective at best, and violence broke out in Bosnia and Herzegovina in April 1992. There were divisions within the NATO alliance over Bosnia, with Britain and France siding together against the US and Germany.[39] That summer NATO warships began to enforce the UN arms embargo in the Adriatic Sea and NATO aircraft enforced the UN-declared no-fly zone. Contingency planning was also underway at SHAPE for a number of possible operations, from enforcing the peace plans being discussed to providing close air support to UN peacekeepers threatened by the warring parties, or assisting in the withdrawal of those peacekeepers.[40]

The 1994 Brussels summit agreed to the development of Combined Joint Task Forces (though the US, UK, and France also developed their own CJTFs). The CJTF's would be important for power projection and signaled an increasing willingness to go "out of area." The summit also saw NATO offer to consider on a case-by-case basis requests to undertake peacekeeping and other operations under the authority of either the United Nations Security Council or the Organization for Security and Cooperation in Europe (OSCE, an offshoot of the Conference on Security and Cooperation in Europe, a multilateral forum for dialogue between East and West). This was important as the United Nations was significantly overstretched, having launched seventeen peacekeeping operations during the period 1991–1994 (compared to fifteen between 1945 and 1988[41]). Interestingly, NATO's offer did not define whether or how NATO should limit its area of operation for peace support operations."[42] This lack of definition may have been designed to avoid the disputes over out-of-area, but in practice provided the alliance with considerable flexibility.

In 1992–1994 the situation in the Balkans became critical, encompassing both classic interstate war between the newly independent states of Serbia, Croatia, and Bosnia and Herzegovina, intrastate wars because populations were not homogenous, and a major humanitarian crisis with millions of people (willingly or unwillingly) on the move. In 1993 the no-fly zone was violated and bombs dropped on what was supposed to be the "safe area" of Srebrenica. This led to a more proactive use of force in protection of UN forces and implementation of the air restrictions. In February 1994 NATO fighter aircraft shot down four Bosnian-Serb military aircraft over Bosnia and Herzegovina, the most active air engagement of NATO's history to that point.

In 1995 Srebrenica's existence as a "safe area" was once again violated, this time with genocidal consequences, and Dutch UN peacekeepers were forced to stand by (per their mandate) as troops under Serbian General Ratko Mladic took away more than 8,000 Bosnian Muslim men and boys. They were subsequently slaughtered in the "worst crime on European soil since the Second World War," according to UN Secretary-General Kofi Annan.[43] This, and many other acts of aggression such as the deliberate targeting of civilians in the siege of Sarajevo, led to an August 1995 NATO decision to respond to a UN request and launch Operation Deadeye, a series of air strikes designed to compel Serbia to comply with UN demands to withdraw from Bosnia. The failure of this tactic led to the launch of Operation Deliberate Force: air strikes against the Serb artillery and other military targets. Thus, as international efforts to confront the crisis diplomatically met with limited success, the conflict became more peace enforcement than peacekeeping. Operation Deliberate Force is cited by NATO as the "key factor" bringing the Serbs to the negotiating table and ending the conflict in Bosnia.[44] The resulting peace treaty, the Dayton Accords of December 1995, was to be implemented by a NATO Implementation Force (I-FOR) under UN mandate. Sixty thousand NATO troops were deployed in Operation Joint Endeavor, followed a year later by a 32,000-strong NATO Stabilization Force (S-FOR).

Even five years after the decisions had been taken to retain NATO and the New Strategic Concept had been operationalized and NATO was actively engaged in the Balkans, the institution's future was not necessarily ensured because the US commitment to European security was in doubt. Writing in 1995, Stanley Sloan commented: "In spite of numerous post–Cold War US government pronouncements about the US commitment to European security, the basic directions of US policy toward NATO have not yet been tested and confirmed in US political decision-making and public opinion."[45] This problem led to a flurry of publications addressing why the US had a central role in European security, and indeed needed NATO.[46] However, once NATO began to evolve beyond Europe, the case for relevance was more easily made.

An important strand of debate within NATO concerned expansion: whether, how, and when to expand. The reaction of Russia to any enlargement was an important element of these debates, with some members wishing to bring Russia into the organization (something Russia itself proposed early on), while others were keen to expand in the face of Russian objections. Typically for NATO, the outcome of these debates was somewhat of a fudge: the creation of a "Partnership for Peace" mechanism to put states on a pathway to entry, also giving NATO a means to keep potential members at arm's length for a period. In essence, it was a hedging strategy. However, during the Clinton administration US policy began to propel NATO expansion forward.

At the 1997 Madrid summit invitations were extended to the Czech Republic, Hungary, and Poland to join NATO in 1999. The enlargement reflected effective lobbying of President Bill Clinton by East European state leaders, combined with the policy preferences of an influential cadre of appointees within the administration.[47] There was significant dissent from the enlargement agenda, both within the US government and in the broader strategic community.[48] The expansion agenda was seen by the Europeans as a "socialization" process to ensure that the Central and East European states formerly in the Soviet empire would be so fully integrated into the alliance that no future conflict could be contemplated. Arguably the Russians saw expansion partly in the same way, which is why Moscow objected to it so much.

The 1990s also saw NATO move into the areas of activity that were beyond even an expanded definition of security. As Todd Sandler noted, "NATO is more than a military alliance, since it is also an international organization that promotes inter-allied cooperation and consultation on scientific affairs, traffic control and myriad other mutual concerns. These activities have also bolstered the contribution of the institution."[49] They were also a means to perpetuate the existence of NATO at a time when its military security role was not necessarily as successful (for example, in Bosnia) as was desirable.

The 1999 Washington summit addressed the burgeoning Kosovo crisis. The authorization of a NATO operation in Kosovo was again precedent-setting because the alliance in so doing acknowledged that it would not be possible to gain a UN mandate for military action against the Federal Republic of Yugoslavia. NATO intervened in June 1999 to end the widespread violence and halt the humanitarian crisis. The upshot was a twenty-two-month NATO campaign to oust Serbian forces from Kosovo. Again, NATO's operational activities had evolved far beyond peacekeeping to *peace enforcement*. Today the NATO Kosovo Force (KFOR) is engaged in security sector reform activities.

In 1999 NATO reviewed the 1991 New Strategic Concept. This exercise resulted in the 1999 Strategic Concept (see Documents section). The 1999 Strategic Concept reemphasized that the core purpose of NATO was collective defense, but acknowledged that the security interests of the alliance could be affected by risks and events beyond NATO territories, necessitating attention to the global context.

NATO was not only operationally engaged in peace enforcement activities, but launched an unprecedented *conflict prevention* operation in the former

Yugoslav republic of Macedonia. Operation Essential Harvest involved disarming ethnic Albanian groups operating across the country. This was followed by Operation Amber Fox to protect international monitors from the European Union and OSCE overseeing the implementation of the peace plan, and Operation Allied Harmony in December 2002 to "provide advisory elements to assist the government in ensuring stability throughout the country."[50] Sixteen years later, NATO Headquarters Skopje is still assisting the Macedonian government with the military aspects of *security sector reform*, another post–Cold War mission, evolving out of practical need.

In 2001, NATO launched its first-ever *counterterrorism operation* in response to the September 11 attacks on the United States. Operation Eagle Assist was an eight-month operation to help patrol the skies over North America, deploying seven NATO AWACS planes. Indeed, the invocation of Article 5 of the NATO Charter after the attacks on the United States was a reversal of all expectations of how that article would be used.[51] A month after the attacks NATO launched Operation Active Endeavor to monitor the Mediterranean Sea for terrorist activities. Since April 2003 the operation has involved systematically boarding suspect ships (with the agreement of the ships' captains and flag states).

Most NATO members actively supported the ensuing intervention in Afghanistan. Nevertheless, as with involvement in Bosnia, the organization came late to involvement in Afghanistan. In each case NATO was used when it was clear that the interventions were going to be protracted and required significant coordination. NATO took over leadership of the International Security Assistance Force (ISAF) in August 2003 and concluded the operation in December 2014. This is NATO's most significant operational commitment to date, and has been a complex operation involving coordinating allies from forty-eight countries.

The Prague summit of 2002 returned to the expansion agenda, and seven more countries were invited to join NATO. The summit, the first after 9/11, also emphasized being ready to meet new threats:

> In order to carry out the full range of its missions, NATO must be able to field forces that can move quickly to wherever they are needed, upon decision by the North Atlantic Council, to sustain operations over distance and time, including in an environment where they might be faced with nuclear, biological and chemical threats, and to achieve their objectives. Effective military forces, an essential part of our overall political strategy, are vital to safeguard the freedom

and security of our populations and to contribute to peace and security in the Euro-Atlantic region."[52]

The Prague summit returned to the issue of where NATO might conduct operations and reinforced the flexibility provided by lack of definition at the Brussels summit. The Prague communiqué stated that NATO needed to be able to field forces that could be quickly transported "to wherever they are needed." It was therefore agreed to create a NATO Response Force (NRF). According to Mamuka Metreveli, "This change essentially ends the 'out-of-area' debate that has raged within the Alliance in the last few years."[53]

This summit also agreed on some moves to streamline NATO's military command arrangements, and, responding to US zeal, established a strategic command for Transformation. Although headquartered in the US, the command was to have a presence in Europe and would be responsible for the continuing transformation of military capabilities and for the promotion of interoperability of alliance forces, in cooperation with the Allied Command Operations as appropriate."[54] Again, this is an example of a policy advocated by the US that did not really gain traction within NATO.

The 2002 summit also addressed the problem of terrorism by upgrading and expanding the Mediterranean Dialogue. "We reaffirm that security in Europe is closely linked to security and stability in the Mediterranean. We therefore decide to upgrade substantially the political and practical dimensions of our Mediterranean Dialogue as an integral part of the Alliance's cooperative approach to security."[55] From the mid-2000s NATO was accelerating its process of "globalization," for example, forging close, institutionalized partnerships in Southeast Asian and East Asian democracies. According to Bruce Weinrod, as a consequence of all these activities: "[w]ithout *deliberate decisions*, NATO has taken on several new roles. First, NATO has become a global security forum; second, it serves as a global security network; and third, NATO is a de facto framework for a global democratic security community."[56]

The 2003 US invasion of Iraq brought new discord to NATO. Member states France and Germany were opposed to the operation, while Britain was the most active partner in the intervention. New NATO member countries offered forces to the subsequent peacekeeping/counterinsurgency operation, leading US Secretary of Defense Donald Rumsfeld to opine about the difference between "new Europe" and "old Europe" (he liked the former). Alliance relations have taken time to heal after the rift caused by the Iraq intervention. Many member states deployed forces to the NATO ISAF mission in order to avoid having to deploy forces to Iraq or face a new round of accusations about not "sharing" the "burden."

Reflecting NATO's more global purview, in 2007 the organization began supporting the African Union (AU) mission in Somalia (AMISOM) by providing airlift support to the peacekeepers. The mission has been extended several times, and "NATO is also working with the AU in identifying further areas where it could support the African Standby Force."[57] NATO also cooperated to support the AU mission in Sudan.

During the 2000s NATO also took on more naval missions, including Operation Active Endeavour in the Mediterranean. NATO also branched out at the formal request of the United Nations into *counterpiracy activities* off the Horn of Africa.[58] This has led to increasing cooperation with non-NATO maritime powers; indeed this is a growing feature of NATO activities. An important expansion of these activities was the 2008 launch of Operation Allied Provider, to counter piracy off the coast of Somalia targeting UN World Food Program vessels taking aid to Africa. The same forces also escorted African Union vessels carrying military equipment for the Burundian contingent in AMISOM. Subsequently, Operation Allied Protector of March to August 2009 took up the mission, as piracy was seen as "threatening sea lines of communication and economic interests."[59] This operation was immediately succeeded by Operation Ocean Shield, which is additionally mandated to work with states in the region that request help in improving their own capacities for countering piracy.

At the 2008 Bucharest summit *cyber-security* became a major priority for NATO, having been noted as important in 2002. The prompt for this was the Russian cyber-attacks on Estonia and Georgia in 2007. The North Atlantic Council also gave NATO accreditation to the Cooperative Cyber Defense Center of Excellence in Estonia, and the organization's membership and reach have expanded since then.[60] When Estonia experienced another major denial-of-service attack in 2009, NATO provided technical assistance to help restore critical services in the country.[61] Also, *energy security* was identified as a key issue for NATO.[62]

The 2009 Strasbourg sixtieth-anniversary summit both welcomed two additional member states (Albania and Croatia, leading to cries of derision from NATO critics) and began the process of developing a new strategic concept.[63] The summit emphasized: "NATO nations and the world are facing new, increasingly global threats," with members' "security increasingly tied to that of other regions." The summit called for enhanced cooperation with other international actors "to improve our ability to deliver a comprehensive approach to meeting these new challenges."[64] Some saw this—both positively and negatively—as a call for a global NATO.[65] At the summit there was also discussion of the situation in Afghanistan, with newly installed President Barack Obama seeking increased voluntary troop contributions from the allies.[66] These hopes were not fulfilled.

The 2010 Strategic Concept (see Documents section) emphasized the threat posed by organized crime.[67] This is interesting as it potentially broadens the scope of NATO operations yet again. In some senses this development reflects the reality of globalization, where economic security is considered crucial and is under threat from various types of nonstate actors, from pirates to hackers to organized crime. However, there are still critics who consider that these types of problems do not reach a level that demands NATO engagement.

The 2014 Wales summit was preoccupied with how NATO should respond to Russian provocations in Ukraine. Nevertheless, the summit did take an important decision about cyber-attacks. "The Wales Summit Declaration expressly paved the way for interpreting cyber-strikes as physical attacks, thus embedding them in Art. 5 of the Washington Treaty, which rules that an attack on any NATO ally will be treated as an attack on all allies and requires necessary action to be taken on behalf of the collective defence of NATO."[68] This enhanced priority to cyber-security reflects the evolving nature of warfare in the twenty-first century.

NATO's evolution has been driven by member states, particularly by its leading light, the United States, but also at times by other powers. Not all member-state initiatives have been successfully incorporated into NATO's operational mandate. For example, *counterproliferation* (a more active military policy than the political approach of nonproliferation) was pushed by the United States as a vital mission for NATO in the mid-1990s.[69] This was somewhat grudgingly accepted by the European member states. However, there was disquiet about the military-intervention implications of counterproliferation, and the response of European members and the NATO bureaucracy was to put the issue into a committee structure before allocating any budget to it, thereby ensuring that the initiative suffered "death by a thousand paper cuts" without the European allies having to confront the US directly or spend money on something that they did not want to do.[70] The US-sponsored Smart Defense Initiative seems to be suffering the same fate.

CONCLUSION

During the Cold War NATO faced many challenges to its internal cohesion. There were many disputes that tore at the fabric of the institution, but after each the NATO members (with the exception of France) fully recommitted to the alliance, a signal of its geostrategic importance. However, after the end of the Cold War this strategic "glue" was lost, with less to unify the member states and more to pull them apart. In response, NATO went into overdrive, and we saw a myriad of new missions and priorities being set: crisis management, crisis prevention, humanitarian operations, peacekeeping, Combined Joint Task Forces, enlargement, peace enforcement, security sector reform, counterterrorism, counterpiracy, counterproliferation, transformation, Smart Defense, cyber-security, energy security, and combating organized crime. And this does not count NATO's myriad new low-level institutional relationships being built with non-European states, and initiatives dealing with issues only broadly related to security. Many of the new missions were the result of deliberate decision-making, but undoubtedly some were driven by the operations NATO was undertaking in the field.

NATO has survived the loss of its core mission by finding new things to do. This is how NATO has survived. There is more emphasis placed on finding new roles and missions when there is an absence of a consuming security problem to occupy NATO attention. If this logic holds, the withdrawal from Afghanistan might have been expected to yield new initiatives for NATO, keeping it as relevant as possible. However, the crisis in Ukraine has brought back to the center NATO's role in Europe, negating the need to develop any new initiatives at this point.[71]

Notes

1. Ellen Hallams and Benjamin Schreer, "Towards a 'Post-American' Alliance? NATO Burden-Sharing after Libya," *International Affairs*, Vol. 88, No. 2 (March 2012), pp. 313–27. Ironically, there has been surprisingly little debate over the way the alliance moved beyond its mission of protecting civilians to actually assisting in the dismantlement of the Gaddafi regime; there seems to be tacit approval of that "mission creep." Rather, there has been celebration. Ivo H. Daalder and James G. Stavridis, "NATO's Victory in Libya," *Foreign Affairs*, Vol. 91, No. 2 (March/April 2012), pp. 2–7; http://www.foreignaffairs.com/articles/137073/ivo-h-daalder-and-james-g-stavridis/natos-victory-in-libya. M. J. Williams, "Enduring, but Irrelevant? Britain, NATO and the Future of the Atlantic Alliance," *International Politics*, Vol. 50, No. 3 (May 2013), pp. 360–86. Richard Milne and Katherine Hille, "Estonian Agent's Seizure by Russia Stirs Fears in Baltic States," *Financial Times*, October 10, 2014; http://www.ft.com/intl/cms/s/0/103f5d b8-5082-11e4-8645-00144feab7de.html#axzz3FypUE3XX.

2. Mary E. Sarotte, *1989: The Struggle to Create Post–Cold War Europe* (Princeton: Princeton University Press, 2009); Sten Rynning, *NATO Renewed: The Power and Purpose of Transatlantic Cooperation* (Basingstoke: Palgrave Macmillan, 2005).

3. SEATO was initiated in 1954 as a bulwark against communism. "Consistently driven by the U.S., there were nevertheless different and frequently ambivalent attitudes of its founding members towards it, even at the time of its birth": Justus M. van der Kroef, *The Lives of SEATO*, Occasional Paper No. 45, Institute for Southeast Asian Studies (Singapore: ISEAS, 1976), p. 5. These divisions were fatally exposed by the US intervention in Vietnam, which other member states were disinclined to become seriously involved in. As the Vietnam intervention became a protracted, unpopular conflict, SEATO began to fall apart. The organization's final military exercise involved a paltry 188 personnel undertaking civil projects in the Philippines. "February 20, 1976: SEATO Disbands," http://www.history.com/this-day-in-history/seato-disbands.

4. See, for example, Fred C. Ikle, "How to Ruin NATO," *New York Times*, January 11, 1995; http://www.nytimes.com/1995/01/11/opinion/how-to-ruin-nato.html (accessed November 18, 2014); Michael E. Brown, "The Flawed Logic of NATO Expansion," *Survival*, Vol. 37, No. 1 (Spring 1995), pp. 34–52; James H. Wyllie, "NATO's Bleak Future," *Parameters*, Vol. 28, No. 4 (Winter 1998/1999), pp. 113–23.

5. NATO, Secret Memorandum from the Executive Secretary to the Secretary General, "Record of a Private Meeting of the Council held on Saturday, 27 October, 1956, at 3.30 pm," declassified document; http://www.nato.int/nato_static_fl2014/assets/pdf/hungarian%20revolution%201957%20-%20private%20records/20130917_PR_56_44-ENG.pdf.

6. See the NATO archives on the Hungarian Revolution of 1956: http://www.nato.int/cps/en/natolive/102641.htm.

7. Tore T. Petersen, *The Middle East between the Great Powers: Anglo-American Conflict and Cooperation, 1952–7* (Basingstoke: Macmillan, 2000), p. 72.

8. Memorandum by the President, 1 November 1956, *FRUS, 1955–57*, Volume XVI: *Suez Crisis* (Washington, DC: Government Printing Office, 1990), p. 924. Cited in Simon C. Smith, ed., *Reassessing Suez 1956* (Aldershot: Ashgate, 2008), p. 7.

9. W. Scott Lucas, *Divided We Stand: Britain, the US and the Suez Crisis* (London: Hodder and Stoughton, 1991).

10. Memorandum from the Executive Secretary to Secretaries of Delegations to NATO, "The Impact of the Present Crisis on the Economies of NATO Countries," restricted document RDC/524/56, December 7, 1956; http://archives.nato.int/uploads/r/null/3/7/37947/RDC_56_524_ENG.pdf.

11. NATO Secret, "Record of a Private Meeting of the Council held on Tuesday, 13th November, 1956, at 10.15 am," Section IV: *Assessment of the Situation by the Turkish Representative*, 13 (b) Middle East, 14 November, 1956, pp. 3–4, declassified document; http://www.nato.int/nato_static_fl2014/assets/pdf/hungarian%20revolution%201957%20-%20private%20records/20130917_PR_56_56-ENG.pdf.

12. Stephen D. Kertsez, "NATO's Disarray and Europe's Future," *Review of Politics*, Vol. 28, No. 1 (January 1966), pp. 3–18; Morris Janowitz, "The Future of NATO," *Survival*, Vol. 13 (1971), pp. 412–25.

13. Mary E. Sarotte, *Dealing with the Devil: East Germany, Détente, and Ostpolitik, 1969–1973* (Chapel Hill: University of North Carolina Press, 2001).

14. Gordon A. Craig, "Did Ostpolitik Work?" *Foreign Affairs*, January/February 1994; http://www.foreignaffairs.com/articles/49450/gordon-a-craig/did-ostpolitik-work.

15. Werner D. Lippert, *The Economic Diplomacy of Ostpolitik: Origins of NATO's Energy Dilemma* (Germany: Berghahn, 2010).

16. Lippert, *The Economic Diplomacy of Ostpolitik*, pp. 102–03.

17. Fotios Moustakis, *The Greek-Turkish Relationship and NATO* (London: Frank Cass, 2003), p. 33.

18. Moustakis, *The Greek-Turkish Relationship*, p. 34.

19. Margaret Thatcher, *The Downing Street Years* (New York: Harper Collins, 1993), pp. 470–71.

20. Cited in Gregory W. Pedlow, ed., *The Evolution of NATO Strategy 1949–1969*, NATO (1997), pp. viii–ix; http://www.nato.int/docu/stratdoc/eng/intro.pdf.

21. "NATO's Strategy of Flexible Response and the Twenty First Century," Marine Corps University, Command and Staff College (Quantico, VA, 1986); http://www.globalsecurity.org/wmd/library/report/1986/LLE.htm.

22. Fred Halliday, *The Making of the Second Cold War* (London: Verso, 1983).
23. NATO, "Protocol to the North Atlantic Treaty on the Accession of Greece and Turkey," October 22, 1951; http://www.nato.int/cps/en/natolive/official_texts_17245.htm.
24. Cohen, *Strategy and Politics*, p. 30.
25. Michael Cohen, *Strategy and Politics in the Middle East, 1954–1960: Defending the Northern Tier* (Abingdon, Oxon: Frank Cass, 2005), p. 215.
26. For a bold refutation of this argument, see Michael Shafer, "No Crisis: The Implications of U.S. Dependence on South African Strategic Minerals," Occasional Paper, South African Institute of International Affairs, November 1983; http://dspace.africaportal.org/jspui/bitstream/123456789/29860/1/No%20crisis.pdf?1.
27. Michael Cox, *US Foreign Policy after the Cold War: Superpower without a Mission?* (London: Royal Institute of International Affairs, 1995), p. 83.
28. On this see Mary E. Sarotte, "A Broken Promise? What the West Really Told Moscow about NATO Expansion," *Foreign Affairs*, Vol. 93, No. 5 (September/October 2014), pp. 90–97; http://www.foreignaffairs.com/articles/141845/mary-elise-sarotte/a-broken-promise.
29. Cited in NATO, "20 Years Ago: London Declaration Marks Birth of New NATO," July 2, 2010; http://www.nato.int/cps/en/natolive/news_64790.htm?selectedLocale=en.
30. Mamuka Metreveli, "Legal Aspects of NATO's Involvement in the Out-of-Area Peace Support Operations," Final Report of a NATO-EAPC Research Fellowship (Tbilisi, 2003), p. 16; http://www.nato.int/acad/fellow/01–03/metreveli.pdf.
31. NATO official text, "The Alliance's New Strategic Concept (1991), November 7, 1991"; http://www.nato.int/cps/en/natolive/official_texts_23847.htm.
32. NATO, "The Alliance's New Strategic Concept."
33. NATO, "The Alliance's New Strategic Concept."
34. Rome Declaration on Peace and Cooperation, issued by the heads of state and government participating in the meeting of the North Atlantic Council in Rome, November 8, 1991; http://www.nato.int/docu/comm/49–95/c911108a.htm.
35. NATO Ministerial Communiqué, "The Situation in Yugoslavia," Rome, 1–8 November 1991, Press Release S-1(98)88; http://www.nato.int/docu/comm/49–95/c911108b.htm.
36. Noam Chomsky, *The New Military Humanism* (Monroe, Maine: Common Courage Press, 1999), pp. 197–99.
37. Ethan Chorin, *Exit the Colonel: The Hidden History of the Libyan Revolution* (New York: Public Affairs, 2012), pp. 48–49.
38. Final Communiqué, Ministerial Meeting of the North Atlantic Council in Oslo, June 4, 1992; http://www.nato.int/docu/comm/49–95/c920604a.htm.
39. Zbigniew Brzezinski, "NATO Expand or Die?" *New York Times*, December 28, 1994, p. A15; http://www.nytimes.com/1994/12/28/opinion/nato-expand-or-die.html.
40. Allied Command Operations, "1994–1998: One Team, One Mission! NATO Begins Peacekeeping in Bosnia"; http://www.aco.nato.int/page14672955.aspx.
41. Oliver Ramsbotham and Tom Woodhouse, eds., *Peacekeeping and Conflict Resolution* (London: Frank Cass, 2000), p. 122.
42. Metreveli, "Legal Aspects of NATO's Involvement," p. 6.
43. UN Press Release SG/SM/9993UN, Nov. 11, 2005, "Secretary-General Kofi Annan's message to the Ceremony Marking the Tenth Anniversary of the Srebrenica Massacre in Potocari-Srebrenica"; http://www.un.org/press/en/2005/sgsm9993.doc.htm.
44. NATO, "NATO Operations and Missions," December 1, 2014; http://www.nato.int/cps/en/natolive/topics_52060.htm.
45. Stanley R. Sloan, "US Perspectives on NATO's Future," *International Affairs*, Vol. 71, No. 2 (April 1995), p. 222.

46. Jonathan Dean, *Ending Europe's Wars: The Continuing Search for Peace and Security* (New York: Twentieth Century Fund, 1994).
47. James M. Goldgeier, "NATO Expansion: The Anatomy of a Decision," *Washington Quarterly*, Vol. 21, No. 1 (Winter 1998), pp. 85–102; Brzezinski, "NATO Expand or Die?"
48. Michael G. Roskin, "NATO: The Strange Alliance Getting Stranger," *Parameters*, Vol. 28, No. 2 (Summer 1998), pp. 30–38; James H. Wyllie, "NATO's Bleak Future," *Parameters*, Vol. 28, No. 4 (Winter 1998/1999), pp. 113–23.
49. Todd Sandler, "The Future of NATO," *Economic Affairs*, Vol. 17, No. 4 (1997), p. 15.
50. NATO, "NATO Operations and Missions."
51. NATO, "Invocation of Article 5 Confirmed," *NATO Update*, October 2, 2001; http://www.nato.int/docu/update/2001/1001/e1002a.htm.
52. Prague Summit Declaration, issued by the heads of state and government participating in the meeting of the North Atlantic Council in Prague, November 21, 2002; http://www.nato.int/docu/pr/2002/p02-127e.htm.
53. Metreveli, "Legal Aspects of NATO's Involvement," p. 6.
54. Prague Summit Declaration, 4(b).
55. Prague Summit Declaration, 10.
56. W. Bruce Weinrod, "The Future of NATO," *Mediterranean Quarterly*, Vol. 23, No. 2 (Spring 2012), pp. 7–8 (emphasis added).
57. NATO, "NATO Operations and Missions."
58. NATO, "Counter-Piracy Operations"; http://www.nato.int/cps/en/SID-21B6BDD8-F423BDC4/natolive/topics_48815.htm.
59. NATO, "NATO Operations and Missions."
60. NATO Cooperative Cyber Defense Center of Excellence, "About Us: History"; https://ccdcoe.org/history.html.
61. Josephine Wolff, "NATO's Empty Cybersecurity Gesture," *Slate*, September 10, 2014; http://www.slate.com/articles/technology/future_tense/2014/09/nato_s_statement_on_cyberattacks_misses_some_fundamental_points.html.
62. Bucharest Summit Declaration, April 3, 2008; http://www.nato.int/cps/en/natolive/official_texts_8443.htm.
63. Patrick Keller, "The Future of NATO: Between Overstretch and Irrelevance," *American Foreign Policy Interests*, Vol. 29 (1997), pp. 207–17.
64. "Strasbourg Kehl Summit Declaration," issued by the heads of state and government participating in the meeting of the North Atlantic Council in Strasbourg Kehl, April 4, 2009; http://www.nato.int/cps/en/natolive/news_52837.htm?mode=pressrelease.
65. Theodore Couloumbis, Bill Ahlstrom, and Gary Weaver, "NATO: Out of Area, Not Out of Business," *Real Clear World*, April 29, 2009; http://www.realclearworld.com/articles/2009/04/nato_out_of_area_not_out_of_bu_1.html. Ted Galen Carpenter, "NATO at 60: A Hollow Alliance," *Policy Analysis* No. 635 (Washington, DC: Cato Institute, March 30, 2009).
66. "NATO's 60th Birthday: Alliance Views Its Future Cautiously," *Strategic Comments*, Vol. 15, No. 2 (March 2009), 2 pp.
67. Wibke Hansen, "The Organized Crime - Peace Operations Nexus," *Prism*, Vol. 5, No. 1 (2014), p. 63.
68. Yavuz Yener, "NATO Reaffirmed Its Commitment to Cyber Security," *Journal of Turkish Weekly*, November 12, 2014; http://www.turkishweekly.net/news/175398/nato-reaffirmed-its-commitment-to-cyber-security.html.
69. Ashton B. Carter and David Omand, "Countering Proliferation Risks: Adapting the Alliance to the New Security Environment," *NATO Review*, No. 5 (September 1996), pp. 10–15; Robert Joseph, "Proliferation, Counter-Proliferation, and NATO," *Survival*, Spring 1996.

70. Joanna Spear, "Organizing for International Counterproliferation: NATO and U.S. Nonproliferation Policy," in Janne E. Nolan, Bernard I. Finel, and Brian D. Finlay, eds., *Ultimate Security: Combatting Weapons of Mass Destruction* (New York: Century Foundation, 2003), pp. 203–28.

71. Cited in Steven Erlanger, "Europe Begins to Rethink Cuts to Military Spending," *New York Times*, March 26, 2014; http://www.nytimes.com/2014/03/27/world/europe/europe-begins-to-rethink-cuts.html?_r=0.

Chapter 7

NATO's Charter:
Adaptable but Limited

James Goldgeier

The NATO Charter is a fairly simple document, yet it provided the alliance with its purpose and scope during the four-decade-long Cold War, and remarkably, has enabled the organization to move forward in the decades after the original rationale for its existence disappeared. Designed to combat the Soviet threat to Western Europe after World War II, the alliance has spread across the Continent in the years since the collapse of the USSR, and has engaged in missions and areas of operations that its founders could never have imagined. While its ability to incorporate the formerly Communist states of Central and Eastern Europe was written into the charter in Article 10, the Alliance's response to a range of threats and challenges in recent years goes well beyond that which was originally envisioned by Articles 4 and 5, which provide for consultation and action in the event of a threat to security.

The primary limitation of the alliance in an era of global threats is the territorial scope of the charter. It explicitly focused on the transatlantic community, a sensible decision as the paramount concern was to prevent a Soviet assault across Europe at a time when there were few other countries worldwide that adhered to the principles of democracy, individual liberty, and the rule of law. While the 2014 Russian invasion of Ukraine refocused NATO's immediate attention to its original defense and deterrence mission, the threat environment the alliance faces is global, and democracies exist across the globe. Moreover, many countries outside of North America and Europe have participated in NATO operations, most notably in Afghanistan, yet the charter, whose regional orientation appears anachronistic in the twenty-first century, limits the extent of these external partnerships to formalized arrangements short of membership.

This geographical limitation is particularly notable as there exists no other organization in the world that can do what NATO does, which is why it has been called upon to act in a variety of situations from disaster relief to counterpiracy to humanitarian intervention. Doing so outside of Europe, however, raises questions of legitimacy given a membership limited to the West.[1]

ARTICLE 5

At NATO's core lies its famous Article 5, which outlines the provisions for collective defense: "The Parties agree that an armed attack against one or more of them in Europe or North America shall be considered an attack against them all . . . ." Perceiving the Soviet threat through the lens of a devastating world war initiated through territorial aggression, NATO was founded to prevent the possibility of the most feared conventional threat of the time: a Soviet invasion of a Western European country or group of countries. Collective defense by all members of the alliance was the anticipated response. In reality, the core function of NATO was to provide confidence that the United States would come to the aid of its Western European allies, effectively serving to decrease the likelihood of a Soviet attack and curtailing the development of mass hysteria in the West over the Soviet threat. In addition, NATO would minimize security dilemmas within Western Europe (where countries continued to fear a future German threat, given the origins of World Wars I and II), enabling alliance members to regain their economic vitality, and in turn strengthening the US economy and global position.

After the end of the Cold War and the collapse of the Soviet Union, the then-sixteen members of NATO no longer faced a conventional military threat. Following the dissolution of the Warsaw Pact, many scholars and analysts suggested that NATO had become obsolete. Moreover, some analysts and policymakers advocated for the emergence of the pan-European Conference on Security and Cooperation in Europe (CSCE) as the lead security organization on the Continent. But NATO enabled the United States to dominate European security affairs for four decades, and US officials were loath to lose that standing, particularly as the European Community, which excluded the United States, was forming a closer union. Europeans, meanwhile, had grown dependent on the US provision of security, and many remained concerned about the newly unified Germany. While the CSCE eventually did upgrade to an organization (the OSCE), NATO remains the most significant security institution in Europe.

In the decades since the collapse of the USSR, NATO has responded to a range of threats, developing a broad set of missions and operating throughout the globe. In doing so, it has largely enabled events to define its priorities. And just as it seemed new questions regarding its purpose and relevance would arise as the most complex operation in its history—the mission in Afghanistan—wound down, NATO turned its attention to the threat posed by the Russian takeover of Crimea, statements by President Vladimir Putin that Russia reserved the right to protect ethnic Russian populations in neighboring states,[2] and continued Russian aggression in Eastern Ukraine.

Debates about NATO's scope and area of operations began in 1999, as the alliance prepared to celebrate its fiftieth anniversary while determining whether to act to save the population of Kosovo, which faced the prospect of mass killings ordered by the government of Serbia. NATO's subsequent bombing of Serbia, the first major military operation in its history, was controversial for a number of reasons. There had been no attack on a NATO member, and despite talk of the threat of refugees, there was no real threat of the type envisioned even by Article 4, which provides for consultations "whenever, in the opinion of any of them, the territorial integrity, political independence or security of any of the Parties is threatened." Serbia had threatened an ethnic group within its territory, and thus any external intervention would undermine its national sovereignty. Given the certainty of a Russian and Chinese veto in response to a Security Council resolution to interfere in the affairs of a sovereign state, NATO would have to act without United Nations authorization.

NATO, however, did act. With American reassurances to France that such an operation outside of the UN Charter would serve as the exception and not the rule, NATO acted out of what came to be called the "responsibility to protect." As British Prime Minister Tony Blair argued in April 1999, "[T]hose nations which have the power, have the responsibility."[3]

NATO's operation to defend the Albanian Kosovars was highly consequential. The United Nations system had been founded on the principle of respect for sovereignty and territorial integrity. At the beginning of the 1990s, when Iraq invaded Kuwait, US President George H. W. Bush formed an international coalition to enforce the rationale for the United Nations' founding: to protect smaller countries from being invaded by larger ones. Now, at the end of the decade, the United States and its partners had declared that leaders who grossly violated human rights norms within their states ceded their right to invoke sovereignty as protection against an international coalition using force against them.

Since 1999, NATO has engaged in a variety of missions that have neither involved the threat of armed attack nor taken place near the territory of member states. In Libya in 2011, the alliance once again acted to prevent a humanitarian catastrophe in war-ravaged Benghazi. It airlifted supplies to Indonesia after the 2004 tsunami and has partnered with the United Nations and the European Union to combat piracy in the Indian Ocean. In 2008, the alliance created the NATO Cooperative Cyber Defense Center of Excellence in Estonia.[4]

The closest NATO came in the period after the Cold War to acting as originally envisioned by the NATO Charter was in the aftermath of the terrorist attacks in the United States on September 11, 2001. Indeed, for the first and only time in its history, NATO members invoked Article 5. Contrary to the expectations of 1949, when the purpose of Article 5 was to commit the United States to come to the aid of its allies in Western Europe, in 2001 the European members of the alliance offered to come to the defense of the United States, not in response to a conventional armed attack but rather in the aftermath of the use of hijacked American civilian airplanes as weapons against populations in New York and Washington.

The administration of George W. Bush, however, chose not to accept the offer of support from alliance members. The Bush administration believed that the prior NATO operation in Kosovo was inefficient, hampered by the requirement to work through the alliance infrastructure to determine bombing targets. Instead, the administration opted to assemble a US-led "coalition of the willing," whereby the United States would work with a few select allies to pursue al-Qaeda in Afghanistan rather than through NATO. The only Article 5 mission to emerge from the aftermath of the attacks was the maritime counterterrorism operation in the Mediterranean known as Operation Active Endeavor.

After the United States became bogged down in Iraq, NATO accepted the Bush administration's request to assume leadership of the International Security Assistance Force (ISAF) in Afghanistan in August 2003. While NATO was initially responsible for postconflict reconstruction in Kabul, over time the alliance expanded its operations throughout the countryside. Nearly fifty nations from around the world, including Azerbaijan, Finland, and the United Arab Emirates, sent troops to Afghanistan in support of ISAF's mission.

The mission was not without controversy. While participating coalition members like Germany and Italy hailed their countries' support of ISAF despite their "caveats" restricting military action, US military personnel bitterly joked that ISAF stood for "I saw Americans fight."[5] Although Article 5 envisioned an alliance in which every member could contribute, over time military spending as a percentage of GDP has remained low in Europe, and the gap between American fighting capabilities and those of its allies has grown larger and larger.

As the mission in Afghanistan began winding down in 2013, NATO members again were confronted with a few overriding questions that remain unresolved since the conclusion of the Cold War: What is the purpose of the alliance, and how do we understand Article 5 going forward? In its 2010 Strategic Concept (see Documents section), the alliance reaffirmed that it will "deter and defend against any threat of aggression, and against emerging security challenges where they threaten the fundamental security of individual Allies or the Alliance as a whole."[6] Despite this reassertion, there exists a range of opinions within the alliance on what constitutes an emerging security challenge and the appropriate responses.

In one sense the Russian annexation of Crimea in March 2014 clarified Article 5, but in another it simply muddied the waters. For those NATO members who have argued all along that the Russian threat remains paramount, the events of 2014 were an "ah-ha" moment. While it seems clear that Putin believed he could act in Ukraine precisely because his neighbor was not a member of NATO and therefore not protected formally by Article 5, Russia's intervention also produced anxiety in the Baltic countries and in Poland about the certainty of NATO's collective defense commitment. The United States in particular was eager to reassure NATO's eastern members that the alliance is prepared to defend its member states should Russia threaten them, but Putin had exposed the fact that NATO had done little to plan for this contingency. Moreover, Putin had succeeded in clarifying his competing vision for Europe, one that was not a "Europe whole, free and at peace," a notion the United States and its partners had promoted since 1989.

NATO leveraged its September 2014 summit in Wales and the one that followed in Warsaw in July 2016 to respond to the threat Russia now poses to the post–Cold War European order. NATO increased sea patrols in the Baltic and Black Seas and stepped up its air defense over its eastern territory. The alliance created a small high-readiness rotational force for deployments in the Baltic countries and Poland to deter any Russian aggression. Unfortunately, while NATO member states continue to commit to spending 2 percent of their GDP on defense, that promise will remain unfulfilled in all but a handful of NATO countries. And NATO remains unprepared to respond to covert aggression in places like Estonia, where, while a direct Russian military assault is unlikely, the Kremlin's use of the country's Russian population to foment instability remains a serious concern.

While the ongoing Ukraine crisis reminds us that countries covered by Article 5 have become part of Europe's institutional fabric and have less to fear than countries such as Ukraine, Moldova, and Georgia, which are not members of the alliance, the conflict is less clarifying than it might seem at first glance. After all, the reminder that Russia opposed the post–Cold War path Europe has taken does not diminish the threats posed to alliance members from outside of Europe. If NATO reverts to its mission to exist solely as an alliance that defends against a threat from Russia, it will neglect to combat the substantial transnational threats that continue to plague its members. The 113-paragraph 2014 NATO Wales summit declaration indicated the range of threats NATO seeks to address alongside Russian aggression, including terrorism, cyber-security, nonproliferation, piracy, and drug trafficking—a heavy burden to bear for an alliance in which most member states fail to meet the 2 percent defense spending target.[7]

Moreover, in order to combat the broad range of global threats it faces, NATO must venture beyond Europe to engage more deeply with potential partners with shared concerns. The biggest change in the security environment between Wales and Warsaw (whose summit produced a 139-paragraph document) was the rise of the Islamic State of Iraq and Syria (ISIS): "Our security," stated the Warsaw summit communiqué,

> is also deeply affected by the security situation in the Middle East and North Africa, which has deteriorated significantly across the whole region. Terrorism, particularly as perpetrated by the so-called Islamic State of Iraq and the Levant (ISIL)/Da'esh, has risen to an unprecedented level of intensity, reaches into all of Allied territory, and now represents an immediate and direct threat to our nations and the international community. Instability in the Middle East and North Africa also contributes to the refugee and migrant crisis.[8]

To address the range of threats NATO members face requires deeper partnerships with non-NATO countries outside of Europe that by the terms of the North Atlantic Treaty will continue to remain ineligible to join the alliance.

ARTICLE 10

Twelve nations founded NATO in 1949, though the charter exhibited flexibility and a willingness to grow by laying out the basis for enlargement. Article 10 states, "The Parties may, by unanimous agreement, invite any other European State in a position to further the principles of this Treaty and to contribute to the security of the North Atlantic area to accede to this Treaty." Prospective members were required to be committed to democracy and the rule of law and could not simply be consumers of security; rather, they would be obligated to contribute to a collective defense.

Greece and Turkey joined NATO in 1952, and West Germany followed in 1955. Post-Franco Spain entered the organization in 1982. Greek military rule in the 1960s raised questions about the democratic principles underpinning membership in the alliance, exposing a charter omission: whereas there exists a provision for accepting new members based on core principles, there exists no provision for expelling them for violating these norms, a concern that has arisen in recent years with the antidemocratic rhetoric and behavior emanating in particular from Hungarian leader Viktor Orban and Turkish President Recep Tayyip Erdogan.

Although NATO pursued modest enlargement during the Cold War, the meaning of Article 10 only became clear when formerly Communist nations clamored to join the alliance in the 1990s.

Debates regarding the virtues of welcoming Central and Eastern European nations into the alliance were deeply divisive. On one side were those who believed that the main goal of Western policy after 1991 should be to engage Russia with hopes of developing stronger ties with the West. These scholars and practitioners regarded enlargement as undermining that goal by threatening Moscow with the shift of NATO's borders to the east. On the other side were those who saw an opportunity to support democratization in Central and Eastern Europe and to extend the Western zone of peace and prosperity across Europe.[9]

While the debate died down after the initial round of post–Cold War enlargement in 1999, it resumed with a vengeance in 2014. Alongside the Russians, led by Putin, who criticized the West's expansion and the perceived harm to Russian interests, many observers in the West considered the threat NATO posed to Russia, particularly if it were to consider Ukrainian membership, as a motivation for Putin's move into Crimea.

Russian opposition to enlargement has often been predicated on the belief that the West promised Soviet President Mikhail Gorbachev that NATO would not enlarge. Supporters of enlargement dismiss the notion that a binding commitment was made. Both sides reference statements and declassified documents from the period supporting their positions, rendering a potential resolution to this debate improbable given the competing interests.

As discussions regarding German unification emerged in 1990, West German Foreign Minister Hans-Dietrich Genscher declared on January 31 of that year, "What NATO must do is state unequivocally that whatever happens in the Warsaw Pact, there will be no expansion of NATO territory eastwards, that is to say closer to the borders of the Soviet Union." US Secretary of State James A. Baker III traveled to Moscow shortly thereafter and assured Gorbachev that "there would be no extension of NATO's jurisdiction for forces of NATO one inch to the east." When Gorbachev said, "any extension of the zone of NATO is unacceptable," Baker replied, "I agree."[10]

For many Russians, any argument about promises made ends there. But the story is not so simple. Back in the White House, officials were concerned about Baker's statements and spent the balance of February 1990 ensuring that no such commitment was articulated in any agreement that would emerge from the "two-plus-four" talks taking place on German unification. In June 1990, in a meeting with Gorbachev, George H. W. Bush got the Soviet leader to recommit to the principle enshrined in the 1975 Helsinki Final Act that Germany, like other signatories, was free to choose with whom to ally.[11] In the final agreement, signed in Paris in September 1990, restrictions were placed on German troop presence in the former German Democratic Republic (East Germany) during the Soviet withdrawal, and nuclear weapons were permanently barred from that region, but this was the extent of any binding accord on NATO's extension. Whatever had been said early in 1990 was superseded by the formal agreement signed later that year, further supporting the Americans' assertion that any so-called promise to Russia not to enlarge did not exist. Most important, the discussions in 1990 were about the future status of what had been East Germany not the rest of Eastern Europe.

Contributing to the Russian sense of betrayal, however, was a conversation that took place between US Secretary of State Warren Christopher and Russian President Boris Yeltsin in October 1993. Christopher described the Clinton administration's plan to create a Partnership for Peace for all CSCE members (including Russia) that would be announced in January 1994. Christopher noted, "There would be no step taken at this time to push anyone ahead of others." When Yeltsin asked for clarification that partnership did not mean membership, Christopher stated, "Yes, that is the case, there would not be even an associate status." Yeltsin replied, "This is a brilliant idea, it is a stroke of genius." Christopher then added, "We will in due course be looking at the question of membership as a longer term eventuality. There will be an evolution, based on the development of a habit of cooperation, but over time. Those who wish to can pursue the idea over time, but that will come later."[12] For Yeltsin, what was likely most important was the feeling that he had dodged an immediate bullet, and certainly he did not anticipate the push to enlarge would come so soon. He understood Christopher as saying that NATO would not enlarge; Christopher, a lawyer by training, had not said anything quite so specific.[13]

The debate over what was said in the early 1990s between US and Russian leaders is ironic in that the very subjects of these negotiations, countries such as Poland, Hungary, and Romania, were not party to the discussions. Any conversations about these newly independent nations' aspirations needed to include them. Moreover, the debate over promises made or not made fails to address the real issues: namely, the dissimilar visions emerging from the West and from Russia for how best to foster security in Europe in the aftermath of the Cold War, and the dissimilar power that the West and Russia possessed to implement their respective visions. Article 10 of the NATO Charter provided a roadmap for enlargement and impeded efforts to block the pursuit of membership by Central and Eastern Europeans. After all, the charter explicitly offered the possibility of membership to "any other European State in a position to further the principles of this Treaty and to contribute to the security of the North Atlantic area." For those who hoped to use enlargement to provide security to Central and Eastern European countries that had been invaded by Germany during World War II and subsequently occupied by the Soviet Union for four decades, Article 10 offered an extraordinary opportunity.

Although the language of Article 10 regarding what it meant to further the principles or contribute to security was vague, the basic points were largely understood and enabled NATO to leverage the incentive of membership to foster political and economic reforms in the formerly Communist countries. Poland, for example, committed to civilian control of the military, and Hungary agreed to respect existing territorial borders. Initial expectations were that Poland, Hungary, the Czech Republic, and Slovakia would be the first from the East to join, but Slovakia found itself on a nondemocratic course in the mid-1990s, delaying its entrance into the alliance until it could demonstrate its commitment to democracy.

After Poland, Hungary, and the Czech Republic joined in 1999, the alliance decided that it should better define the expectations of Article 10, establishing the "Membership Action Plan" in order to ensure that aspirant nations committed to the principles and the idea of a shared contribution to overall security. Given the decline in military spending across Europe, the United States in particular feared that countries would join in order to acquire security guarantees without actually contributing their share. After all, those security guarantees were the primary rationale for countries like Poland and Estonia to join, viewing NATO membership as finally putting to rest any future threat from Russia.

While Russian elites continued to argue that their country had been betrayed by promises the government thought it had received from the United States not to enlarge and reacted with great alarm to NATO's inclusion of its former client states, the alliance continued to grow, from sixteen to twenty-eight members. Montenegro was formally invited to join the alliance as its prospective twenty-ninth member at the 2016 Warsaw summit. Only a handful of countries in southern and Eastern Europe that have expressed an interest in joining remain outside NATO: Macedonia has not convinced Greece to abandon its opposition to the country's name, and Georgia's ongoing conflict with Russia prevents its accession. Ukrainians previously demonstrated great ambivalence regarding membership, but public support grew as a result of the Russian annexation of Crimea and the continuing war in Eastern Ukraine. Russia has also now demonstrated in going to war with Georgia in 2008 and invading Ukraine in 2014 that it will use force to prevent the non-Baltic countries of the former Soviet Union from joining the alliance, and the insecurity of those countries lying between NATO and Russia remains a significant challenge for Europe. Nevertheless, the alliance has maintained its stated commitment to its Article 10. As the 2014 Wales Summit Declaration succinctly put it: "NATO's door will remain open to all European democracies which share the values of our Alliance, which are willing and able to assume the responsibilities and obligations of membership, which are in a position to further the principles of the Treaty, and whose inclusion will contribute to the security of the North Atlantic area."[14]

As the alliance neared completion of the enlargement process, as threats to members originated from well beyond Europe, and as missions across the globe followed, the limitation inherent in Article 10 to enable only European nations to join NATO has become glaringly obvious. In an era in which threats are global, why should an alliance of democracies remain regional in scope?

While any effort to open membership outside of Europe would require a revision to the NATO Charter, other obstacles exist to developing a "Global NATO."[15] Most European nations view the organization as central to a special relationship with the United States. In addition, countries that have contributed greatly to NATO missions, like Australia, would be wary of the commitments underlying membership and, in that particular case, of creating antagonisms with China. Moreover, some members fear a much larger alliance would lose its cohesion and focus, particularly those in Central and Eastern Europe who regard the alliance as a bulwark against Russian intimidation.

Despite the apprehension, NATO secretaries general since 2006 have stressed that global partnerships are essential for the future of the alliance. When NATO's Charter was drafted, the formalization of a special bond among the North Atlantic democracies to protect against the Soviet threat required no explanation. The idea that countries would band together in the event of an attack on any one of them was completely legitimate.

Today, however, when NATO acts, it largely acts "out of area." Global partners provide additional capacity and greater legitimacy when the alliance acts far from home. An alliance that can foster global partnerships and greater participation from outside the transatlantic community will act with greater credibility and legitimacy in the eyes of non-Western populations. Since it would be impossible for NATO members to agree on a revision of Article 10, we are likely to continue to see NATO countries leverage developing partnerships with others outside of the alliance to respond to emerging threats. At the Wales summit in 2014, for example, ten countries announced their intention to work together in a "core coalition" to defeat ISIS: nine NATO countries plus Australia.[16] For operations in the Middle East, NATO countries will look to partner with nondemocratic countries such as the United Arab Emirates, as occurred during both the 2011 Libyan campaign and the 2014 initiation of air strikes against ISIS.

CONCLUSION

There is no organization in the world that can do what NATO does. Its leaders have repeated for decades their staunch support for NATO as the most successful alliance in history, and in recent years it has combated a range of challenges. But it is much more than simply an alliance. As a collective security arrangement it has served since the end of the Cold War as an engine of democratization in Europe (its provision of security enabled the European Union to enlarge across the Continent) and as an enforcer of international norms in places like Kosovo and Libya. As long as no other institution is capable of acting like NATO, the international community will turn to the alliance for help in a crisis.

And yet the elements of the charter that have made NATO so successful, in particular Articles 5 and 10, also limit the organization going forward. In an era when an "armed attack" from one state toward another is not the only risk, what threats rise to an Article 5 level? European member states invoked Article 5 in the aftermath of the terrorist attacks of September 11, but NATO did not do so in the wake of a major cyber-attack on Estonia in 2007.

The notion of a regional alliance in an era of global threats seems like a mismatch. To put it another way, if the alliance did not exist today, the United States would not seek to create it in its current form.[17] Were we to start from scratch in the twenty-first century, US officials would have no reason to foster an alliance including only Canada and democratic countries in Europe in light of the current threat environment. Article 10 has enabled NATO to create a more peaceful Europe (though we witnessed in 2008 and 2014 that insecurity persists for those left out of Article 5 coverage), but it has limited the potential of the alliance to create global capabilities and legitimacy.

It is critical for the alliance to clarify its understanding of Article 5 today, when distant challenges can threaten the prosperity and security of its member states, and to foster a robust network of partnerships worldwide. Enlargement in Europe is essentially over. The mission in Afghanistan is greatly reduced. Since the end of the Cold War, NATO has faced many questions about its relevance that both enlargement and the war in Afghanistan quieted to a great degree.

The Ukraine crisis appears to have rejuvenated NATO, but many questions remain both about the alliance's commitments to all member states and about NATO's capacity to respond to the threat environment. Defense spending remains paltry in most countries. In the aftermath of the Russian invasion of Crimea in 2014, NATO Secretary General Rasmussen and US Secretary of Defense Chuck Hagel, among others, called for alliance members to spend more, as did President Donald Trump on his visit to NATO headquarters in May 2017, but most member states are unlikely to increase their military spending to any significant degree given pressing domestic needs. Most significant, the anxiety Putin created in the Baltic countries and in Poland is not easily addressed. When the United States Senate ratified NATO enlargement, there was little thought given to the commitment the United States was making to the defense of countries in the region through Article 5. Putin does not need to invade Estonia to threaten it. We have seen how he has deployed Russian populations in Ukraine for his purposes; he could leverage similar populations in Estonia or Latvia to undermine those countries' security and stability. What would NATO do in such a situation? Whereas going to war with Serbia or combating the Taliban in Afghanistan were tests of the alliance, reassuring a country like Estonia that NATO will be there to defend it goes to the heart of why the alliance was created in the first place, and it remains to be seen if NATO is truly up to the task before it.

Notes

1. Ivo Daalder and James Goldgeier, "Global NATO," *Foreign Affairs* (September/October 2006).
2. Address by President of the Russian Federation, March 18, 2014, at http://eng.kremlin.ru/news/6889.
3. Tony Blair, speech before the Economic Council in Chicago, April 22, 2009, at http://www.pbs.org/newshour/bb/international-jan-june99-blair_doctrine4-23/.
4. On the latter, see https://www.ccdcoe.org/423.html.
5. http://www.usnews.com/news/world/articles/2008/06/05/in-afghanistan-the-nato-led-force-is-underresourced-for-the-fight-against-the-taliban.
6. http://www.nato.int/cps/en/natolive/official_texts_68580.htm.
7. Wales Summit Declaration at http://www.nato.int/cps/en/natohq/official_texts_112964.htm.
8. Warsaw Summit Communiqué at http://www.nato.int/cps/en/natohq/official_texts_133169.htm.
9. See James M. Goldgeier, *Not Whether but When: The U.S. Decision to Enlarge NATO* (Washington, DC: Brookings Institution Press, 1999).
10. James M. Goldgeier and Michael McFaul, *Power and Purpose: U.S. Policy toward Russia after the Cold War* (Washington, DC: Brookings Institution Press, 2003), pp. 184–85.
11. Svetlana Savranskaya and Thomas Blanton, "The Washington/Camp David Summit 1990: From the Secret Soviet, American and German Files," at http://www2.gwu.edu/~nsarchiv/NSAEBB/NSAEBB320/.
12. Goldgeier and McFaul, *Power and Purpose*, pp. 186–87.

13. James Goldgeier, "Promises Made, Promises Broken? What Yeltsin Was Told About NATO in 1993 and Why It Matters," *War on the Rocks*, July 12, 2016; available online at http://warontherocks.com/2016/07/promises-made-promises-broken-what-yeltsin-was-told-about-nato-in-1993-and-why-it-matters/.
14. Wales Summit Declaration, paragraph 92.
15. Daalder and Goldgeier, "Global NATO."
16. Patrick Wintour, "U.S. Forms 'Core' Coalition to Fight ISIS Militants in Iraq," *Guardian*, September 5, 2014, at http://www.theguardian.com/world/2014/sep/05/us-core-coalition-fight-isis-militants-iraq-nato.
17. James M. Goldgeier, "The Future of NATO," Council on Foreign Relations Special Report, 2010, available at http://www.cfr.org/nato/future-nato/p21044.

Chapter 8

NATO, Regionalism, and the Responsibility to Protect
Anne Orford

With the ending of the Cold War, it might have been expected that the age of spheres of influence and of regional hegemons had also finally ended. Yet the twenty-first century has been marked by a return to battles over regional influence between expansionist powers, particularly in Eastern Europe and the Middle East. Given that context, it is perhaps unsurprising that the role of a regional alliance such as the North Atlantic Treaty Organization has continued to be the subject of debate and contention. What is perhaps more surprising is that post–Cold War justifications for extending the reach of NATO have extended beyond the traditional vocabulary of collective self-defense to embrace more controversial and, at least prima facie, less self-interested concepts of humanitarian intervention and the responsibility to protect civilians.

This chapter considers the implications of the expansive role that NATO has claimed for itself in protecting civilians not only within but also beyond the North Atlantic area, beginning with NATO's 1999 "humanitarian" intervention in Kosovo and extending to the use of the responsibility to protect concept to frame the use of force against Libya in 2011 as part of Operation Unified Protector. Part 1 of the chapter considers the initial mandate of NATO and its relationship to the uneasy compromise between universalist and regionalist visions of international security embedded in the UN Charter. Part

2 examines the challenges posed to traditional understandings of the NATO mandate and area of operation by the ending of the Cold War, and analyzes the Kosovo intervention as a turning point in the history both of NATO and of international law relating to intervention. Part 3 explores the use of the responsibility to protect concept to frame the UN Security Council resolutions mandating the use of force against Libya in 2011 and the role that NATO played in taking up that Security Council mandate. Part 4 concludes by critically assessing the turn to regionalism in the development of policies and practices relating to civilian protection, and asks what that turn might mean for the universalist ambitions of the existing international legal order.

1. THE FOUNDING OF NATO AND THE UN CHARTER

NATO has been an important player in the emergence and consolidation of the responsibility to protect concept. The concept is premised on the notion that "the primary raison d'être and duty" of every state is to protect its population.[1] If a state manifestly fails to protect its population, the responsibility and authority to do so shift to the international community. The responsibility to protect concept was initially developed by the International Commission on Intervention and State Sovereignty (ICISS) as a response to debates over the legitimacy of NATO's 1999 intervention in Kosovo and the implications of that intervention for the existing international order.[2] The concept came of age with its adoption by the UN General Assembly at the World Summit of 2005.[3] The emphasis in the World Summit Outcome and in subsequent General Assembly debates on the need to ensure that military intervention undertaken in furtherance of the responsibility to protect is conducted through the United Nations was designed to ensure that actors such as NATO could not use the concept to justify unilateral humanitarian action.[4]

Yet the responsibility to protect concept has since been taken up to justify another "out of area" mission by NATO, this time when members of the alliance, acting under Security Council Resolution 1973, undertook Operation Unified Protector to secure the protection of civilians in Libya. In the aftermath of the NATO operation in Libya, commentators began to focus on the potential of regional actors as agents for realizing the responsibility to protect.[5] More radically, UK and US policymakers sought to reassert the legitimacy of military interventions undertaken without Security Council authorization where necessary to prevent mass atrocities,[6] including interventions conducted by NATO.[7] The international community was urged to adopt the concept of a "regional responsibility to protect" modeled on NATO action in Kosovo.[8]

In order to comprehend the radical nature of the claim that NATO has a legitimate role to play as a regional actor with a responsibility to protect civilians outside the North Atlantic area, it is necessary to recall two aspects of the role initially conceived for NATO. The first role relates to the place envisaged for NATO within the system of collective security established under the UN, and the second relates to the limited sphere of operations claimed for NATO, particularly in relation to the defense of European colonies.

NATO, Regionalism, and the UN System of Collective Security

The collective security system established under the UN Charter in 1945 was an extension of earlier twentieth-century attempts to outlaw war and maintain international peace and security through international institutions. The use of force in international relations was formally prohibited under the UN Charter except in self-defense or where authorized by the Security Council, and members committed themselves to settling disputes by peaceful means and to regulating armaments. At the heart of the UN system of collective security was a commitment to universalism and the idea that it was possible to constitute a community of states, or at least of peace-loving states, that would act forcefully only in the name of that community to counter aggressive actions. In joining the UN, states gave up their right unilaterally to resort to force other than in self-defense, and pledged to use force only in the name of the international community. The principle of collective security meant not that force would be abolished, but that it would be "collectivized" or "denationalized."[9] More specifically, the UN system sought to collectivize the judgment that there had been an illegal breach of the peace or act of aggression, and the decision to resort to force in response. That model of collective security seemed to render regional military alliances a thing of the past.

Nonetheless, the UN inherited a more accommodating orientation toward regionalism from its predecessor organization, the League of Nations.[10] The drafters of the League Covenant had been forced to find a place for regional arrangements in the covenant due to the significance that the US Senate placed upon preserving the Monroe Doctrine. The doctrine had been a core plank of US foreign policy since its articulation by President James Monroe in 1823.[11] In his initial articulation of the doctrine, Monroe declared that "the American continents, by the free and independent condition which they have assumed and maintained, are henceforth not to be considered as subjects for future colonization by any European powers." As the "political system of the allied Powers was essentially different" from "that of America," the US would consider any attempt by European powers to "extend their system to any portion of this hemisphere as dangerous to our peace and safety" and view any attempt to interfere with, oppress, or control the destiny of the independent governments of the American continent as "the manifestation of an unfriendly disposition towards the United States."[12] Monroe's formulation linked the space of the American continents to the political idea of republicanism, which was represented as "essentially different" from the political system of the European alliance. His message was "intended to carry specific information" to the nations of Europe that they should not "contemplate the vindication of monarchical principles in the territory of the New World."[13] The doctrine thus expressed a new sense of regionalism, grounded in a differentiation between the monarchic-dynastic political system governing Europe and the republican system governing America.[14]

US commentators insisted that the Monroe Doctrine was a policy of self-defense and not a policy of aggression.[15] Yet already by the late nineteenth century, the measures required to defend the US were being interpreted in an expansive manner. The announcement by President Theodore Roosevelt in 1904 that an "international police power" was a corollary of the Monroe Doctrine left a generation of Latin American governments skeptical about the implications of the doctrine for the political independence of states in the region.[16] US Secretary of State Charles Evans Hughes spelled out in 1923 that the right of self-defense of which the Monroe Doctrine was a particular expression allowed the US to resist the foreign possession or control of any place that could be prejudicial to the safety and communications of the US.[17] This meant, for example, that in building the Panama Canal, the US had "not only established a new and convenient highway of commerce," but it had also created "new exigencies and new conditions of strategy and defense." "It is up to us," said Hughes, "to protect that highway."[18] It was only with the introduction of the good neighbor policy in President Franklin D. Roosevelt's 1933 inaugural address that this concern began to ease.[19]

In line with that longstanding foreign policy tradition, the US sought to ensure that joining the League of Nations would not require it to abandon the Monroe Doctrine or submit the right to interpret it to any other authority. At the insistence of the US drafters, the League Covenant was amended to include Article 21, which provided that "[n]othing in this Covenant shall be deemed to affect the validity of international engagements, such as treaties of arbitration or regional understandings like the Monroe doctrine, for securing the maintenance of peace." The result of this odd compromise formulation was that "regional understandings like the Monroe doctrine" were deemed compatible with the universal system established under the League Covenant.[20] The meaning of "regional understanding" was, however, nowhere defined in the covenant, with some commentators interpreting the phrase to mean understandings between states of a particular region, and others interpreting it to mean an understanding between perhaps widely separated states concerning a particular geographically defined region. The Monroe Doctrine could be used in support of either interpretation, as on the one hand it could be viewed as an understanding between American states concerning their own region, and on the other as an agreement between the US and European states concerning the destiny of Latin America.[21]

The league's recognition of regional understandings fueled claims for recognition of other forms of extended spatial order during the interwar period. During the 1930s and 1940s lawyers, political thinkers, economists, and politicians debated whether other forms of spatial order were better suited to emerging economic arrangements, the need for states to access raw materials, new forms of energy and the infrastructure that supported those forms, and issues related to the distribution of population. Colonialism offered one alternative model for organizing space on a global scale to address such questions; the Monroe Doctrine, with its approach to regional hemispheric control, offered a second; and fascist expansionist policies, whether in the form of the Italian invasion of Abyssinia or the expansionist German policy of *Volk ohne Raum*, offered a third.

To geopolitical thinkers such as Rudolf Kjellén and Friedrich Ratzel, it was apparent that "the nation-state was becoming too small to correspond to the twentieth century's political and economic necessities."[22] The German jurist Carl Schmitt translated this geopolitical thinking into international law, arguing that it was necessary to think about a new concept of space—a greater space, or *Großraum*, that extended beyond the state, involving a vision of the world in which nation-states coexisted with other kinds of territories (such as protectorates and border states), all of which were guaranteed their independence and security by a great power. For Schmitt, this greater space concept was related to forms of ordering that more closely mapped onto energy economies, strategic interests, and the relation of people to territory, while also dependent upon shared values, ethnicity, allegiance, and identity. He argued that this principle of spatial order had already been introduced into international law by the Monroe Doctrine.[23] Schmitt imagined Central Europe as just such a future *Großraum*, with Germany as its leading force.

More liberal European and American commentators expressed some sympathy with the position that fascist expansionism was in part a response to an unfair world order, in which colonial powers enjoyed a monopoly of access to "essential colonial raw materials" and to the space perceived as necessary for addressing problems of metropolitan overpopulation.[24] Thus during the 1930s internationalists began to question the exceptional status and privileges of colonial powers and to link the resolution of the world crisis to the development of mechanisms for "peaceful change" toward decolonization.[25]

After World War II, these models of spatial ordering, in which hegemonic powers exercised control over the people and territory of the greater spaces they controlled, were largely discredited. Nonetheless, the UN inherited the uneasy recognition of regionalism introduced into the League Covenant to placate the US, and with it the resulting tension between universal aspirations, regional alliances, and imperial ambitions. The relationship between the UN and regional arrangements became a source of bitter debates during the drafting of the UN Charter. The US and Soviet delegations, as well as the Latin American republics, pushed to maintain recognition for regional defense arrangements in the text.[26]

The resulting compromise between universalist and regionalist visions of internationalism was enshrined in two sections of the UN Charter. First, Chapter VIII provided a very confined place for regionalism. It contained three articles regulating the relationship between the UN and regional arrangements, including Article 53 requiring Security Council authorization of any enforcement action taken under regional arrangements or by regional agencies. Second, and more significant, the drafters included Article 51, which provides an exception to the requirement for Security Council authorization of collective enforcement action in cases where states take measures in individual or collective self-defense. That article was introduced to placate the US and the USSR and ensure that Article 53 would not make it possible for extraregional powers to veto regional action against external aggressors through their dominance in the Security Council.[27]

This was the complicated legal and political context concerning the role of regional arrangements into which NATO was born in 1949. From the outset NATO's relation to the collective security system envisaged under the UN Charter was a matter of debate. Under Article 5 of the North Atlantic Treaty, parties agreed that armed attack against one or more of them in Europe or North America would be considered armed attack against them all. Consequently, if such an armed attack occurred, each of them, in exercise of the right of individual or collective self-defense recognized by Article 51 of the UN Charter, would assist the party or parties so attacked in order to "restore and maintain the security of the North Atlantic area." Thus the North Atlantic Treaty made clear that NATO was constituted under Article 51 of the UN Charter, recognizing the rights of states to take individual and collective self-defense against armed attack.

The parties to the North Atlantic Treaty consistently asserted that NATO was a self-defense organization constituted under Article 51 and not a regional organization regulated by Chapter VIII of the Charter (as did the parties to the subsequent Warsaw Pact). That characterization mattered, because a regional organization could not take enforcement action without Security Council authorization. The characterization of NATO as a defensive alliance was designed to ensure that the Security Council was not given a legal basis for exerting influence over it. The first secretary general of NATO, Lord Ismay, consistently stressed the defensive nature of NATO, declaring early in his tenure that "no gun or ship or airplane that is provided for NATO will be used except in legitimate self defence."[28] The position that NATO is not a regional organization in the sense set out in Chapter VIII of the charter was later expressly clarified in a letter from then-Secretary General Willy Claes to the UN secretary-general.[29]

NATO and the Colonial Question

NATO's relation to the international order established under the UN was also shaped by the broad anti-imperial sentiments held by former colonies (among them Canada and the US), as embodied in the UN Charter's commitment to the principles of equal rights and self-determination. The anti-imperial climate of the 1940s had a strong influence on decisions about the geographical scope of the alliance's operations.[30] Article 5 of the North Atlantic Treaty makes clear that the obligation of allied defense arises only if there is an armed attack against one or more of the parties in Europe or North America. Article 6 defined armed attack against one or more of the parties in Article 5 to mean an attack "on the territory of any of the Parties in Europe or North America," as well as on "the Algerian Departments of France" (a clause that became inapplicable from July 3, 1962) and "Islands under the jurisdiction of any of the Parties in the North Atlantic area north of the Tropic of Cancer." The definition consciously excluded the colonial territories of members (with Algeria at that point being considered legally and administratively part of France), so that the obligation to provide military support did not extend to mutual defense of colonial possessions. The US had insisted that military aid pursuant to NATO was strictly for use in Europe only,[31] at one point warning the Dutch government that it would not receive any military aid under the treaty until it resolved its relationship with Indonesia.[32] During the Cold War, Article 6 was regularly invoked to prevent discussion of the possibility of "out-of-area" military action.[33] This caused much dissatisfaction on the part of Cold War warriors such as Henry Kissinger, who was scathing about the "legalism" of the European position that NATO's operational boundaries did not extend to include the Middle East, and criticized the use of Article 6 to reject American calls for assistance in supporting Israeli forces during the 1973 Yom Kippur War.[34]

However, Article 6 did not block all considerations of situations outside the North Atlantic area. Article 4 of the treaty provided a basis for consultation whenever a party considered that "the territorial integrity, political independence or security of any of the Parties is threatened." According to the report of the Committee of Three prepared in response to the Suez crisis (see Documents section), Article 4, while limited in its terms, was included because of an "insistent feeling that NATO must become more than a military alliance."[35] The deterrent role of NATO, "based on solidarity and strength," could only be discharged if the members of the alliance had cooperative and close political and economic relations, and took account of each other's interests. Article 4 therefore provided the basis for discussions in the North Atlantic Council on matters of common concern outside the defined NATO area. By the end of the Cold War, the development of Article 4 consultations and processes of coordination in response to situations in Goa, the Suez, Angola, Indochina, and Cuba, together with growing US pressure for a broader interpretation of the alliance's area of responsibility, had begun to move NATO toward a broader interpretation of its geographic mandate.

2. OUT OF AREA: NATO'S INTERVENTION IN KOSOVO AND THE RESPONSIBILITY TO PROTECT

During the Cold War, it had been possible to see NATO simply as a defensive alliance of independent states arrayed against an external enemy. The fact that NATO survived and indeed became more significant as a global force after the fall of the Soviet Union suggests that it was all along something more integrated than an alliance.³⁶ The sense that NATO might become a Cold War relic did not last long, in part due to its actions in the Balkans, first in Bosnia in 1995, then in Kosovo from 1999, and later in Macedonia from 2001. These operations, together with other out-of-area actions in Iraq, Afghanistan, and Libya, made it clear that with the ending of the Cold War, NATO was developing a new sense of its mission and of its defensive area of operations. By 2007, Daniel Fried, US assistant secretary of state for European and Asian affairs, could suggest that during the 1990s NATO had been transformed "into a transatlantic institution with global missions, global reach, and global partners."³⁷ According to Fried, the old 'in area/out of area' debate was over: "There is no 'in area/out of area.' Everything is NATO's area, potentially. That doesn't mean it's a global organization. It's a transatlantic organization, but Article 5 now has global implications."

The Kosovo intervention of 1999 played a major role in the development of that perception of NATO as a transformed institution with a global mission that was no longer constrained by an allegedly narrow and legalistic conception of its "area."

NATO's Intervention in Kosovo

NATO's Operation Allied Force, launched on March 24, 1999, was the first major military campaign undertaken by the alliance in its history. The eleven-week bombing campaign was conducted without Security Council authorization. NATO intervened in response to evidence of a pending humanitarian catastrophe in Kosovo, and in the context of an ongoing civil war between the Kosovo Liberation Army and the Yugoslav army, concerns that Belgrade was planning the systematic ethnic cleansing of Kosovar Albanians, and a potential regional crisis caused by the growing numbers of internally displaced persons and refugees from the conflict.

To the extent that NATO governments offered a legal defense for their action, it was premised on the controversial principle of humanitarian intervention. According to a UK Foreign and Commonwealth Office note of October 1998, military intervention by NATO was "lawful on grounds of overwhelming humanitarian necessity."³⁸ In general, even international lawyers sympathetic to NATO's position tended not to accept that argument for the legality of the intervention, but many nonetheless considered it to be legitimate.³⁹ The action was widely considered to be illegal because NATO acted in violation of the UN Charter by using force without Security Council authorization. The "relative freedom of action" granted to NATO by Article

51 of the charter to act in self-defense did not apply to situations where NATO sought to take broader enforcement measures by military means.[40] Many international lawyers considered that the action was nonetheless legitimate, because it was an urgent measure to avert a humanitarian catastrophe and defend the values of the international community. Such interpretations of the legitimacy of the NATO intervention supported the position put by political leaders such as British Prime Minister Tony Blair, who portrayed the NATO intervention in Kosovo as a "just war, based not on territorial ambitions, but on values."[41]

Yet the legitimacy of the intervention undertaken by NATO, as well as the legality of humanitarian intervention, remained extremely questionable for many states outside the NATO alliance, as was made clear in collective statements issued by the Non-Aligned Movement, the Rio Group, and the Commonwealth of Independent States,[42] and in addresses before the Security Council and General Assembly over the following year.[43] India's representative summed up the nature of the opposition to NATO's intervention during a Security Council debate concerning NATO's actions:

> Those who take the law into their hands have never improved civic peace within nations; neither will they help in international relations. Those who continue to attack the Federal Republic of Yugoslavia profess to do so on behalf of the international community and on pressing humanitarian grounds. They say that they are acting in the name of humanity. Very few members of the international community have spoken in this debate, but even among those who have, NATO would have noted that China, Russia and India have all opposed the violence which it has unleashed. The international community can hardly be said to have endorsed their actions when already representatives of half of humanity have said that they do not agree with what they have done.[44]

In addition, critics argued that the conduct of NATO's bombing campaign had put civilians at risk rather than protecting them. The air campaign appeared to have caused minimal damage to the Yugoslav military, but rather to have succeeded through putting pressure on the Serbian government as a result of the destruction caused to roads, bridges, energy infrastructure, and industry, all of which also harmed the civilian population. The use of depleted uranium projectiles and cluster bombs by NATO created a hazardous environment for the population. It became clear that the killing and displacement of Kosovar Albanians had increased dramatically after the bombing commenced, creating doubts as to "whether, in the absence of the NATO bombing, ethnic cleansing would have proceeded with such speed and viciousness."[45]

The precedent represented by Kosovo was also seen to pose a potential threat to the authority of the UN. The argument that a defensive regional alliance representing only a small percentage of the UN membership had a right and perhaps even a duty to take on the role of enforcing international law ran the risk of undermining constraints on resort to force. The treatment of NATO as somehow interchangeable with the UN threatened to open the way to a system of competing regional counteralliances, all claiming the authority to intervene to defend universal values. In an address to the General Assembly, then-Secretary-General Kofi Annan described the Kosovo intervention as posing a stark dilemma that had to be faced by the UN: "on one side, the question of the legitimacy of an action taken by a regional organization without a United Nations mandate; on the other, the universally recognized imperative of effectively halting gross and systematic violations of human rights with grave humanitarian consequences."[46]

From NATO's Humanitarian Intervention to the Responsibility to Protect

In response to that challenge, the Canadian government announced at the General Assembly in 2000 its establishment of the International Commission on Intervention and State Sovereignty, tasked with producing a report on the issues raised by NATO's intervention. The resulting ICISS report, entitled *The Responsibility to Protect*, sought to transcend the perceived tension between sovereignty and humanitarian intervention that had divided opinion in relation to Kosovo.[47] The ICISS report argued that "the changing international environment" required a rethinking of the fundamental notion of authority. ICISS proposed a "necessary re-characterization" of sovereignty from "*sovereignty as control* to *sovereignty as responsibility*."[48] According to ICISS, thinking of sovereignty in those terms enabled a clearer focus upon the "functions" of "state authorities."[49] The responsibility to perform the functions of protecting citizens and promoting their welfare "resides first and foremost with the state whose people are directly affected."[50] However, in circumstances where the state does not have the power, the capacity, or the will to meet its responsibility to protect, the need for international action arises. In that situation, a "residual" or "fallback" responsibility to protect on the part of the "broader community of states" is activated.[51]

The responsibility to protect came of age with its unanimous adoption by the General Assembly in its World Summit Outcome of 2005.[52] The articulation of the responsibility to protect concept in the World Summit Outcome offered something to both sides of the debate over NATO intervention in Kosovo. On the one hand, the General Assembly endorsed the notion that both the state and the international community have a responsibility to protect populations from genocide, war crimes, ethnic cleansing, and crimes against humanity. It accepted that if a state manifestly fails in that task of protecting its population from genocide, war crimes, ethnic cleansing, or crimes against humanity, the responsibility to do so vests with the international community. On the other hand, the World Summit Outcome stressed that the responsibility to protect was entrusted to the international community only when acting through the UN, and in the case of the use of force, acting "through the Security Council, in accordance with the Charter," and "in cooperation with relevant regional organizations as appropriate." At subsequent General Assembly meetings to discuss the concept, states continued to endorse the concept provided it was not misused by powerful states to justify intervention outside the UN Charter framework.[53]

3. REGIONAL RESPONSIBILITIES? LIBYA AND NATO'S CONDUCT OF OPERATION UNIFIED PROTECTOR

The emphasis in the World Summit Outcome on the need to ensure that military intervention in furtherance of the responsibility to protect be undertaken through the Security Council was designed to ensure that actors such as NATO would not again take humanitarian action into their own hands. Thus it is perhaps surprising that for much of 2011 in the context of Libya, it was largely NATO that effectively exercised the power to make decisions about how protection could be realized in North Africa, and by whom.

NATO and Operation Unified Protector

The UN and regional organizations began to focus on the situation in Libya in February 2011, when the combination of violent repression of protesters by Libyan security forces, the deteriorating humanitarian situation, and threatening statements made by Colonel Gaddafi as his forces surrounded the town of Benghazi gave rise to concerns that a large-scale massacre of civilians might be about to take place. Following the defection of several members of Gaddafi's government and the condemnation of the violence by Libya's ambassador to the UN, the Security Council met in an extraordinary session on February 26 and unanimously adopted Resolution 1970.[54] The resolution recalled "the Libyan authorities' responsibility to protect its population," demanded an immediate end to the violence, referred the situation in Libya to the prosecutor of the International Criminal Court, imposed sanctions on Colonel Gaddafi, members of his family, and his accomplices, and established an embargo on arms destined for Libya.

On March 17 the Security Council passed Resolution 1973. The resolution demanded the establishment of a ceasefire in Libya and a complete end to violence against and abuses of civilians, and required that Libyan authorities comply with their obligations under international law and take all measures to protect civilians.[55] The resolution authorized member states, acting nationally or through regional organizations or arrangements and in cooperation with the secretary-general, to take all necessary measures to protect civilians and civilian populated areas under threat of attack in Libya, while "excluding a foreign occupation force of any form on any part of Libyan territory."[56] The resolution recognized "the important role of the League of Arab States in matters relating to the maintenance of international peace and security in the region," and called upon members of the league to cooperate in implementing the necessary measures required to protect civilians.[57] It established "a ban on all flights" in Libyan airspace "in order to help protect civilians," with the exception of flights for humanitarian purposes and those necessary to enforce the resolution.[58] The adoption of Resolution 1973 was the first time that the Security Council had invoked the responsibility to protect concept to authorize the use of military force for the primary purpose of protecting the civilian population of an individual state without its consent.[59]

It was not immediately evident that NATO would have a role to play in the Libyan intervention. Resolution 1973 had referred specifically to the League of Arab States, but had made no mention of NATO. In the days after the resolution was passed, a "coalition of the willing" involving France, the UK, and the US began to undertake air strikes against Gaddafi's forces. While that US-led coalition operation was underway, NATO members debated whether the alliance would become involved. The US and UK argued for NATO control of the operation, on the basis that it would have greater legitimacy than a coalition of the willing and already had command structures and facilities in place to facilitate the operation. Other NATO members were less enthusiastic. France opposed NATO involvement on the grounds that it would undermine Arab support, Germany was in favor of nonmilitary responses to the Libyan situation, Turkey was skeptical about the motivations behind the intervention, suggesting it was driven by oil interests rather than civilian protection, and a number of members were concerned at the prospect that NATO might take action beyond enforcing the arms embargo and no-fly zone.[60] Eventually it was agreed that NATO would take control of all aspects of the military operations under UN Security Council Resolutions 1970 and 1973. On March 31, 2011, NATO commenced Operation Unified Protector, formally assuming responsibility for enforcing the arms embargo, enforcing the no-fly zone, and protecting civilians and civilian-populated areas under threat of attack.

While the threat to civilians in Benghazi was the primary basis on which Security Council support was obtained for a no-fly zone, that threat was averted very early. According to senior NATO officials, the initial US-led intervention "rescued the people of Benghazi, obliterated Libya's air defense system within 72 hours, and deployed aircraft and naval vessels to enforce the UN resolution."[61] No further Security Council resolution was sought to authorize intervention in support of rebel forces advancing on other parts of Libya, or the use of force to overthrow the Gaddafi government. Nonetheless, NATO governments interpreted the civilian protection mandate broadly. The NATO campaign continued until October 2011, during which time NATO conducted a bombing campaign targeting government forces, command and control centers, and perhaps Gaddafi himself. As a result of the combined effects of NATO air attacks and the growing competence of rebel forces, rebels began to capture government-controlled areas and on August 20 took control of Tripoli. On October 20 Gaddafi was killed. Operation Unified Protector was concluded eleven days later, on October 31.

During the operation in Libya, national militaries adopted dedicated communications strategies that were integrated with NATO policies. The idea that force was being used to protect civilians was at the core of those strategies.[62] Presenting the NATO operation in Libya as an exercise in civilian protection "helped convince domestic audiences that the campaign was worthwhile."[63] NATO was far less successful in persuading people in Libya or the Middle East and North Africa region more generally of the justice of its cause. News coverage in the region remained neutral to negative throughout the campaign, and appeared to have been influenced far more strongly by the "strategic communication" of the Gaddafi regime and the rebel forces. A NATO report concluded that its "traditionally rather negative image in the region has not yet changed," and that although NATO's operation in Libya "very likely saved a large number of civilian lives, the role it played in this respect might well be obscured."[64] As had been the case with NATO's campaign in Kosovo, public opinion was thus split over questions about the conduct and effectiveness of the campaign, and over NATO's motivations for undertaking it.

The Conduct of NATO's Operation Unified Protector

The question of whether NATO had exceeded the mandate provided by Resolution 1973 in its conduct of Operation Unified Protector was hotly debated. A number of NATO states considered that the mandate was far-reaching, and in particular that the authorization of all necessary measures to protect civilians and civilian-populated areas under threat of attack authorized the alliance to take any measures that would stop Gaddafi's forces from winning the civil war, including if necessary targeting Gaddafi. This interpretation was made clear two weeks into the campaign, when the foreign ministers of the allies and operational partners participating in Operation Unified Protector made a statement strongly endorsing the call for Gaddafi to "leave power."[65] The same day, Presidents Barack Obama and Nicolas Sarkozy and Prime Minister David Cameron published an open letter in the New York Times, stating: "Our duty and our mandate under U.N. Security Council Resolution 1973 is to protect civilians, and we are doing that. It is not to remove Qaddafi by force. But it is impossible to imagine a future for Libya with Qaddafi in power."[66]

In contrast, many states that had supported or abstained from vetoing Resolution 1973 considered that NATO had exceeded its mandate and that the conduct of the operation caused unnecessary harm to civilians and long-term instability in Libya and the region. Within weeks of NATO forces beginning their campaign, a number of states began to express concerns that the conduct of the air strikes went beyond the scope of the mandate. On March 19, 2011, the High-Level Committee of the African Union called for an immediate stop to NATO attacks against Gaddafi's government.[67] Brazil, Russia, India, China, and South Africa, all represented on the Security Council, repeatedly voiced concerns in council meetings over the course of 2011 that the civilian protection mandate was being exceeded, and that the NATO intervention had blurred the line between civilian protection and regime change.

China's about-face was particularly marked. Up to early 2011, China had appeared to be softening its longstanding foreign policy support for the principle of nonintervention, as suggested by China's willingness to endorse the inclusion of the responsibility to protect concept in the World Summit Outcome, its support for Resolution 1970, and its abstention from the debate on

Resolution 1973. China watchers speculated that the expansion of China's overseas investments had necessitated a revised foreign policy, and that China was prepared to consider intervening in other states' internal affairs in order to safeguard Chinese interests or protect Chinese citizens.[68] Yet China quickly began to distance itself from NATO's conduct of the Libyan intervention.[69] In a series of Security Council meetings held during May 2011, China declared that "the internal affairs and fate of Libya must be left up to the Libyan people to decide,"[70] and stated that "there must be no attempt at regime change under the guise of protecting civilians."[71]

Russia also specifically referred to the conduct of the Libyan intervention to explain its first veto of a resolution on Syria in October 2011. At that meeting, the Russian representative argued that the situation in Syria could not be considered separately from the "Libyan experience." It rejected the suggestion that "the NATO interpretation" should be a model for "implementing the responsibility to protect."

> The demand for a quick cease-fire turned into a full-fledged civil war, the humanitarian, social, economic and military consequences of which transcend Libyan borders. The situation in connection with the no-fly zone has morphed into the bombing of oil refineries, television stations and other civilian sites. The arms embargo has morphed into a naval blockade in western Libya, including a blockade of humanitarian goods. These types of models should be excluded from global practices once and for all.[72]

Brazil was also a vocal critic of the conduct of the Libyan intervention. Brazil directed its comments to "the transformation of the civilian protection landscape" during Operation Unified Protector, criticizing "excessively broad interpretations of the protection of civilians" that threatened to exacerbate the conflict, compromise the impartiality of the UN, and create the perception that civilian protection was "being used as a smokescreen for intervention or regime change." It argued that when, as in the case of Libya, the council did authorize the use of force, it had "the responsibility to ensure the appropriate implementation of its resolutions."[73] In November 2011 Brazil circulated a concept note entitled "Responsibility while protecting: Elements for the development and promotion of a concept,"[74] which initiated an institutional discussion within the UN about the need to set limits on the power of those carrying out protection mandates.

Other critics argued that while NATO technically conducted its campaign from the air and sea, the success of the operation depended on support provided for rebel forces by individual NATO members and partner states, among them Qatar, France, the UK, and the US.[75] Rebel forces were able to receive air support because of intelligence provided by covert Allied special forces on the ground. This systematic use of covert and semicovert operations formed a "shadow Land Component" of the broader NATO campaign,[76] and appeared to be in breach of the comprehensive arms embargo imposed by Resolution 1970 and the specification in Resolution 1973 that there be no "foreign occupation force of any form." The legitimacy both of NATO and of the responsibility to protect concept will be influenced by whether it proves possible to address the political instability in Libya and rise of ISIS in the region that have followed NATO's intervention and the proxy wars that accompanied it.[77]

Protecting North Atlantic Security or Libyan Civilians? Motivations for NATO'S Intervention

The international community was also divided over the question of whether NATO's intervention was primarily motivated by the goal of protecting North Atlantic security or protecting Libyan civilians. Many political leaders and analysts from non-NATO states, as well as peace activists and liberal commentators from within NATO states, charged that Operation Unified Protector, like the post-9/11 intervention in Iraq, was another US-led coalition fighting a war for self-interested ends, among them securing access to Libya's oil reserves and halting the flow of refugees from North Africa to Europe.[78] Such criticisms open up the broader question of the relation between NATO's new role as "unified protector" and its strategic goals.

The general framework for NATO's strategy in any given period is articulated in its current strategic concept document. The 2010 Strategic Concept (see Documents section), which was operative at the time of Operation Unified Protector, clearly set out NATO's perception of the links between protection of energy security, the management of crises beyond NATO's borders, and North Atlantic defense. The Strategic Concept stated that ensuring the security of foreign energy supply is part of NATO's "security environment," and committed the organization to deterring and defending "against any threat to the safety and security of our populations," including through developing NATO's "capacity to contribute to energy security, including protection of critical energy infrastructure and transit areas and lines."[79] It envisaged that "[c]rises and conflicts beyond NATO's borders can pose a direct threat to the security of Alliance territory and populations," and that NATO would therefore intervene "to prevent crises, manage crises, stabilize post-conflict situations and support reconstruction."[80]

The situation in Libya in the lead-up to Operation Unified Protector undoubtedly involved threats to Europe's foreign energy supply. The Middle East and North Africa in general, and Libya in particular, are vital to European energy security.[81] Libya has the world's fifth-largest oil reserves, and the largest in Africa.[82] Eighty-five percent of Libyan oil was sold to European markets by early 2011. Production costs of Libyan oil were cheaper than those of the two other main European suppliers, Norway and Russia. The shift in Colonel Gaddafi's stance toward the UK and the US after 2003 had opened Libya up to foreign investments, with Italian ENI, Spanish Repsol, and French Total all investing in the Libyan oil industry. Much of the fighting between rebels and Gaddafi's forces took place around key oil reserves, pipelines, and refineries in the Tobruk, Ajdabiya, Benghazi, and Tripoli areas.[83] Stabilizing the situation in Libya was thus extremely important for European energy interests.

Securing the Mediterranean had also been a strategic priority for NATO since 2001, when NATO naval forces were dispatched to the Mediterranean to patrol shipping in the region in the aftermath of the terrorist attacks of September 11. Operation Active Endeavor had subsequently focused on monitoring shipping, deterring trafficking, combating terrorism, and securing global trade. Its ambition was to ensure that the Mediterranean was a space in which the proper movements of people and goods could take place and improper movements be prevented.[84] The naval component of Operation Unified Protector consolidated that control over the Mediterranean. It sought to enforce the arms embargo and ensure the protection of civilians, but also to minimize the impact on other forms of shipping. The commander of the Maritime Component Command, Vice Admiral Rinaldo Veri, announced in 2011:

> This mission is not only about enforcement. There are ships out there trying to carry out legitimate business with Libya. The country needs supplies. There are ships carrying out humanitarian roles. My headquarters and the crews of the NATO maritime group carry out an essential coordination role to allow these legitimate movements to take place. We tell these ships exactly what they must do and if they follow all our instructions they can proceed with minimum disturbance.[85]

A sense of what this entailed can be gained from NATO's final mission statistics in carrying out the arms embargo: it covered a maritime surveillance area of 61,000 nautical miles, hailed over 3,100 vessels, boarded around 300 vessels, and denied 11 ships transit to or from Libyan ports because the vessel or its cargo posed a risk to the Libyan civilian population.[86]

Yet while NATO had declared the Mediterranean a military zone under its control, it did not consider that rescuing refugees fleeing Libya by sea was its responsibility.[87] At least 1,500 people died attempting to cross the Mediterranean during 2011. One incident that received a great deal of attention involved a small boat that left Tripoli with seventy-two people on board in late March, and after two weeks at sea drifted back to Libya with only nine survivors. According to a Council of Europe report into the incident, the boat's distress calls were ignored by a number of fishing boats, at least two military vessels, and a military helicopter, indicating that despite controlling the maritime zone, NATO failed to respond to distress calls sent out by the Rome Maritime Rescue Coordination Center.[88] Although the Security Council invoked concerns about the plight of refugees fleeing Libya in the preambular paragraphs of Resolutions 1970 and 1973, NATO read its civilian protection mandate to exclude responsibility for protecting those civilians seeking to survive by fleeing Libya.

More broadly, the collective European response to refugees fleeing the Middle East and North Africa during that period indicated greater concern with protecting Europe from refugees than with offering protection to them. The Balkans and North Africa, both areas in which NATO has conducted civilian protection operations, are perceived as key sites in the attempt to manage the "risk" posed by migration to Europe from the east and south.[89] According to Frontex, the European border management agency, "the security and economic well-being of Europe's millions" depend on controlling movement across those borders, including the "new flows of Europe-bound migrants" escaping the repressive responses to the Arab spring.[90]

4. PROTECTION AND REPRESENTATION: RETHINKING THE BASIS OF REGIONAL AUTHORITY

While NATO's intervention in Libya did stop attacks on protesters and prevent a potential massacre in Benghazi, it also led to a regime change that was desired by Western powers, served to defend the energy security of Europe, consolidated NATO's dominance in the Mediterranean, and protected against refugee flows perceived as a threat to European security. Serious reservations about the legitimacy of NATO's implementation of the Security Council mandates in Libya have had flow-on effects in relation to future support for the responsibility to protect concept. Yet rather than seeing the backlash against the Libyan intervention as a reason to rethink the privileging of North Atlantic security interests through out-of-area operations, US officials and commentators have argued instead that NATO's intervention in Kosovo should serve as a model for the transformation of international law.

For example, in a 2013 discussion of possible grounds for US intervention in Syria, Harold Hongju Koh, former legal adviser to the US Department of State, argued that any analysis of the law governing military intervention that treats a Security Council veto on use of force for civilian protection purposes as a barrier to action rather than a systemic problem is "overly simplistic."[91] According to Koh, "such an absolutist position amounts to saying that international law has not progressed since Kosovo." Koh argued instead for a revived doctrine of humanitarian intervention modeled on NATO's intervention in Kosovo, in which the involvement of regional organizations increases the legitimacy of intervention by ensuring that action is collective.

Similarly, Anne-Marie Slaughter has proposed the concept of a "regional responsibility to protect" as a means of redrawing the terms of the debate about intervention.[92] In Slaughter's view, while interventions in response to gross and systematic violations of human rights are becoming more feasible and legitimate, they are likely to remain illegal given the use of the veto by permanent members and the lack of collective will to revise the UN Charter. As a result, Slaughter proposes "a collective reinterpretation of the UN Charter" so that regional organizations are given the primary responsibility for authorizing military interventions, subject to later approval or disapproval by the Security Council. For Slaughter, devolving collective decision-making to regional organizations large enough to represent a diverse range of views and interests would protect against "aggression masquerading as humanitarian intervention." Regional organizations would offer a "collective check" because "multiple nations, large and small, with different histories and perspectives" would have to approve the resort to military force. At the same time, these regional organizations would be able to reach agreement on the collective authorization of force more readily. In Slaughter's account, such a shift in practice would lead to an effective amendment of Article 53 of the charter, as "authorization of intervention by regional organizations" would become a rule of customary international law.

Slaughter's argument offers a way of grasping the stakes of NATO's expanded mission for the contemporary international legal order, and thus understanding the role that regionalism is coming to play in security thinking. Under the UN Charter, international law has been organized around the nation-state as the central political form of spatial order. Yet that was not inevitable, as Part 1 showed. Slaughter's call for a regional responsibility to protect echoes the arguments made during the 1930s, in which lawyers were urged to escape from the false alternatives of maintaining a conservative respect for sovereignty and waiting for a universalistic global law to be realized through international institutions. Instead, like the lawyers of the 1930s, Slaughter argues that regionalism offers the new form of spatial order for our time.

That way of thinking about space has been expressed through NATO's adoption of the responsibility to protect mission and its focus upon a mandate of civilian protection. The focus on civilian protection as a new ground for authority has been used to extend the scope of NATO's area of operations. Since 1999, NATO has claimed for itself a new global role as protector of civilians and preventer of mass atrocities on a world scale. Commentators have begun to place NATO in the company of other regional organizations, and to suggest that NATO is well placed to understand the dynamics of conflicts in its "region" and to be able to protect civilians effectively. The interventions in Libya and Kosovo are presented as turning points, in which regional organizations assumed a new role in supporting and undertaking civilian protection operations.[93] Yet NATO has never claimed to be a regional organization as envisaged in Chapter VIII of the UN Charter.[94] It remains a defensive alliance representing the security interests of Western Europe and North America. The effect of such representations is to ignore the specificity and particularity that differentiate NATO from other regional organizations.

During the first decades of the twenty-first century, NATO increasingly came to be portrayed as if it were simply the armed wing of the European Union, committed not only to the welfare of North Atlantic populations but also to the populations of neighboring territories. This required ignoring the fact that NATO unapologetically uses force in the service of protecting the economic and national security of the alliance. In addition, to understand NATO as committed in a deep sense to the welfare and protection of the inhabitants of territories surrounding the North Atlantic area requires ignoring the enormous number of refugees and displaced persons caused by Western interventionism and controlled by forces policing the Mediterranean and the western Balkans.[95] While the model proposed by Western internationalists such as Koh and Slaughter offered an attempt to revive regionalism as a founding principle of spatial order connecting people and territory in international jurisprudence, it is unlikely that the return to a geopolitics of regional ordering would be a positive development from the perspective of those who inhabit the territories that surround the North Atlantic area.

Notes

1. United Nations Secretary-General (2005), Report of the Secretary-General, *In Larger Freedom: Towards Development, Security and Human Rights for All*, delivered to the General Assembly, UN Doc A/59/2005 (March 21, 2005).

2. International Commission on Intervention and State Sovereignty, *The Responsibility to Protect* (Ottawa: International Development Research Centre, 2001).

3. 2005 World Summit Outcome, GA Res. 60/1, 24 October 2005, para 139.

4. Anne Orford, *International Authority and the Responsibility to Protect* (Cambridge: Cambridge University Press, 2011), 25, 179–181.

5. See the discussions in UN Secretary-General, *The Role of Regional and Sub-regional Arrangements in Implementing the Responsibility to Protect: Report of the Secretary-General*, 27 June 2011, UN Doc A/65/877-S/2011/393; Luke Glanville, "Intervention in Libya: From Sovereign Consent to Regional Consent," *International Studies Perspectives* 14 (2013): 325; Anne-Marie Slaughter, "A Regional Responsibility to Protect," in David Held and Kyle McNally, eds., *Lessons from Intervention in the Twenty-first Century: Legality, Feasibility and Legitimacy: Global Policy e-book* (2014), available at http://www.globalpolicyjournal.com/blog/01/05/2014/regional-responsibility-protect.

6. UK Prime Minister's Office, *Chemical Weapon Use by Syrian Regime: UK Government Legal Position*, 29 August 2013, available at https://www.gov.uk/government/publications/chemical-weapon-use-by-syrian-regime-uk-government-legal-position/chemical-weapon-use-by-syrian-regime-uk-government-legal-position-html-version; Daniel Bethlehem, "Stepping Back a Moment: The Legal Basis in Favour of a Principle of Humanitarian Intervention," *EJIL: Talk!*, 12 September 2013, available at http://www.ejiltalk.org/?s=bethlehem; United Nations, *Remarks by President Obama in Address to the United Nations General Assembly*, 24 September 2013, available at http://gadebate.un.org/sites/default/files/gastatements/68/US_en_0.pdf; Harold Hongju Koh, "Syria and the Law of Humanitarian Intervention, Part II: International Law and the Way Forward," *Just Security*, 2 October 2013, available at http://justsecurity.org/1506/koh-syria-part2/.

7. Slaughter, "A Regional Responsibility to Protect."

8. Ibid.

9. Arnold D. McNair, "Collective Security," *British Year Book of International Law* 17 (1936): 150, 161.

10. Nico Krisch and Christian Walter, "Introduction to Chapter 8" in Bruno Simma et al., eds., *The Charter of the United Nations: A Commentary*, Volume 2, 3rd edition (Oxford: Oxford University Press, 2012), 1431–44, at 1434.

11. See Charlemagne Tower, "The Origin, Meaning and International Force of the Monroe Doctrine," *American Journal of International Law* 14 (1920): 1; Charles E. Hughes, "Observations on the Monroe Doctrine," *American Journal of International Law* 17 (1923): 611.

12. Hughes, "Observations on the Monroe Doctrine," 613–14.

13. Elihu Root, "The Real Monroe Doctrine," *Proceedings of the American Society of International Law* 8 (1914): 6, 8.

14. Tower, "Origin, Meaning and International Force," 1; Alejandro Alvarez, "Latin America and International Law," *American Journal of International Law* 3 (1909): 269, 310 (describing the Monroe Doctrine's

message that "the political system of Europe is different from that of the American states" as "the Gospel of the New Continent"); Carl Schmitt, "The Großraum Order of International Law with a Ban on Intervention for Spatially Foreign Powers: A Contribution to the Concept of Reich in International Law (1939–1941)," in Timothy Nunan, ed., *Carl Schmitt: Writings on War* (Cambridge: Polity Press, 2011), 75–124, at 87–88.

15. See Root, "The Real Monroe Doctrine," 11; Hughes, "Observations on the Monroe Doctrine," 615; John H. Spencer, "The Monroe Doctrine and the League Covenant," *American Journal of International Law* 30 (1936): 400, 402.

16. Charles G. Fenwick, "The Monroe Doctrine and the Declaration of Lima," *American Journal of International Law* 33 (1939): 257, 259.

17. Hughes, "Observations on the Monroe Doctrine," 616.

18. Ibid., 620.

19. Fenwick, "Monroe Doctrine and the Declaration of Lima," 260–61.

20. Krisch and Walter, 'Introduction to Chapter 8, 1435.

21. Spencer, "Monroe Doctrine and the League Covenant," 409–10.

22. Ola Tunander, "Swedish-German Geopolitics for a New Century: Rudolf Kjellén's 'The State as a Living Organism,'" *Review of International Studies* 27 (2001): 451, 458.

23. Schmitt, "Großraum Order," 83–95.

24. Moves in favor of "doing something about raw materials" at an institutional level were partly fueled by the speech of Sir Samuel Hoare to the League of Nations Assembly in September 1935, the aim of which was understood to be dissuading Mussolini from invading Abyssinia. See further McNair, 'Collective Security,' 158; Harold Nicolson, "The Colonial Problem," *International Affairs* 17 (1938): 32; International Institute of Intellectual Co-operation, *Peaceful Change: Procedures, Population, Raw Materials, Colonies, Proceedings of the Tenth International Studies Conference, Paris, June 28th July 3rd, 1937* (Paris: League of Nations, 1938).

25. See, for example, Frederick Sherwood Dunn, *Peaceful Change: A Study of International Procedures* (New York: Council on Foreign Relations, 1937); C. A. W. Manning, ed., *Peaceful Change: An International Problem* (New York: MacMillan, 1937).

26. Neil Smith, *American Empire: Roosevelt's Geographer and the Prelude to Globalization* (Berkeley and Los Angeles: University of California Press, 2003), 406.

27. Smith, *American Empire*, 407–09; Michael Akehurst, "Enforcement Action by Regional Agencies with Special Reference to the Organization of American States," *British Year Book of International Law* 42 (1967): 175, 180.

28. "Lord Ismay's Talk to French Diplomatic Correspondents, 12 June 1952," available at http://www.nato.int/cps/en/natohq/opinions_17323.htm?selectedLocale=en.

29. Bruno Simma, "NATO, the UN and the Use of Force: Legal Aspects," *European Journal of International Law* 10 (1999): 1, 10.

30. Allan K. Henrikson, "The Creation of the North Atlantic Alliance, 1948–1952," *Naval War College Review* 32 (1980): 4, 20.

31. Winfried Heinemann, *Vom Zusammenwachsen des Bündnisses. Die Funktionsweise der NATO in ausgewählten Krisenfällen 1951–1956* (Munich: Oldenbourg, 1998), 177–91.

32. Henrikson, "Creation of the North Atlantic Alliance," 20.

33. Douglas Stuart, "NATO's Future as a Pan-European Security Institution," *NATO Review* 41 (1993): 15.

34. Henry Kissinger, *Years of Upheaval* (New York: Simon and Schuster, 1982).

35. North Atlantic Council, *Report of the Committee of Three on Non-Military Co-operation in NATO*, 10 January 1957, C-M(56)127 (revised).

36. Tunander, "Swedish-German Geopolitics," 460.

37. Daniel Fried, assistant secretary, European and Eurasian affairs, "Transatlantic Security: NATO and Missile Defense," Washington, DC, 17 April 2007, US Department of State Archive, available at http://2001-2009.state.gov/p/eur/rls/rm/83176.htm.

38. The note is reproduced in Adam Roberts, "NATO's 'Humanitarian War' over Kosovo," *Survival* 41 (1999): 102, 106.

39. Simma, "NATO, the UN and the Use of Force"; Antonio Cassese, "*Ex iniuria ius oritur*: Are We Moving Towards International Legitimation of Forcible Humanitarian Countermeasures in the World Community?" *European Journal of International Law* 10 (1999): 23; Michael J. Glennon, "The New Interventionism: The Search for a Just International Law," *Foreign Affairs* 78 (1999): 2.

40. Simma, "NATO, the UN and the Use of Force," 10.

41. Tony Blair, "Doctrine of the International Community," speech given to the Economic Club of Chicago, Chicago, 22 April 1999.

42. Movement of Non-Aligned Countries, Statement, Geneva, 9 April 1999; Declaration Adopted by the Inter-Parliamentary Assembly of States Members of the Commonwealth of Independent States, 3 April 1999, UN Doc A/53/920-S/1999/461, Annex II, 22 April 1999, reprinted in Heike Krieger, *The Kosovo Conflict and International Law: An Analytical Documentation 1974–1999* (Cambridge: Cambridge University Press, 2001), 487, 496–97.

43. See, for example, UN Security Council, 3989th Meeting, 26 March 1999, S/PV.3989 (statements made by Russia, India, Ukraine, Belarus, and Cuba); UN General Assembly, 54th session, 4th plenary meeting, 20 September 1999, A/54/PV.4 (statement made by Algeria); UN General Assembly, 55th session, 24th plenary meeting, 20 September 2000, A/55/PV.24 (statements made by Namibia, Cyprus, Ecuador, China, Malaysia, and Russia); UN General Assembly, 55th session, 30th plenary meeting, 27 September 2000, A/55/PV.30 (statements made by the Democratic People's Republic of Korea, India, Cuba, Iraq, and Namibia).

44. UNSC, 3989th Meeting, 26 March 1999, S/PV.3989, 16.

45. Roberts, "NATO's 'Humanitarian War,'" 113–14.

46. UN General Assembly, 54th session, 4th plenary meeting, 20 September 1999, A/54/PV.4, at 4.

47. International Commission on Intervention and State Sovereignty (ICISS), *The Responsibility to Protect* (Ottawa: International Development Research Centre, 2001).

48. ICISS, *Responsibility to Protect*, 13 (emphasis in original).

49. Ibid.

50. Ibid., 17.

51. Ibid.

52. 2005 World Summit Outcome, UN Doc A/RES/60/1, 24 October 2005, paras 138–39.

53. See further the discussion in Anne Orford, *International Authority*.

54. S/RES/1970 (2011), 26 February 2011.

55. S/RES/1973 (2011), 19 March 2011, paras 1, 3.

56. Ibid, para 4.

57. Ibid, para 5.

58. Ibid, paras 6 and 7.

59. See A. J. Bellamy, "Libya and the Responsibility to Protect: The Exception and the Norm," *Ethics and International Affairs* 25 (2011): 1; Catherine Powell, "Libya: A Multilateral Constitutional Moment?" *American Journal of International Law* 106 (2012): 298.

60. Jeffrey H. Michaels, "Able but Not Willing: A Critical Assessment of NATO's Libya Intervention," in Kjell Engelbrekt, Marcus Mohlin, and Charlotte Wagnsson, eds., *The NATO Intervention in Libya: Lessons Learned from the Campaign* (London and New York: Routledge, 2014), 17, 23–24.

61. Ivo H. Daalder and James G. Stavridis, "NATO's Victory in Libya: The Right Way to Run an Intervention," *Foreign Affairs*, 2 February 2012.

62. See Rikke Bjerg Jensen, "Managing Perceptions: Strategic Communication and the Story of Success in Libya," in Engelbrekt, Mohlin, and Wagnsson, *The NATO Intervention in Libya*, 171.

63. Ibid.

64. Florence Gaub, *Six Strategic Lessons Learned from Libya: NATO's Operation Unified Protector*, NATO Defense College Research Report, March 2012, 5.
65. NATO, *Official Text: Statement on Libya Following the Working Lunch of NATO Ministers of Foreign Affairs with Non-NATO Contributors to Operation Unified Protector*, 14 April 2011, available at http://www.nato.int/cps/en/natohq/official_texts_72544.htm.
66. Barack Obama, David Cameron, and Nicolas Sarkozy, "Libya's Pathway to Peace," *New York Times*, 14 April 2011, available at http://www.nytimes.com/2011/04/15/opinion/15iht-edlibya15.html.
67. Glanville, "Intervention in Libya," 337.
68. Andrew Garwood-Gowers, "China and the 'Responsibility to Protect': The Implications of the Libyan Intervention," *Asian Journal of International Law* 2 (2012): 375, 382.
69. Ibid., 386–88.
70. UN Doc S/PV.6528 (2011), at 10.
71. UN Doc S/PV.6531 (2011), at 20.
72. UN Doc S/PV.6627 (2011), at 4.
73. UN Doc S/PV.6531 (2011), at 11.
74. Annex to the letter dated 9 November 2011 from the Permanent Representative of Brazil to the United Nations, addressed to the Secretary-General, *Responsibility while Protecting: Elements for the Development and Promotion of a Concept*, UN Doc A/66/551 S/2011/701, 11 November 2011.
75. Gaub, *Six Strategic Lessons*, 2; Michaels, "Able but Not Willing," 35; Ian Davis, "How Good Is NATO after Libya?" *NATO Watch Briefing Paper No. 20*, 8 September 2011, at 2.
76. Marcus Mohlin, "Cloak and Dagger in Libya: The Libyan *Thuwar* and the Role of Allied Special Forces," in Engelbrekt, Mohlin, and Wagnsson, *The NATO Intervention in Libya*, 195, 196.
77. See Gaub, *Six Strategic Lessons*; Patrick Haimzadeh, "Libya's Second Civil War," *Le monde diplomatique*, April 2015: 5–6.
78. Davis, "How Good Is NATO after Libya?" 1–2.
79. NATO, *Active Engagement, Modern Defence: Strategic Concept for the Defence and Security of the Members of the North Atlantic Treaty Organization*, Adopted by Heads of State and Government at the NATO Summit in Lisbon, 19–20 November 2010, at 17.
80. Ibid., 19.
81. Gaub, *Six Strategic Lessons*, 6.
82. Kjell Engelbrekt and Charlotte Wagnsson, "Introduction," in Engelbrekt, Mohlin, and Wagnsson, *The NATO Intervention in Libya*, 1, 3–4; Richard Reeve, "Libya's Proxy Battlefield," *Oxford Research Group Briefing Paper*, 13 January 2015.
83. Engelbrekt and Wagnsson, Introduction, 3–4.
84. Barry J. Ryan, "A Mediterranean Police Assemblage," in Jan Bachmann, Colleen Bell, and Caroline Holmqvist, eds., *War, Police and Assemblages of Intervention* (London and New York: Routledge, 2015), 147–52.
85. NATO Unified Protector, "VADM Veri Holds Press Conference aboard ITS Etna," 4 April 2011, available at http://www.jfcnaples.nato.int/page167503642.aspx.
86. NATO, *Operation Unified Protector, Final Mission Stats*, 2 November 2011.
87. Fredrik A. Holst and Martin D. Fink, "A Legal View on NATO's Campaign in Libya," in Engelbrekt, Mohlin, and Wagnsson, *The NATO Intervention in Libya*, 63, 88.
88. Council of Europe Parliamentary Assembly, Committee on Migration, Refugees and Displaced Persons Report, *Lives Lost in the Mediterranean Sea: Who Is Responsible?*, 29 March 2012, available at http://assembly.coe.int/CommitteeDocs/2012/20120329_mig_RPT.EN.pdf.
89. Frontex, *Western Balkans Annual Risk Analysis 2015*.
90. Frontex, *Twelve Seconds to Decide. In Search of Excellence: Frontex and the Principle of Best Practice*, 2014.
91. Koh, "Syria and the Law of Humanitarian Intervention, Part II."

92. Slaughter, "A Regional Responsibility to Protect."
93. Glanville, "Intervention in Libya," 330.
94. It is worth noting that the UN Secretary-General's 2011 report *The Role of Regional and Sub-Regional Arrangements in Implementing the Responsibility to Protect* nowhere mentions NATO, despite being written and presented to the General Assembly while Operation Unified Protector was being conducted.
95. Ryan, "A Mediterranean Police Assemblage," 147.

Chapter 9

Conclusion:
Another Cold War? NATO and the New Russia

Adam Tooze and Ian Shapiro

The first forty years of NATO's history were defined by the Cold War confrontation with the Soviet Union. As a uniquely powerful alliance with a uniquely binding commitment on the US, NATO was both shaped by that standoff and helped to sustain it, a standoff that was not simply between military powers but between economic and social systems. Even in the early 1980s, the Cold War confrontation was still urgent and hotly contested. Europe was riven over the politics of twin track and the deployment of cruise and Pershing missiles. Then, suddenly, between 1989 and 1991 the enemy against which the Western alliance defined itself disappeared. First the Iron Curtain, then the Warsaw Pact, and finally the Soviet Union itself dissolved. By the time of the financial crisis in 1998, Russia was reduced to a charity case dependent on Western goodwill for its economic survival.

NATO was, by most measures, a Cold War success. George Kennan might have been right to warn in 1949 that it would militarize the standoff with the Soviets unnecessarily,[1] but NATO forces were never deployed against the USSR or any of its allies, and it seems plausible, if not likely, that the Soviets would have been tempted to seek opportunistic gains in Western Europe but for the Article 5 threat. NATO also helped bury, perhaps permanently, conflicts among the Western European powers that had torn the Continent for centuries. Despite the challenges facing the European Union, it is hard to imagine a scenario in which Britain, France, and Germany would go to war with one other, or, indeed with any other NATO power in Europe. In the Far East, by contrast, where the US pursued security via bilateral agreements instead of an umbrella alliance during the Cold War, longstanding animosities continue to simmer many decades after they last exploded into open warfare.[2]

For NATO today, as reflected in the essays in this volume, the Cold War is in the rear-view mirror. For some of our contributors, the Cold War offers a history to be examined and reevaluated with the benefit of hindsight. For others, it is the end of the Cold War that poses the question: If the mission of containing and facing down the Soviet threat was triumphantly accomplished, what is there left to do? Is NATO the right vehicle to address the challenges that are on the international security agenda of its members? President Donald Trump left many commentators aghast by declaring NATO obsolete on the eve of his inauguration.[3] His other comments on the subject, and those of his cabinet nominees during Senate confirmation hearings, suggested that this headliner reflected Trump's proclivity for hyperbole more than likely future US policy,[4] but we have seen here that fundamental questions about NATO's nature, composition, and purposes do indeed have to be addressed.

For the first twenty years after the end of the Cold War, expansion and mission-creep kept the alliance in business. There was even talk of "global NATO." But with the winding down of the Afghanistan operation and the half-hearted intervention in Libya, questions about NATO's raison d'être inevitably resurged. With European commitment to common defense visibly waning, the parting shot of US Defense Secretary Robert Gates in the summer of 2011 was to ask whether Europe still wanted the alliance.

If the Europeans were not willing to contribute, the US had other issues on its agenda. Most notably, the US was "pivoting" to face China in East Asia, a strategic arena to which Europe seemed largely irrelevant. As the story in Libya turned from self-satisfaction to self-doubt, this only increased the worries. Analysts asked whether the Libyan operation was NATO's swan song.[5] Meanwhile opinion polls in Germany, where Angela Merkel's second coalition government (with the right-wing liberals of the FDP) had opposed the Libyan intervention, suggested plunging support for the Western alliance.[6] Further disillusionment followed in 2013, when European-US relations were driven to a low ebb by Edward Snowden and the National Security Agency scandal. The documents that Snowden released showed that US and European intelligence agencies, NATO, and even the EU were embroiled in embarrassing allegations of spying on each other and on their own citizens, in flagrant denial of basic privacy rights and without adequate democratic oversight.[7] NATO's targeted killing program in Afghanistan was subject to unprecedented scrutiny.[8] In scenes reminiscent of the Cold War, Snowden fled to Moscow airport, where after an embarrassing interlude he was given safe harbor. But unlike in the Cold War this defector to the East was lionized by liberal opinion, precisely because Snowden's revelations cast such a stark light on the inner workings of the discredited Western alliance. In October 2015 Europe's parliamentarians in Strasbourg went so far as to pass a motion calling on their national governments to drop all criminal charges against Snowden and to offer him protection against extradition to the US.[9]

But within months of the Snowden debacle, over the winter of 2013–2014, the dominant Western narrative changed. The crisis in Ukraine, followed by Russia's aggressive moves to annex Crimea and support breakaway movements in Eastern Ukraine, sent NATO scrambling. With the Russian army taking control of Crimea, armored units on Ukraine's northern border, and dark rumors of Russian activity in the Baltic, the Russian specter was back. And Ukraine was not the limit of Putin's activism. In September 2015 Moscow shifted focus to Syria, bringing it into dangerously direct conflict with NATO's easternmost member, Turkey. After Russian military aircraft invaded Turkish air space, Turkey responded by shooting one down. With Russia and Turkey bombarding each other's chosen proxies in Syria, there was a very real risk that a Russo-Turkish conflict might suck in the rest of NATO.

Does Moscow's aggression answer the questions posed by the skeptical critics about NATO's raison d'être? Is this a new Cold War? Can NATO get back to the future?

For many the answer is a clear yes. Putin's often polarizing rhetoric seems bent on affirming Russia's hostility to its old antagonist. Russia has been rearming systematically since 2010. Its nuclear forces are being modernized.[10] It can mobilize a substantial strike force of conventional troops. In 2014 the Baltic states began clamoring for the kind of American bases that once dotted West Germany, asking President Obama to restore the missile shield that his predecessor had promised. Meanwhile Jaroslaw Kaczynski, the kingmaker in Poland's nationalist government, called for NATO to return to its glory days: "One needs to make this path to imperialism completely irrational and not lead to any success whatsoever," Kaczynski told the *Financial Times* in an interview. "This is what Ronald Reagan did, and this resulted in the collapse of the Soviet Union." But, Kaczynski admonished, "NATO back then was different than NATO now. Back then it was an organisation living in the tension of the cold war. It was a military organisation that was prepared for war. A defensive war, sure, but still a war. It has stopped functioning that way."[11] RAND agrees. Having run a series of war games on the possibility of a Russian invasion of the Baltic, the think tank concluded that there was an urgent need for the deployment of heavy conventional forces to the region. Washington responded by quadrupling the funding for the European Reassurance Initiative to $3.4 billion in 2017, enabling a heavily armed US combat brigade of 5,000 personnel to be held permanently on guard in Eastern Europe.[12]

The echoes of the past are powerful. But this ought not to obscure the reality of historical disjuncture and the novelty and complexity of the new situation.

The differences start with Russia itself. Putin's resurgent Russia poses a different kind of threat than that of the Soviet Union. The Soviet Union was a largely self-sufficient Communist colossus. Putin's regime, by contrast, is an unstable hydrocarbon oligarchy. Its wealth leaks out into the billionaire enclaves of the West. Conversely, the economies of the NATO members and particularly those of Europe are significantly interconnected with Russia's, most notably through the massive infrastructure of gas supply.

Though Putin and his Russian nationalists have sought to construct the new tensions in ideological terms, the fact that they have had to resort to issues like LGBT rights to mark the supposed cultural divide points to the vast gap that separates them from the era of Soviet Marxism. Even those who are most adamant about the need to confront a resurgent Russia often choose to refer not to the Cold War, but to deeper and even more troubling historical associations. It is not so much the struggles of 1949 that need to be refought as those of 1939. Putin is as much Hitler as he is Stalin. Alternatively, Putin is the reincarnation of ancient Russian aggression, a symbol of authoritarianism and expansionism rooted deep in his nation's past. This specter provides legitimacy for a strong Western stance, but it smacks more of Samuel Huntington's "culture wars" than it does of reviving NATO's Cold War mission.[13]

Though Russia's military is potent enough both to bully its neighbors and to project force into the eastern Mediterranean, its military spending is dwarfed by that of the US. Even after the largesse of the Putin years, Russia's military budget fluctuates between 50 and 100 billion dollars, depending on the unstable value of the ruble. This is less than half what the Soviet Union was spending, and between a fifth and a tenth of the current US budget, depending on the budget year and conversion factor. Russian military performance may have improved since the shambles of Chechnya and Georgia, but Putin's forces are a far cry from the Red Army of old. In 1968 the Warsaw Pact swamped rebel Czechoslovakia with over 400,000 troops. Today Moscow's largest conventional deployments involve no more than 50,000 troops. Where possible, it prefers to dispatch the "little green men."

In many respects Russia's most effective weapons may be its new versions of information war. The old Cold War was an information war as well. Both sides operated through open propaganda and covert surrogates. NATO had a cultural wing. And since 1989 the West has never dropped out of the soft power game. Democracy promotion through NGO activism and the like has attracted substantial investment. With news outlets like the TV station *Russia Today*, Moscow responds in kind. Its hacking and internet campaign are more innovative, as the scandalous revelations around the 2016 US presidential election underscored.[14] But if today Moscow is exporting anything to the West, it is the radical post-truth cynicism of Russia's managed democracy, the kind of "political engineering" that replaced the official ideology and propaganda of the Communist period. In their work online, the Russian trolls are as effective as they are because they operate not from without, but from within the self-corrosive inner logic of the West's commercialized media sphere.

In 2016 the US Defense Intelligence Agency did not list Russia among the fully-fledged global antagonists America faces.[15] Russia was classed instead as regional threat and a spoiler. The fact that it can be seen even as that reflects not a return to Cold War conditions, but NATO's own changed priorities. Most of America's forces are deployed in other theaters. The European members of NATO have since 1990 pursued a historically unprecedented program of demilitarization, amplified by the policy of austerity pursued since 2010 and the never-ending national rivalries that prevent efficient integration of what is left of Europe's armed forces. The opportunities for action that Moscow has seized upon since 2014 were presented to it by the weaknesses of the West's own politics. And the international crises that Putin has taken advantage of are in no small part of the West's own making. The challenges that Ukraine and Syria pose to NATO derive in large part from the fact that they do not conform to the logic of the Cold War.

The defining feature of the Ukraine crisis is simply its setting in what used to be the heartland of Russian power. The original flash point in the conflict was the Association Treaty that would have linked Kiev to Brussels, 1,141 miles away. In 2008 the hasty push to extend membership of NATO to Georgia and Ukraine had already triggered Russia's short and decisive punishment campaign against Georgia. Five years later the EU's botched diplomacy with Kiev and the corrupt vacillation of Viktor Yanukovych's regime triggered a revolution and another Russian intervention. What Georgia and Ukraine have in common is that they proposed radical eastward expansions of Western influence, sure to antagonize Russia. In both cases, these moves were supported by a fraction of the local population and local elites, well short of overwhelming majorities. And they had the support of some members of NATO. But neither initiative was backed by a concerted grand strategy on the part of the Western alliance. The EU feigned innocence, insisting that it did not pursue geopolitics at all. When these gambits ran into resistance, and not just from Russia, the result, unsurprisingly, was crisis and disunity.

If Poland, leading the new Eastern European member states of NATO, and the hawks in Washington had had their way, the response to Russia's seizure of Crimea and sponsorship of uprising in Donetsk might have been massive. But President Obama stalled, giving Chancellor Merkel time to rally the EU for a united response based on modest economic sanctions. There was no majority in Germany for any more aggressive response, nor in many of the other EU countries. Powerful business interests were opposed to sanctions tout court. It was only the shooting down of Malaysian airliner MH17 that shifted the balance. But when united EU sanctions did not produce a Russian withdrawal and violence escalated in eastern Ukraine to the point where a military intervention by the West became ever more probable, Berlin opted for a diplomatic approach based on bilateral cooperation with France, not the EU external action service, or NATO. Holding the aggressive military command of NATO at bay was the entire point. By the spring of 2015 Berlin was so alarmed at the apparent efforts of NATO SACEUR General Philip M. Breedlove to undermine the Minsk process that it lodged a formal protest with the NATO secretary general.[16]

The experience of dealing with Russia over Ukraine hardened attitudes in Berlin, notably around Chancellor Merkel. After 2014 she allowed members of her coalition government to advocate a more expansive and assertive German security policy. The 2016 White Paper on German defense strategy called for a stronger commitment to NATO, an emphasis on deterrence, and a major new investment in the Bundeswehr. But the European members of NATO and the EU remained deeply divided. The East Europeans considered

Minsk a sellout, another dangerous example of German unilateralism. Meanwhile, a large part of the German public remained deeply averse to any strong action against Russia. And many southern European EU members, notably Italy, displayed little patience for sanctions. Surveys conducted by the Pew Foundation showed no appetite among the populations of the leading Western European NATO members for a clash with Russia.[17] Not only did they oppose a closer embrace of Ukraine, with well over half of German respondents opposing either Ukrainian membership in NATO or the EU; they also expressed profound skepticism about the rationale of fulfilling basic Article 5 obligations of mutual defense even of existing NATO members. Majorities not only in Germany, but also in France and Italy, opposed the use of force to defend an Eastern European NATO member involved in a conflict with Russia.[18]

This was how the dilemma stood in the summer of 2016 for those who viewed Putin's aggression as the basis for reenergizing NATO. It is hardly the stuff of which a rerun of the Cold War is made. And if events since 2013 had not been enough to indicate the degree of disjuncture, what happened in the autumn of 2016 in the United States surely made irrevocably clear the gap that divides us from the era of the Cold War. On November 8 Donald Trump was elected president on a platform that explicitly repudiated confrontation with Russia and presented cooperation with Russia, rather than Germany or the EU, as a pillar on which America's strategy should rest. This did not mean that the US public was won over. Opinion toward Russia remained largely hostile. But the fronts were dizzyingly inverted. It was the Democrats whose candidate was attacked by Russian-sponsored hackers who were solidly against any détente. By contrast, a substantial minority of Republicans rallied reluctantly around their new hero and his peculiar affection for Putin. The electorate did not seem to mind that Trump and his entourage were exceptional among the US elite for the tight connections they maintained to Russia. They did not even seem to mind that America's intelligence agencies accused the Russian secret service of seeking to influence the election. And they were not fazed by allegations that the president might be vulnerable to Russian blackmail. For all this, he did not quite fit the bill of a Manchurian candidate.

Nor was Trump's stance on Russia merely a personal idiosyncrasy. He was able to recruit senior military figures to his cause. The most notable was retired General Michael T. Flynn, former head of the Defense Intelligence Agency. What propelled Flynn into Trump's camp was the fact that America's relationship to Russia and NATO was crosscut by the ongoing crisis in the greater Middle East. If the priority was the war against Islamic extremism, if the emergence of ISIS in Syria had raised those stakes, should Russia not be an ally? As the president-elect put it, NATO was out of date. Why should America go on paying for the defense of a free-riding Europe against a nonexistent Russian threat? There were more important battles to fight—against ISIS, against China.

How to deal with the spillover from the war on terror is one of the basic issues with which NATO has been struggling to come to terms since the beginning of the new millennium. The only military operation the alliance has ever conducted under Article 5 is the war in Afghanistan. During the Cold War a dividing line of sorts was maintained between America's wider engagement in the Middle East and NATO, which remained concentrated on Europe. It was a boundary defended by the Europeans who wanted to stay clear of America's clash with Iran. But the partition had at least two further preconditions. The first was that the Mediterranean functioned effectively as a geographic barrier. At its eastern end, Turkey stood as a geopolitical buffer between the Middle East and Europe. The complexity of our current moment is that these separations can no longer be taken for granted.

Turkey's rivalry with Russia goes deep, and it was happy to join the anticommunist front in 1952 as a loyal NATO member. This set boundaries for repeated phases of domestic political instability and regime change. In the first fifty years of NATO membership, Turkey's soldiers undertook three coups against civilian administrations they considered unreliable in their commitment to Mustafa Kemal Atatürk's legacy. But stabilization of civilian rule since 2002 under Recep Tayyip Erdogan's AKP had seemed to usher in a new phase. Widely seen as an Islamic form of Christian Democracy, the AKP was at first lionized in the West. Erdogan, for his part, sought to secure his version of Islamic politics against military intervention by flaunting his pro-American and pro-European credentials. He was rewarded by President George W. Bush's open advocacy of Turkish membership in the EU, which would have rounded out the alignment of the boundaries of the EU and NATO. But not only did European Islamophobia and the opposition of Cyprus stall Turkey's accession negotiations, Erdogan's own attitude became progressively more ambiguous. Amid a popular anti-Western turn, his regime has been drawn ever more to the mode of nonpluralist democracy, for which Putin serves as a figurehead. Furthermore, the sheer havoc created in the wider Middle East by the disastrous war in Iraq, and the pivotal role that gave to the Kurds as a force of stability, put Turkey at odds with the drift of US policy.

Come the Arab Spring in 2011 and NATO's intervention in Libya, Erdogan was determined not to be left behind. For Erdogan in his new, expansive neo-Ottomanist phase, it was an irresistible opportunity to promote his brand of "moderate" Sunni geopolitics. Geopolitical entrepreneurship by the lesser NATO members was not in and of itself new; the British and French initiative that hustled the alliance into intervention against Muammar Gaddafi was only the latest instance. But Turkey's new assertiveness posed novel challenges. Not that Turkey had much option. By the spring of 2016 Syria's disintegration had made Turkey into the destination for 2.5 million refugees. Further complicating matters, many thousands of them were Kurdish Syrians. Along with Saudi Arabia, Ankara was one of the main backers of Sunni resistance to Syrian President Bashar al-Assad, including a more or less open toleration of extremist Islamic groups. It was only opposition by the Turkish military command that prevented Erdogan from intervening directly in Syria to establish safe zones in the north and to assist in the toppling of Assad.

To be comfortable with intervention, Turkey's military needed approval from NATO. But Europe was disinterested. France and Britain were chastened by the chaos they had helped to unleash in Libya. Nominally, the Obama administration lined up with Turkey. The CIA helped to ship the abandoned arsenals of Libya to the Syrian opposition. But the Obama administration refused open involvement. Washington was torn among three factions: those who favored intervention on the side of "moderate" resistance forces; the cautious Obamaians, who after Libya put safety first; and those who advocated an exclusive focus on the war against Islamic radicalism even if that meant cooperating with Assad's odious regime and its supporters in Teheran and Moscow. The result was paralysis. In September 2013, in the "red line crisis," the worst foreign policy crisis of his administration, Obama stepped back from striking Assad over his use of chemical weapons and instead cooperated with Russia in trying to dismantle Syria's poisonous arsenal.

Ankara was left to twist and turn. The result was a wild oscillation that repeatedly reshuffled Turkey's affiliations with and within NATO. In 2013, furious at the failure of its Western allies to act, Ankara tacked toward Russia, placing giant orders for atomic power plants in Russia and buying a missile shield system in China. As Turkish domestic politics radicalized and the struggle between police and protesters in Istanbul's Gezi Park took an ugly turn over the summer of 2013, Western journalists asked: Is "Erdogan's Turkey the next Putin's Russia?"[19] As Ukrainian protesters were assembling on the Euromaidan, Erdogan signaled to Putin that he would be happy for his country to be considered for membership in the Eurasian Union and the Sino-Russian Shanghai Cooperation Organization.[20] Nor, despite appeals from NATO headquarters in Brussels, did Turkey fall into line with the EU and the US in enforcing economic sanctions against Russia over Ukraine.[21] There were calls from some pundits for Turkey to be expelled from NATO.[22]

But this Russo-Turkish rapprochement could persist only so long as the two powers chose to ignore their differences over Syria. Moscow's decision to intervene on the side of Assad blew this harmony apart. The result was to drive Turkey back into the NATO fold. Following the shooting down of a Russian warplane by American F15 fighters flown by the Turkish air force and the close-quarter fighting around Aleppo, by early 2016 anxieties were running high about NATO being drawn into a clash with Russia.[23] Meanwhile, the refugee crisis escalated, and in response Merkel gambled on Erdogan to help contain the human flow. In early 2016 Erdogan teamed up with Chancellor Merkel to prod NATO into deploying naval units to the Aegean to interdict the people smugglers.

At the same time, however, Turkey faced a profound contradiction. Insofar as the US and NATO had an answer to ISIS, it consisted in using the Kurds to build a buffer zone across northern Syria and Iraq. For Ankara, the prospect of a unified Kurdish state was a nightmare. For domestic political purposes Erdogan had previously pursued a policy of coopting the conservative Kurds of eastern Turkey in support of the AKP. Now he reversed direction and in July 2015 unleashed the Turkish military in a high-intensity anti-insurgency campaign that laid waste to entire towns and city districts in Kurdish Turkey. To provide this campaign with political cover, Turkey invoked Article 4 of the North Atlantic Treaty to force a general debate among NATO ambassadors—only the fourth time in NATO's history that Article 4 had been invoked—and granted the US permission to use the Incirlik air base for its strikes against ISIS.[24] Despite its implications for the broader Kurdish question, NATO chose simply to look away. And the situation became even more tense on the night of July 15, 2016, when a faction of the Turkish military sought to overthrow Erdogan by force. It was the fourth coup attempt during Turkey's NATO membership. Unlike the others, this one failed, but not thanks to any Western intervention on behalf of Turkish democracy. Russia and Iran were far quicker to condemn the coup and to throw their weight behind Erdogan. The US secretary of state called simply for calm and stability.

The AKP's response was drastic. Along with tens of thousands of civil servants, Erdogan purged the vast majority of Turkey's military representatives at NATO headquarters. Having subordinated the military leadership, he then unleashed military operations across the border into northern Syria. Their goal was to prevent the linking up of Kurdish cantons. The upshot was that different members of NATO were backing rival warring factions in northern Syria. Turkey's incursion might also have led to direct military confrontation with Russia and Assad's forces around Aleppo. In the event, rather than leading to clashes with Russia, it sent Ankara lurching back toward Moscow. In December 2016 Turkey participated in peace talks for Syria at which no other NATO member was present. Not surprisingly, 2017 began with renewed talk of Turkey exiting NATO.

Meanwhile, unprecedented confusion reigned in Washington. President-elect Trump had to defend himself against accusations of being in the pocket of Russian intelligence. Nevertheless, he doggedly stuck to a pro-Russian line, and repeated to British and German reporters his highly critical stance on NATO and the EU. At the same time, General James Mattis, the nominee for US secretary of defense, upheld a standard NATO line. In his confirmation hearings Mattis described NATO as "the most successful military alliance, probably, in modern world history, maybe ever," with which it was vital for the US to preserve the "strongest possible relationship." Not only that, Mattis outlined a view of the stakes involved that was diametrically opposed to that of the incoming president. The West, he argued, is "under the biggest attack since World War II" from Russia, from terrorist groups, and China in the South China Sea. "History is not a straitjacket," but "since Yalta, we have a long list of times that we've tried to engage positively with Russia. We have a relatively short list of successes in that regard."[25] How allies and adversaries would respond to such mixed messages remain to be seen.

Though the shambles of the incoming Trump administration was spectacular, the US was not the only Western NATO member to be deeply divided over basic issues of strategy. The same was true in France. Following the terrorist attacks of 2015, President François Hollande joined the attack in Syria and made no secret of his willingness to cooperate with Putin in coordinating the aerial assault on common targets. But by 2016 Russia's targeting of a wide range of opposition forces and support for the annihilation of

Aleppo had led Paris to sponsor motions at the UN accusing Russia of human rights abuses. In May of 2017, France's incoming President Emmanuel Macron reaffirmed France's traditional stance, openly challenging Putin's indulgence of Syria's use of chemical weapons against civilian populations and blasting the Kremlin's state-owned media organizations as "organs of influence and propaganda."[26] What might happen if America were to actually align itself with Russia was not a scenario that European statecraft has had to deal with since 1947.

In the face of the new uncertainty in Washington, many in Europe looked to Germany for leadership. There was talk of reviving a European policy based on a Franco-German axis. The official policy of Merkel's coalition was to throw its weight behind NATO. But whether this could be maintained in the face of Trump's casual hostility and cynical contempt for the EU remained an open question. Furthermore, Merkel's strong stance against Russia had opened the door for the Social Democratic Party to position itself ahead of the 2017 elections as the "party of peace" and the advocate of détente with Russia.[27]

Security is NATO's promise, and there is plenty of insecurity to address. At the time this volume is going to press, the international scene both inside and outside NATO is more disturbed than at any time since the end of the Cold War. But there is no way back to the future. The complex issues in Ukraine and the Middle East are not reruns of the confrontations of an earlier era. They entangle NATO members in so many cross-cutting ways that they do not provide the alliance with any ready made raison d'être. Moreover, NATO members now confront political upheavals in what at the founding in 1949 were the two anchoring states of the alliance, the US and the UK. If in the summer of 2013 NATO was an alliance in search of a mission, the subsequent increase in tension does not so much answer the question as to make it more urgent. As NATO heads toward its seventieth anniversary, it is not just that the answer is unclear. It is not even apparent where the answer might come from.

Notes

1. John Lewis Gaddis, *Strategies of Containment* (New York: Oxford University Press, 1982), pp. 71–74.

2. See Victor D. Cha, "Powerplay: Origins of the U.S. Alliance System in Asia," *International Security*, Vol. 34, No. 3 (Winter 2009/10), pp. 158–96; and Kimie Hara, "50 Years from San Francisco: Re-examining the Peace Treaty and Japan's Territorial Problems," *Pacific Affairs*, Vol. 74, No. 3 (Autumn 2001), pp. 361–82.

3. See Pamela Engel, "Trump's Nominee for Secretary of State Breaks with President-elect on Defending America's NATO Allies," *Business Insider*, January 11, 2017, http://www.businessinsider.com/tillerson-trump-nato-article-5-2017-1?r=UK&IR=T; and Michael Gordon and Niraj Chokshi, "Trump Criticizes NATO and Hopes for 'Good Deals' with Russia," *New York Times*, January 15, 2017, https://www.nytimes.com/2017/01/15/world/europe/donald-trump-nato.html?_r=0.

4. John Grady, "Mattis Puts Russia on Top of His Threat List, Defends NATO," *U.S. Naval Institute News*, January 12, 2017, https://news.usni.org/2017/01/12/mattis-puts-russia-top-threat-list-defends-nato.

5. Steven Metz, "New Republic: Libya Could Be NATO's Swan Song," *NPR Online*, April 15, 2011, http://www.npr.org/2011/04/18/135434396/new-republic-libya-could-be-natos-swan-song.

6. "NATO Topline and Methods," *Pew Research Center*, August 28, 2013, http://www.pewglobal.org/2013/08/28/nato-topline-and-methods/.

7. James A. Lewis, "The Snowden Effect: Can We Undo the Damage to American Power?" *Global Forecast 2014*, https://csis-prod.s3.amazonaws.com/s3fs-public/legacy_files/files/publication/131112_chap2_Lewis.pdf.

8. "Obama's Lists: A Dubious History of Targeted Killings in Afghanistan," *Spiegel Online*, http://www.spiegel.de/international/world/secret-docs-reveal-dubious-details-of-targeted-killings-in-afghanistan-a-1010358.html.

9. Conor Friedersdorf, "European Lawmakers Vote in Favor of Edward Snowden," *Atlantic*, October 29, 2015, http://www.theatlantic.com/international/archive/2015/10/european-parliament-edward-snowden/413257/.

10. Steven Pifer, "Overblown: Russia's Empty Nuclear Sabre Rattling," *Brookings Online*, March 17, 2015, http://www.brookings.edu/research/opinions/2015/03/17-russia-nuclear-weapons-modernization-pifer.

11. "NATO Damned as a 'Lightweight Boxer' by Polish Political Leader," *Financial Times*, February 26, 2016, https://www.ft.com/content/bf41cb0e-dbd5-11e5-98fd-06d75973fe09.

12. David A. Shlapak and Michael W. Johnson, "Reinforcing Deterrence on NATO's Eastern Flank," RAND Corporation 2016, https://www.rand.org/content/dam/rand/pubs/research_reports/RR1200/RR1253/RAND_RR1253.pdf; and "Fact Sheet: The 2017 European Reassurance Initiative Budget Request," White House Press Office, February 2, 2016, https://www.whitehouse.gov/the-press-office/2016/02/02/fact-sheet-fy2017-european-reassurance-initiative-budget-request.

13. Samuel P. Huntington, *The Clash of Civilizations and the Remaking of World Order* (New York: Simon and Schuster, 2011).

14. Mark Mazzetti and Eric Lichtbrau, "C.I.A. Judgment on Russia Built on Swell of Evidence," *New York Times*, December 11, 2016, https://www.nytimes.com/2016/12/11/us/politics/cia-judgment-intelligence-russia-hacking-evidence.html.

15. Vincent R. Stewart, "Statement for the Record: Worldwide Threat Assessment," Defense Intelligence Agency, February 9, 2016, http://www.dia.mil/News/SpeechesandTestimonies/ArticleView/tabid/11449/Article/653278/statement-for-the-record-worldwide-threat-assessment.aspx.

16. "Ukraine Crisis: Transcript of Leaked Nuland-Pyatt Call," *BBC News Online*, February 7, 2014, http://www.bbc.com/news/world-europe-26079957; "Breedlove's Bellicosity: Berlin Alarmed by Aggressive NATO Stance on Ukraine," *Der Spiegel Online International*, March 6, 2015, http://www.spiegel.de/international/world/germany-concerned-about-aggressive-nato-stance-on-ukraine-a-1022193.html.

17. Kate Simmons, Bruce Stokes, and Jacob Poushter, "NATO Publics Blame Russia for Ukrainian Crisis, but Reluctant to Provide Military Aid," Pew Research Center, June 10, 2015, http://www.pewglobal.org/files/2015/06/Pew-Research-Center-Russia-Ukraine-Report-FINAL-June-10-2015.pdf.

18. Ian Shapiro, *Politics against Domination* (Cambridge, MA: Harvard University Press, 2016), pp. 142–71.

19. Mark Champion, "Is Erdogan's Turkey the Next Putin's Russia?" *Bloomberg View Online*, June 5, 2013, http://www.bloombergview.com/articles/2013-06-05/is-erdogan-s-turkey-the-next-putin-s-russia.

20. Kemal Kirişci, "Warming Up Turkey: The Importance of Economic Engagement," *Brookings Online*, April 6, 2015, http://www.brookings.edu/blogs/order-from-chaos/posts/2015/04/06-turkey-economic-engagement-kirisci.

21. Sevil Erkuş, "NATO Calls on Turkey to Join EU Sanctions against Russia as Putin Visits Ankara," *Hürriyet Daily News Online*, http://www.hurriyetdailynews.com/nato-calls-on-turkey-to-join-eu-sanctions-against-russia-as-putin-visits-ankara.aspx?pageID=238&nID=75048&NewsCatID=510.

22. Jonathan Schanzer, "It's Time to Kick Turkey Out of NATO," *Politico Magazine Online*, October 9, 2014, http://www.politico.com/magazine/story/2014/10/time-to-kick-turkey-out-of-nato-111734?o=1.

23. Dion Nissenbaum, Emre Peker, and James Marson, "Turkey Shoots Down Russian Military Jet," *Wall Street Journal*, November 24, 2015, http://www.wsj.com/articles/turkey-shoots-down-jet-near-syria-border-1448356509.

24. "Why Turkey Called a NATO Article Four Consultation," *Economist*, July 28, 2015, http://www.economist.com/blogs/economist-explains/2015/07/economist-explains-21.

25. Natasha Bertrand, "Trump Secretary of Defense Nominee Mattis: Current World Order Is 'Under Biggest Attack since World War II,'" *Business Insider*, January 12, 2017, http://www.businessinsider.com/james-mattis-on-putin-russia-and-nato-2017–1.

26. James McAuley, "French President Macron Blasts Russian State-owned Media as 'Propaganda,'" *Washington Post*, May 29, 2017, https://www.washingtonpost.com/world/europe/french-president-macron-blasts-russian-state-run-media-as-propaganda/2017/05/29/4e758308-4479-11e7-8de1-cec59a9bf4b1_story.html?utm_term=.4382d32c084c.

27. Christian Kerl, "Ukraine Krise: Putin treibt einen Keil in die Berliner Koalition," November 23, 2014, https://www.nrz.de/politik/ukraine-krise-putin-treibt-einen-keil-in-die-berliner-koalition-id10069212.html; and Fabian Klask, "Wohin soll das führen?" *Die Zeit Online*, http://www.zeit.de/2016/46/spd-wahlkampf-friedenspartei-russland-annaeherung.

Contributors

IAN DAVIS, PhD (University of Bradford) is the founding director of NATO Watch and an independent human security and arms control consultant, writer, and activist. His expertise ranges from British and US defense and foreign policy to NATO and transatlantic security issues, the international arms trade, and arms control and disarmament. He has worked in government, academia, and nongovernmental organizations (NGOs). He was formerly executive director of the British American Security Information Council (BASIC; 2001–2007) and program manager at Saferworld (1998–2001). He blogs for the *Guardian* online and is an advisor to the United Nations Association-UK, Saferworld, ISIS Europe (Brussels), and Open Briefing.

ALEXANDRE DEBS, PhD (Massachusetts Institute of Technology) is an associate professor of political science at Yale University, where he is also a research fellow at the Whitney and Betty MacMillan Center for International and Area Studies. He is interested in the causes of war, nuclear proliferation, and democratization. His work has appeared in the *American Political Science Review*, the *Economics of Peace and Security Journal*, *International Organization*, *International Security*, *International Studies Quarterly*, the *Journal of Conflict Resolution*, the *Journal of the History of Economic Thought*, and the *Quarterly Journal of Political Science*. His book manuscript *Nuclear Politics: The Strategic Causes of Proliferation* (with Nuno Monteiro) is under contract with Cambridge University Press.

FRANCIS J. GAVIN, PhD (University of Pennsylvania) is the first Frank Stanton Chair in Nuclear Security Policy Studies and professor of political science at the Massachusetts Institute of Technology. He is the author of *Nuclear Statecraft: History and Strategy in America's Atomic Age* (Cornell University Press, 2012). He is an associate of the Managing the Atom Program at the Belfer Center for Science and International Affairs at Harvard University, senior fellow of the Clements Program in History, Strategy, and Statecraft, a distinguished scholar at the Robert S. Strauss Center, an adjunct senior research fellow at the Center for a New American Security in Washington, DC, and a senior advisor to the Nuclear Proliferation International History Project at the Woodrow Wilson Center.

JAMES GOLDGEIER, PhD (University of California, Berkeley) is dean of the School of International Service at American University and president of the Association of Professional Schools of International Affairs (APSIA). Previously, he directed George Washington University's Institute for European, Russian and Eurasian Studies and held a number of public policy appointments, including director for Russian, Ukrainian, and Eurasian affairs on the National Security Council staff, Whitney Shepardson Senior Fellow at the Council on Foreign Relations, Henry A. Kissinger Chair at the Library of Congress, and Edward Teller National Fellow at the Hoover Institution. He is the recipient of the Edgar S. Furniss book award in national and international security and corecipient of the Georgetown University Lepgold Book Prize in international relations. His books include *Power and Purpose: U.S. Policy toward Russia after the Cold War* (cowritten with Michael McFaul) and *Not Whether but When: The U.S. Decision to Enlarge NATO*.

GRAEME LAMB (Lt. Gen. Sir) is a retired British Army officer of thirty-eight years' experience. In 2009, he stepped down as commander of the Field Army and returned to Afghanistan at the direct request of General David Petraeus and General Stanley McChrystal of the US Army to head a program designed to repeat the success of that in Iraq whereby insurgents were persuaded to give up their arms. He remains the colonel commandant of the Special Air Service, is a trustee of the charity Walking with the Wounded, is on the advisory board of the Good Governance Group (G3), is a partner with FirstHaven, a nonexecutive director with AEGIS, a global private security company, and continues to undertake work for both the UK and US governments.

NUNO P. MONTEIRO, PhD (University of Chicago) is an associate professor of political science at Yale University, where he teaches international relations theory and security studies. He is also a research fellow at the Whitney and Betty MacMillan Center for International and Area Studies. His research focuses on great-power politics, power transitions, nuclear proliferation, the causes of war, deterrence theory, nationalism, and the philosophy of science. His book *Theory of Unipolar Politics* was published by Cambridge University Press in 2014. His articles have appeared in *International Organization*, *International Security*, and *International Theory*, and his commentary has appeared in *Foreign Affairs*, the *Guardian*, *The National Interest*, Project

Syndicate, and *USA Today*, and been featured in the media, including radio (BBC World Service), television (C-SPAN), and print (the *Boston Globe*).

ANNE ORFORD, PhD (University of Helsinki) is Redmond Barry Distinguished Professor and Michael D. Kirby Chair of International Law and director of the Laureate Program in International Law at Melbourne Law School. She is a coconvenor of the Annual Junior Faculty Forum for International Law, past president of the Australian and New Zealand Society of International Law (2013–2015), and founding director of the Institute for International Law and the Humanities at Melbourne Law School (2005–2012). She has been awarded the degree of doctor of laws honoris causa by Lund University (2012) and the University of Gothenburg (2012), and the Woodward Medal for Excellence in Humanities and Social Sciences by the University of Melbourne (2013). Her publications include *International Authority and the Responsibility to Protect* (Cambridge University Press, 2011), *Reading Humanitarian Intervention* (Cambridge University Press, 2003), the edited collection *International Law and Its Others* (Cambridge University Press, 2006), and, as coeditor, *The Oxford Handbook of the Theory of International Law* (Oxford University Press, 2016).

MARY ELISE SAROTTE, PhD (Yale University) is professor of history and of international relations at the University of Southern California and a visiting professor in both the Government and History Departments at Harvard. Her most recent book, *1989: The Struggle to Create Post–Cold War Europe* (2009), was a Financial Times Book of the Year. It became the first book to win both the Ferrell Prize (for distinguished scholarship on US foreign policy) and the Shulman Prize (for distinguished scholarship on Communist bloc foreign policy); it also received the DAAD Prize for distinguished scholarship in German and European studies.

IAN SHAPIRO, PhD, JD (Yale University) is Sterling Professor of Political Science at Yale University, where he also serves as Henry R. Luce Director of the MacMillan Center for International and Area Studies. He has written widely and influentially on democracy, justice, and the methods of social inquiry. His current research concerns the relations between democracy and the distribution of income and wealth. He is a fellow of the American Academy of Arts and Sciences and the American Philosophical Society. He is a past fellow of the Carnegie Corporation, the Guggenheim Foundation, and the Center for Advanced Study in the Behavioral Sciences. He has held visiting appointments at the University of Cape Town, Keio University in Tokyo, Sciences Po in Paris, the Institute for Advanced Study in Vienna, the University of Oslo, and Nuffield College, Oxford. His most recent books are *Politics against Domination*; *The Real World of Democratic Theory*; *Containment: Rebuilding a Strategy against Global Terror*; and *The Flight from Reality in the Human Sciences*.

JOANNA SPEAR, PhD (University of Southampton) is associate professor of international affairs and director of the Elliott School's Security Policy Studies Program at George Washington University (GWU). She was the founding director of the National Security Studies Program, an executive education program serving the needs of the US Department of Defense and other federal agencies. She is also an associate fellow at Chatham House in London. Before joining GWU, she was director of the Graduate Research Programme and a Senior Lecturer at the Department of War Studies, King's College, London; a postdoctoral research fellow at Harvard's Belfer Center for Science and International Affairs; and a visiting scholar at the Brookings Institution.

ADAM TOOZE, PhD (London School of Economics) is a professor of history at Columbia University, and was previously professor of history at Yale University and reader in modern European economic history at the University of Cambridge. He was awarded a Philip Leverhulme Prize for Modern History (2002). He is currently best known for his economic study of the Third Reich, *The Wages of Destruction*, which was one of the winners of the Wolfson History Prize (2006).

Index

Access to Information Disclosure Policy (World Bank), 232
Accountability, xii, 231–52; and funding issues, 237–43; and information classification rules, 235–37; and inner workings of alliance, 234–35; need for, 245–47; and parliamentary oversight, 243–45; and public oversight, 243–45; reform recommendations, 247–50; and secrecy rules, 235–37; and security state, 232–33
Acheson, Dean: radio address (March 18, 1949), viii–ix, 31–39; speech at treaty signing ceremony (April 4, 1949), 40–41
Adenauer, Konrad, 201, 203
Afghanistan: and accountability, 238, 243, 245–48, 250; drone strikes in, 247; NATO operations in, 168, 238, 291–92, 330, 335; and pragmatic functionalism, 265, 279, 282–83; and responsibility to protect, 310; and strategic concept (2010), 168; and UN charter adaptability, 289–92, 299–300
Air and Missile Defence Committee, 234
Air forces: in strategic concept (1991), 136; in strategic concept (1999), 158
Air Traffic Management Committee, 234
Albania: and CSCE process, 112–13; NATO operations in, 279, 290–91
Albright, Madeleine, 246
Allied Command Europe, 65–66, 68, 71
al-Qaeda, 260
Amsterdam Treaty (1997), 144
Annan, Kofi, 277, 312
Arab Spring (2011), 336
Archives Committee, 234
Armed forces: and accountability, 233, 248; Acheson on, 36–37; Military Committee on, 63–64; and nuclear proliferation, 210; post-Cold War evolution of, 220; and pragmatic functionalism, 270; in strategic concept (2010), 167. *See also* Conventional forces
Arms control: North Atlantic Council on, 111, 119–20; and nuclear proliferation, 207, 209; in strategic concept (1991), 123, 127–29, 139; in strategic concept (1999), 133–34, 145, 147, 151, 155; in strategic concept (2010), 164, 169–70
Arms Control and Disarmament Agency (US), 201
Arms embargo, 276, 315, 317, 319–20
Article 1 (NATO Charter), 35, 93; text of, 3
Article 2 (NATO Charter), 35, 95, 116; text of, 3–4
Article 3 (NATO Charter), 35–36; text of, 4
Article 4 (NATO Charter), 125, 290, 309; text of, 4
Article 5 (NATO Charter): and accountability, 238; Acheson on, 36–37; adaptability of, 289–94, 299; and Afghanistan intervention, 335; deterrent effect of, 328; and NATO's Cold War strategy, 254, 256; North Atlantic Council on, 113; and pragmatic functionalism, 279; and responsibility to protect, 307–8; and strategic concept (1991), 125; and strategic concept (1999), 146, 148; text of, 4
Article 6 (NATO Charter), 113, 125, 146, 256, 309; text of, 4–5
Article 7 (NATO Charter): text of, 5
Article 8 (NATO Charter): text of, 5
Article 9 (NATO Charter): text of, 5
Article 10 (NATO Charter), 151, 294–99; text of, 5

347

Article 11 (NATO Charter): text of, 5–6
Article 12 (NATO Charter): text of, 6
Article 13 (NATO Charter): text of, 6
Article 14 (NATO Charter): text of, 6
al-Assad, Bashar, 336
Atatürk, Mustafa Kemal, 335
'Atiyat Allah, Lewis, 260
Atlantic Treaty Association, 100, 114
Atomic Energy Act of 1946 (US), 195
Atomic Energy Commission (France), 197
Atomic weapons. *See* Nuclear weapons and proliferation
Atoms for Peace policy, 195
Australia: accountability and transparency in, 248; defense budget in, 240
Austria: defense budget in, 240; and NATO formation, 21

Baker, James, 218, 221, 295
Balkan Commission, 27
Balkans conflict, 168, 243, 275–79, 310. *See also specific countries*
Bech, Joseph, 49–50
Belgium: and Brussels Treaty (1948), 177; and NATO formation, 19, 31, 41–43
Benediktsson, Bjarni, 47–48
Ben-Gurion, David, 205
Bevan, Aneurin, 264
Bevin, Ernest: Churchill on, 12; Spaak on, 23, 26; speech at treaty signing ceremony (April 4, 1949), 55–56
Blair, Tony, 290, 311
Boegner, Jean-Marie, 197
Bonn Conference on Economic Cooperation in Europe, 112
Bosnia and Herzegovina, NATO intervention in, 243, 276–79, 310
Bozo, Frédéric, 226n12
Brandt, Willy, 203, 269
Brazil, Libya intervention opposed by, 316, 317
Breedlove, Philip M., 333
Brussels Treaty (1948), 177
Building security, 79
Bulgaria, end of Cold War changes in, 117

Bundy, McGeorge, 209n62
Burden sharing, 179, 265, 271, 282–83, 287
Bush, George H. W.: and German reunification, xi, 212–13, 215–17, 219–21, 295; and Gulf War, 290–91; and strategic concept (1991), 123
Bush, George W., 291, 335

Caeiro Da Matta, José, 53–55
Cameron, David, 316
Canada: defense spending in, 240; and Kosovo intervention, 312; and NATO formation, 19, 31, 43–44; US defense treaty with, 12
Charter of Fundamental Rights of the European Union, 233
Chatham House, 261
Chemical weapons, 110, 136
Chemical Weapons Convention, 145
China: and Korean War, 180, 183; and Libya intervention, 316–17; Nixon's diplomacy in, 269
Christopher, Warren, 296
Churchill, Winston, 254; "The Sinews of Peace" speech by, 7–17
Cicconi, Jim, 227n29
Civil Emergency Planning Committee, 234
Civilian Intelligence Committee, 234
Civilian protection, 277, 302–27. *See also* Responsibility to protect (R2P)
CJTFs. *See* Combined Joint Task Force
Claes, Willy, 308
Classified information, 74–79, 236, 251
Climate change, 166
Clinton, Bill, 213, 223, 278
CNAD (Conference of National Armaments Directors), 234
Cockran, Bourke, 11
Cold War: end of, 215, 217, 222, 224, 226–28; force postures during, 256–58, 261, 263–64; and NATO Charter adaptability, 289, 291–92, 294, 296, 299–300; and non-military cooperation, 88; North Atlantic Council on, 117; and nuclear proliferation, 177–79, 184, 187, 189–92,

INDEX 349

203, 206, 212–13; pragmatic functionalism of NATO during, 266–67, 271–74; and regionalism, 302–3, 309–10; and strategic concept (1999), 140, 143; and strategic concept (2010), 169; and transparency issues, 231, 236, 239–40; Truman on, 59
Collective defense and security: and force postures, 255; and responsibility to protect, 304–8, 323–24; strategic concept (1991), 130, 131; strategic concept (2010), 164
Colombo Plan, 107n1
Colonialism, 307, 308–9
Combined Joint Task Force (CJTF), xiii, 143, 156, 276, 283
Committee on Non-Military Cooperation, 81. *See also* Non-military cooperation
Committee on the Challenges of Modern Society, 114
Common foreign and security policy (CFSP), 144
Commonwealth of Independent States, 311
Communism, 15, 85. *See also* Soviet Union
Comprehensive Concept of Arms Control and Disarmament (1989), 111
Comprehensive Nuclear Test Ban Treaty, 145
Conference of National Armaments Directors (CNAD), 234
Conference on Security and Cooperation in Europe (CSCE): and end of Cold War, 215–16, 219–21, 227; and NATO Charter adaptability, 289–90; North Atlantic Council on, 111–12, 118, 120–21; and pragmatic functionalism, 274, 276; and strategic concept (1991), 127, 129
Conflict prevention: strategic concept (1991), 130–31; strategic concept (1999), 148–49
Consultation, Command and Control Board, 234
Conventional Armed Forces in Europe Treaty (CFE, 1990): North Atlantic Council on, 109, 111–12, 118, 119–20; and strategic concept (1991), 123, 124; and strategic concept (1999), 145, 151
Conventional forces: air forces, 136, 158; ground forces, 64, 136, 158; naval forces, 64–69, 136, 158, 319–20; strategic concept (1991), 135–37; strategic concept (1999), 157–60
Cooperation: strategic concept (1991), 128, 129–30; strategic concept (1999), 149–51; strategic concept (2010), 164, 170–71
Cooperative Cyber Defense Center of Excellence, 281, 291
Corbyn, Jeremy, xi
Costigliola, Frank, 209n62
Counter-sabotage, 79–80
Counter-terrorism, 172, 279
Cox, Michael, 272
Crimes against humanity, 313
Crisis management: strategic concept (1991), 130–31; strategic concept (1999), 142–43, 148–49, 152–53, 154; strategic concept (2010), 164, 167–69
CSCE. *See* Conference on Security and Cooperation in Europe
Cultural cooperation, 99–100
Cyber attacks and cyber-security, 165, 167, 281–83, 293, 332
Cyprus conflict (1974), 269
Czechoslovakia/Czech Republic: accession to NATO, 278, 297; and end of Cold War, 108, 117; parliamentary oversight in, 244; Soviet control of, 14; Soviet withdrawal from, 122

DATAMAT, 237
Davis, Ian, xii, 232
Dayton Accords (1995), 277
Debs, Alexandre, x, 193
Decolonization, 307
Defence Committee (UK), 247
Defence Planning Committee, 115
Defense Intelligence Agency (US), 332
Defense Investment Pledge, 240, 262
Defense spending, 240–41, 261–62, 271, 300, 331–32
De Gaulle, Charles, xi, 197, 198, 199, 201, 268
De Margerie, Caroline, 217, 226–27
Democracy, 34, 126
Democratic deficit, 245–46

Democratic Institutions Fellowship
    Programme, 114
Denmark: and NATO formation, 18, 19,
    44–45; parliamentary oversight in, 244
Deterrence: and non-military cooperation,
    82–83; strategic concept (1999), 142;
    strategic concept (2010), 166–67
Dialogue: strategic concept (1991), 128, 129;
    strategic concept (1999), 149–51; strategic
    concept (2010), 170
Diehl (company), 237
Disarmament: North Atlantic Council on,
    111; strategic concept (1991), 127–28;
    strategic concept (1999), 147, 151;
    strategic concept (2010), 164, 169–70; and
    transparency, 251. *See also* Arms control;
    Nuclear weapons and proliferation
Drone strikes, 247
Drug trafficking, 293
Dulles, Allen, 268
Dulles, John Foster, 197, 199, 205

EADS Astrium, 237
Eastern Europe: Churchill on, 13; and end of
    Cold War, 213, 216, 220, 222–23; and
    NATO expansion, 236, 288, 294–98; and
    non-military cooperation, 85–86; North
    Atlantic Council on, 108, 110, 112, 114,
    116–19; and nuclear proliferation, 190,
    202; and regionalism, 302; strategic
    concept (1991), 122, 124–25, 129; strategic
    concept (1999), 150
East Germany: and end of Cold War, 218–19,
    222; and nuclear proliferation, 200, 206,
    209; Soviet withdrawal from, 122. *See also*
    German reunification
Economic cooperation, 95–99; conflict
    resolution, 96–97; consultation on
    economic problems, 98–99; scientific and
    technical cooperation, 97–98
Egypt, Suez Crisis in (1956), 267–68, 309
Eisenhower, Dwight D., 182, 195, 197,
    204–5, 268
Electronic warfare, 165–66. *See also*
    Cyber attacks and cyber-security

Emergency plans, 79
Energy security, 165, 281, 318
Erdogan, Recep Tayyip, 294, 335–38
Erlander, Tage, 204
ESDI. *See* European Security and Defence
    Identity
Eshkol, Levi, 206
Espionage, 75, 77
Estonia: Cooperative Cyber Defense Center
    of Excellence in, 291; defense spending
    in, 240, 261; and NATO expansion, 297;
    and pragmatic functionalism, 281; Russia
    as military threat in, 265, 293, 299–300
Ethnic cleansing, 313
Eurasian Union, 337
Euro-Atlantic Partnership Council (EAPC),
    149, 172, 236
European Defense Community, 181
European Reassurance Initiative, 331
European Scrutiny Committee (UK), 247
European Security and Defence Identity
    (ESDI), 137, 143–44, 147–48, 152–53,
    156, 159–60
European Union: and accountability, 231,
    233, 247, 251; information classification
    system in, 236, 25n19; and NATO Charter
    adaptability, 289, 291, 299; North Atlantic
    Council on, 117; and pan-Europeanism,
    215–16, 219; and pragmatic functional-
    ism, 273, 279; and responsibility to
    protect, 322; strategic concept (1991), 123,
    127, 129, 131; strategic concept (1999),
    143–44, 148; strategic concept (2010),
    162, 171–72
Expansion of NATO: in Eastern Europe, 236,
    288, 294–98; and end of Cold War, 223–24;
    strategic concept (1999), 151; strategic
    concept (2010), 170. *See also specific countries*

Federal Republic of Germany. *See* West
    Germany
Finland, defense budget in, 240
Fisher, Adrian, 201
Five-Power Treaty (1948), 18–21, 25–26
Flynn, Michael T., 334–35

Force planning, 132
Force posture: alert system, 72; North Atlantic Military Committee on, 58–73; nuclear capability, 72; strategic concept (1991), 132–38; strategic concept (1999), 147–48, 152–61. *See also* Conventional forces; Nuclear forces
Forces-in-being, 65–66, 72
Foreign Affairs Committee (UK), 247
Four Freedoms (Roosevelt), 29
Fragile States Index, 259
France: and Brussels Treaty (1948), 177; and Libya intervention, 314, 318, 336; and NATO formation, 18, 19, 45–46; nuclear weapons program in, 138, 160, 188, 194–95, 196–200, 208n42; parliamentary oversight in, 244; and Suez Crisis (1956), 268; and Syria intervention, 338–39; and US invasion of Iraq, 280; US relations with, xi, 214–16, 226n12
Freedom of Information Act of 1966, 231, 233
Fried, Daniel, 310

Gaddafi, Muammar, 313–14, 315, 316, 319, 336
Gaillard, Félix, 199
Game theory, 255, 258
Gates, Robert, 213, 329
Gavin, Francis J., x, 177
General Agreement on Tariffs and Trade (GATT), 107n1
General Assembly (UN), 22, 29–30, 303, 311–13, 323, 325, 327
Genocide, 313
Genscher, Hans-Dietrich, 217–18, 219, 295
Georgia: defense budget in, 240; Russia as military threat in, 259, 297, 333; and strategic concept (2010), 172–73
German reunification: NATO role in, 178, 295; North Atlantic Council on, 113, 117; and pan-Europeanism, 213, 214, 219, 221, 225–26; strategic concept (1991), 123
Germany: defense spending in, 240–41; and Libya intervention, 314, 329; and NATO formation, 21; and NATO membership, 113, 123; nuclear program in, 194; parliamentary oversight in, 244; threat perspective in, 261; and Ukraine crisis, 334; and US invasion of Iraq, 280. *See also* East Germany; West Germany
Global Principles on National Security and the Right to Information (Tshwane Principles), 233
Goldgeier, James, xiii, 272, 288
Gorbachev, Mikhail, x, 117, 213, 218, 221–22, 273, 295
Greece: accession to NATO, 294; and Cyprus conflict, 269; defense spending in, 240, 261
Grotius, Hugo, 253
Ground forces, 64, 136, 158

Hagel, Chuck, 300
Harmel, Pierre, 252n24
Harmel Report (1967), 124, 188, 252n24
Helsinki Process. *See* Conference on Security and Cooperation in Europe
Hennekine, Loïc, 216
Herbst, John, 223
High-Level Committee on the African Union (UN), 316
Hoare, Samuel, 324n24
Hobbes, Thomas, 253
Hollande, François, 338
Hughes, Charles Evans, 305
Humanitarian intervention, 275–76, 289, 302, 310–12, 321, 323, 326
Human rights, 126, 145, 248, 249
Hungary: accession to NATO, 278, 296–97; and end of Cold War, 117; and non-military cooperation, 88; Soviet suppression of revolution in, 267–68; Soviet withdrawal from, 122
Huntington, Samuel, 331

IABG (company), 237
IBAN (International Board of Auditors for NATO), 241–42
IBRD (International Bank for Reconstruction and Development), 107n1

Iceland, NATO formation role of, 18–20, 47–48
ICISS. *See* International Commission on Intervention and State Sovereignty
IFC (International Finance Corporation), 107n1
India: and Kosovo intervention, 311; and Libya intervention, 316
Indonesia, Dutch interests in, 309
Information: classification rules, 74, 79, 235–37, 251n8; cooperation on, 100–102; disclosure policies, 232; protection of, 79, 80
INF Treaty (1987), 123
Intelligence and Security Committee (UK), 248
Intelligence operations, 62, 72
Inter-member disputes, 82, 93–94, 105
International Bank for Reconstruction and Development (IBRD), 107n1
International Board of Auditors for NATO (IBAN), 241–42
International Commission on Intervention and State Sovereignty (ICISS), 303, 312, 323, 325
International Criminal Court, 314
International Finance Corporation (IFC), 107n1
International law, 321–22
International Monetary Fund (IMF), 107n1
International Security Assistance Force (ISAF), 265, 279, 291–92
International Staff (NATO), 100, 104–5
Inter-Parliamentary Union (IPU), 254
Iran nuclear program, 193
Iraq: and Israel's nuclear program, 205; and Turkey's accession to NATO, 271; US invasion of, 280–81
Ireland, NATO formation role of, 19
ISAF. *See* International Security Assistance Force
ISIS. *See* Islamic State of Iraq and Syria
Islamic State of Iraq and Syria (ISIS), 258, 293, 299, 318, 335, 337
Ismay, Hastings, vii, 183, 308

Israel: defense budget in, 240; nuclear program in, 186, 195, 198, 204–6, 210; and Suez Crisis, 268; Yom Kippur War (1973), 309
Istanbul Cooperation Initiative, 172, 173
Italy: defense spending in, 240; and NATO formation, 18, 19, 48–49; parliamentary oversight in, 244

Japan: defense budget in, 240; nuclear program in, 194
Johnson, Lyndon, 196
Joint Standing Committee on Treaties (Australia), 248
Joliot-Curie, Frédéric, 197
Jordan: defense budget in, 240; and Israel's nuclear program, 205

Kaczynski, Jaroslaw, 330–31
Kelleher, Catherine M., 209n62
Kennan, George, 328
Kennedy, John F., 195–96, 201, 202, 205–6
Kennedy, Joseph, viii
KFOR (Kosovo Force), 278
Khrushchev, Nikita, 200, 202, 209n57
Kiesinger, Kurt, 203
Kissinger, Henry, 269, 309
Kjellén, Rudolf, 306
Koh, Harold Hongju, 321, 323
Kohl, Helmut, xi, 213, 215, 217, 218, 221
Korean War, 180, 183
Kornblum, John, 223
Kosovo: NATO operations in, 238, 243, 250, 278, 290–91, 299, 302–4; nongovernmental organizations in, 245; and responsibility to protect, 309–13, 321, 325
Kosovo Force (KFOR), 278
Kosygin, Alexei, 202
Küntzel, Mathias, 209n62

Lamb, Graeme, xii, 253
Lange, Halvard M., vii, 51–53
League of Arab States, 314
League of Nations, viii, 9, 16, 254, 304–5, 324
Legitimacy, 289, 298–99, 311–14, 318

INDEX 353

Leviathan (Hobbes), 253
Libya: and accountability, 243, 250; and force posture, 262; NATO operations in, xiv, 238, 265, 275, 283n1, 291, 299, 302–3, 322, 329, 336; and responsibility to protect, 262, 310, 313–20, 325–26
Lodge, Henry Cabot, 254
Logistics Committee, 234
London Declaration (July 6, 1990), 116–21, 126
Luxembourg: and Brussels Treaty (1948), 177; freedom of information law in, 233; and NATO formation, 19, 31, 49–50

Macedonia: accession to NATO, 297; NATO operations in, 279, 310
Macron, Emmanuel, 339
MAD (mutual assured destruction), ix, xii, 182, 255
Maritime forces. *See* Naval forces
Marshall Plan, 28, 50, 200, 208
Mattis, James, 338
McGhee, George, 202–3
McNamara, Robert, 184
Mediterranean Dialogue, 150, 155, 172, 236, 280
Mediterranean region: naval forces in, 319–20; and strategic concept (1999), 150–51, 155; and strategic concept (2010), 172, 173
Meir, Golda, 205
Mendès, Pierre, 197, 198, 207n20
Merkel, Angela, 329, 333, 337, 339
Metreveli, Mamuka, 280
Middle East: and energy security, 319; and Israel's nuclear weapons program, 204–6; NATO relations with, 125; and strategic concept (2010), 173; Yom Kippur War (1973), 309
Military Committee (NATO): on defensive aims of NATO, 59; on deterrent and defensive value of NATO forces, 72–73; on effective pattern of NATO military strength, 58–73; on factors affecting outcome of initial phase of conflict, 61–63; on factors affecting outcome of subsequent operations, 63; on probable nature and duration of future war involving NATO, 59–61; recommendations of, 71; on sea communications, 67–69; on Soviet capabilities and probable strategy, 63–65; on task of NATO forces in Europe, 65–67
Minimax theorem, 255
Missile defense, 237
Mitterrand, François, xi, 215–16, 219–25, 227n31
Mladic, Ratko, 277
Mollet, Guy, 198
Monroe, James, 304–5
Monroe Doctrine, 304–7, 323–24
Monteiro, Nuno P., x, 193
Montenegro, accession to NATO, 297
Montgomery, Bernard, ix
Morgenthau, Henry, Jr., 210n68
Morgenthau Plan, 210n68
Morocco, defense budget in, 240
Moscow Treaty (1970), 203
Multilateral Force initiative, 187, 195, 196, 201–2, 209n55, 209n62
Multinational forces, 136–37, 159–60
Mutual assured destruction (MAD), ix, xii, 182, 255

NAC. *See* North Atlantic Council
Nash Equilibrium, 255, 258
Nasser, Gamal Abdel, 198, 268
National security, 34–35, 75, 210, 233, 246, 251, 261, 322
National Security Agency (US), 329–30
NATO: Charting the Way Forward (Chatham House), 261
NATO Charter: adaptability of, 288–301; and force posture, 254–56, 258; and pragmatic functionalism, 282; signing of, vii; and strategic concept (1991), 125–26, 128; and strategic concept (1999), 141–42, 144, 146–47, 151–52; and strategic concept (2010), 163–64, 166; text of, 3–6. *See also specific Articles*

NATO Fellowship and Scholarship Program, 100
NATO Response Force (NRF), 166, 280
NATO–Russia Founding Act on Mutual Relations, Cooperation and Security, 150, 172
Naval forces: and Libya intervention, 319–20; Military Committee on, 68–69; and sea communications, 67–69; Soviet, 64–65; strategic concept (1991), 136; strategic concept (1999), 158
Netherlands: and Brussels Treaty (1948), 177; and colonial territories, 309; and NATO formation, 19, 31, 50–51; parliamentary oversight in, 244
Netherlands Court of Audit (NCA), 241–42
New Zealand, defense budget in, 240
Nixon, Richard, 269
"No-first-use" doctrine, 184
Non-Aligned Movement, 311
Nongovernmental organizations (NGOs), 245
Non-military cooperation, 81–107; cultural cooperation, 99–100; economic cooperation, 95–99; information field cooperation, 100–102; and organizational structure, 102–5; political cooperation, 89–94
Non-Proliferation Treaty (NPT), 194–96, 202–4, 207, 209–10
North Atlantic Council (NAC): and accountability, 234–35, 242, 245, 249; creation of, 6; links with member governments, 103; London Declaration (July 6, 1990), 116–21; meetings of, 102–4; and Military Committee, 71; and non-military cooperation, 81, 102–5; and pragmatic functionalism, 267, 279, 281; resolutions, 105–6; and responsibility to protect, 309, 324; strategic concept (1991), 122–39; strategic concept (1999), 140–61; strategic concept (2010), 162–74; Truman on, 58; Turnberry, Scotland meeting (June 7, 1990), 108–15
North Korea, nuclear weapons program in, 193

Norway: and NATO formation, 18, 19, 31, 51–53; oil exports from, 319; threat perspective in, 261
NPT. *See* Nuclear Non-Proliferation Treaty
NRF (NATO Response Force), 166, 280
Nuclear forces: and end of Cold War, 220; North Atlantic Council on, 109, 111, 115, 118–19; and regionalism, 330; strategic concept (1991), 123, 132, 137–38; strategic concept (1999), 145, 152, 160–61; strategic concept (2010), 166, 167. *See also* Nuclear weapons and proliferation
Nuclear Non-Proliferation Treaty (1968), x, 145, 169, 187, 194, 210n69
Nuclear Planning Group, 115, 187, 234
Nuclear weapons and proliferation: and end of Cold War, 217, 222, 224; in France, 196–200; in Iran, 193; in Israel, 186, 195, 198, 204–6, 210; Military Committee on, 58–73; NATO's response to, 177–211; and non-military cooperation, 85; North Atlantic Council on, 119–20; in North Korea, 193; strategic concept (1991), 132–33; strategic concept (1999), 145, 151, 153; strategic concept (2010), 162, 165–67, 169–70; in Sweden, 203–4; in West Germany, 200–203. *See also* Nuclear forces
Nunn, Sam, 249–50
Nye, Joseph S., Jr., 209n57

Obama, Barack: and Afghanistan alliance, 282; and European security, 330; and Libya intervention, 316, 336; and transparency initiatives, 231; and Ukraine crisis, xii, 333
Oder-Neisse line, 209n63
OECD (Organisation for Economic Cooperation and Development), 107
Open Data Initiative (World Bank), 232
Open Skies initiative, 110, 118, 123
Open Society Justice Initiative, 233
Operation Ace Guard, 273–74
Operation Active Endeavor, 279, 281, 291, 319
Operation Allied Force, 310
Operation Allied Goodwill I and II, 275

Operation Allied Harmony, 279
Operation Allied Protector, 281
Operation Allied Provider, 281
Operation Amber Fox, 279
Operation Anchor Guard, 273
Operation Deadeye, 277
Operation Deliberate Force, 277
Operation Eagle Assist, 279
Operation Essential Harvest, 279
Operation Fragile Genie, 275
Operation Joint Endeavor, 277
Operation Ocean Shield, 281
Operation Unified Protector, 243, 302–3, 313, 315–19, 326–27
Orban, Viktor, 294
Orford, Anne, xiv, 302
Organisation for Economic Cooperation and Development (OECD), 107n1
Organisation for Security and Cooperation in Europe (OSCE), 143–44, 149, 276, 279, 290
Organized crime, 259, 261, 282–83
OSCE. *See* Organisation for Security and Cooperation in Europe
Ottawa Convention (1997), 145

Pakistan, drone strikes in, 247
Palmerston, Lord, vii–viii
Pan-Europeanism, 215, 217, 223, 225
Parliamentary oversight, 94, 243–45
Parodi, Alexandre, 197
Parsons, J. Graham, 204
Partial Test Ban Treaty (PTBT), 189, 195, 204
Partnership for Peace (PfP), 149–50, 155, 172, 236, 277, 296
Partnerships: strategic concept (1999), 149–51; strategic concept (2010), 170–73
Peacekeeping operations, 149, 256, 263, 268, 275–78, 281
Peace of Westphalia (1648), 253
Pearson, Lester B., 43–44
Personnel security, 77–78
Persson, Göran, xiii
PfP. *See* Partnership for Peace
Physical security, 78–79

Piracy, 172, 281, 291, 293
Poland: accession to NATO, 278, 297, 333; defense spending in, 262; and end of Cold War, 108, 117; nuclear forces in, 189–90; Soviet control of, 14; Soviet withdrawal from, 122; threat perspective in, 261
Political cooperation, 89–94; annual political appraisals, 92–93; consultation on foreign policies, 90–93; inter-member disputes, 93–94, 105; parliamentary associations, 94
Politkovskaya, Anna, 224
Portugal: Britain's alliance with, 12; and NATO formation, 19, 53–55
Pragmatic functionalism, 265–87; in Cold War period, 267–72; in post-Cold War period, 272–82
Propaganda, 25–26, 86, 87, 260, 332
PTBT (Partial Test Ban Treaty), 195, 204
Public oversight, 243–45
Putin, Vladimir, xi, 224, 292, 330, 339

Qatar: defense budget in, 240; and Libya intervention, 318
Qinetiq, 237
Qutb, Sayyd, 260

Radford plan (1956), 201
Rasmussen, Anders Fogh, 239, 246, 250, 300
Rasmussen, Gustav, 44–45
Ratzel, Friedrich, 306
Raytheon, 237
Reagan, Ronald, x, 214, 269–70
Refugees, 320, 337
Regionalism, 304–8
Resource Policy and Planning Board, 234, 242
Responsibility to protect (R2P), xiv, 302–27; and collective security, 304–8; and colonial territories, 308–9; and force posture, 262; and founding of NATO, 303–4; Kosovo intervention, 309–13; Libya intervention, 313–20; and regionalism, 304–8; and UN Charter, 303–4
Rice, Condoleezza, 227n29
Rio Group, 311

Rio Treaty (1947), 20
Roberts, Alasdair, 236
Romania, 117
Rome Maritime Rescue Coordination Center, 320
Roosevelt, Franklin D., viii, 29, 305
Roosevelt, Theodore, 305
Rosenberg, David, 180
Royall, Janet Anne, 243
Rule of law, 34, 126
Rumsfeld, Donald, 280
Rusk, Dean, 202
Russell, Bertrand, x
Russia: Churchill on, 13, 17; defense spending in, 331–32; and end of Cold War, 223–24, 252; and force posture, 257–58, 275; force posture of, 332; and Libya intervention, 316, 317; and NATO expansion, xi, 223–24, 292–97; and nuclear proliferation, 178, 180–81, 190; oil exports from, 319; and responsibility to protect, 311, 316–17, 319, 325; as security challenge, 328–39; and strategic concept (1999), 143, 150, 154–55; and strategic concept (2010), 167, 169, 172; and Syria intervention, 330, 337, 339; threat posed by, 331–32; Turkey's relations with, 330, 335–37; US relations with, 224. *See also* Soviet Union

Sabotage, 75, 77
SAIC (Science Applications International Corporation), 237
SALT I and SALT II, 184, 191
Sandler, Todd, 278
Sarkozy, Nicolas, 316
Sarotte, Mary Elise, xi, 212
Saudi Arabia, defense budget in, 240
Schmitt, Carl, 306
Schuman, Robert, 45–47
Science Applications International Corporation (SAIC), 237
Sea communications, 67–69
SEATO (Southeast Asia Treaty Organization), 266, 284n3

Secrecy rules, 235–37
Security approach: strategic concept (1991), 128–31; strategic concept (1999), 146–51
Security Council (UN): Acheson on, viii–ix, 37; and NATO Charter, 4–5; and responsibility to protect, 303–4, 307–8, 313–14, 316, 320–21, 325; and strategic concept (1999), 144, 149; and strategic concept (2010), 163
Security Investment Programme (NATO), 153, 242
"Security Within the North Atlantic Treaty Organization" (NATO), 74–80; classified information, 79; coordination on information on espionage, sabotage, terrorist, and other subversive activities, 77; counter-sabotage, 79–80; information protection, 79, 80; organization of security, 76–77; personnel security, 77–78; physical security, 78–79; safeguards against malicious willful damage, 79; security agreement, 74–75; security standards, 75–80
Senate Foreign Relations Committee (US), 35
September 11, 2001 terrorist attacks, 279, 291, 299
Serbia, 276–77, 290, 300
Sforza, Carlo, 48–49
Shanghai Cooperation Organization, 337
Shapiro, Ian, 328
Shevardnadze, Eduard, 218–19
Slaughter, Anne-Marie, 321–22, 323
Sloan, Stanley, 277
Slovakia, 117
Smart Defense Initiative, 237, 282
Snowden, Edward, 329–30
Social Justice in Islam (Qutb), 260
Somalia, NATO support for peacekeeping mission in, 281
South Africa, 316
Southeast Asia Treaty Organization (SEATO), 266, 284n3
South Korea: defense budget in, 240; nuclear program in, 194; US security guarantees for, 193

INDEX 357

Soviet Union: Britain's treaty with, 12; Churchill on, 12–13, 15–16; conventional forces in, 192n14; and economic conflict, 98; NATO military strategy and, 180–92; Nixon's diplomacy in, 269; North Atlantic Military Committee on future war with, 59–73; Spaak on, 22–30; US summit with, 109; and Yalta Agreement, 15
Spaak, Paul-Henri: treaty signing ceremony speech (April 4, 1949), 41–43; "Why We Fear Russia" speech, 22–30
Spain: accession to NATO, 294; freedom of information law in, 233; and NATO formation, 21
Spear, Joanna, xiii, 265
Special United Nations Fund for Economic Development (SUNFED), 107n1
Sputnik, 199, 201
Stalin, Joseph, 13
START Treaty (1991), 109, 123, 145
State Department (US), 210, 223, 228
Stikker, Dirk U., 50–51
Stimson, Henry, 31
Stockholm Conference on Confidence- and Security-Building Measures and Disarmament in Europe (CDE, 1986), 123
Stoltenberg, Jens, 239
Strategic Air Command, 183
Strategic concept (January 6, 1950), 270
Strategic concept (November 8, 1991), 122–39; alliance objectives and security functions, 126–28; collective defense, 130; conflict prevention, 130–31; context for, 122–26; conventional forces, 135–37; cooperation, 129–30; crisis management, 130–31; defense guidelines, 131–38; dialogue, 129; force posture, 132–38; mission of alliance military forces, 133; nuclear forces, 137–38; protection of peace in Europe, 128–29; security approach, 128–31, 318; security environment, 124–26, 274–75
Strategic concept (April 24, 1999), 140–61; arms control, 151; conflict prevention, 148–49, 278–79; conventional forces, 157–60; cooperation, 149–51; crisis management, 142–43, 148–49; deterrence and defense, 142; dialogue, 149–51; disarmament, 151; enlargement of alliance, 151; force posture, 147–48, 152–61; non-proliferation, 151; nuclear forces, 160–61; partnerships, 149–51; purposes and tasks of alliance, 141–42; security approach, 146–51; security challenges and risks, 145–46; security tasks, 142–43; strategic environment, 143–46, 278–79
Strategic concept (November 19, 2010), 162–74; arms control, 169–70; collective defense, 164; cooperative security, 164; core tasks and principles, 163–64; crisis management, 164, 167–69; deterrence, 166–67, 292; disarmament, 169–70; enlargement of alliance, 170; non-proliferation, 169–70; partnerships, 170–73; reform and transformation of alliance, 173; security environment, 164–66, 261, 282
Strauss, Franz Josef, 201, 203
Study of the Supreme Allied Commander Europe, 66
Subversive activities, 77
Suez Crisis (1956), 205, 267–68, 309
SUNFED (Special United Nations Fund for Economic Development), 107n1
Supreme Allied Commander Europe, vii
Supreme Headquarters Allied Powers Europe (SHAPE), 268–69, 276
Sweden: and accountability, 240; defense budget in, 240; and NATO formation, 18, 19; nuclear program in, 186, 195, 203–4, 210n73
Switzerland, defense budget in, 240
Syria: humanitarian intervention in, 321, 330, 332, 335–38; and Israel's nuclear program, 205; and responsibility to protect, 317, 321, 323, 326; Russia as military threat in, 259–60, 337

Talbott, Strobe, 223
Tennyson, Alfred, Lord, 253, 257

Terrorism: coordination on information on, 77; and force posture, 258, 260, 335; strategic concept (2010), 165, 172
Thales Raytheon System Company, 237
Thatcher, Margaret, 214, 215, 270
TNO (company), 237
Tooze, Adam, 328
Trachtenberg, Marc, 180
Transparency, xii, 231–52; and funding issues, 237–43; and information classification rules, 235–37; and inner workings of alliance, 234–35; military, 123; need for, 245–47; North Atlantic Council on, 110, 123; and parliamentary oversight, 243–45; and public oversight, 243–45; reform recommendations, 247–50; and secrecy rules, 235–37; and security state, 232–33; strategic concept (1991), 129, 133; strategic concept (1999), 145, 150, 155; strategic concept (2010), 169–72
Transparency International, 235
Treaty of Collaboration and Mutual Assistance (Britain–Soviet Russia), 12
Treaty of Moscow (1970), 203
Treaty of the European Union, 144
Treaty on the Functioning of the European Union, 233
Truman, Harry, viii, 35, 38–39, 57
Trump, Donald: on burden sharing, 241, 300; on NATO being obsolete, xii, 266, 329; and US–Russia relations, 334, 338
Tshwane Principles (Global Principles on National Security and the Right to Information), 233
Turkey: accession to NATO, 271–72, 294, 335; as buffer between Middle East and Europe, 335; and Cyprus conflict, 269; and Libya intervention, 314; NATO operations in, 273–74; Russia's relations with, 330, 335–37; Soviet influence in, 14; and Syria intervention, 336, 337

Ukraine: and Nuclear Non-Proliferation Treaty, 145; Russian invasion (2014–2015), xi, 224, 259, 265, 282, 288, 292–93, 297, 300, 330, 332–34; and strategic concept (1999), 143, 150, 155; and strategic concept (2010), 172–73
Union of Soviet Socialist Republics (USSR). *See* Soviet Union
United Arab Emirates, defense budget in, 240
United Kingdom: accountability and transparency in, 247–48; and Brussels Treaty (1948), 177; defense spending in, 240, 261, 271; freedom of information law in, 233; and German reunification, 214–15; and Kosovo intervention, 310; and Libya intervention, 314, 318, 336; and NATO formation, 18, 19, 31, 55–56; nuclear forces in, 138, 160–61, 188, 194; Portugal's alliance with, 12; Soviet Russia's treaty with, 12; and Suez Crisis (1956), 268; and US invasion of Iraq, 280; US relations with, 11–12
United Nations: Acheson on, 32–35, 37–39; and Balkans conflict, 290, 310–11; Bech on, 49–50; Benediktsson on, 47; Churchill on, 9, 12, 15, 17; Committee on Disarmament, 202; High-Level Committee on the African Union, 316; and Korean War, 180; Lange on, 52–53; NATO Charter on, 3–6, 291; and non-military cooperation, 87–89, 93, 107; and nuclear proliferation, 197; and pragmatic functionalism, 267, 273, 275–76, 281; and responsibility to protect, 303, 312, 323, 326, 327n94; Schuman on, 45; Spaak on, 22, 27–29, 41–42; and strategic concept (1991), 129, 131; and strategic concept (1999), 143, 147; and strategic concept (2010), 162–63, 171; Truman on, 57
United Nations Charter: and inter-member disputes, 93; and international law, 322; and NATO formation, 35; North Atlantic Council on, 117; and responsibility to protect, 303–4, 307–8
United States: Britain's relations with, 11–12; Canada's defense treaty with, 12;

INDEX   359

Churchill on, 8; congressional oversight in, 244; defense budget in, 183, 240, 261, 271; France's relations with, 214–16, 226n12; and Libya intervention, 314, 318; and NATO formation, 18; NATO relationship with, 178–79; nuclear forces in, 138, 160, 180; Soviet summit with, 109; threat perspective in, 261
USSR. *See* Soviet Union

Védrine, Hubert, 217, 219, 221
Veri, Rinaldo, 319
Versailles Treaty (1919), 15
Vienna Convention on the Law of Treaties, 244
Vietnam War, 188, 197
Vishinsky, Andrey, 23–25
Von der Leyen, Ursula, 241
Von Neumann, John, 255, 258

Wampler, Robert, 180
War crimes, 313
Warsaw Treaty Organization, 117, 122, 257
Washington, George, viii
Washington Treaty. *See* NATO Charter
Water supply, 166
Weapons of mass destruction (WMDs), 146

Weinrod, Bruce, 280
Western European Union, 131, 143–44, 148, 153
West Germany: accession to NATO, 294; and end of Cold War, 213–14, 216–17, 220, 225; military power in, 178, 181; North Atlantic Military Committee on, 66–67; nuclear aspirations of, 186, 200–203, 209n65; and nuclear proliferation, 178, 181–90, 196, 199–203, 206, 208–10; and pragmatic functionalism, 269. *See also* German reunification
Wilson, Harold, 209n55
Wilson, Woodrow, viii, 29, 254
Woerner, Manfred, 219
World Bank, 232, 241, 249
Worner, Manfred, 118

Yalta Agreement (1945), 15
Yanukovych, Viktor, 333
Yeltsin, Boris, 223, 296
Yom Kippur War (1973), 309
Yugoslavia, NATO operations in, 275, 276

Zelikow, Philip, 227n29
Zero-sum competition, 255, 258
Zoellick, Robert, 221, 222, 223